English Vocabulary for Academic Success

Practicing Academic English Words and Grammar

2nd Edition

Bill Walker

22.44

Published and printed on demand by CreateSpace.
www.CreateSpace.com
CreateSpace is a DBA of On-Demand Publishing LLC, part of the Amazon group of companies.

Credits: Many thanks to Nate Soelberg, my esteemed colleague at the University of Oregon, whose keen proofreading has made this book as error-free as is humanly possible.

Cover photo: University of Oregon campus, Eugene, Oregon, USA

Contents

To the Student

This book is for you if you are preparing for study at the university (college) level.

You probably already know about 2,000 English words or more.

To do well at a university, you need more words. This book will help you to learn 540 "academic" words. These 540 words plus the 2,000 you already know will let you understand almost 90% of what you might read in an academic textbook.

How long will it take?

If you study for one hour every day, it will take about one week to learn one unit. There are ten units in this book. If you study one unit per week, it will take ten weeks to learn these 540 words.

What will you learn?

You will learn not only what the words mean, but you will also practice *grammar* and *spelling*.

You must write the answers to every question. As you write, think about the spelling of each word. Also, think about the grammatical form of each word: some nouns need to be made plural, some verbs need to change their tense. Also, according to the context, you will need to change the part of speech of the word (noun, verb, adjective, adverb).

What kind of exercises will you do?

Each unit begins with a list of the target words, followed by these activities:

- **Definition**
  You write the words in sentences by matching words with definitions.
- **Parts of Speech**
  You change the form of the word to fit the grammar of the sentence. You must also write correct plurals and verb tenses, and sometimes capital letters.
- **Collocations**
  Given highlighted collocation clues, you will produce the correct grammatical form of the word in contextualized sentences.
- **Synonyms** Crossword Puzzle
  Given synonyms as clues, you can try to solve crossword puzzles.
- **Review**
  You choose the best word for each sentence. Many sentences contain collocation, synonym or other context clues.

How can you memorize the words?

You will work with each word an average of *eight* times. That means you will have an excellent chance of keeping each word in your long term memory. In addition, you can make **flash cards**:

On one side of the flash card, write the vocabulary word in your language.

On the other side, you should write the vocabulary word and all of its parts of speech, synonyms and collocations.

概 念

```
concept (n) conceptualize (v) conceptual (adj)
synonyms: idea, theory, thought
collocations: an abstract concept
              a key concept
              to grasp a concept
```

Carry the flash cards with you everywhere you go. Study them frequently and study them over a period of several days so that they stay in your "long-term memory."

Use the flash cards to give yourself quizzes. Review the ones you miss, then mix them up with the ones you know and quiz yourself again.

What is a collocation?

A collocation is a word or group of words that native speakers naturally associate with a particular word. For example, a non-native speaker might say:

"scientists have *made* the theory of global warming."

However, a native speaker would say

"scientists have *formulated* the theory …".

In this case, "formulate" is the word that collocates with the word "theory".

Here are some more examples of **collocations**:

to take a different approach **a constructive** approach	**to take … out of** context **to put … into** context
evidence **comes to light** **to gather** evidence	identity **crisis** **a case of mistaken** identity
to adopt legislation **a piece of** legislation	to proceed **with a plan** to proceed **on the basis of**

This book does not provide all of the possible collocations. You can find more collocations in a good "collocation dictionary" such as *Oxford Collocations: Dictionary for Students of English*.

Dictionary

At the end of each unit is a dictionary section containing:

Definitions: Some words have more than one definition.

Parts of speech: noun, verb, adjective, adverb, conjunction, preposition

Collocations: Collocations are listed according to part of speech and/or meaning.

Many *sample sentences* are included.

Synonyms: Synonyms are listed at the end of the dictionary section.

Answer Key

You can check your answers at the end of each unit. Pay attention to spelling!

What do these words sound like? How do you pronounce these words?

The best way to learn how to pronounce these words is to listen to them as they are spoken by a native speaker. Also, there are many dictionary web sites that let you click and listen to individual words. Find a web site that you like, and visit it often. Listen to each word and say it out loud several times.

Success!

Yes, you will be successful, but only if you do the exercises in this book carefully, thoughtfully and regularly. Do a few pages every day, rather than try to do a whole unit all at once the day before a quiz. By spreading your studies over many days, you will be able to remember the words much more easily and for a longer period of time.

These are the English words you will need *for the rest of your life*, so take the time to study them in the best possible way.

To the Teacher

The Academic Word List

The Academic Word List was created by Averill Coxhead. By analyzing millions of words from a wide range of academic subject areas (excluding literature), she compiled 570 high frequency academic words in the Academic Word List (AWL). These words, when combined with the 2,000 most frequent words in general English, give the learner nearly 90% of the words they need to know in order to understand academic English. For more detailed information, please read:

Coxhead, A. (2000). A new academic word list. TESOL quarterly, 34(*2*), 213–238.

Vocabulary and Grammar: Lexicogrammatical Production

English Vocabulary for Academic Success covers 540 of the words in the AWL. Every exercise requires the student to produce the target word with accurate spelling and grammar. It is important to realize how intricately vocabulary (lexis) and grammar are related to each other as "lexicogrammar." In a lexical approach to language teaching, it can be said that vocabulary acquisition comes first, then word patterns are "refined" by the application of grammar rules. This vocabulary book capitalizes on the lexicogrammatical relationship by requiring students not only to learn the meaning of the word, but also to produce (write) the correct forms of words: noun plurals, verb tenses, gerunds and participles, parts of speech (noun, verb, adjective, conjunction, preposition) and other grammatical forms.

There are two ways to look at vocabulary acquisition. **Depth** refers to the number of words learned. Thus, a student who knows 3,000 words has greater vocabulary depth than a student who knows only 2,000 words. **Breadth** refers to how much the student knows *about* each word. Paul Nation, Norbert Schmidt and others suggest that a broad knowledge would include such things as the sound of the word and how to pronounce it, spelling, the various meanings of the word, connotations, register constraints, grammatical preferences, collocations and other associations (including synonyms), and how the word is related to other words in its family (e.g., by the addition of prefixes and affixes). This book endeavors to increase a student's depth and breadth of vocabulary knowledge by focusing on definitions, spelling, parts of speech, collocations and synonyms.

Organization of the Book

Students who study for an hour or two every day should be able to cover one unit per week.

This book contains ten units. Each unit covers 54 words. There are five sections in each unit:

- **Definition**
  For every three target words, students are given six answer choices. They read the definition of each word, then write the answer in contextualized sentences.
- **Parts of Speech**
  For each target word, students must change the form of the word (noun, verb, adjective, adverb, preposition, conjunction) to fit the grammar of two contextualized sentences. They must also, if necessary, write correct plurals, verb tenses, and sometimes capital letters.
- **Collocations**
  In each set, there are ten target words and twelve answer choices. In each group of sentences, the student write the *one* word that goes with the highlighted collocations. The student will also have to produce the correct grammatical form of the word.
- **Synonyms** Crossword Puzzle
  Given synonyms as clues, students try to solve crossword puzzles. Some of the synonym clues may be unknown to the students, so this can be an opportunity for them to expand their vocabulary depth.
- **Review**
  For every three target words, students are given six answer choices. Many sentences contain collocations, synonyms or other context clues.

Spelling

Note that *accurate spelling* is required in each exercise. Because the students write each word seven or eight times, there is an increased likelihood that orthographic accuracy will improve. Of course, there are vocabulary learning "apps" that allow students to click on answers, but that involves little more than word recognition. By having to write out the answers with correct spelling and attention to grammatical forms, much more mental effort is required; thus, much better retention and more accurate written production are achieved.

Self-study or Classroom Activities?

English Vocabulary for Academic Success is a *workbook* intended for students to use at home so as not to take up valuable class time. To that end, there is an answer key at the end of each unit.

However, there may be opportunities for your students to engage in vocabulary activities in class. Writing teachers, for instance, might want to extend students' ability to use the target words more productively in their written assignments. One way to do this would be to have them try to write sentences using collocations which they can find either in the exercises or in the dictionary section of each unit. For speaking and listening practice, pairs of students can dictate individual words (or entire sentences) to each other, with special attention to pronunciation and spelling.

Dictionary: Note that the embedded dictionary is unique in that it provides collocations arranged according to the different meanings and different parts of speech of the target words. Also note that when a collocation creates an idiomatic usage, an explanation is given in brackets. The dictionary provides hundreds more sentences in addition to the nearly 4,000 sample sentences in the exercises in the ten units.

Free Quizzes

Instructors may receive via email 40 professionally prepared quizzes (4 quizzes per unit).

This offer is strictly for bona fide instructors whose program of 50 or more students adopts this textbook. You will be required to submit proof of your status as an instructor at a recognized institute and proof that the book has been adopted. There is no charge for the quizzes.

Please send your request to the author, Bill Walker: billwalk@uoregon.edu

The quizzes will be sent to you as Word documents so that you can modify them as you wish. A template will be provided so that you may develop your own quizzes.

Each quiz comes with an answer key.

About the author

Mr. Walker is a retired senior instructor with over 25 years of experience teaching English at San Francisco State University in California, in Saudi Arabia and Qatar, and at the University of Oregon in Eugene, Oregon. He has specialized in teaching reading and vocabulary. He has done extensive research into vocabulary acquisition and supplemented his research readings with a great deal of practical classroom observation. In addition to teaching, he has worked as a journal editor, has written research articles, and has given many professional presentations at TESOL and other conferences in the United States and abroad.

He has also written another vocabulary book:

Academic English Vocabulary for International Students IS N 978-1442113138 (Available from Amazon.com). This is a shorter version of *English Vocabulary for Academic Success* with fewer exercises (all multiple choice).

Acknowledgements

The author wishes to thank his astounding colleagues at the University of Oregon who contributed their expert opinions, suggestions and kind encouragement without which this book would not be possible: Jeff Magoto, Kay Westerfield, Donna Shaw and Brendan DeCoster.

Unit 1

Unit 1

Word List
Parts of speech: **n** = noun   **v** = verb   **adj** = adjective   **adv** = adverb

analysis (n)
    analyze (v)
    analytical (adj)
    analytically (adv)
approach (n)
    approach (v)
    approachable (adj)
area (n)
assessment (n)
    assess (v)
assumption (n)
    assume (v)
authority (n)
    authorize (v)
    authoritative (adj)
    authoritatively (adv)
    authorization (n)
available (adj)
    availability (n)
benefit (n)
    benefit (v)
    beneficial (adj)
    beneficially (adv)
concept (n)
    conceptualize
    conceptual (adj)
    conceptually (adv)
consist of (v)
    consist in (v)
    consistency (n)
constitute (v)
    constitution (n)
context (n)
    contextualize (v)
    contextual (adj)
    contextually (adv)
contract (n)
    contract (v)
    contractual (adj)
    contractually (adv)
    contraction (n)
creation (n)
    create (v)
    creative (adj)
    creatively (adv)
data (n pl)
    datum (n s)
derive (v)
    derivation (n)
    derivational (adj)
    derivationally (adv)
distribute (v)
    distribution (n)

environment (n)
    environmental (adj)
    environmentally (adv)
establish (v)
    establishment (n)
evident (adj)
    evidently (adv)
    evidence (n)
export (n)
    export (v)
    exportable (adj)
factor (n)
    factor (v)
finance (n)
    finance (v)
    financial (adj)
    financially (adv)
formula (n)
    formulate (v)
    formulaic (adj)
function (n)
    function (v)
    functional (adj)
    functionally (adv)
identity (n)
    identify (v)
    identification (n)
income (n)
indicate (v)
    indication (n)
    indicative (adj)
    indicatively (adv)
individual (n)
    individualize (v)individual (adj)
    individually (adv)
interpret (v)
    interpretation (n)
    interpretive (adj)
issue (n)
    issue (v)
labor (n) [British: labour]
    labor (v)
legal (adj)
    legally (adv)
    legality (n)
    legalization (n)
    legalize (v)
legislate (v)
    legislation (n)
    legislative (adj)
    legislatively (adv)

major (adj)
    major (n)
    majorly (adj)
method (n)
    methodical (adj)
    methodically (adv)
occur (v)
    occurrence (n)
percent (n)
    percentage (n)
period (n)
    periodical (adj)
    periodically (adv)
    periodical (n)
policy (n)
proceed (v)
process (n)
    process (v)
require (v)
    requirement (n)
research (n)
    research (v)
role (n)
section (n)
sector (n)
significant (adj)
    significantly (adv)
    signify (v)
    significance (n)
similar (adj)
    similarly (adv)
    similarity (n)
source (n)
specific (adj)
    specifically (adv)
    specify (v)
    specification (n)
structure (n)
    structure (v)
    structural (adj)
    structurally (adv)
theory (n)
    theorize (v)
    theoretical (adj)
    theoretically (adv)
vary (v)
    variety (n)
    variation (n)
    various (adj)
    variously (adv)

Unit 1

Definitions Use the definition clues to write the correct words in the blanks.

<table>
<tr>
<td>

1. to happen or take place
   Earthquakes _____ frequently in Japan.

2. to manage or get money
   My father will help me _____ my new business by loaning me $5,000.

3. to go toward or near
   When you _____ the baby, you should be very quiet.

</td>
<td>

approach
proceed
occur
benefit
analyze
finance

</td>
</tr>
<tr>
<td>

4. something which is made or brought into being
   The government is working on the _____ of new jobs.

5. an established or accepted way of doing something
   She used the same _____ for all of her love stories.

6. a point or problem which people are thinking about and discussing
   Each student wrote about a difficult _____ such as abortion, genetic engineering or nuclear energy.

</td>
<td>

role
formula
section
creation
issue
factor

</td>
</tr>
<tr>
<td>

7. allowed by or relating to the law
   If you need _____ advice, get a good lawyer.

8. more important, bigger or more serious than others of the same type
   A _____ difference between the two women is their views on divorce.

9. able to be used, purchased, obtained or reached
   Mr. Keller will be _____ to see you at 3:00 today.

</td>
<td>

available
similar
major
legal
formulaic
periodical

</td>
</tr>
<tr>
<td>

10. to change, alter or modify
    In a chemistry experiment, if you _____ the temperature, you will get different results.

11. to form, compose or make
    Women _____ nearly 80% of healthcare workers.

12. to make laws
    It is difficult to _____ controls on the Internet.

</td>
<td>

require
vary
analyze
assume
constitute
legislate

</td>
</tr>
<tr>
<td>

13. the set of circumstances or events in which a particular event occurs
    Freedom has a special meaning in the _____ of American history.

14. a clear or logically formed principle or idea
    "Human rights" is a western _____ that has a different meaning in the East.

15. a systematic series of actions or events used to produce something
    The planning _____ is slow, but the results are great.

</td>
<td>

process
creation
availability
concept
export
context

</td>
</tr>
</table>

Unit 1

16. helpful or providing an advantage *This book is _____ for student who study English.* 17. existing as a single, distinct, or separate thing *Different opinions were held by _____ members of the group.* 18. especially meaningful, important; considerable *Technology plays a _____ role in everyone's life.*	evident beneficial functional individual methodical significant
19. the surrounding objects, influences and conditions *A good social _____ in the classroom helps students to learn better.* 20. separation into parts for a close look in order to discover more *The _____ of the food showed that it was poisonous.* 21. the money derived from doing work or investing *Her _____ was more than $50,000 a year.*	concept analysis labor environment research income
22. to start or continue doing or saying something after a delay *You can _____ with your game after you finish your homework.* 23. to make something necessary; to demand or insist upon *Law and medicine degrees _____ many years of study.* 24. to divide into parts and give out to each of several people or groups *The manager will _____ the pay checks every Friday.*	distribute function benefit proceed require legislate
25. resembling or being almost the same, but not exactly *The sisters are quite _____, but they are not identical.* 26. relating or pertaining to one definite thing and not others *When water reaches a _____ temperature, it freezes.* 27. clearly, obviously or easily seen or understood *It was _____ that the girl was not telling the truth.*	specific available evident legal similar significant
28. the amount, value, or quality of something that has been decided *The teacher's _____ of my essay pleased me. She said it was thoughtful and rich with excellent ideas.* 29. controlled area or region, such as in society or in a political system *The government should not try to do things that are better done in the business _____.* 30. the purpose or role for which an object or person is naturally used *I soon learned my _____ as a new team member.*	function creation assessment factor sector identity

Unit 1

31. to show, point out or make clear *The test _____ that you have a healthy heart.* 32. to be made of, composed of or formed of *Mud _____ dirt mixed with water.* 33. to send or transport goods to other countries for sale or trade *China _____ many goods to the US and Europe.*	indicates exports requires consists of assumes constitutes
34. detailed, systematic study to obtain and analyze information especially in order to learn something new *Our _____ shows that cigarettes cause cancer.* 35. a legal document that states and explains a formal agreement *According to the _____ , you must pay me $2,000 for the work that I have done for you.* 36. one of the parts that something is divided into, separate or distinct from the whole *The first _____ of the book was short but funny.*	research section method environment structure contract
37. to get, obtain or extract something from an original source *It is possible to _____ gas from rock formations.* 38. to explain or determine what the intended meaning of something is *We didn't know how to _____ his joke.* 39. to bring into being something that will last a long time *It is time for us to _____ a new advertising program.*	identify interpret constitute derive establish require
40. a place or region *It is safe to walk around most _____ of our town at night.* 41. information, especially facts or numbers *These _____ do not support your conclusion.* 42. proper or assigned position and function or behavior of a person or thing in a particular situation *She does well in two _____ :housewife and businesswoman.*	data benefits roles areas concepts contracts
43. a system consisting of a number of parts joined together or arranged in a certain way *The students learned more about the _____ of atoms.* 44. the moral or legal right, power, or ability to give orders, make decisions, or control *Mark has the _____ to hire and fire workers.* 45. one part for every one hundred *Ten _____ of the students said they would like to have all of their textbooks in electronic form.*	structure legislature authority percent method assessment

46. a set of principles, ideas or a plan that is officially agreed on and used as a guide for action *The new_____ gives workers the right to stay at home for six weeks after the birth of a child.* 47. the cause of something; where something comes from *The birth of our first child was a _____ of great happiness for us.* 48. the qualities or characteristics which make a person or group different from others *We had trouble guessing the _____ of the woman who donated all the money for our project.*	identity analysis income export source policy
49. a particular way or procedure for doing something *The old _____ of testing the students was not as good as the new way.* 50. something which is supposed to be true without evidence or proof *The teacher gave the students more time to work on her essay on the _____ that the essays would be much better.* 51. a fact or situation which influences or partially affects the result of something *The most important _____ in his recovery was the support of his family.*	legislature assumption sector structure factor method
52. practical work requiring either physical or mental effort *We decided on a division of _____ in order to get the work done faster.* 53. a specific or limited length of time *We did not have to pay for the equipment during a trial _____ of one month.* 54. a proposed formal explanation of a fact or event; usually an opinion or explanation based on abstract reasoning *Many uneducated people do not believe in the _____ of global warming.*	labor contract period variety theory income

Unit 1

Parts of Speech

Write the parts of speech (noun, verb, adjective or adverb form).
Be careful with nouns and verbs:

   Some *nouns* might need to be plural (~**s**).
   Some *verbs* might need ~**s, ~ed, ~ing**.

analysis
1. It is difficult to _____ this problem.

   She is using an _____ approach to solve the problem.

approach
2. You will like Donna. She is a very _____ person.

   Jason usually _____ his work very slowly.

area
3. Many people in the _____ had to leave their homes.

   Several _____ of the city were under police control.

assessment
4. Our house was _____ at $200,000.

   The bank made an _____ of our house.

assumption
5. We left the office on the _____ that our work was finished.

   I think we can _____ that Jill no longer wants the job.

authority
6. You have no _____ to make that decision.

   We were impressed by Kendall's _____ manner.

available
7. They built a factory here because of the _____ of cheap labor.

   The new cameras will be _____ in a few months.

benefit
8. The warm weather in Florida usually _____ the tourist industry.

   The weather was _____ for the farmers' crops.

concept
9. Some physics _____ are too difficult for me to understand.

   It's hard to _____ multiple universes.

consist of
10. Water _____ oxygen and hydrogen.

    Until recently, the committee _____ ten members.

constitute
11. The government officials cannot agree on what _____ a "rural" area.

    We could easily solve the problem after we broke it down into its _____ parts.

Unit 1

context   12. Her views make more sense in the broader _____ of social conservatism.

Some educators believe that _____ learning has a beneficial effect on most students.

contract   13. The company failed and broke its _____ with us.

We have to fulfill our _____ agreement by tomorrow.

creation   14. We decided to _____ a new logo for our website.

Elaine used a _____ approach to solve the problem.

data   15. According to the latest _____, climate change is real.

In the entire report, only one _____ was inaccurate.

derive   16. Most people have trouble understanding the _____ of Einstein's formula: $E = MC^2$.

The Russian word *czar* is _____ from *Caesar*.

distribute   17. The hungry people went home after the food was _____.

The police are _____ pictures of the suspect.

environment   18. By the mid-1990s, the _____ movement was becoming stronger.

The new regulations will be bad, _____ speaking.

establish   19. The war ended after the _____ of a no-fly zone.

We have _____ a friendship with our new neighbors.

evident   20. The police could not find any _____ linking Melissa to the crime.

It is fairly _____ that you did not write this essay.

export   21. Every year, China _____ many products other countries around the world.

Wood is one of Oregon's most _____ products.

factor   22. One of the most important _____ in Alek's success was his willingness to work hard.

When we _____ in how much it would cost to rent a car, we decided not to drive.

Unit 1

finance
23. Sam could not find the _____ records he needed for his bank loan.

Last year, we _____ our home at National Bank.

formula
24. The chemical _____ for water is H$_2$0.

It took him two years to _____ his new theory.

function
25. In her _____ as director of the school, she was responsible for hiring and firing teachers.

We are happy now that everything is _____ so well.

identity
26. It was dark, so I could not _____ the man in the back of the room.

You will need some _____ when you go for your driver's license.

income
27. Clara is beautiful and she has a good _____.

People whose _____ are below $20,000 can get some government assistance.

indicate
28. The latest report _____ that the economy is getting better.

The early _____ is that the hurricane will miss Florida.

individual
29. Some doctors _____ the cost of treatments for each patient.

Many _____ do not have health care.

interpret
30. For some reason, Paul _____ my behavior the wrong way yesterday.

We love Mr. Burhonesque's _____ of Beethoven's Fifth Symphony.

issue
31. By Friday, the court will _____ its final judgment.

One of the _____ that concerns me is the lack of good textbooks.

labor
32. Last night, the students _____ on their report until 11:30.

Women constitute only 40% of the _____ force.

legal
33. Some people think that we should _____ drugs.

The protesters questioned the _____ of the police action.

Unit 1

legislate   34. The Parliament is the British _____ body.

                Congress was slow to pass the _____ .

major   35. When you decide to become a college student, you have several _____ decisions to make.

                When I was in college, I _____ in Art History.

method   36. Kim is an excellent business woman. She is _____ and precise.

                The mechanic _____ put all of the pieces of the engine back together again.

occur   37. None of this would have _____ if you had stayed at home.

                We fixed the computer to prevent a further _____ of the problem.

percent   38. Fewer than three _____ of Americans can find Burkina Faso on a map.

                Here, the sales tax is six _____ of the price.

period   39. After a _____ of two weeks, we decided to try again.

                We should do a _____ review of our work.

policy   40. According to my car insurance _____ , I will be provided with a rental car if my car is damaged in an accident.

                The CEO decided to make a _____ change.

proceed   41. After she told me her name, she _____ to tell me her life story.

                The cows stopped suddenly without _____ to the barn as they usually would.

process   42. We are still trying to solve the mystery. We are _____ all of the information that we have so far.

                You would feel better if you ate less _____ food.

require   43. Local farmers are _____ to get a business license.

                A passport is a _____ for entering Canada.

research   44. Much _____ has been done on the effects of coffee on the heart.

                The university is _____ ways to use solar energy.

Unit 1

role   45. President Obama is a good _____ model for young African Americans.

The actor played two different _____ in the play.

section   46. This new software will allow you to create a _____ on your web site for additional information.

The teacher divided the class into two _____.

sector   47. A _____ of a circle looks like a piece of pie.

Certain stock _____ are doing very well despite the poor economy.

significant   48. The airplane could not fly because of _____ problems with its engines.

Houses are _____ cheaper today than they were a few years ago.

similar   49. Recent research shows that the body responds _____ to physical and emotional pain.

The only _____ shared by the sisters was their blond hair.

source   50. "Facebook" is a _____ of entertainment for many people.

If it does not rain soon, we will have to find new _____ of water.

specific   51. We are concerned _____ with the possibility that laws concerning the separation of church and state will change over time.

You need to _____ the color before you send in your purchase request.

structure   52. Astrophysicists study the overall _____ of the universe.

The inspectors found the building to be _____ safe.

theory   53. The Journal of _____ Biology is published four times a year.

Most of her _____ about child-raising are quite strange.

vary   54. The ability to smell different odors _____ from person to person.

There are a _____ of ways to catch wild animals.

Unit 1

Collocations

In each group of sentences, write *one* word from the list which goes with the **highlighted collocations**. Use the *correct form* of the word.

Exercise 1	approach data contract benefit area policy
	concept authority issue theory factor source

1. They **took a conservative** _____ to the problem.

   When we got near the gate, we _____ it **with caution**.

   We all **took different** _____ but we came to the same conclusion.

2. Albert Einstein **formulated the** _____ of relativity.

   In education, it is best to **combine** _____ **and practice**.

   Sheila **has several pet** _____ about why some men are poor listeners.

3. Tim needs to **exercise** his _____ in the next meeting.

   Some college students like to **challenge** _____.

   You can't make the purchase until the manager _____ **the payment**.

4. They must finish the work because they **are under** _____ to do so.

   The lawyers will **write up** both _____ tomorrow.

   My father's company **landed a** _____ with Microsoft.

5. The weather was a **contributing** _____ in the accident.

   The bad economy _____ **into** the way people will vote.

   The patient's attitude is a **critical** _____ in her recovery.

6. The President seemed to **adopt a** _____ of being tough on terrorism.

   We need a **sound** _____ for dealing with energy consumption.

   Professor Hans has **an open-door** _____. You can visit him anytime.

7. Exxon is looking for a way **to tap** new _____ of oil.

   You need **to cite** all the _____ that you use in your research paper.

   According to **an undisclosed** _____, Mrs. Markus is going to resign.

8. Gay marriage is a **controversial** _____ in the United States.

   Because of her mistake, Ms. Stevens wants to _____ **an apology**.

   Yesterday, the mayor _____ **a statement** that shocked everyone.

9. In Florida, you can **enjoy the** _____ **of** lots of sunshine.

   Plants **derive** many _____ **from** the excellent climate.

   The swimming pool is shallow **for the** _____ **of** children.

10. Today's computers can **store** _____ very efficiently.

    Statistical _____ show that the climate is changing.

    Our decision is **based on solid** _____.

Unit 1

Collocations

Exercise 2	available	labor	role	analysis	income	legislation
	method	identity	research	major	environment	interpret

1. They used an _____ **approach** to solve the mystery.

    In the final _____, Democrats proved stronger than Republicans.

    It will take time to _____ **the data in detail**.

2. Addictive substances are **readily** _____ to teenagers.

    Thanks for **making yourself** _____ to help us.

    The Internet is not **widely** _____ in some African countries.

3. You should protect yourself from possible _____ **theft**.

    I thought you were someone else. Sorry, it's a case of **mistaken** _____.

    Criminals sometimes **assume a false** _____ in order to commit a crime.

4. They didn't _____ **my remarks** the way I meant them.

    Well, that **puts a different** _____ on the matter.

    A strict _____ **of** the rules prohibits using the money for parties.

5. Some farmers are using **traditional** _____ for growing crops.

    They **developed a sure-fire** _____ for catching fish.

    We need to **devise a new** _____ for scaring away the raccoons.

6. Congress wants to **enact** _____ to limit government spending.

    The _____ **branch** passed a law concerning illegal immigrants.

    The President can **veto** _____ that she disagrees with.

7. This professor is **carefully** _____ the effects of certain drugs on animal behavior.

    Professors need **to publish** _____ from time to time.

    Marketing _____ shows that people prefer to eat fatty, sugary food.

8. What can you do **to protect the** _____?

    Some _____ **organizations** are challenging the new laws.

    This is an **unfriendly** _____ for people who are not religious.

9. Many old people **live on a fixed** _____.

    The **yearly** _____ of many Americans have been declining lately.

    It is hard for most people **to live within their** _____.

10. The oldest daughter **took on the** _____ of mother when Mary died.

    Tariq and Mariam **played the leading** _____ in the performance.

    Fathers **perform a major** _____ in children's development.

Unit 1

Collocations

Exercise 3	area concept formula period establish distribute
	vary section consist process individual assess

1. These notes _____ **entirely of** unimportant details.

    His lecture yesterday _____ **largely of** PowerPoint presentations.

    The first step in forming the committee _____ **in** deciding how many people will be on it.

2. The professor wrote **a chemical** _____ on the blackboard.

    Amy memorized several **mathematical** _____ before the test.

    We are _____ **a plan for** getting the two sides to agree.

3. He is not interested in **abstract** _____. He wants facts.

    We tried to **grasp the** _____ of dark energy.

    Focal length is **a key** _____ in photography.

4. The organizers wanted **to close off** two _____ near the stage.

    The local government **declared** the entire city **a disaster** _____.

    The definition of mental illness is **a gray** _____ in law.

5. There have been several **dark** _____ in American history.

    The birds sat quietly for **a short** _____ **of time**, then flew away.

    After my presentation, there will be **a question and answer** _____.

6. The **random** _____ of the numbers puzzled the researchers.

    Food was **unevenly** _____ after the earthquake.

    The Internet promotes the **global** _____ of goods and services.

7. This neighborhood is **a cross** _____ of the population of the city.

    A short _____ of the street was closed for repairs.

    The teacher **divided** the class **into** _____ according to student ability.

8. The gold rings were _____ at $1,000 each.

    Before we change the curriculum, we must do **a needs** _____.

    The experts will **undertake an** _____ of our new program.

9. Sergeant Monroe is **an outstanding** _____.

    Which camera setting to use is **a matter of** _____ **preference**.

    Sally uses clothes **to express** her _____.

10. Mr. Obama has _____ **himself as** an intelligent leader.

    The business sector favors **the gradual** _____ of new guidelines.

    Congress **is calling for the** _____ of a peace-finding mission.

Unit 1

Collocations

Exercise 4	vary	function	proceed	legality	structure	occur
	labor	evidence	sector	context	process	require

1. Engineers design bridges to be _____ **sound**.

    Organic molecules are **complex** _____ based on carbon.

    The CEO wants to simplify **the financial** _____ of the corporation.

2. If you **meet** all of **the minimum** _____ , you can become a team member.

    They have **a strict** _____ that everyone remains quiet during the talk.

    Does everyone know what is _____ **of** them?

3. More people want to work in **the business** _____ these days.

    The public and **private** _____ are under attack.

    Hispanics represent **a growing** _____ of the population.

4. The temperature _____ **from** day **to** day during the summer.

    Opinions _____ **considerably** as to who should be nominated.

    The results _____ **slightly**, depending on the density of the water.

5. She gets **the creative** _____ started by meditating.

    Judicial _____ can sometimes be slow, but they are necessary.

    Scientists are trying **to slow down the** _____ of aging.

6. Diabetes is **a common** _____ among certain indigenous people.

    Wild fires will **likely** _____ all summer.

    There is a **high** _____ **of** pregnancy in the inner city.

7. Some citizens want **to** _____ **drugs** such as marijuana.

    My lawyer **has doubts about the** _____ **of** school's right to expel my daughter.

    It **is perfectly** _____ **to** fish in this area.

8. After the light changed to green, they _____ **with caution**.

    Grab your things and _____ **quickly** to the exit.

    The chairwoman is _____ **with the plan** to lower the fees.

9. The leaf's tiny hairs **serve an important** _____ .

    Grooming can **perform the** _____ **of** social bonding.

    His job is to make sure that the computer _____ **properly**.

10. The detectives **are searching for** _____ in the woods near his home.

    We will **examine the** _____ before we give our opinion.

    It is **clearly** _____ **that** no one knows where the key is.

Unit 1

Synonyms Use the synonym clues to solve this crossword puzzle.

Across

1. origin, cause, root
4. control, power, strength
8. idea, theory, thought
9. method, system
13. happen, take place, exist
14. revenue, profit, salary
16. facts, statistics, information
20. good, productive, helpful
23. study, inquiry, investigation
27. alter, change, modify
30. single, alone, separate
31. part, place, spot, locale
32. explain, translate, clarify
33. pass out, share, spread

Down

2. agreement, deal, pact
3. part, capacity, use, place
5. gather, get, obtain, acquire
6. name, point out, show
7. time, term, interval
8. compose, form, make up
10. alike, close, related
11. go, move, continue, advance
12. develop, form, start, make
15. function, aspect, cause
17. work, job, task
18. way, plan, technique, mode
19. examination, study
21. model, recipe, plan
22. division, part, piece, portion
24. zone, territory, department
25. go, arrive, near, reach
26. greater, larger, dominant
28. clear, plain, noticeable
29. concept, idea, guess

Unit 1

Review

Write the correct word in each sentence.

1. The new law allows for the _____ of a new school district in our city. 2. Teachers take care of the _____ of textbooks to their students on the first day of class. 3. Karen and her daughter have one _____ : they have the same taste in clothes.	creation distribution approach similarity interpretation contract
4. After resting for a few minutes, she _____ with caution to the top of the mountain. 5. The damage to the car was _____ at over $1,000. 6. Glen's smile _____ that he was in love with this beautiful young woman.	assumed indicated proceeded available assessed exported
7. We _____ his comment to mean that he doesn't want to help us. 8. The senators _____ the president's speech in depth in order to critique it. 9. Honesty, love and truth _____ my value system.	require analyze vary constitute interpret export
10. Last week, thunderstorms frequently _____ in the afternoon on those hot summer days. 11. The book he "wrote" _____ entirely of a cover and a hundred empty pages! 12. We were _____ to take our shoes off before entering the temple.	occurred established consisted of financed conceived required
13. It's important that the rules do not _____ from one person to another. 14. Scientists can _____ many useful products from tropical plants. 15. We should _____ the dog with caution. It looks angry.	authorize derive consist of approach vary legislate
16. Congress _____ against gays in the military. 17. When I met Frieda, I _____ her to be your friend. 18. The wealthy businessman _____ a new school for children of poor families.	established identified legislated required varied assumed

Unit 1

Review

19. Korea's _____ are worth billions of dollars every year. 20. The _____ of these devices are unknown to me. 21. Terrorism and poverty are important _____ today.	exports issues sections functions periods labors
22. During the _____ from 1930 to 1940, many people were out of work. 23. My _____ is to help you learn because I'm a teacher. For your part, you have to make an effort to learn. 24. The _____ of this paragraph is logical and clear.	sector variety role data period structure
25. One of the _____ of working here is that you get a discount. 26. According to the _____, the number of Asian students is increasing. 27. He used secret _____ to make his high-quality furniture polishes.	formulas definitions benefits concepts environments data
28. Building your own home requires a lot of physical _____. 29. The managers are in the _____ of developing a new system. 30. My _____ is that children will behave if they are respected.	areas labor finance process theory legislature
31. You have to interpret his behavior in the _____ of recent events. 32. She's really bad at personal _____. She spends more than she earns. 33. My _____ of making bread requires a lot of patience.	context policy method role theory finance
34. We put the chairs in one _____ of the room, and the tables in another. 35. You don't have the _____ to tell me what to do. 36. Lack of water was one _____ that caused the plants to die.	variety factor benefit section authority approach

Unit 1

Review

37. Six _____ of all men in this room are over 21 years old.	income analysis contract environment concept percent
38. It is difficult for me to understand the _____ of selfishness.	
39. Her _____ was not high, but she knew how to live well without very much money.	
40. Each _____ in the group had his or her own idea.	export individual source area interpretation legislation
41. The _____ of her strength is her religion.	
42. We live in the _____ where the weather is usually quite nice.	
43. According to recent _____ it may be possible to clone a human.	research identity similarity sector contract process
44. The police could not establish the _____ of the bank robber.	
45. According to your _____ you have to work one more year.	
46. Life in the Jewish _____ of town was beginning to improve.	policy analysis sector assessment concept environment
47. I can't relax in a noisy _____ .	
48. The company's _____ prohibits workers from smoking inside.	
49. The president was not _____ to comment on the accident.	structural significant evident available formulaic analytical
50. It was _____ that she was too sick to walk home.	
51. They donated a _____ amount of money to the university.	
52. Your question is too general. You need to be more _____ .	specific conceptual beneficial financial major legal
53. He made some minor mistakes, but his _____ error was that he had lied.	
54. Get a lawyer because you need _____ advice right away.	

Unit 1

Definitions ° Parts of Speech ° Collocations

analysis (n) separation into parts for a close look in order to discover more
>   to carry out an analysis, to make an analysis, to perform an analysis
>   a careful analysis, a thorough analysis, comprehensive analysis, detailed analysis, in-depth analysis
>   systematic analysis, brief analysis, objective analysis, subjective analysis, comparative analysis
>   cost-benefit analysis, discourse analysis [= analysis of written, spoken or sign language]
>   critical analysis; quantitative analysis [= analysis of factual data]
>   a subjective analysis [= analysis based on personal opinion or point of view]: *More accurate x-ray images can eliminate most of the mistakes that result from subjective analysis.*
>   an objective analysis [= analysis without personal opinion]: *We need someone outside the company to give us an objective analysis.*
>   upon/on further analysis: *Upon further analysis, we decided not to continue with the project.*
>   in the final analysis, in the last analysis

analyze (v) [British: analyse]
>   to carefully analyze, to critically analyze, to fully analyze, to painstakingly analyze [= to analyze thoroughly and with great care]: *After painstakingly analyzing the data, we made our decision.*
>   to analyze in depth, to analyze fully, to analyze in detail
>   to analyze scientifically, to analyze systematically

analytical (adj)
>   (to use/take) an analytical approach

analytically (adv)

analyst (n)
>   a leading analyst, business analyst, financial analyst, data analyst, market analyst
>   military analyst, policy analyst, retail analyst, systems analyst

approach (n) near in space, time, quality or amount
>   to make an approach; to take (a different) approach, to adopt an approach
>   to begin an approach: *The pilot began his approach to the airport.*
>   a creative approach, a conservative approach, a realistic approach
>   an objective approach, a constructive approach, an indirect approach
>   conventional approach, orthodox approach, traditional approach, cautious approach
>   creative approach, positive approach, pragmatic approach
>   analytical approach, scientific approach, systematic approach, theoretical approach
>   with the approach of (something): *Birds go south with the approach of winter.*
>   an approach to: *He has an interesting approach to the problem.*

approach (v)
>   to approach (someone) about: *She approached me about my views on abortion.*
>   to approach (someone) for: *He approached me for a cigarette.*
>   to approach from: *We should approach this problem from a different angle.*
>   to approach with caution: *You should approach a poisonous snake with caution.*
>   to approach slowly, cautiously, warily
>   the time is fast approaching: *The time is fast approaching when you will have to leave home.*
>   easy to approach, difficult to approach

approachable (adj.) friendly and easy to talk to
>   *You will like your new teacher. She is very approachable.*

approachable (adj.) able to be reached in a certain way
>   *The village is only approachable by way of a narrow mountain trail.*

area (n) a place or region
>   to close off an area, to rope off an area, to seal off an area [= to close an area]: *The police sealed off the area around the governor's mansion when they received the bomb threat.*
>   to be scattered over an area, to be spread over an area, to cover an area
>   an urban area, a rural area, a built-up area, a residential area, metropolitan area
>   a vast area, a wide area, a huge area, a small area, the local area
>   a smoking area, a service area, a storage area
>   a key area, a sensitive area, a complex area, a problem area
>   a mountain area, coastal area, remote area, outlying area
>   dining area, play area, picnic area
>   a disaster area: *The governor declared the flooded towns a disaster area.*

area (n) subject or activity
>   to identify an area, to cover an area
>   a gray area [=an unclear or uncertain subject or idea]: *It would be difficult to decide whether or not you can keep the money you found on the beach. The law is not clear. It is a gray area.* an important area
>   key area, main area, sensitive area, problem area, area of interest
>   an area of life, an area of concern, an area of difficulty

assessment (n) the amount, value, quality or importance of something that has been decided upon

to undertake an assessment, to carry out an assessment, to make an assessment

a broad assessment, a general assessment, an overall assessment

an individual assessment, a personal assessment, an independent assessment, an objective assessment

quality assessment, needs assessment, risk assessment, performance assessment

continual assessment, regular assessment

assessment measures, assessment procedures, assessment criteria, assessment process

assess (v)

to attempt to assess, to try to assess, to be difficult to assess

to fully assess, to accurately assess, to correctly assess, to properly assess

to assess (something) at: *The ring was assessed at $5,000.*

to assess the damage

assumption (n) something which is supposed to be true without evidence or proof

to make an assumption, to start from the assumption, to work on the assumption

a basic assumption, a fundamental assumption. an underlying assumption

a hidden assumption, implicit assumption, tacit assumption, unspoken assumption

a common assumption, conventional assumption, widespread assumption

a reasonable assumption, correct assumption, valid assumption

a number of assumptions, a set of assumptions, a series of assumptions

on the assumption that: *We booked our flight for the 5ᵗʰ of June on the assumption that our vacation would start that day.*

assume (v)

to be fair to assume, to be safe to assume

it would be a mistake to assume, wrong to assume, easy to assume

automatically assume: *Why do you automatically assume that I will order a hamburger?*

naturally assume: *We naturally assumed that Kate and Tom were going to get married.*

reasonably assume, safely assume: *We can safely assume that the law protects minors in this case.*

assume (someone/something) to be (something): *He was assumed to be an authority.*

authority (n) the moral or legal right, power, or ability to give orders, make decisions, or control

to assert authority, to demonstrate authority, to show authority

to exercise authority, have authority, to use authority, to assume authority [= to take authority]: *Bob won the election and he will assume authority on January 1.*

to give authority, to yield authority, to delegate authority

to relinquish authority [= to give up authority]: *Because she lost the election, Ellen had to relinquish authority when the new mayor took over the office.*

to challenge authority, to question authority, to reject authority

to abuse authority, to overstep one's authority

to have authority over: *Ms. Hubert has authority over everyone in this office.*

to have authority for: *Robert has authority for operating all of this equipment.*

(to be) in authority: *In this office, the director is in authority, not the manager.*

to have it on good authority: *We have it on good authority that the mayor will soon step down.*

to act on someone's authority: *We are acting on the authority of the captain.*

appropriate authority, competent authority, reliable authority

local authority, regional authority, public authority, government authority

absolute authority, complete authority, full authority, supreme authority

authority (n) a person who is an expert on a subject

to cite an authority, to invoke an authority

a leading authority, a respected authority, a well-known authority

authorization (n)

to require authorization, to ask for authorization, to seek authorization

to refuse authorization, to revoke authorization [= to take away authorization]: *Kay did not want the hospital to share her medical records with anyone, so she revoked that authorization in writing.*

formal authorization, official authorization, written authorization

without (prior) authorization

authorize (v)

to authorize a payment

authoritative (adj)

authoritatively (adv)

available (adj) able to be used, purchased, obtained or reached

to make oneself available: *There's a meeting at noon. Can you make yourself available?*

easily available, readily available, freely available, widely available

available to: *The information is available to anyone.*

available for (a meeting, etc.) *Are you available for a movie after work tonight?*

available from: *Application forms are available from our web site.*

Unit 1

availability (n)
    to check availability: *Before we go to the concert, we need to check the availability of tickets.*
    to ensure availability: *To ensure the availability of vegetarian meals, you must check the appropriate box on our web site.*
    subject to availability [= according to whether or not something is available]: *Premier members may receive upgrades to first class, subject to availability of seats.*

benefit (n) anything that provides an advantage or is helpful
    to get benefit, to obtain the benefit of, to receive the benefit of
    to derive benefit, to reap benefit from [= to get benefit from]: *If you work hard, you will reap the benefits of your labor.*
    to enjoy the benefit of, to have the benefit of: *He has the benefit of a good upbringing.*
    to be of benefit to: *Take this dictionary on your trip. It will be of benefit to you.*
    to give someone the benefit of the doubt [=to trust that someone is telling the truth]: *He claims that he is the only one who can help us, so we have to give him the benefit of the doubt.*
    for the benefit of: *We need to develop a program for the benefit of small businesses.*
    mutual benefit, considerable benefit, enormous benefit, great benefit, major benefit
    a fringe benefit [= an extra benefit] *Free cafeteria lunches are a fringe benefit of working here.*

benefit (n) money
    to be eligible for a benefit, to be entitled to a benefit, to qualify for a benefit
    to draw benefits [= to receive benefits]: *You can draw your Social Security benefits when you are 68.*
    to be dependent on benefits, to lose benefits
    a death benefit [= insurance money paid to survivors of someone who has died]

benefit (v)
    to benefit greatly, to benefit considerably
    to clearly benefit, to obviously benefit
    to benefit from

beneficial (adj)
beneficially (adv)

concept (n) a clear or logically formed principle or idea
    to formulate a concept, to frame a concept, to have a concept
    to understand a concept, to grasp a concept [= to understand a concept]: *I didn't grasp the concept of the space-time continuum until you explained it to me. Thanks!*
    an abstract concept, a vague concept, a theoretical concept
    a clear concept, a precise concept
    an ambiguous concept, a nebulous concept, a vague concept [= unclear concept]: *The idea that wealthy people are "job creators" is a rather vague concept.*
    a basic concept, a simple concept
    a key concept, a central concept, a fundamental concept, an important concept
    the overall concept, the wider concept, the broad concept

conceptualize (v)
conceptual (adj)
conceptually (adv)

consist of (v) to be made of, composed of or formed of
    consist of: *Molecules consist of atoms.*
    consist entirely of, consist largely of, consist mostly of, consist mainly of
    consist primarily of, consist principally of, consist predominantly of
    consist only of, consist simply of, consist solely of

consist in (v):
    The first step of the process will consist in organizing a meeting.

consistency (n) degree of firmness or density
    thick consistency, soft consistency, creamy consistency, smooth consistency
    to have the consistency of: *Mix the ingredients with milk until they have the consistency of soft butter.*

constitute (v) to form, compose or make
    to constitute a problem for: *This new law constitutes a problem for us.*
    to constitute a source: *The survey constitutes the best source of data that we can rely on.*

constitution (n) The form of a set of laws
    to draft a constitution, to draw up a constitution [= to write a constitution]: *The military announced that it would meet next week to draw up a new constitution.*
    to adopt a constitution, to ratify a constitution [= to officially approve or vote on a constitution]: *The constitution of the United States was ratified in 1790.*
    to violate the constitution
    to be enshrined in a constitution [= to be solidly set in a set of laws]: *Freedom of expression is enshrined in the U. S. Constitution.*
    federal constitution, state constitution, written constitution

unwritten constitution, draft constitution, proposed constitution
an amendment to a constitution, the provisions of a constitution
constitution (n) condition that the body is in
   a weak constitution
   a strong constitution: *Peggy seldom gets sick. She has a strong constitution.*
context (n) the set of circumstances or events in which a particular event occurs
   to provide a context, to place something in context, to consider something in context
   to put in (into) context: *To make that more clear to you, let me put it into context.*
   to consider, to examine, to see, to understand, to view something in the context of
   to put something into context
   to take or cite something out of context, to quote something out of context
   a broad context, a larger context, a wider context, an appropriate context
   the right context, the correct context, the proper context, the human context
   historical context, political context, religious context, social context
   normal context, everyday context, modern context
   global context, international context
   appropriate context, realistic context, normal context
   theoretical context, practical context; conversational context, communicative context
   context for ~ing: *We need a neutral context for discussing our different ideas.*
   within the context of
contextualize (v)
contextualized (adj)
contextual (adj)
contextually (adv)
contract (n) a legal document that states and explains a formal agreement between two different people
   or groups specifying things that should or should not be done
   to sign a contract; to make or conclude a contract; to negotiate a contract, to land a contract
   to be under contract: *Our company is under contract to build a new web site for the City of Portland.*
   to draw up or write (up) a contract; to cancel, break or violate a contract
   a contract expires, a contract is in force [= a contract is still valid]: *This contract is in force until the*
   end of the year, at which time we can negotiate a new one.
   an oral, verbal, or written contract; a marriage contract
   terms of a contract, a contract worker, contract law
   a long-term contract, a verbal contract, a valid contract
   a major contract, a business contract, a lucrative contract [= a contract worth a great deal of money]
   a commercial contract, an employment contract, a marriage contract
   in breach of contract [= done against the terms of the contract]
contractual (adj)
contractually (adv)
contract (v) to enter into a legal agreement
   to contract with, to contract for
contract (n) an agreement to kill someone
   to put out a contract on someone: *The Mafia put out a contract on one of its enemies.*
contract (v) to become shorter or smaller: *Most metals contract when they become colder and expand*
   when they become warmer.
contraction (n)
creation (n) something which is made or brought into being
create (v)
   to create friction, to create difficulty; to create a dilemma
creative (adj)
   creative energy
creatively (adv)
creativity (v)
   to develop creativity, to stimulate creativity, to encourage creativity
   to stifle creativity [= to stop or prevent creativity]
   artistic creativity, musical creativity
data (n. pl) [datum = n. sing] information, esp. facts or numbers, collected for examination and
   consideration and used to draw a conclusion
   to process data, to analyze data, to interpret data, to evaluate data, to manipulate data, to manage data
   to collect data, to gather data, to access data, to retrieve data, to store data
   to cite data, to be based on (concrete/solid) data: *Ken received high marks for his research paper*
   because he cited data from many recent sources.
   data indicate, data suggest, data show
   biographical data, statistical data; available data
   comparative data, concrete data, raw data, solid data

Unit 1

accurate data, reliable data, raw data [= unprocessed or unanalyzed data]
data collection, data entry, data storage, data access, data retrieval, electronic data processing

derive (v) to get, obtain or extract something from an original source
 clearly derive, largely derive, mainly derive, primarily derive
 originally derive, ultimately derive
 to derive from: *Many English words are derived from Latin.*
 to derive a benefit from; derive benefits from: *Banks will derive huge benefits from the new law.*
 to derive power from

derivation (n)
derivational (adj)
derivationally (adv)

distribute (v) to divide into parts and give out to each of several people or groups, or to spread out,
 scatter or supply
 to distribute fairly, to distribute equitably, to distribute evenly
 to distribute unfairly, to distribute inequitably, to distribute unevenly
 to distribute among, to distribute to

distribution (n)
 normal distribution, random distribution, smooth distribution, skewed distribution
 general distribution, broad distribution, wide distribution
 equitable distribution, fair distribution, optimal distribution
 global distribution, regional distribution, worldwide distribution

environment (n) the surrounding objects, influences and conditions that affect how you feel or how
 effectively you can work
 to create an environment, to provide an environment: *The new building provides a clean and safe
 working environment.*
 to adapt to an environment, to improve an environment, to explore an environment
 a social environment, a work environment, a classroom environment
 a hostile environment, an unfriendly environment, a harsh environment, an unstable environment
 an alien environment, a new environment, an unfamiliar environment, a competitive environment
 a changing environment, a friendly environment, a stimulating environment

environment (n) the natural world
 to protect the environment, to preserve the environment, to safeguard the environment
 to improve the environment, to clean up the environment
 to pollute the environment, to damage the environment, to harm the environment
 natural environment, local environment, world environment, global environment
 conservation of the environment, protection of the environment, pollution of the environment
 harmful to the environment

environmental (adj)
 environmental hazards; environmental organizations
 to raise environmental concerns

environmentally (adv)

establish (v) to bring into being something that will last a long time
 to seek to establish, to try to establish, to attempt to establish: *The French attempted to establish a
 military base inside the Russian border.*
 to agree to establish, to help to establish
 recently established, newly established, firmly established, securely established
 to establish oneself (as)

establishment (n)
 to support an establishment, to allow the establishment of, to enable the establishment of
 to call for the establishment of, to provide for the establishment of, to agree to the establishment of to
 consent to the establishment of, to lead to the establishment of
 an educational establishment, a financial establishment, a political establishment
 formal establishment, gradual establishment, rapid establishment

Establishment (n) The dominant (strongest) group, especially in government, the military and the church
 to fight the Establishment
 the literary Establishment, the Church Establishment, the armed forces Establishment

evident (adj) clearly, obviously or easily seen or understood
 to be evident that: *It is evident that you have not studied for the quiz.*
 to seem evident, become evident, remain evident
 fairly evident, clearly evident, plainly evident, strongly evident, painfully evident, perfectly evident
 evident from, evident in, evident to: *Her guilt was evident to everyone.*

evidently (adv)
evidence (n)
 to search for evidence, to gather evidence, to obtain evidence, to collect evidence

Unit 1

to offer evidence, to provide evidence, to show evidence

to consider evidence, to examine evidence, to review evidence, to cite evidence

abundant evidence, considerable evidence, substantial evidence, widespread evidence, overwhelming evidence, compelling evidence, convincing evidence

clear evidence, conclusive evidence, hard evidence, solid evidence, strong evidence

flimsy evidence, weak evidence, insufficient evidence

circumstantial evidence, anecdotal evidence: *There is only anecdotal evidence to suggest that Vikings established a colony in the New World before Columbus arrived.*

evidence comes to light, evidence emerges, evidence accumulates, evidence grows

in the face of evidence, in the light of evidence

a lack of evidence, not a scrap of evidence, not a shred of evidence [= no evidence at all]: *There is not a shred of evidence to suggest that Putin is interested in peace in the region.*

export (v) to send or transport goods to other countries for sale or trade

to export widely, to export legally, to export illegally

to export from, to export to

export (n)

to encourage the export of, to promote the export of

to reduce the export of, to restrict the export of

chief export, leading export, major export

a ban on exports, a decline in exports, a fall in exports

a rise in exports, an increase in exports

exporter (n)

leading exporter: *Saudi Arabia is a leading exporter of light crude oil.*

major exporter, food exporter, oil exporter

exportable (adj)

factor (n) a fact or situation which influences or partially affects the result of something

a contributing factor, a relevant factor, an additional factor

a crucial factor, a critical factor, a vital factor: *Cindy's optimism is a vital factor in her recovery.*

an important factor, a key factor, a major factor; a determining factor, an essential factor

a complicating factor, a limiting factor

the fear factor; a risk factor, a causal factor

the common factor: *The police discovered a common factor in all of the recent burglaries.*

environmental factor, genetic factor, psychological factor

a factor which affects, factor which influences, factor which contributes to, factor which determines

a factor behind: *One of the key factors behind her success is her husband's support.*

a factor in: *A major factor in the pollution of the environment is industrial discharge.*

factor (v)

to factor into: *How do these data factor into our decision?*

finance (n) the management of a supply of money or other assets

public finance; high finance

long-term finance, short-term finance

outside finance, private sector finance, public sector finance

housing finance, mortgage finance

finance company, finance sector

the world of high finance (finance involving huge corporations or nations)

consumer finance, government finance, public finance

finance director, finance officer, finance consultant

finances (n. pl,) monetary resources or funds

to keep finances in order, to manage finances, to handle finances, to sort out finances

to lack finances, shaky finances [= not having enough money]: *I can't buy a new car right now because of my shaky finances.*

household finances, state finances, government finances, public finances

to improve one's finances, to boost finances

to be a drain on finances, to strain one's finances

finance (v)

mainly finance, privately finance, publically finance

financing (n) the act of providing funds

to get finance (financing), to obtain finance (financing)

deficit financing [= government getting money by borrowing]; equity financing [= selling stocks to raise money]

financial (adj)

financially (adv)

formula (n) an established group of words or symbols or standard way of doing or making something

to devise a formula, to come up with a formula, to follow a formula, to devise a formula a formula for (for ~ing): *Charles devised a formula for improving the strength of the explosives.*

a mathematical formula, an algebraic formula, a chemical formula

a complex formula, a simple formula

a magic formula: *I wish there were a magic formula for memorizing vocabulary words.*

a traditional formula, a time-honored formula; a face-saving formula [= a formula for preventing someone from feeling embarrassed]

formulate (v)

to carefully formulate, to clearly formulate, to fully formulate, to properly formulate

to formulate a plan: *The prisoners formulated a plan for escaping from the prison.*

formulaic (adj)

function (n) the purpose, role or duty for which an object or a person is naturally used or suited

to perform a function, to fulfill a function, to carry out a function, to serve a function

important function, useful function, valuable function, main function, primary function, major function: *the marsh plants serve the valuable function of filtering impurities out of the water.*

function (n) a social event

to attend a function, to hold a function

a charity function, a gala function, a social function: *The city plans to hold a gala function to celebrate its 200th birthday.*

function (v)

to function properly, to function efficiently, to function normally, to function smoothly

fully functioning: *Elena Makarova has described the fourteen characteristics of a fully functioning person.*

to function as: *This table could function as a desk if we just remove the tablecloth.*

functional (adj)

functionally (adv)

identity (n) the qualities or characteristics which make a person or group different from others

to establish someone's identity, to discover identity, to find out identity, to guess identity

to conceal one's identity; to assume the identity of, to assume a false identity

to disclose identity, to reveal identity

racial identity, sexual identity

true identity, assumed identity, false identity, mistaken identity: *That wasn't Robin we saw at the restaurant. It was a case of mistaken identity.*

identity theft; identity crisis: *Don't mind him. He's just having an identity crisis.*

identity bracelet, identity tag, identity card, identity documents

a sense of identity: *Seeing the place where I was born has given me a better sense of identity.*

a search for identity; proof of identity

identify (v) to determine who or what something is

identification (n)

income (n) the money derived from doing work or investing

to earn an income, to have an income, to generate income, to provide income

to live within one's income

an annual income, a yearly income, a monthly income

average income, below average income; sufficient income; above average income, high income

gross income, net income, taxable income, after-tax income

disposable income [= money that you are free to spend after you spend money on necessities]: *With her recent pay raise, Samara found that she had much more disposable income than before.*

fixed income, limited income, low income, retirement income

income exceeds expenditures: *When your income exceeds your expenditures, you can live comfortably.*

income level, income bracket [= income level]

source of income: *Many married couples have two sources of income.*

income per capita [= income per person]

indicate (v) to show, point out or make clear

to clearly indicate; to indicate something to someone

to be used to indicate: *The dollar sign is used to indicate the relative cost of each hotel.*

indication (n)

to give an indication, to provide an indication, to find an indication: *We found no indication that anyone had lived in the house recently.*

to be regarded as an indication, to be taken as an indication

a clear indication, a reliable indication, an accurate indication, a sure indication: *When his left eye closes, it's a sure indication that he is becoming angry.*

preliminary indication, initial indication; outward indication, visible indication

positive indication, valuable indication, useful indication

amid indications: *The military was on high alert amid indications that the populace was growing uneasy.*

Unit 1

there is every indication that: *There is every indication that spring will arrive late this year.*
indicative (adj)
    to be considered indicative (of), to be regarded as indicative (of), to be seen as indicative (of)
    clearly indicative, not necessarily indicative: *A gray sky is not necessarily indicative of rain.*
indicatively (adv)
individual (n) existing as a single, distinct, or separate person or thing
    to treat someone as an individual, to have concern for the individual
    outstanding individual, talented individual, creative individual
    average individual, ordinary individual, unique individual, private individual
    like-minded individual, qualified individual: *We will give every qualified individual an interview.*
    no single individual, no one individual: *No one individual was responsible for the team's win.*
individuality (n)
    to express individuality, to show individuality, to recognize individuality
    a sense of individuality, a feeling of individuality
    suppression of individuality [= not letting a person express himself/herself as an individual]
individualize (v)
individual (adj)
    a matter of individual preference, individual taste; an individual effort
    individual freedom
individually (adv)
interpret (v) to explain or determine what the intended meaning of something is
    to interpret one's remarks
    to interpret something to mean something: *Ginny interpreted my smile to mean that I like her.*
    to interpret for; to interpret as: *They interpreted my silence as hostility.*
    to interpret with caution; to be difficult to interpret
    to be variously interpreted as
    not know how to interpret: *We did not know how to interpret Natasha's silence.*
    correctly interpret, rightly interpret, wrongly interpret
    narrowly interpret, broadly interpret: *The constitutionality of the health care law depends on how broadly or narrowly one interprets the law.*
interpretive (adj)
    interpretive dance
interpretation (n) explaining what something means or is supposed to mean
    to make an interpretation
    to put a certain interpretation on: *I put a totally different interpretation on her story.*
    a broad interpretation, a free interpretation, a liberal interpretation
    a narrow interpretation, a strict interpretation
    to be open to interpretation: *Jill's remarks were unclear and so were open to interpretation.*
interpretation (n) translating a language
    simultaneous interpretation [= immediately interpreting from one language to another]
interpretive (adj)
issue (n) a point, problem or matter which people are thinking about and discussing
    to raise an issue, to debate an issue, to discuss an issue
    to examine an issue, to address an issue, to explore an issue: *Today, we will explore the issue of the government's role in protecting the environment.*
    to tackle an issue [= to go to work on an issue with determination]
    to settle an issue, to decide an issue; to touch on an issue [= to mention an issue]
    to focus on an issue, to clarify an issue, to highlight an issue
    to confuse the issue, to avoid the issue, to evade the issue [= to avoid the issue]
    controversial issue, big issue, burning issue, serious issue
    controversial issue, thorny issue [= complicated issue that upsets people]: *Gay marriage is a thorny issue in many communities.*
    real issue, fundamental issue, basic issue, underlying issue, unresolved issue
    at issue, issue about, issue concerning: *This is an issue concerning individual freedom.*
    on this issue: *What is your thinking on this issue?*
issue (v) to announce something or make something officially available
    to issue a threat, to issue a warning; to issue an apology, to issue a statement
    to issue stamps, to issue money: *Only the federal government can issue money.*
    to issue equipment, to issue clothing
issue (n) a publication
    the issue came out [= was published]
    current issue, special issue, back issue [= previous issue]
labor (n) [British: labour] practical work requiring either physical or mental effort
    to do labor, to perform labor

Unit 1

to sentence someone to hard labor [= to send someone to prison where he or she must perform hard physical labor]: *Jean was sentenced to twenty years of hard labor for stealing a loaf of bread.*
backbreaking labor, manual labor, physical labor, mental labor
productive labor; a division of labor; forced labor, hard labor; slave labor, child labor, migrant labor
organized labor; skilled labor, unskilled labor

labor (v) [British: **labour**]
to labor over: *She labored over her love poem for several days.*
to labor as: *They labored as construction workers for many years.*

laborer (n) [British: **labourer**]
manual laborer, migrant laborer, seasonal laborer, farm laborer
skilled laborer, unskilled laborer
gang of laborers [= group or team of laborers] *A gang of peasant laborers worked on the railroad line.*

legal (adj) allowed by or relating to the law
completely legal, perfectly legal
legal to: *It isn't legal to smoke marijuana in most states.*

legally (adv)

legality (n)
to challenge the legality of, to have doubts about the legality of
to uphold the legality of, to recognize the legality of
doubtful legality, dubious legality [= doubtful legality]

legalization (n)

legalize (v)
to legalize drugs, to legalize marijuana

legislate (v) to make a law or laws
to legislate for, to legislate against

legislation (n)
to adopt legislation, to enact legislation, to pass legislation
to draft legislation, to introduce legislation, to call for legislation, to initiate legislation
to veto legislation, to vote down legislation, to repeal legislation, to block legislation
legislation comes into effect, legislation comes into force
emergency legislation
social legislation
a piece of legislation: *Congress will debate this piece of legislation before they vote on it later today.*

legislative (adj)
the legislative branch (of government): *The legislative branch passed a law that the President likes.*

legislatively (adv)

legislature (n)
to be elected to the legislature
federal legislature, national legislature, state legislature, provincial legislature

major (adj) more important, bigger or more serious than others of the same type; great in position or reputation
major aim, major objective; major area, major concern, major problem
major effort, major factor, major part, major responsibility
major source of: *A major source of funding for NPR comes from members like you.*
of major importance

majorly (adj)

major (v) to formally focus one's studies on a specific subject in college
major in: *Latisha wants to major in psychology at Michigan State University.*

major (n) the formal focus of one's studies in college. *Laurie's major is business.*

major (n) a military officer

method (n) a particular way or procedure for doing something
to apply a method, to employ a method, to use a method, to develop a method
to adopt a method, to devise a method (for ~ing): *We need to devise a new method for growing corn.*
an effective method, an efficient method, a practical method, a reliable method: *Abstinence is the most reliable method of birth control.*
an antiquated method [= very old method], an obsolete method [= a method which is no longer used]
a crude method, a devious method, a sure method, a sure-fire method: *She has a sure-fire method to get students to understand and use the present perfect tense.*
a modern method, a traditional method; a sophisticated method
the empirical method, the deductive method, the Socratic method [= a method in which the teacher asks questions to make students discover knowledge.]
a method for: *She knows a good method for growing tomatoes in the winter.*
a method in: *There is a method in her teaching. There's a method in his madness.*

methodical (adj)

a methodical approach
methodically (adv)
occur (v) to happen or take place
    commonly occur, frequently occur, rarely occur, naturally occur
    to be likely to occur, to tend to occur, to be unlikely to occur
occurrence (n)
    a common occurrence, a daily occurrence, everyday occurrences, regular occurrences
    frequent occurrence, infrequent occurrence, rare occurrence, unusual occurrence
    frequency of occurrence, high frequency of occurrence, low frequency of occurrence
percent (n) [also: per cent] one part for every one hundred
    to give a hundred percent [= to work or play to the best of one's ability]
    account for X percent of, amount to X percent of, be equal to X percent of
    grow by X percent, improve by X percent, increase by X percent, rise by X percent
    decrease by X percent, decline by X percent, drop by X percent, to be down by X percent
percentage (n)
    high percentage, low percentage
    to calculate the percentage, to express the percentage
    in percentage terms, on a percentage basis
period (n) a specific or limited length of time
    (after) a short period of time
    a rest period, a cooling-off period [= a rest period]: *The angry teens were advised to stop arguing and come back after a cooling-off period.*
    an extended period, a long period, a brief period, a limited period
    a set period, a trial period, a waiting period
    a dark period, a difficult period, a bleak period
    a question and answer period: *After the PowerPoint presentation, there will be a ten-minute question and answer period.*
    a transitional period, a period of transition; an intervening period
    the period from X to Y, the period between X and Y
    for a period of time, in a certain period, within a period of, during a period of, after a period of: *After a short period of time, the bears stopped trying to catch the salmon.*
periodical (adj)
periodically (adv)
periodical (n) a publication that comes out on a regular basis, such as a magazine or journal
policy (n) a set of principles, ideas or a plan that is officially agreed on and used as a guide for action
    to adopt a policy, to establish a policy, to set a policy
    to adhere to a policy, to follow a policy
    to carry out a policy, to form a policy, to make a policy, to introduce a policy, to shape a policy
    to change a policy, to modify a policy, to revise a policy, to violate a policy
    a clear policy, a sound policy, a wise policy
    an official policy, a government policy
    a friendly policy, an open-door policy
    a financial policy, an environmental policy, a social policy, a controversial policy
    domestic policy, monetary policy, fiscal policy
    a policy on, a policy towards
    a policy decision, a policy change, a policy review
    a matter of policy
proceed (v) to start or continue doing or saying something, especially after a delay
    to proceed in an orderly fashion
    to proceed quickly, to proceed rapidly, to proceed smoothly
    to proceed carefully, to proceed cautiously, to proceed with caution
    to proceed on the basis of: *We have no choice but to proceed on the basis of what we know so far.*
    to proceed against, to proceed from ~ to
    to proceed with (a plan/research)
process (n) systematic series of actions or events used to produce something or achieve a particular result
    to slow down the process, to speed up the process, to go through the process
    a creative process, a democratic process, the aging process, a natural process
    the judicial process, legal process; mental processes
    a gradual process, a lengthy process, a long process, a slow process
    a complex process, a difficult process, a complicated process
    decision-making process, planning process, assessment process
    political process, election process, democratic process; judicial process, legal process
    peace process: *It was painful to watch the long, slow peace process, but we knew it had to be done.*
    chemical process, manufacturing process; ageing process, evolutionary process

by a/the process of elimination: *By a process of elimination, we figured out who had last used the computer.*

process (v)

    to efficiently process, to quickly process, to automatically process

    to process for, to process into: *Old glass can be processed into road paving material.*

require (v) to make something necessary; to demand or insist upon

    to urgently require, to reasonably require

    to require from, to require of; to know what is required of: *By the end of the orientation session, every new student knew what was required of him or her.*

requirement (n)

    to fulfill requirements, to establish requirements, to set requirements, to meet requirements

    to relax requirements, to waive requirements [= to drop or eliminate requirements]

    to comply with the requirements, meet the requirements, fulfill the requirements, satisfy the requirements

    to suit the requirements: *We cannot accept these textbooks because they do not suit our requirements.*

    to be subject to the requirements of

    legal requirements, minimum requirements, physical requirements, entrance requirements

    absolute requirement, strict requirement, minimum requirement, basic requirement, key requirement

research (v) to do detailed, systematic study to obtain and analyze information especially in order to learn something new

    to carefully research, to extensively research, to fully research

    to research for, to research into

research (n. sing) *(This noun is never plural!)*

    to carry out research, to conduct research, to do research, to pursue research, to publish research

    detailed research, painstaking research, solid research, original research

    academic research, clinical research, historical research, scientific research

    collaborative research [= research done by many people working together]

    marketing research, animal research, space research

    qualitative research, quantitative research

role (n) proper or assigned position and function or behavior of a person or thing in a particular situation

    to take on a/the role: *When she married a man with two children, she had to take on the role of mother.*

    to be on a role [= to be successful]: *He keeps on winning. He's really on a role now.*

    to perform a role, to play a role

    to assign a role, to hand out roles

    a decisive role, an important role, a key role, a leading role

    an active role, a passive role

    a major role, a key role, a central role, an essential role, a leading role, a primary role

    a minor role, a secondary role, a minor role, a subordinate role,

    an advisory role, a managerial role, a maternal role, a paternal role

section (n) one of the parts that something is divided into, separate or distinct from the whole

    the business section, the classified section, the news section, the sports section, the travel section

    a vertical section, a large section, a long section; a small section, a short section

    a business section, a residential section, an industrial section; a smoking section

    a section of society; a cross section of society [= a small group that represents the larger social group]

    to come in sections: *The desk came in sections, so we had to put it together ourselves.*

    to divide into sections

sector (n) controlled area or region, such as in society or in a political system

    the public sector, the private sector, the business sector

    in the ~ sector: *Martin worked in the private sector for many years before moving to the public sector.*

    an important sector, a key sector, a growing sector

    a sector of the economy, a sector of the market

significant (adj) especially meaningful, important; considerable

    significant for: *This coin is significant for the fact that it is made of gold.*

    significant to: *That monument is not significant to me at all.*

    significant that: *It is significant that Norman decided not to attend the meeting.*

significantly (adv)

signify (v)

significance (n)

    to be of great significance, considerable significance, enormous significance, major significance

    to be of limited significance, of minor significance, of no particular significance: *These old copper coins are of no particular significance to a collector like me.*

    to acquire significance, to assume significance, to gain significance, to take on significance

    the significance lies in (the fact that): *The significance of her promotion lies in the fact that is that she is now her husband's boss.*

Unit 1

similar (adj) resembling or being almost the same, but not exactly
    in a similar manner, in a similar vein
    a similar feel, a similar look, a similar sound
    to have similar tastes
    strikingly similar
similarly (adv)
similarity (n)
    to bear a similarity to: *Janice bears a great similarity to her mother.*
    a similarity among/between
    a strong similarity, considerable similarity, striking similarity: *There is a striking similarity in the way the two poets describe fear.*
    a point of similarity
source (n) the cause of something; where something comes from
    to locate a source, to track down a source
    to tap a source [= to use a source]: *We need to tap a new source of petroleum.*
    to cite a source, to document a source; to disclose a source, to reveal a source
    to provide, prove or constitute a source: *The recent survey constitutes the best source of data that we can rely on.*
    an informed source, a reputable source, an excellent source, a reliable source
    a major source, principle source; an undisclosed source
    the sources dried up: *All of our energy sources have dried up.*
specific (adj) relating or pertaining to one definite thing and not others
    specific about: *She was very specific about what she wanted us to do.*
    specific to: *This bird is specific to a small region in Tanzania.*
    be specific: *That's not clear. Can you be more specific?*
specifically (adv)
specify (v)
    to specify (something) by (~ing): *They specified their wishes by putting them in writing.*
    to specify someone or something by name
    to specify that; to specify how to
specification (n)
structure (n) a system consisting of a number of parts joined together or arranged in a certain way
    to lack structure, to create structure, to establish structure
    a basic structure, a complex structure, a solid structure
    corporate structure; economic structure, financial structure, corporate structure, price structure
    tax structure, wage structure
structure (v)
structural (adj)
structurally (adv)
    structurally sound [= structurally strong]: *The bridge collapsed because it was not structurally sound.*
theory (n) a proposed formal explanation of a fact or event; usually an opinion or explanation based on abstract reasoning
    to have a theory about; to put forth a theory, to set forth a theory
    to formulate a theory, to advance a theory, to advocate a theory, to propose a theory
    to test a theory, to confirm a theory, to grasp a theory
    to discredit a theory, to disprove a theory, to explode a theory
    to combine theory and practice
    a pet theory [= a favorite theory] *Nate's pet theory is that "Nowadays 'good' can be defined as anything that is popular over time."*
    in theory
theorize (v)
theoretical (adj)
theoretically (adv)
vary (v) to change, alter or modify from one situation or thing to another, usually within a group
    to vary considerably, to vary greatly, to vary significantly
    to vary slightly
    to vary between ~ and ~
    to vary from ~ to ~; to vary in
variety (n)
    amazing variety, considerable variety, good variety, huge variety, impressive variety
    a rare variety, an unusual variety, a new variety, an old variety
variation (n)
various (adj)
variously (adv)

Unit 1

Synonyms

analysis:	examination, study, diagnosis
approach:	come near, go near, arrive, reach
area:	part, place, spot, locale
assessment:	estimate, judgment, calculation
assumption:	supposition, guess, conjecture
authority:	control, command, power, strength
available:	accessible, obtainable, ready
benefit:	good, productive, helpful
concept:	idea, theory, thought
consist of:	amount to
constitute:	compose, form, make up
context:	locality, milieu
contract:	agreement, deal, pact, understanding
create:	develop, form, start, make
data:	facts, statistics, information
derive:	gather, get, obtain, acquire
distribute:	pass out, share, spread
environment:	surroundings, background, setting
establish:	create, begin, initiate, originate
evident:	clear, plain, noticeable, obvious
export:	send out
factor:	function, aspect, cause, element
finance:	capital
formula:	model, recipe, plan
function:	role, use, job, duty
identity:	sameness, self, individuality
income:	revenue, profit, salary, gains
indicate:	name, point out, show, signal
individual:	single, alone, separate
interpret:	explain, translate, clarify
issue:	pour out, discharge, publish
labor:	work, job, task
legal:	lawful, rightful, valid
legislate:	enact
major:	greater, larger, dominant
method:	way, plan, technique, mode
occur:	happen, take place, exist
percent:	percentage, fraction
period:	time, term, interval
policy:	program, system, practice
proceed:	go, move, continue, advance
process:	method, procedure, system
requirement:	demand, necessity, need
research:	study, inquiry, investigation
role:	part, capacity, use, place
section:	division, part, piece, portion
sector:	zone, territory, department
significant:	big, important, major, substantial
similar:	alike, close, related, equivalent
source:	origin, cause, root, beginning
specific:	certain, particular, definite
structure:	construction, building, form
theory:	concept, idea, guess
vary:	alter, change, modify

Unit 1

Answers

Definitions

1. occur
2. finance
3. approach
4. creation
5. formula
6. issue
7. legal
8. major
9. available
10. vary
11. constitute
12. legislate
13. context
14. concept
15. process
16. beneficial
17. individual
18. significant
19. environment
20. analysis
21. income
22. proceed
23. require
24. distribute
25. similar
26. specific
27. evident
28. assessment
29. sector
30. function
31. indicates
32. consists of
33. exports
34. research
35. contract
36. section
37. derive
38. interpret
39. establish
40. areas
41. data
42. roles
43. structure
44. authority
45. percent
46. policy
47. source
48. identity
49. method
50. assumption
51. factor
52. labor
53. period
54. theory

Parts of Speech

1. analyze / analytical
2. approachable / approaches
3. area / areas
4. assessed / assessment
5. assumption / assume
6. authority / authoritative
7. availability / available
8. benefits / beneficial
9. concepts / conceptualize
10. consists of / consisted of
11. constitutes / constituent
12. context / contextual / contextualized
13. contract / contractual
14. create / creative
15. data / datum
16. derivation / derived
17. distributed / distributing
18. environmental / environmentally
19. establishment / established
20. evidence / evident
21. exports / exportable / exported
22. factors / factored
23. financial / financed
24. formula / formulate
25. function / functioning
26. identify / identification
27. income / incomes
28. indicates / indication
29. individualize / individuals
30. interpreted / interpretation
31. issue / issues
32. labored / labor
33. legalize / legality
34. legislative / legislation
35. major / majored
36. methodical / methodically
37. occurred / occurrence
38. percent / percent/ percentage
39. period / periodical
40. policy / policy
41. proceeded / proceeding
42. processing / processed
43. required / requirement
44. research / researching
45. role / roles
46. section / sections
47. sector / sectors
48. significant / significantly
49. similarly / similarity
50. source / sources
51. specifically / specify
52. structure / structurally
53. Theoretical / theories
54. varies / variety

Unit 1

Answers

Collocations			
Exercise 1	**Exercise 2**	**Exercise 3**	**Exercise 4**
1. approach	1. analytical	1. consist	1. structurally
approached	analysis	consisted	structures
approaches	analyze	consists	structure
2. theory	2. available	2. formula	2. requirements
theory	available	formulas	requirement
theories	available	formulating	required
3. authority	3. identity	3. concepts	3. sector
authority	identity	concept	sectors
authorizes	identity	concept	sector
4. contract	4. interpret	4. areas	4. varies
contracts	interpretation	area	vary
contract	interpretation	area	vary/varied
5. factor	5. methods	5. periods	5. process
factors	method	period	processes
factor	method	period	process
6. policy	6. legislation	6. distribution	6. occur
policies	legislative	distributed	occurrences
policy	legislation	distribution	occurrence
7. sources	7. researching	7. section	7. legalize
sources	research	section	legality
source	research	sections	legal
8. issue	8. environment	8. assessed	8. proceeded
issue	environmental	assessment	proceed
issued	environment	assessment	proceeding
9. benefits	9. income	9. individual	9. function
benefits	income	individual	function
benefit	income/incomes	individuality	functions
10. data	10. role	10. established	10. evidence
data	roles	establishment	evidence
data	role	establishment	evident

Unit 1

Answers

Synonyms (Crossword)

Across
1. source
4. authority
8. concept
9. process
13. occur
14. income
16. data
20. benefit
23. research
27. vary
30. individual
31. area
32. interpret
33. distribute

Down
2. contract
3. role
5. derive
6. indicate
7. period
8. constitute
10. similar
11. proceed
12. create
15. factor
17. labor
18. method
19. analysis
21. formula
22. section
24. sector
25. approach
26. major
28. evident
29. theory

Review

1. creation
2. distribution
3. similarity
4. proceeded
5. assessed
6. indicated
7. interpret
8. analyze
9. constitute
10. occurred
11. consisted of
12. required
13. vary
14. derive
15. approach
16. legislated
17. assumed
18. established
19. exports
20. functions
21. issues
22. period
23. role
24. structure
25. benefits
26. data
27. formulas
28. labor
29. process
30. theory
31. context
32. finance
33. method
34. section
35. authority
36. factor
37. percent
38. concept
39. income
40. individual
41. source
42. area
43. research
44. identity
45. contract
46. sector
47. environment
48. policy
49. available
50. evident
51. significant
52. specific
53. major
54. legal

Unit 2

Word List
Parts of speech: **n** = noun   **v** = verb   **adj** = adjective   **adv** = adverb

achieve (v)
   achievement (n)
acquire (v)
   acquisition
administer (v)
   administration (n)
   administrative (adj)
   administratively (adv)
affect (n)
   affect (v)
   affective (adj)
   affectively (adv)
appropriate (adj)
   appropriately (adv)
   appropriate (v)
   appropriation (n)
aspect (n)
category (n)
   categorize (v)
   categorization (n)
   categorical (adj)
   categorically (adv)
chapter (n)
commission (n)
   commission (v)
community (n)
compute (v)
   computation (n)
   computational (adj)
   computationally (adv)
conclude (v)
   conclusion (n)
   conclusive (adj)
   conclusively (adv)
conduct (n)
   conduct (v)
   conductive (adj)
consequence (n)
   consequent (adj)
   consequently (adv)
construct (v)
   construct (n)
   construction (n)
consume (v)
   consumption (n)
   consumptive (adj)
   consumptively (adv)
credit (n)
   credit (v)

culture (n)
   cultural (adj)
   culturally (adv)
design (n)
   design (v)
distinct (adj)
   distinctly (adv)
element (n)
   elementary (adj)
   elementarily (adv)
   elemental (adj)
   elementally (adv)
equate (v)
   equation (n)
evaluate (v)
   evaluation (n)
feature (n)
   feature (v)
focus (n)
   focus (v)
impact (n)
   impact (v)
injure (v)
   injury (n)
   injurious (adj)
institute (n)
   institute (v)
invest (v)
   investment (n)
   investor (n)
item (n)
   itemize (v)
   itemization (n)
journal (n)
   maintenance (n)
   normalize (v)
   normality (n)
obtain (v)
   obtainable (adj)
participate (v)
   participation (n)
perceive (v)
   perception (n)
   perceivable (adj)
   perceivably (adv)
positive (adj)
   positively (adv)
   positive (n)

potential (adj)
   potentially (adv)
   potential (n)
primary (adj)
   primarily (adv)
   primary (n)
purchase (n)
   purchase (v)
range (n)
   range (v)
region (n)
   regional (adj)
   regionally (adv)
regulate (v)
   regulation (n)
   regulatory (adj)
relevant (adj)
   relevantly (adv)
   relevance (n)
reside (v)
   resident (n)
   residency (n)
resource (n)
   resourceful (adj)
restrict (v)
   restriction (n)
   restricted (adj)
seek (v)
select (v)
   selection (n)
   selective (adj)
   select (adj)
site (n)
   site (v)
strategy (n)
   strategic (adj)
   strategically (adv)
   strategize (v)
survey (n)
   survey (v)
text (n)
   text (v)
   textual (adj)
transfer (n)
   transfer (v)

Unit 2

Definitions Use the definition clues to write the correct words in the blanks.

1. to make a choice as a result of a decision *When Dan failed to arrive, we* _____ *that he had changed his mind about joining us.* 2. to buy *Ahmed* _____ *a new BMW.* 3. to establish or start a system, rule, legal action, etc. *The new government* _____ *reforms to the legal system.*		maintained instituted selected constructed purchased concluded
4. to determine, judge or calculate the quality or importance of *We need to* _____ *how well the new plan is working.* 5. to acquire or get something *You can* _____ *more information on our web site.* 6. to hurt; to cause physical harm *Football players sometimes* _____ *themselves during games.*		consume invest obtain evaluate achieve injure
7. a distinct section of a book or period of time *The first* _____ *of the book was very interesting.* 8. a large or continuous part of the world, a country or a body *The southern* _____ *of the country was hit by a strong storm.* 9. a comprehensive overview or general look at opinions, etc. *The lecture began with a* _____ *of the course.*		chapter community region resource survey design
10. most important; main, most essential *My* _____ *reason for calling you is to invite you to my party.* 11. without a doubt; certain, hopeful and confident *We are* _____ *about our chances to win the game.* 12. suitable for certain requirements *It is not* _____ *for students to drink coffee in class.*		distinct positive regional primary strategic appropriate
13. to order a certain piece of work or task *The museum will* _____ *a painting of its founder.* 14. to control or manage the operation of *Mrs. Yamada knows how to* _____ *the test.* 15. to act in a particular way *The police in our city usually* _____ *themselves like gentlemen.*		commission impact affect conduct administer transfer

Unit 2

16. something which is a separate part of a list or group of things *The first _____ on the list is the most important one .* 17. a regularly published magazine or newspaper *The latest issue of the _____ has an article about a new financial system.* 18. different parts put together to form a whole *The _____ of the new science building is expensive.*	resident item journal region aspect construction
19. to move or convey from one place or person to another *The police will _____ the criminal to the new jail.* 20. to calculate by using a machine or by using mathematical operations *It took me more than an hour to _____ how much money I would need for my trip.* 21. to reach something successfully, especially after a lot of effort *Ahmed hopes to _____ fame and fortune by becoming a great tennis player.*	achieve survive compute evaluate transfer regulate
22. a particular feature, element or part of a situation, idea, plan, etc. *One interesting _____ of this cell phone is its ability to translate text messages automatically.* 23. the quality being trusted, believed, praised, approved or honored *Lionel failed the test, but, to his _____, he tried very hard to succeed.* 24. a useful or valuable possession, source of aid or support of a country, organization or person *The most valuable _____ in Saudi Arabia is oil.*	credit text aspect range resource consequence
25. to have an influence on something or cause a change in something *Scientists know that temperature can _____ the way people behave.* 26. to become aware of by seeing, smelling, etc. *Some bacteria can _____ tiny amounts of chemicals in their environment.* 27. to control or direct by making something work in a particular way *Certain chemicals _____ activity in the brain.*	transfer regulate perceive equate purchase affect
28. a type or group of things having some elements that are the same *I wouldn't put Dr. Li in the same _____ as Einstein.* 29. a typical or outstanding quality, important part, characteristic, or trait *The best _____ of this camera is its video recording.* 30. the limits, extents or area something is contained in *The _____ of the test scores is 18 points.*	chapter range category culture feature focus

Unit 2

31. the people living in one well defined area *All the families in our* _____ *have children.* 32. a place where something is or will happen or will be built *There are no trees on the* _____ *of the new building.* 33. an influence or powerful effect of one thing on another *The higher taxes should have only a small* _____ *on our business.*	site community conclusion institute purchase impact
34. connected with or related to what is happening or being discussed *What you are saying is not* _____ *to the discussion.* 35. usual, regular, ordinary; conforming to a standard or general average *It is* _____ *for new babies to sleep all day.* 36. capable of coming into existence when the necessary conditions exist *There is a* _____ *for rain tomorrow.*	survey resource aspect relevant potential normal
37. to use, especially in large amounts; to eat, devour or destroy *An elephant can* _____ *450 kg of food every day.* 38. to consider something to be the same as something else *More investment doesn't* _____ *with better care.* 39. to come to possess; to obtain *The terrorists want to* _____ *new weapons.*	acquire consume equate compute injure survive
40. the way of life, especially the general customs, beliefs, language and art of a particular group of people at a particular time *They couldn't understand each other due to* _____ *differences.* 41. clearly set apart or separate and different *There are two* _____ *forms of dissociation.* 42. according to a plan, method or series of actions for achieving success *We need to do some* _____ *thinking for our plan to work.*	journal regional distinct strategic primary cultural
43. an important or significant result, often bad or inconvenient *A slowdown of the economy was a* _____ *of the banks' failures.* 44. the central point of greatest concentration, attention, or interest *Today, London is the* _____ *of my talk.* 45. printed material or oral theme or subject *You should not copy and paste* _____ *from websites into your essay.*	investment residence consequence construct focus text

46. to make or draw plans for the structure or form of something *She uses colored pencils to _____ garden plans.* 47. to make a choice as a result of a decision *Jack likes to _____ the most expensive things on the menu.* 48. to live in or to occupy a place for an extended period of time *Greeks _____ in a nice neighborhood in our town.*	design reside select administer restrict transfer
49. taking part in, sharing in or becoming involved in an activity *We enjoyed your _____ in the discussion.* 50. to limit or reduce something or prevent it from increasing *Parents put a _____ on how much money their children can spend.* 51. a part or a component of any whole *Clean water is an important _____ for raising fish.*	perception site participation restriction credit element
52. to search for, look for or try to discover or obtain *If you need help, you can _____ advice from the librarian.* 53. to continue or keep in existence, usually in good condition *After Mary graduates from college, she wants to _____ contact with her professors.* 54. to put money, effort or time into something to make a profit or get an advantage *It would be smart for you to _____ in the new digital technology.*	maintain regulate design seek invest select

Unit 2

Parts of Speech

Write the parts of speech (noun, verb, adjective or adverb form).
Be careful with nouns and verbs:

      Some *nouns* might need to be plural (~s).
      Some *verbs* might need ~s, ~ed, ~ing.

achieve
1. Everyone was happy with Jon's _____ .
   Steve Jobs _____ fame for the work he did for Apple.

acquire
2. The lab's newest _____ is an electron microscope.
   Some people don't like coffee. It's an _____ taste.

administer
3. Right now, we are _____ a test to new students.
   We will have to put Lisa on _____ leave until she can prove that she is innocent.

affect
4. The change in regulations should only _____ new members.
   Teachers need to be aware of the _____ variables that influence learning.

appropriate
5. Their huge dog is _____ named Titan.
   I do not think it is _____ to drink coffee in class.

aspect
6. One of the most unusual _____ of the case was that the defendant never stopped smiling.
   Our new basketball star resembles Michael Jordan in almost every _____ .

category
7. There are three different _____ that these products can be divided into.
   Journalists sometimes _____ new social groups according to the way they use language.

chapter
8. None of the _____ in this book is over three pages long.
   When he retired, he ended one _____ of his life and began a new one.

commission
9. The company charged us a _____ for buying stocks.
   Last year, Congress _____ a statute to honor Martin Luther King.

community
10. The _____ organizers will meet tonight at 8:00.
    The new law should help many _____ develop independence.

compute
11. You can _____ how much you can save each month if you know what your monthly expenses are.
    Without using a computer, Jed made an accurate _____ in his head.

Unit 2

conclude
12. Lionel came to the _____ that he should major in engineering.

Let's think about this more carefully. Let's not jump to _____.

conduct
13. Yesterday we _____ an experiment with the rats.

Inappropriate _____ will be punished.

consequence
14. We stayed at home. _____, we missed the game.

The economy crashed. As a _____, Jan lost her job.

construct
15. Twelve new homes will be _____ next year.

The _____ should take about ten months.

consume
16. Coffee _____ has increased over the years.

The fans _____ over 90,000 hot dogs.

credit
17. Tax _____ are normally paid to a bank account.

At any rate, I give you _____ for trying.

culture
18. Immigrants sometimes lose their _____ identity.

We wish to promote a _____ of equality.

design
19. The architects will soon begin _____ the new Law School.

Pauline regularly _____ some of the most beautiful fashions.

distinct
20. Critical thinkers make _____ between facts and opinion.

I _____ heard you say "buzz off."

element
21. Cooperation will be a key _____ in our team's success.

The people were unhappy with two key _____ in the president's plan for economic reform.

equate
22. It would be hard to _____ President Bush with President Obama.

The ancient Romans _____ Zeus with their own supreme god, Jupiter.

Unit 2

evaluate   23. The nurses can make a fair _____ of your child.

The new players were _____ to determine if they could play in this week's game.

feature   24. One of the most distinctive _____ of the Mall of America is the indoor amusement park.

One of the unique _____ of the new phone is its ability to understand human speech.

focus   25. All of your pictures seem to be out of _____ .

Her new book _____ on Iran's nuclear program.

impact   26. Her advice had a lasting _____ on me.

We are looking at how the video _____ children.

injure   27. Not all food additives are _____ to your health.

A knee _____ ended Juliet's dancing career.

institute   28. The CSC is a fully-funded research _____ of the medical research council.

The IDM is a marketing _____ in Europe.

invest   29. Right now, _____ in the stock market seems like a bad idea.

We are thinking of _____ in oil futures.

item   30. I read an interesting _____ in the newspaper today.

You need to _____ all of your expenses.

journal   31. The teachers' organization plans to put out a _____ this year.

Hank wrote more than twenty _____ articles.

maintain   32. It is becoming more and more difficult for many people to _____ their standard of living.

The old car was nicely _____ by the previous owner.

normal   33. The two countries tried to _____ their relationship.

Under _____ circumstances, you would have to take the test over again.

Unit 2

obtain

34. Somehow, she always _____ her goals.

    Is peace _____ in the Middle East?

participate

35. With physical therapy, the wounded soldier will be able to fully _____ in sports activities.

    We can't succeed without your _____.

perceive

36. When we _____ that the meeting was over, we all started to yawn.

    They had the mistaken _____ that Bernard was rich.

positive

37. Beth has a very _____ attitude about her job.

    Overall, the _____ outweigh the negatives.

potential

38. Some endangered species do not have the _____ to recover.

    There is enormous _____ to develop solar energy.

primary

39. We were _____ concerned with our children's safety.

    Poverty is sometimes the _____ cause of crime.

purchase

40. Their food was _____ with food stamps.

    Vera made too many _____ with her credit card.

range

41. Night school classes are available for all age _____.

    His complaints covered a _____ of topics.

region

42. The _____ conference starts in two weeks.

    This drug affects several _____ of the brain.

regulate

43. Army _____ prevent me from telling you details about my job.

    The new medicine does a better job of _____ blood sugar levels.

relevant

44. Take notes only on those issues which are directly _____ to the subject in question.

    In your email, please keep your comments _____ to the subject indicated in the subject line.

.

Unit 2

reside

45. They have three homes, but they _____ chiefly in Arizona.

The king has been _____ at his mountain home for the past three months

resource

46. Kevin found a website that has many educational _____ for his children.

Nora is a highly _____ person, which is why we hired her in the first place.

restrict

47. Congress is thinking of imposing new _____ on some of our country's trading partners.

Access to the senate's offices is _____ .

seek

48. Yolinda _____ a solution for her financial problem, but she did not find one.

More students are _____ permission to take the new French class.

select

49. Our grocery store has a wide _____ of great wine.

Only one child will be _____ to go to the science fair.

site

50. The land on the edge of our town would be a good _____ for the new hospital.

There are many possible _____ for the new hospital.

strategy

51. Castles were _____ built all along the river.

Good learners use several different _____ for remembering new material.

survey

52. Unfortunately, the customer satisfaction _____ backed up what the newspaper had reported.

They hired college students to conduct these _____ quickly.

text

53. Some of the _____ used in the geology class are over twenty years old.

Sally _____ her friends and told them she was OK.

transfer

54. The overall heat _____ performance of both types of material is expected to be similar.

The lawyers will help us _____ ownership.

Unit 2

Collocations

In each group of sentences, write *one* word from the list which goes with the **highlighted collocations**. Be sure to change the form of the word if necessary.

Exercise 1	category distinction regulate impact potential achieve strategy resource element range invest community

1. There is an **obvious** _____ **between** the two brothers.

   He had trouble **making a** _____ **between** fact and fiction.

   There are **clear-cut** _____ **between** the Republicans and the Democrats.

2. She **makes good** _____ in the Stock Market.

   A college education is a **long-term** _____.

   He is _____ **with the authority** to hire new employees.

3. Guy is a strong football player. He **has great** _____.

   The team found itself in a _____ **dangerous situation.**

   Sally is intelligent and **has the** _____ to be a great leader someday.

4. The enemy had the _____ **of surprise** on us.

   I tried to have fun at the party, but I was **out of my** _____.

   Certain **criminal** _____ are trying to hack into our computers.

5. We need **to map out a** _____ for increasing our finances.

   The senator uses many excellent **campaign** _____.

   Nike has **a global** _____ for increasing its business.

6. The Pietà was Michelangelo's most **brilliant** _____.

   The cell phone is **a great** _____ **in** technology.

   Hugo made many **outstanding** _____ in writing.

7. Marius does not seem **to fit into any particular** _____.

   We can probably **put** this bacterium **into a special** _____.

   This plant can be _____ **as** a weed or a flower.

8. The crowded classes are going to **have an** _____ **on** the students.

   Give her the good news first to **lessen the** _____ of the bad news.

   The uplifting film **emotionally** _____ me.

9. Yesterday's test results _____ **from** 84% **to** 99%.

   We try **to make long** _____ plans, but we don't always succeed.

   They could not hear us because they were **out of** _____.

10. We are running out of money, so we have **to reserve** our _____.

    Fresh water is an important **natural** _____.

    Bill Gates **has the** _____ **to** help developing nations in Africa.

Unit 2

Collocations

Exercise 2	region	credit	focus	restrict	conclusion	purchase
	feature	normal	survey	regulate	commission	maintain

1. The City Council **adopted** several new _____.

   None of the police want **to enforce this** _____.

   This machine will help **to** _____ **your breathing**.

2. After hours of thinking, she **arrived at a** _____.

   I still don't know how you **came to that** _____.

   Last night's concert _____ **with** a sonata by Beethoven.

3. Lenny always wants **to take** _____ **for** everything.

   To her _____, Tillie is a great mother.

   The neighbors _____ Lassie **with** saving Timmy's life.

4. Please help me **get the** problem **into** _____.

   We all _____ **on** what the old woman had to say.

   Beer-making **is the** _____ **of** today's talk.

5. Last night, we watched **a** _____ **film** on TV.

   His strange face has several **distinctive** _____.

   The most **notable** _____ of the garden is the old maple tree.

6. If Terry does not get better grades, we will have to **impose a** _____ **on** his after-school activities.

   You should not **place** _____ **on** your child's creative outlets.

   Access is _____ after 9:00 this evening.

7. They **carried out a** _____ to see how people felt about gays.

   If you want to know more, you should **conduct a** _____.

   Before we went farther, we _____ **the surroundings**.

8. I'll be happy **when things get back to** _____ around here.

   When Dan is sick, he performs **below** _____.

   The prince finally **restored some semblance of** _____ to the country.

9. A few people live in the one **mountainous** _____ of this state.

   In **a remote** _____ of Borneo, the explorer discovered a new tribe.

   Many Mexicans live in **the border** _____ of Texas and Mexico.

10. Tomorrow, the web site will be shut down **for routine** _____.

    Preventative _____ on your car can save you a lot of money.

    It is more and more difficult for us to _____ **a high standard of living**.

Unit 2

Collocations

Exercise 3	acquire	chapter	seek	obtain	purchase	commission
	primary	select	design	relevant	administer	consequence

1. During the 16th Century, Spain _____ **power** in the New World.

   You might not like this spice. It's an _____ **taste**.

   He is smart and he _____ **languages** very easily.

2. The mayor put together **a fact-finding** _____.

   The next step is **to appoint a** _____ to study the problem.

   Regina _____ **a new opera** to celebrate her marriage.

3. Father promised **to** _____ **revenge for** the destruction of his home.

   Pam is **eagerly** _____ **to** establish a new business in our town.

   Ted went to his tutor and _____ **help on** his essay.

4. **Nothing of** _____ came from the two-hour meeting.

   Freedom of speech in public schools **is a matter of great** _____ for some very religious people.

   They could not deal with all of **the unintended** _____ **of** their actions.

5. Retirement **began a new** _____ **in** Bill's life.

   Forget what you did. That's **a closed** _____ now.

   Kevin could **quote** the law _____ **and verse**.

6. No one liked the way she _____ **justice to** criminals.

   We are required **to** _____ **the test to** all students.

   I always have trouble _____ **medicine to** my dog.

7. My _____ **concern** is that you learn these words well.

   Elaine hopes to win the _____ **election**.

   You should **give** my proposal your _____ **consideration**.

8. This room **is** _____ **for** meditation.

   Our house is energy-efficient **by** _____.

   Here are some samples of **creative** _____ layouts.

9. Last week, Irene was _____ **as** the chairperson of the new committee.

   The store **offers a wide** _____ **of** herbs and spices.

   Evolution depends on **natural** _____.

10. You need to _____ **permission** before you hike on that trail.

    We need to _____ 5,000 **signatures** on our petition.

    They thought they had _____ **a lasting peace** in the Middle East.

Unit 2

Collocations

Exercise 4	culture	aspect	journal	seek	consume	evaluate
	transfer	text	conduct	range	appropriate	participate

1. Elwood paid his loan by making **an electronic** _____.

   After the elections, there was **a peaceful** _____ **of power**.

   He _____ his wallet **from** his back pocket **to** his front pocket.

2. Democracy works when people **actively** _____ **in** the elections.

   All of the students are _____ **fully** in class.

   Wendy loves to _____ **in** after-school **activities**.

3. People **keep a** _____ to remember events in their life.

   Dr. Kramer publishes articles in several **academic** _____.

   When you graduate, you should **subscribe to a** _____ in your field.

4. We will **make an** _____ **of** your work and give you feedback.

   Omar was afraid to **critically** _____ my **performance**.

   It is sometimes hard to **make a realistic** _____ of our lives.

5. New TV programs are influenced by **pop** _____.

   Most new students from abroad **suffer from** _____ **shock**.

   We can learn things from studying various **tribal** _____.

6. Nancy shakes because she _____ **a lot of** coffee.

   When we saw the ambulance, we **were** _____ **with fear**.

   The entire apartment building **was** _____ **by fire**.

7. After the lecture, we _____ **an experiment** and proved the theory.

   Carbon does not _____ **electricity**.

   He wants to _____ a **survey** to see what we think about the plan.

8. The most **frightening** _____ **of** the construction is its cost.

   The book is serious, but it does have some **humorous** _____.

   In every _____ **of** my work, I try to be useful to society.

9. If you do not follow the rules, we will **take** _____ **action**.

   The reporter was respected for her _____ **behavior** during the interview.

   Chocolate and flowers are _____ **gifts** to give when you are invited to dinner.

10. You can **annotate** _____ on your Kindle.

    Aaron needs to **edit the** _____ of his speech to make it shorter.

    As you write your essay, do not **stray from the** _____ of the article you are criticizing.

Unit 2

Synonyms Use the synonym clues to solve this crossword puzzle.

Across
9. eat, use up, devour
10. aspect, member, part
11. obtain, get, accumulate
13. take, acquire, receive
18. possible, probable, likely
21. keep, retain, continue
24. build, assemble, raise
25. plan, outline, picture
27. end, terminate; decide
28. design, plan, scheme
29. transport, send, hand over

Down
1. merit, approval, praise
2. class, kind, sort, set
3. influence, change, modify
4. neighborhood, group
5. buy, obtain, acquire
6. control, organize, adjust
7. choose, pick, identify
8. related, appropriate
12. live, stay
14. proper, right, reasonable
15. separate, special, different
16. article, thing, piece
17. detect, notice, sense
19. damage, hurt, harm
20. oversee, direct, manage
22. ordinary, usual, accepted
23. first, main, key
26. emphasis, center, aim

Unit 2

Review

Write the correct word in each sentence.

1.	There are many nice families living in our _____.	community chapter conclusion aspect potential range
2.	There was only one _____ of the plan that Sam didn't like.	
3.	A black bear's _____ is about 200 km.	
4.	All countries have limited natural _____.	resources transfers consequences purchases surveys elements
5.	Several _____ indicated that the senator was no longer popular.	
6.	He does things without thinking, disregarding the possible _____ of his actions.	
7.	The prize money will have a huge _____ on your life.	chapter commission site impact range feature
8.	We told the children to stay away from the construction _____.	
9.	Sarah received a _____ to write a new opera in honor of the birth of the new prince.	
10.	Each _____ in the box had once belonged to my grandfather.	item distribution function issue text credit
11.	According to the ancient _____, flood waters once covered the land.	
12.	The teacher gave everyone _____ for doing well on the exam.	
13.	One interesting _____ of the symphony is its use of African instruments.	feature culture element sector theory factor
14.	I like to study the history and _____ of foreign countries.	
15.	Can a substance be composed of only one _____?	
16.	In a dry _____ such as the Sahara, water is very valuable.	process method purchase category region journal
17.	According to an article in this _____, the world's climate is slowing becoming warmer.	
18.	These items belong in a different _____.	

Unit 2

Review

19. The Civil War was a terrible _____ in American history.	labor
20. The _____ of his speech was that we should question authority.	strategy
21. It will be difficult to win if you don't have a good _____.	chapter research structure focus

22. Over the years, we have _____ too many possessions.	derived
23. The school _____ the policy of no smoking on campus.	perceived instituted
24. We acted quickly to take care of our _____ weaknesses.	acquired functioned benefited

25. The engineers told us the best way to _____ the bridge.	construct
26. We will _____ more land when we get more money.	consist derive
27. My brother can _____ the answer to many math problems in his head.	calculate export purchase

28. The instructor made it very clear how she would _____ us on the work we are doing.	indicate
29. Jane can _____ the sums of large numbers in her head.	evaluate transfer
30. With the Internet, you can _____ money from one account to another.	proceed compute require

31. John and Sam _____ enormous amounts of water on hot days.	consume
32. Before you enter his library, you need to _____ permission.	select occur obtain
33. You have a choice, but if you _____ the wrong one, you will be sorry.	vary establish

34. The police will _____ a search for the missing child.	analyze
35. I would like to _____ in the search.	function administer
36. The court will _____ justice to the kidnapper.	identify participate conduct

Unit 2

Review

37. If you _____ in the stock market, you will be taking a chance.	achieve
	conduct
38. We _____ the best results when we plan carefully.	invest
	maintain
39. We started the hike by walking very quickly, but we were unable to _____ the pace for very long.	categorize
	acquire
40. Weather can _____ the way you feel.	site
	affect
41. The concert will _____ with a Beethoven symphony.	survive
	equate
42. Architects _____ beautiful buildings.	conclude
	design
43. Work carefully, or you might _____ yourself.	injure
	purchase
44. The government tried to _____ the flow of money.	conclude
	regulate
45. Many Hispanics _____ in Florida and Texas, while fewer live in the northern states.	achieve
	reside
46. We were using too much paper, so the boss decided to _____ our use of the copy machine.	consume
	restrict
47. If you have been injured, you should _____ medical attention.	seek
	equate
48. Some people _____ high prices with better quality.	commission
	feature
49. I'm sure we'll have higher taxes. It's a _____ possibility.	relevant
	cultural
50. Marcia is a _____ player for the women's basketball team. We hope they choose her to play this year.	positive
	distinct
51. None of these examples are _____ to your argument.	potential
	individual
52. Flowers are _____ gifts for hospital patients.	primary
	legal
53. There was nothing _____ about him. He was unusual in every way.	appropriate
	available
54. Her _____ mission is to find new funding for the history museum.	evident
	normal

Unit 2

Definitions ◦ Parts of Speech ◦ Collocations

achieve (v) to reach an aim or carry something through successfully, especially after a lot of effort
> to achieve fame: *The writer did not achieve fame within his lifetime.*
> to achieve an aim, to achieve a goal
> hard to achieve, impossible to achieve, fail to achieve: *Gordon failed to achieve his goal of becoming a Hollywood actor.*

achievement (n)
> a brilliant achievement, crowning achievement, glorious achievement, great achievement, major achievement, notable achievement, outstanding achievement, fine achievement
> an achievement in: *The computer is a great achievement in technology.*
> a sense of achievement, a lack of achievement, a standard of achievement
> quite an achievement: *Reaching the summit was quite an achievement for the 80-year old woman.*

acquire (v) to come to possess; to obtain
> to acquire riches, to acquire wealth, to acquire power; to acquire language
> to acquire a taste for: *I have never acquired a taste for beer.*
> an acquired taste: *You might not like this cheese. It's an acquired taste.*

acquisition (n)
> to make an acquisition, to complete an acquisition
> the latest acquisition, a new acquisition, a recent acquisition: *The painting by Renoir is the museum's latest acquisition.*
> language acquisition: *Second language acquisition is more difficult for adults than it is for children.*

administer (v) to control or manage the operation or arrangement of something
> to administer justice to
> to administer a test to: *We will administer the test to the students at 6:00 tonight.*
> to administer medicine to: *Nurses administer medicine to patients in hospitals.*
> to jointly administer [= to share the administration]

administration (n)

administrative (adj)
> (to put on) administrative leave: *While the police investigated the accusations, Nelly was put on administrative leave.*

administratively (adv)

affect (v) to have an influence on something or cause a change in something
> to be likely to affect: *Andrew's lack of sleep is likely to adversely affect his performance on the test.*
> to adversely affect, seriously affect, deeply affect, profoundly affect, strongly affect

affect (n) a feeling or emotion: *Embarrassment is an affect that teachers need to watch out for in the classroom.*

affective (adj)
> affective variables: *According to H. D. Brown, three affective variables that influence language acquisition are imitation, egoism and inhibition.*

affectively (adv)

appropriate (adj) suitable for or fitting the requirements of a particular situation
> to consider (to be) appropriate, to think something (to be) appropriate
> to deem something appropriate [= to consider something to be appropriate]: *In the law office, wearing blue jeans is not deemed appropriate.*
> to take appropriate (action, steps): *If the neighbors do not remove the junk cars from their front lawn, we will have to take appropriate action.*
> highly appropriate, entirely appropriate
> appropriate for: *Flowers are an appropriate gift for a hostess.*
> appropriate behavior

appropriately (adv)

appropriate (v) to take something for one's own purposes: *When the war started, the government appropriated all of the property belonging to the gentry.*

appropriation (n) something that has been taken to be used for a different purpose

aspect (n) a particular feature, element or part of a situation, idea, plan, etc.
> to take on an aspect: *Eventually, the debate took on the aspect of a comedy.*
> to consider (every) aspect, to deal with (each) aspect, to discuss an aspect, to focus on an aspect
> a frightening aspect, grim aspect, alarming aspect, humorous aspect, serious aspect
> central aspect, fundamental aspect, major aspect, main aspect, principal aspect, key aspect: *The key aspect of the health reform law is the requirement that all citizens buy health insurance.*
> exciting aspect, pleasing aspect, remarkable aspect: *The most remarkable aspect of the Joao's victory is that he succeeded despite suffering from asthma.*
> curious aspect, intriguing aspect, puzzling aspect
> in all aspects; in every aspect: *The son resembles his father in every aspect.*

from a ~ aspect: *From a political aspect, Spencer's advice seemed quite reasonable.*

category (n) a specific type, class or a group of things having some features that are the same

to establish or set up a category; to assign to or put into a category

fit into a category: *This new microorganism does not fit into any previously known category.*

to fall into a category: *I think Paul's criticism falls into the category of sarcasm.*

a separate, a special category, a narrow category; a broad category, a general category

social category, age category; (to belong to or be in) a category of its own

categorize (v)

to be difficult to categorize, to be impossible to categorize

easily categorized, conveniently categorized

to categorize according to: *These books need to be categorized according to topic.*

to categorize as: *These plants can be categorized as either weeds or flowers.*

to categorize by, to categorize into: *Next, you must categorize the leaves into two groups.*

categorization (n)

categorical (adj)

categorically (adv) according to each and every part in a group or class

categorically deny: *Madoff categorically denied any wrongdoing.*

chapter (n) a distinct part of a book or period of time which is part of a larger period of time

a closed chapter [= the end of an event] *Let's not talk about Sue's involvement in the affair. That's a closed chapter now.*

introductory chapter, opening chapter; closing chapter, final chapter

a chapter in one's life: *His first marriage was just a short chapter in his whole life.*

a chapter about: *There are no chapters about technology in this book.*

a chapter on: *I just read a chapter on the history of Iraq.*

to quote chapter and verse [= to quote or cite the relevant part or parts of an authoritative document]: *The actions of the committee are allowed by our organization's regulations. If you don't believe me, I can quote chapter and verse.*

commission (n) a group formed especially to carry out a specific task

to appoint, establish or set up a commission

to head a commission, to preside over a commission, to chair a commission: *Ralph has been elected to chair the commission on public safety.*

a fact-finding commission; a planning commission

commission (n) a special piece of work or the order granting authority to perform a certain task

to resign one's commission

commission (v) to order a certain piece of work or task

commission a play, commission an opera, commission a symphony, commission a statue

commission (n) amount of money paid for marketing and selling services

to charge a commission, to pay a commission, to receive a commission

to earn ~ in commission: *Della earned $500 in commission last week.*

community (n) the people living in one well defined area or people who are considered as a unit due to their common interests, background, etc.

to form a community

academic community, college community, university community

business community, gay community, religious community, scientific community, retirement community

community care, community center, community college, community service: *Alice engages in community service whenever possible.*

tight-knit community, close-knit community [= a community where everyone knows everyone else quite well]: *Everyone in the close-knit community was thrilled when Hilda won the gold medal.*

a thriving community, a vibrant community

a pillar of the community [= a strong, supporting person in the community]: *Mayor Buckley has been a pillar of the community for more than 25 years.*

compute (v) to calculate by using a machine or by using mathematical operations

to compute the answer

that does not compute [= does not make sense; cannot be true]: *He said he was in Chicago last weekend, but that does not compute. We saw him in Cleveland on Saturday.*

computation (n)

computational (adj)

computationally (adv)

conclude (v) to end, finish, complete

to conclude by: *I would like to conclude by saying that I have enjoyed hearing what you had to say.*

to conclude with: *The concert will conclude with a symphony by Takemitsu.*

conclusion (n) the end, finish, or completion of something

at the conclusion of: *At the conclusion of the play, everyone stood up and applauded.*

in conclusion: *In conclusion, we can see that there are many causes for poverty.*

conclusion (n) the final thought or decision

to arrive at a conclusion, to come to a conclusion, to draw a conclusion, to reach a conclusion

to jump to (leap to) a conclusion [= to make a decision too soon]: *She jumped to a conclusion before she heard everything I had to say.*

an erroneous conclusion, false conclusion, invalid conclusion, wrong conclusion

hasty conclusion [= a conclusion that is made too quickly]: *Don't jump to a hasty conclusion. Make sure you get all the facts before you decide on your final answer.*

a correct conclusion, logical conclusion, reasonable conclusion, valid conclusion

satisfactory conclusion, successful conclusion

foregone conclusion [= has already been decided]: *It is a foregone conclusion that Terry will be the next director.*

conclude (v) to judge after some consideration

to conclude from: *I don't know what to conclude from her remarks.*

conclusive (adj) established as a solid, true fact

conclusive evidence; far from conclusive, by no means conclusive [= not established as a fact]: *It is by no means conclusive that raising the minimum wage will harm the economy.*

conclusively (adv)

conduct (v) to act in a particular way

to conduct oneself like: *He conducts himself like a proper gentleman.*

to conduct oneself with: *She conducts herself with great dignity.*

conduct (n) behavior

to regulate conduct, to engage in conduct: *Teenagers sometimes engage in conduct that is silly.*

(to be guilty of) inappropriate conduct

gentlemanly conduct, polite conduct

good conduct: *The prisoner's jail time was reduced due to his good conduct.*

disgraceful conduct, unseemly conduct, aggressive conduct, violent conduct

code of conduct, rules of conduct

conduct (v) to carry out a performance or act

to conduct an experiment

to conduct a survey

conduct (v) to carry heat or electricity

to conduct electricity: *Copper conducts electricity quite well.*

to conduct heat: *Iron cooking utensils conduct heat slowly and evenly.*

conduction (n) moving a liquid, heat, electricity, etc. through a material

Copper is better than aluminum for electrical conduction.

conductive (adj)

consequence (n) an important or significant result, often bad or inconvenient

to suffer the consequences, to accept the consequence(s): *If you decide to spend all of your money on a motorcycle rather than save it for college, you'll just have to accept the consequences.*

nothing of consequence: *Nothing of consequence has happened in the last month or so.*

a matter of some consequence: *Her decision to quit her job became a matter of great consequence to her family.*

in consequence of: *In consequence of her decision, her husband divorced her.*

a person of consequence [= a very important person]: *Although Youkoff is no longer our president, he is still a person of consequence.*

an unintended consequence, far-reaching consequence

devastating consequence, disastrous consequence, horrible consequence

beneficial consequence, positive consequence, intended consequence

natural consequence, logical consequence; long-term consequence, short-term consequence

consequent (adj) resulting from, following

consequently (adv)

construct (v) to build; to put different parts together to form a whole

to be constructed of: *Their homes are constructed of grass and mud.*

construct (n) an idea or theory not based on evidence

construction (n)

to begin construction, to start construction, to finish construction, to complete construction

heavy construction [= using huge machinery to do the construction]: *The entire street is closed to traffic due to heavy construction.*

construction industry, construction sector, construction company, construction firm

construction job, construction work, construction worker

construction yard, construction site

construction (n) language structure

grammatical construction, active construction, passive construction: *The sentence "The essay was written with little thought" is an example of a passive construction.*

consume (v) to use, especially in large amounts; to eat, devour or destroy

consume a lot of something: *These cars consume a lot of gas.*

to be consumed with (fear, passion, envy): *The children were consumed with fear.*

to be consumed by fire: *Within minutes, the entire building was consumed by fire.*

consumption (n)

to encourage consumption, to stimulate consumption

to boost consumption [= to increase consumption]: *Congress hoped that the tax incentives would boost consumption and thus help the economy to recover.*

consumption increases, consumption decreases, consumption declines

heavy consumption, high consumption, excessive consumption

conspicuous consumption [= showing off one's wealth by buying expensive things that everyone can see]: *Nowadays, many people frown on conspicuous consumption.*

per capita consumption, domestic consumption, local consumption, home consumption

for personal consumption

unfit for human consumption: *This tuna must be cat food. It smells unfit for human consumption.*

consumptive (adj)

consumptively (adv)

credit (n) the quality or condition of being trusted, believed, praised, approved or honored

to take credit for, to claim credit for; to give someone credit for

to take all the credit: *Yuki took all the credit for our permission to cross the border.*

due credit: *We should give due credit to Liam for making the banquet a success.*

a credit to: *Your success is a credit to your family.*

to someone's credit: *To his credit, he never stopped trying.*

credit (n) an amount of money that a bank will loan

to provide credit, to extend credit

long-term credit, short-term credit

credit account, credit limit; credit control, credit crunch, credit squeeze [= very limited credit]: *Due to the current credit squeeze, we are unable to borrow money to expand our business.*

credit union, credit card

credit (n) an amount of money that one has in a bank account

a credit balance, credit account

credit (v) to give honor or praise

credit with: *The police credited Tim with saving the little girl's life.*

culture (n) the way of life, especially the general customs, beliefs, language and art of a particular group of people at a particular time

to bring culture to; to foster culture, to spread culture; to develop a culture

(suffer from) culture shock: *Immigrants often suffer from culture shock when they first arrive in a foreign land.*

ancient culture, traditional culture, primitive culture, tribal culture

ethnic culture, human culture, material culture, modern culture

pop culture, dominant culture, mainstream culture

business culture, corporate culture

political culture, religious culture, academic culture, professional culture

a person of culture: *During his term as a university professor, he was known as a man of culture and great intelligence.*

cultural (adj)

cultural heritage

culturally (adv)

design (v) to make or draw plans for the structure or form of something

to be designed for: *This room was designed for children.*

to be designed to: *This car is designed to use less fuel.*

specially designed, specifically designed

design (n)

to come up with a design

simple design, complex design, innovative design, original design, bold design

ergonomic design [= designed to be easy to handle]: *Because of the knife's ergonomic design, your hand won't get tired when you chop vegetables.*

geometric design, abstract design, graphic design

design consultant, design studio, design work

design feature, design solution, design concept

by design: *That's an interesting solution to the problem, but did you arrive at it by accident or by design?*

Unit 2

distinct (adj) clearly set apart or separate and different
    to get the distinct impression: *I get the distinct impression that you find my story boring.*
    to draw a distinction, to make a distinction: *You need to make a distinction between fact and fiction.*
    to blur the distinction: *The new molecules blur the distinction between life and non-life.*
    a clear-cut distinction; a fine distinction, an obvious distinction
    to enjoy the distinction of; to have the distinction of: *Sara enjoys the distinction of being the first woman to head the department.*
    someone of distinction: *She is an artist of great distinction.*
    distinct from: *The warbler's song and the lark's song are distinct from one another.*
    as distinct from: *These sex-linked chicks are all female, as distinct from those straight-run chicks which can be male or female.*
distinctly (adv)
element (n) a part or a component of any whole
    to involve elements of, to contain elements of
    to be in one's element: *Jon loves to act; when he is on stage, he's really in his element.*
    to be out of one's element: *I can't represent you at the meeting. I'd be out of my element.*
    a basic element, an essential element, a key element, a vital element
    a diverse element, an extremist element, a radical element
    a foreign element, a criminal element, an undesirable element
    a racial element, a sexual element
    the element of surprise: *By attacking the enemy before dawn, we are counting on the element of surprise.*
elements (n. pl.) [usually: the elements] bad weather
    to brave the elements, to be exposed to the elements, to battle against the elements
    to be protected from the elements, to be sheltered from the elements
elementary (adj) basic, simple
elementarily (adv)
elemental (adj) referring to basic natural forces
elementally (adv)
equate (v) to consider something to be the same or approximately the same as something else; to connect two things in your mind
    to equate ~ with: *Many people equate money with happiness.*
equation (n)
evaluate (v) to determine, judge or calculate the quality, importance, amount or value of something
    to evaluate a performance
    to be designed to evaluate: *These rubrics are designed to evaluate a variety of oral performances.*
    thoroughly evaluate, carefully evaluate, systematically evaluate
evaluation (n)
    to make an evaluation: *We have to make an evaluation of their plan to modernize the factory.*
    a critical evaluation, a fair evaluation; a realistic evaluation
    a comprehensive evaluation, an objective evaluation
    evaluation process, evaluation procedure
feature (n) a typical or outstanding quality, important part, characteristic, or trait
    to point out a feature: *The guide pointed out a feature of the cathedral that we would have missed.*
    a special feature, a notable feature, a distinctive feature, a distinguishing feature, an important feature, a prominent feature, a striking feature
    an optional feature: *The satellite tracking system is an optional feature on this vehicle.*
    a feature film: *She has been the subject of documentaries and feature films.*
features (n. pl) parts of someone's face
    facial features, delicate features, fine features
    handsome features, rugged features [= strong, masculine features]
feature (v) to put in a prominent or noticeable place
    to feature prominently: *Concern for the underprivileged features prominently in the senator's speeches.*
    regularly feature: *Oprah's TV program regularly featured a book review.*
focus (n) the central point or area of greatest concentration, attention, interest or activity
    to get something into focus, to bring something into focus, to come into focus
    to shift the focus, to change the focus
    to be in focus, to be out of focus [regarding photographs]: *In this picture, the people in the front row are in focus, but the people in the back row are out of focus.*
    to be the focus of: *Climate change will be the focus of tonight's newscast.*
    major focus, prime focus; clear focus, sharp focus; soft focus
focus (v)
    try to focus: *You aren't paying attention. Try to focus!*

to focus heavily on, to focus primarily, to focus largely, to focus entirely

to focus on: *Let's focus on getting the job done right away.*

impact (n) an influence or powerful effect of one thing on another

to have an impact (on), to make an impact (on): *The latest research on cloning will have a dramatic impact on medicine.*

to lessen the impact, to reduce the impact, to soften the impact: *Korean monetary policy helped to soften the impact of the global economic downturn.*

to increase the impact, to heighten the impact, to enhance the impact, to maximize the impact

to resist impact, to appreciate impact, to highlight impact: *New studies highlight the impact of outdoor cats on birds and other creatures.*

strong impact, great impact, lasting impact, powerful impact, massive impact, tremendous impact

emotional impact, profound impact, dramatic impact

negative impact, damaging impact, severe impact, devastating impact, catastrophic impact

positive impact, favorable impact, beneficial impact

immediate impact, initial impact, short-term impact, long-term impact, far-reaching impact

social impact, financial impact, economic impact, cultural impact, political impact

impact (n) the forceful striking or coming together of objects

to lessen the impact, to soften the impact

to survive impact, to withstand impact: *The new windows are designed to withstand the impact of hurricane-force winds.*

the moment of impact, the point of impact, the time of impact

impact crater: *The surface of Mercury is covered with impact craters.*

impact (v)

injure (v) to hurt; to cause physical harm or distress to

to badly injure, to critically injure, to seriously injure, to severely injure

to slightly injure, to accidentally injure: *Sam accidentally injured himself while opening a can of nuts.*

injury (n)

to cause injury, to inflict injury [= to cause injury]

to avoid injury, to escape injury

to overcome injury, to recover from injury, to come back from injury, to shake off injury

to deal with injury, to treat injury

to result from injury, to be hampered by injury, to be troubled by injury

to be dogged by injury [= to be constantly troubled by injury]: *The quarterback was dogged by his shoulder injury all season, so he rarely played.*

to run the risk of injury: *By riding your motorcycle without a helmet, you run the risk of head injury.*

to add insult to injury [= to make a problem worse]: *Allowing the criminals to leave the country would only add insult to the injury to the victims of their crimes.*

nasty injury, serious injury, fatal injury

slight injury, superficial injury [= minor, or just on the surface, injury]

injurious (adj)

institute (n) a special school or place of study, training or rehabilitation

to found an institute [= to establish an institute]: *The Institute of Health was founded in 1897.*

a research institute, scientific institute, technical institute

institute (v) to establish or start something, usually in an official way

to institute research, to institute an investigation, to institute a search

invest (v) to put money, effort or time into something to make a profit, interest or get an advantage

to seek to invest, to plan to invest, to decide to invest, to rush to invest: *When the value of Apple's stock started to increase, many people rushed to invest in the company.*

to invest in; to invest directly in, to invest heavily in: *We invested in new methods of producing electricity.*

carefully invest, safely invest, wisely invest

to invest someone with authority [= to officially give someone authority]: *Only Congress is invested with the authority to declare war.*

investment (n)

to make an investment

to encourage investment, to stimulate investment, to promote investment, to attract investment

to protect investment(s), to recoup investment [= to get the investment back]

a good investment, a sound investment, wise investment, worthwhile investment: *A college education is a very worthwhile investment for most young folks.*

a bad investment, a poor investment, a risky investment

a considerable investment, a huge investment, a sizeable investment, a substantial investment

a small investment, a modest investment, a minimum investment

long-term investment, short-term investment

capital investment, financial investment, overseas investment, corporate investment

investment scheme, investment decision, investment company

a return on an investment, a profit on an investment

investor (n)

    to attract an investor, to advise an investor

    small investor, major investor

    would-be investor, potential investor, prospective investor [= someone who might be an investor in the future]

    investor confidence: *As the economic outlook improves, investor confidence is rising.*

item (n) something which is a separate part of a list or group of things

    to keep an item, to come across an item [= to find an item]

    interesting item, important item, essential item

    expensive item, luxury item, valuable item: *The hotel has a safe where you can keep your valuable items.*

item (n) a particular bit of information, such as in a newspaper or magazine

    an interesting item: *I came across an interesting item in the newspaper about a new kind of nuclear power plant.*

item (n) a dating couple

    to be a real item: *Mark and Alice are dating now. They are a real item.*

itemize (v) to specify the items

    to itemize expenses; to itemize a bill

itemization (n)

journal (n) a regularly published magazine or newspaper, usually about a serious subject

    to publish a journal, to put out a journal, to edit a journal

    to take a journal, to subscribe to a journal

    a learned journal, a scholarly journal, an academic journal

    a trade journal, a business journal, a professional journal, a technical journal

    a major journal, a highly-ranked journal, a prestigious journal [= a very highly valued journal]

journal (n) diary

    to keep a journal

    daily journal, private journal

    a journal entry

maintain (v) to continue or keep in existence, usually in good condition

    to strive to maintain [= to keep trying to maintain]

    to maintain a standard of living

    to maintain a list; to maintain the momentum [= to keep something going]

    properly maintain, poorly maintain

maintenance (n)

    preventative maintenance; routine maintenance; building maintenance, road maintenance, health maintenance

maintain (v) to claim

    to maintain innocence [= to continue to say that one is innocent]: *Despite all of the evidence against him, he continues to maintain that he is innocent.*

normal (adj) usual, regular, ordinary; conforming to a standard or general average

    to feel normal: *I can't go to work. I just don't feel normal today.*

    to be normal to: *It's normal to feel sad sometimes.*

    to consider something as normal, to regard something as normal: *In some countries, drinking wine at lunchtime is regarded as normal.*

    to be above normal, below normal; completely normal, perfectly normal, quite normal

    under normal circumstances: *Under normal circumstances, we would be able to take a vacation this year, but because of the poor economy, we can not.*

    in the normal way

    to get back to normal: *Everything is crazy right now. I can't wait for things to get back to normal.*

normalize (v)

    to normalize relations with

normality (n)

    to restore normality, to return to normality

    some semblance of normality

obtain (v) to acquire or get something

    to obtain admission, to obtain permission, to obtain signatures (for)

    to obtain a lasting peace: *It will be difficult to obtain a lasting peace in the Middle East.*

    a means of obtaining, a way of obtaining, a method of obtaining

obtainable (adj)

participate (v) to take part in, share in or become involved in an activity

    to participate actively, to participate fully

to be required to participate, to be invited to participate, to be encouraged to participate
to have the opportunity to participate, to have a chance to participate
to agree to participate, to refuse to participate
to participate in: *All students are required to participate in group work.*

participation (n)
to invite participation, to encourage participation
active participation: *With the president's active participation, we think that the bill will pass.*
full participation, greater participation, increased participation, limited participation
level of participation, degree of participation, extent of participation
public participation, audience participation: *What made the PowerPoint presentation so much more interesting was the level of audience participation.*

perceive (v) to become aware of by seeing, smelling, etc.
difficult to perceive, impossible to perceive
to perceive ~ differently: *You two will never agree on anything. You both perceive the world differently.*
to perceive color, to perceive time; perceived value, perceived threat, perceived error

perception (n)

perceivable (adj)

perceivably (adv)

positive (adj) without a doubt; certain; hopeful and confident
to sound positive [= to appear to be positive]: *I know the drive to Alaska will be long and difficult, but I'm just trying to sound positive to make you feel better about the trip.*
to remain positive, to seem positive
to be positive about: *You need to be more positive about your chances for winning.*
to be positive that: *I am positive that I left my keys on the table, but they aren't there now.*
positive reinforcement [= giving a reward for behavior in order to increase the chances that it will happen again]: *A good teacher provides positive reinforcement to her students to make sure they will continue to progress.*
fairly positive, quite positive, absolutely positive

positive (adj) indicating the presence of something
to prove positive, to test positive: *None of the subjects tested positive for the HIV virus.*

positively (adv)

positive (n) a test result showing the presence of something
a false positive

potential (adj) capable of coming into existence when the necessary conditions exist
a potential mate, a potential profit; a potential buyer: *I have a potential buyer for your property.*

potential (n) the possibility of becoming something
to live up to the full potential, to use to the full potential
to develop one's potential, to realize one's potential, to have potential, to show potential
to have the potential to: *Lori has the potential to be the top student in the class.*
to have the potential for (~ing): *Tom has the potential for achieving great things.*
great potential, considerable potential, enormous potential

potentially (adv)
a potentially dangerous situation

primary (adj) most important, main, most essential or prevalent
primary concern: *My primary concern is for your safety.*
primary consideration: *Your request will be given primary consideration.*

primarily (adv)

primary (adj) first in time
primary election: *The winner of the primary election will be the party's candidate for president.*

primary (n) primary election

purchase (v) to buy
afford to purchase: *Now that my wife is working, we can afford to buy a new car.*

purchase (n)
to make a purchase
online purchase, cash purchase, credit purchase
purchase price, purchase order
proof of purchase

range (n) the limits, extents or area something is contained in
to extend the range, to broaden the range; to limit the range, to narrow the range
to produce a range, to stock a range, to carry a range
bottom of the range, middle of the range, top of the range
at close range; from close range: *It's easy to hit your target when you are shooting from close range.*

Unit 2

short range plans, long range plans: *My short range plans are to graduate and find a job. My long range plans are to get married and buy a house.*

in range, within range, within a narrow range, within a certain range

wide range, broad range, vast range

narrow range, limited range

a mountain range

out of range: *We couldn't use our cell phones because we were out of range.*

range (v)

widely range; range across

range between ~ and ~ : *The test scores range between 45% and 91%.*

range from ~ to~ : *Prices for new laptops range from $350 to over $1,000.*

region (n) a large or continuous part of the world, a country or a body, etc.

to live in a region, to inhabit a region: *Laplanders inhabit the far northern regions of Norway.*

an entire region, whole region, central region; a region of land

remote region, border region, unexplored region, an outlying region, an unpopulated region

dry region, desert region, a mountainous region, a tropical region

urban region, urbanized region, rural region, sparsely populated region: *The high plateau is a sparsely populated region.*

oil-producing region: *Kenya is the world's newest oil-producing region.*

within the region, throughout the region

regional (adj)

regional conference

regionally (adv)

region (n) approximate area or range

in the region of: *They are paying him in the region of a million dollars a year.*

regulate (v) to control or direct by making something work in a particular way

to attempt to regulate, to try to regulate, to be designed to regulate, to be intended to regulate

strictly regulate, tightly regulate, closely regulate, carefully regulate

to regulate breathing: *It is important to regulate your breathing as you do these exercises.*

to regulate traffic

highly regulated

regulation (n)

to call for regulation, to adopt a regulation, to enact a regulation, to enforce a regulation

to obey regulation, to observe regulation, to comply with regulation

to ignore regulation, to relax regulation, to contravene regulations [= to go against regulation]: *Home owners who do work which contravenes building regulations will be given fines.*

army regulation, safety regulation, government regulation, state regulation

rigid regulation, strict regulation, tight regulation, tough regulation: *People living near the border are calling for tougher regulation of the immigration laws.*

under the regulation: *Under the old regulations, workers could not work overtime.*

in accordance with regulations; rules and regulations

regulatory (adj)

relevant (adj) connected with or related to what is happening or being discussed

to seem relevant, to be considered as relevant, to remain relevant

to deem relevant [= to consider to be relevant]: *None of the witness's comments were deemed relevant to the case.*

not really relevant, hardly relevant, barely relevant, only indirectly relevant

especially relevant, particularly relevant, highly relevant

morally relevant, socially relevant, politically relevant

relevant to: *None of her comments was relevant to the topic we were discussing.*

(to have) relevant information: *I think I have relevant information about this case that you can use.*

relevantly (adv)

relevance (n)

to remain of relevance, to bear relevance, to lose relevance

to demonstrate relevance, to establish relevance

of particular relevance, special relevance, potential relevance, immediate relevance

doubtful relevance, dubious relevance [= doubtful relevance]: *That Dora was not at home at the time of the murder is of dubious relevance to the case.*

reside (v) to live in or to occupy a place for an extended period of time

reside in: *Many retired people reside in Florida.*

resident (n) a person who lives in a particular place

residence (n)

to establish residence, take up residence

permanent residence, principal residence; a change of residence, a place of residence; residence hall

Unit 2

residency (n) the fact of living or staying in a place

to establish residency: *If you want to pay a lower tuition at this university, you need to establish residency by living in the state for at least six months.*

residency (n) the period during which a doctor gets specialized on-the-job training: *Dr. Williams will finish her residency in two more years.*

resident (adj)

resource (n) a useful or valuable possession, source of aid or support

to develop resource, to exploit resource, to tap resource, to mobilize resource

to conserve resource, to pool resource, to share resource

to be rich in resources: *Afghanistan is rich in mineral resources, but lacks the means to mine them.*

to have the resources to: *We don't have the resources to develop our new institution.*

to lack resources: *Jordan lacks the resources to handle the huge number of refugees flooding in from Syria.*

lack of resources, limited resource, non-renewable resource; scarce resource, finite resource

a natural resource, abundant resource

human resources, inner resources, financial resource, capital resource

renewable resource, vital resource, major resource, substantial resource

resourceful (adj)

a resourceful person

highly resourceful

restrict (v) to limit or reduce something or prevent it from increasing

to attempt to restrict, to seek to restrict, to tend to restrict

to restrict to: *From now on, you please restrict your comments to the task at hand.*

to restrict access to

severely restricted, greatly restricted, effectively restricted, unduly restricted [= excessively restricted]: *The committee were unduly restricted by the new rules, so were unable to finish their work.*

restriction (n)

to put restrictions on, to place restrictions on, to impose restrictions on: *The United States wants to impose new restrictions on imports from Mexico.*

to remove restriction, to lift restriction: *The UN is considering lifting restrictions on those countries.*

tight restriction, severe restriction, legal restriction

travel restriction, trade restriction, visa restriction, time restriction, space restriction

without restriction

restricted (adj) limited; excluding certain people or things

restricted information, restricted visibility, restricted diet; restricted access, restricted area

access is restricted: *Access to the Commissary is restricted to military personnel only.*

seek (v) to search for, look for or try to discover or obtain [past: sought]

to seek to do something: *They are seeking to build a new factory in our town.*

to seek help, to seek support, to seek revenge, to seek a solution, to seek advice

to seek refuge [= to seek a safe place]: *When the heavy rain began, we sought refuge in an old barn.*

to eagerly seek, to desperately seek, to urgently seek

to seek in vain: *Charles sought in vain for his lost car.*

select (v) to make a choice as a result of a decision

to carefully select, to select at random, to select randomly; to personally select

to select as: *She was selected as our new president.*

to select for: *He was selected for his good looks.*

to select according to: *The contestants were selected according to the quality of their interview responses.*

selection (n)

to make a selection, to offer a selection

natural selection

selection process, selection criteria, selection procedure, selection committee

careful selection, random selection, final selection, jury selection

wide selection, varied selection, broad selection; representative selection

selective (adv)

select (adj)

select theaters [= a small number of special theatres]: *Brad Pitt's new movie will be shown in select theaters starting next week.*

site (n) a place where something is located or will happen or will be built

to visit a site, to search for a site, to browse a site, to choose a site, to locate a site, to occupy a site

potential site, suitable site, appropriate site

ancient site, historical site; bomb site, crash site; dump site; burial site

web site

at the site of: *Security was tight at the site of the Winter Olympics in Sochi.*

Unit 2

site (v) to locate or position something in a place
>to carefully site, to strategically site, to conveniently site

strategy (n) a plan, method or series of actions for achieving success
>to adopt a strategy, to devise a strategy, to formulate a strategy, to map out a strategy, to outline a strategy, to change a strategy
>to work out a strategy, to apply a strategy, to pursue a strategy, to explore a strategy
>global strategy, comprehensive strategy, long-range strategy, broad strategy, overall strategy
>clear strategy, coherent strategy, viable strategy, grand strategy
>a campaign strategy, a political strategy, a military strategy, a financial strategy
>a change in strategy: *Internet sales are causing a change in strategy for brick-and-mortar stores.*
>a strategy for: *She has an excellent strategy for memorizing new words.*
>a strategy to do something: *France has come up with a new strategy for keeping peace in Ivory Coast.*

strategic (adj)
>strategic defense, strategic plan, strategic thinking, strategic objectives

strategically (adv)

strategize (v)

survey (n) a comprehensive overview of opinions, behavior etc., arrived at by asking people questions
>to carry out a survey, to conduct a survey, to make a survey, to do a survey, to commission a survey
>a detailed survey, a comprehensive survey, an in-depth survey; a brief survey, a quick survey
>customer survey, marketing survey
>an aerial survey

survey (v) to look around
>to survey the environment, to survey the surroundings
>carefully survey, coolly survey

text (n) printed material or oral theme or subject
>to edit a text, to annotate a text
>to stray from the text: *Your analysis does not stray too far from the ideas in the original text.*
>full text, complete text, original text, main text
>accompanying text: *The photograph and the accompanying text made me smile.*
>standard text, recommended text; sacred text [= religious text]: *The Koran is the sacred text for Muslims.*

text (v) to send a written message electronically

textual (adj)

transfer (n) a move from one place or person to another
>to make a transfer
>an electronic transfer, technology transfer
>a peaceful transfer of power; a bus transfer

transfer (v) to move or convey from one place or person to another
>directly transfer, successfully transfer, formally transfer, temporarily transfer
>transfer from: *I transferred from a small college in California.*
>transfer to: *The prisoners were transferred to a new prison.*
>to transfer from one (place, etc.) to another: *I had to transfer money from my savings account to my checking account.*

transferable (adj)
>readily transferable, freely transferable, not necessarily transferable, non-transferable

transferal (n)

Unit 2

Synonyms

achieve:	accomplish, attain, realize, fulfill, get
acquire:	obtain, get, accumulate
administer:	oversee, direct, apply, manage
affect:	influence, change, modify, carry out
appropriate:	proper, befitting, right, reasonable
aspect:	angle, regard, appearance
category:	class, sort, kind, set
chapter:	division, part, section
commission:	authorization, assignment, order
community:	neighborhood, group, society
compute:	calculate, figure
conclude:	end, terminate; decide, determine
conduct:	action, behavior
consequence:	conclusion, outcome, result
construct:	build, assemble, manufacture, raise
consume:	eat, use up, devour
credit:	merit, approval, praise, reliability
culture:	customs, lifestyle, civilization
design:	plan, outline, drawing, picture
distinct:	separate, special, different
element:	aspect, member, part, piece
equate:	identify, liken
evaluate:	measure, grade, judge
feature:	aspect, trait, face
focus:	emphasis, center, aim
impact:	effect, hit, shock, crash
injure:	damage, hurt, harm
institute:	develop, establish, create
invest:	save, speculate, endow
item:	article, thing, piece
journal:	record, periodical, book
maintain:	keep, retain, continue, support
normal:	ordinary, usual, accepted, everyday
obtain:	get, take, acquire, receive
participate:	join, engage, share
perceive:	detect, notice, sense, know
positive:	certain, sure; affirmative
potential:	possible, probable, likely
primary:	first, leading, main, key
purchase:	buy, obtain, acquire
range:	extent, area, reach
region:	area, land, field
regulate:	control, modulate, organize, adjust
relevant:	related, appropriate, applicable
reside:	live, stay
resource:	support, assets, means
restrict:	hold, contain, restrain, control
seek:	look for, hunt for, search for
select:	choose, pick, identify, single out
site:	location, situation, scene
strategy:	design, plan, scheme, tactic
survey:	map, view, overview
text:	writing, book, message
transfer:	transport, send, hand over, relocate

Unit 2

Answers

Definitions

1. concluded	16. item	31. community	46. design
2. purchased	17. journal	32. site	47. select
3. instituted	18. construction	33. impact	48. reside
4. evaluate	19. transfer	34. relevant	49. participation
5. obtain	20. compute	35. normal	50. restriction
6. injure	21. achieve	36. potential	51. element
7. chapter	22. aspect	37. consume	52. seek
8. region	23. credit	38. equate	53. maintain
9. survey	24. resource	39. acquire	54. invest
10. primary	25. affect	40. cultural	
11. positive	26. perceive	41. distinct	
12. appropriate	27. regulate	42. strategic	
13. commission	28. category	43. consequence	
14. administer	29. feature	44. focus	
15. conduct	30. range	45. text	

Parts of Speech

1. achievement(s) / achieved	12. conclusion / conclusions	23. evaluation / evaluated	34. obtains / obtained / obtainable
2. acquisition / acquired	13. conducted / conduct	24. features / features	35. participate / participation
3. administering / administrative	14. Consequently / consequence	25. focus / focusses	36. perceived / perception
4. affect / affective	15. constructed / construction	26. impact / impacts/impacted	37. positive / positives
5. appropriately / appropriate	16. consumption / consumed	27. injurious / injury	38. potential / potential
6. aspects / aspect	17. credits / credit	28. institute / institute	39. primarily / primary
7. categories / categorize	18. cultural / culture	29. investing / investment / investing	40. purchased / purchases
8. chapters / chapter	19. to design / designing / designs	30. item / itemize	41. ranges / range
9. commission / commissioned	20. distinctions / distinctly	31. journal / journal	42. regional / regions
10. community / communities	21. element / elements	32. maintain / maintained	43. regulations / regulating
11. compute / computation	22. equate / equated	33. normalize / normal	44. relevant / relevant

45. reside / residing	49. selection / selected	53. texts / texted
46. resources / resourceful	50. site / sites	54. transfer / transfer
47. restrictions / restricted	51. strategically / strategies	
48. sought / seeking	52. survey(s) / surveys	

Unit 2

Answers

Collocations			
Exercise 1	**Exercise 2**	**Exercise 3**	**Exercise 4**

1. distinction
   distinction
   distinctions
	1. regulations
	   regulation
	   regulate
		1. acquired
		   acquired
		   acquires
			1. transfer
			   transfer
			   transferred

2. investments
   investment
   invested
	2. conclusion
	   conclusion
	   concluded
		2. commission
		   commission
		   commissioned
			2. participate
			   participating
			   participate

3. potential
   potentially
   potential
	3. credit
	   credit
	   credit/credited
		3. seek
		   seeking
		   sought
			3. journal
			   journals
			   journal

4. element
   element
   elements
	4. focus
	   focused
	   focus
		4. consequence
		   consequence
		   consequences
			4. evaluation
			   evaluate
			   evaluation

5. strategy
   strategies
   strategy
	5. feature
	   features
	   feature
		5. chapter
		   chapter
		   chapter
			5. culture
			   culture
			   cultures

6. achievement
   achievement
   achievements
	6. restriction
	   restrictions
	   restricted
		6. administered
		   administer
		   administering
			6. consumes
			   consumed
			   consumed

7. category
   category
   categorized
	7. survey
	   survey
	   surveyed
		7. primary
		   primary
		   primary
			7. conducted
			   conduct
			   conduct

8. impact
   impact
   impacted
	8. normal
	   normal
	   normality
		8. designed
		   design
		   design
			8. aspect
			   aspects
			   aspect

9. ranged
   range
   range
	9. region
	   region
	   regions
		9. selected
		   selection
		   selection
			9. appropriate
			   appropriate
			   appropriate

10. resources
    resource
    resources
	10. maintenance
	    maintenance
	    maintain
		10. obtain
		    obtain
		    obtained
			10. text/texts
			    text
			    text

Unit 2

Answers

<table>
<tr><td colspan="2">Synonyms (Crossword)</td></tr>
<tr><td>Across</td><td>Down</td></tr>
<tr><td>

9. consume
10. element
11. acquire
13. obtain
18. potential
21. maintain
24. construct
25. design
27. conclude
28. strategy
29. transfer

</td><td>

1. credit
2. category
3. affect
4. community
5. purchase
6. regulate
7. select
8. relevant
12. reside
14. appropriate
15. distinct
16. item
17. perceive
19. injure
20. administer
22. normal
23. primary
26. focus

</td></tr>
</table>

<table>
<tr><td colspan="3">Review</td></tr>
<tr><td>

1. community
2. aspect
3. range
4. resources
5. surveys
6. consequences
7. impact
8. site
9. commission
10. item
11. text
12. credit
13. feature
14. culture
15. element
16. region
17. journal
18. category

</td><td>

19. chapter
20. focus
21. strategy
22. acquired
23. instituted
24. perceived
25. construct
26. purchase
27. calculate
28. evaluate
29. compute
30. transfer
31. consume
32. obtain
33. select
34. conduct
35. participate
36. administer

</td><td>

37. invest
38. achieve
39. maintain
40. affect
41. conclude
42. design
43. injure
44. regulate
45. reside
46. restrict
47. seek
48. equate
49. distinct
50. potential
51. relevant
52. appropriate
53. normal
54. primary

</td></tr>
</table>

Unit 3

Word List

Parts of speech: **n** = noun   **v** = verb   **adj** = adjective   **adv** = adverb

alternative (adj)
  alternate (n)
  alternative (adj)
  alternatively (adv)
circumstance (n)
  circumstantial (adj)
  circumstantially (adv)
comment (n)
  comment (v)
compensate (v)
  compensation (n)
  compensatory (adj)
component (n)
consent (n)
  consent (v)
considerable (adj)
  considerably (adv)
constant (adj)
  constantly (adv)
  constancy (n)
constrain (v)
  constraint (n)
contribute (v)
  contribution (n)
  contributor (n)
convene (v)
  convention (n)
coordinate (v)
  coordination (n)
core (n)
  core (v)
corporate (adj)
  corporation (n)
correspond (v)
  correspondence (n)
criteria (n. plural)
  criterion (n. singular)
deduce (v)
  deduction (n)
  deductive (adj)
  deductively (adv)
demonstrate (v)
  demonstration (n)
  demonstrator (n)
  demonstrative (adj)
  demonstratively (adv)
document (n)
  document (v)
  documentation (n)
dominate (v)
  domination (n)
  dominance (n)
  dominant (adj)

emphasis (n. singular)
  emphases (n. plural)
  emphasize (v)
  emphatic (adj)
  emphatically (adv)
ensure (v)
exclude (v)
  exclusion (n)
  exclusive (adj)
  exclusively (adv)
framework (n)
fund (n)
  fund (v)
illustrate (v)
  illustration (n)
  illustrative (adj)
immigrate (v)
  immigration (n)
  immigrant (n)
imply (v)
  implication (n)
initial (adj)
  initially (adv)
  initial (n)
  initial (v)
instance (n)
interact (v)
  interaction (n)
  interactive (adj)
  interactively (adv)
justify (v)
  justification (n)
  justifiable (adj)
  justifiably (adv)
layer (n)
  layer (v)
link (n)
  link (v)
locate (v)
  location (n)
maximize (v)
  maximization (n)
  maximum (n)
  maximal (adj)
  maximally (adv)
minor (n)
  minor (n)
  minor (v)

negate (v)
  negation (n)
  negative (n)
  negative (adj)
  negatively (adv)
outcome (n)
philosophy (n)
  philosophize (v)
  philosophical (adj)
  philosophically (adv)
physical (adj)
  physically (adv)
  physical (n)
proportion (n)
  proportional (adj)
  proportionally (adv)
  proportion (v)
react (v)
  reaction (n)
  reactive (adj)
  reactively (adv)
rely (v)
  reliance (n)
  reliable (adj)
  reliably (adv)
scheme (n)
  scheme (v)
sequence (n)
  sequence (v)
  sequential (adj)
  sequentially (adv)
shift (n)
  shift (v)
specify (v)
  specification (n)
  specific (adj)
  specifically (adv)
sufficient (adj)
  sufficiently (adv)
  suffice (v)
task (n)
technical (adj)
  technically (adv)
  technicality (n)
technique (n)
valid (adj)
volume (n)

Unit 3

Definitions Use the definition clues to write the correct words in the blanks.

1.	one of two or more things, offering the possibility of choice *The road was closed, so we took the _____ route.* 2. of noticeable importance; proportionally large *The weather has _____ power over my emotions.* 3. shared or united as a whole group of individuals *It is our _____ responsibility to generate a profit for our shareholders.*	considerable alternative physical corporate specific valid
4.	a particular situation, occasion or fact, especially an example of something that happens generally *Sometimes, the patient will forget to take the medicine. In this _____, no extra medicine should be given.* 5. a result or consequence of an action, situation, etc *The _____ of today's game will determine which team goes to the playoffs.* 6. to stress or show special importance for something *Some parents put a great deal of _____ on their children's education.*	outcome emphasis deduction instance exclusion location
7.	to have control over or govern by rule or by power *The Ducks _____ most games with their incredible defensive plays.* 8. to give a good reason for something *How can you _____ your decision to quit?* 9. to make various things work harmoniously as a whole *If we carefully _____ with each other, our plan will work.*	coordinate negate justify consent dominate contribute
10.	based on truth, fact, logic or reason; able to be accepted *Sickness is the only _____ excuse for missing the meeting.* 11. concerned with specialized skills or knowledge, especially in science, engineering or industry *Ned's _____ training enabled him to get a great job with a chemical engineering company.* 12. enough or adequate for a particular purpose *Don't worry. You have _____ time to finish your work.*	valid corporate sufficient considerable technical initial
13.	events associated with or having an impact on a situation *In certain _____, the police can ask for identification.* 14. written or printed information, usually official, that provide information, evidence, or proof of something *The secret _____ proved that Lorry was innocent.* 15. tests or standards by which to judge or deal with something *These final exams must have reliable _____, otherwise we cannot use them.*	documents cores criteria circumstances instances outcomes

16. to come into a new country in order to live there permanently *In the 1800s, thousands of Chinese _____ to the US.* 17. to clarify something, especially by giving examples or adding pictures *Bonnie _____ her PowerPoint with her own pictures.* 18. to communicate an idea or feeling indirectly *Her answer _____ that she was not ready to join us.*	implied illustrated ensured commented deduced immigrated
19. continually, never stopping *Connie's mother is _____ calling her.* 20. of the body or material things that can be seen or felt *Marathon runners prepare themselves _____ and mentally to run great distances.* 21. at the beginning; first *_____, we thought that Ursula would be a great employee, but we were wrong.*	specifically alternatively dominantly constantly physically initially
22. a written or spoken observation or opinion *Polly made a nasty _____ about the stale crackers.* 23. an evil plan for obtaining an advantage *The banks devised a _____ for making huge profits.* 24. a bond or connection between two things *The new road establishes a fast _____ between the two cities.*	comment reaction task volume scheme link
25. to make certain something happens *This law _____ that unemployed people will have some hope.* 26. to state or name clearly and exactly *The legal contract _____ that the buyer will pay exactly $150,000 for the services.* 27. to give money, support, or help towards a particular aim or purpose *Frank _____ to his favorite non-profit charity.*	specifies contributes excludes constrains implies ensures
28. a thin sheet of a substance spread over a surface *Irving was covered with a thin _____ of mud from head to toe.* 29. a specific piece of work done regularly, unwillingly or with difficulty *Benjamin was faced with the _____ of cleaning up the mess.* 30. a part or element which combines with other parts to form a whole *Cotton is a major _____ of the new fabric.*	technique outcome outcome component task layer

Unit 3

31. to offset; to be exchanged for something of equal or better value *The insurance must _____ you for your loss.* 32. to reach an answer or draw a conclusion by careful reasoning about the known facts *From the results of the experiment, we can _____ that hydrogen was present in the original gas mixture.* 33. to depend on or trust *The old man can _____ on his children to help him.*		deduce rely alternate compensate correspond maximize
34. having lesser importance, influence or seriousness than other things of the same type *A _____ problem occurred as we set up the experiment.* 35. the central, basic and most important part of something *Saving money is at the _____ of our proposal.* 36. a supporting structure, enclosure or idea *Dr. Rosen worked out the theoretical _____ for the new rocket design.*		emphasis core shift framework link minor
37. to act in a particular way in response to something else *Some people _____ to spiders with great fear.* 38. to increase something in as great an amount as possible *It is natural for a corporation to try to _____ its profits.* 39. move or change slightly from one place or direction to another *Nervous people sometimes _____ their weight from one foot to the other.*		maximize shift react comment coordinate document
40. the number or amount of something *After the senator gave her speech, there was a great _____ of phone calls to her office.* 41. the use of reason in the study of the nature of reality and existence and the principles of moral and aesthetic judgment *Ghandi followed a _____ of non-violence.* 42. a specific way of performing an activity requiring skill in the arts, sports, science, etc. *Van Gogh's brush _____ has often been imitated.*		volume emphasis exclusion component philosophy technique
43. to give your permission, your agreement or your approval *There is no way we will _____ to lower wages.* 44. to match, be similar to, be equal to or in agreement with *The numbers on a clock do not _____ to the 60 minutes in an hour.* 45. to leave out, keep out or omit something or someone *Ken decided to _____ us from the discussions.*		immigrate consent correspond convene constrain exclude

Unit 3

46. a supply of money saved, collected or provided for a particular purpose *I'm setting aside a little money every week for my college.* _____. 47. a process or series of related things or events which follow each other *When a new forest grows back after trees have been removed, new species of trees follow each other in a natural _____.* 48. the relationship of one thing when compared to another *You will be paid in _____ to how hard you work.*	specification emphasis corporation proportion sequence fund
49. to communicate with or react to one another in a social situation *These children are so wonderful. They _____ with each other very calmly.* 50. to show; to make clear; to explain or describe in detail using many examples *The professor knew how to _____ chemical valence so that the students could understand it easily.* 51. to gather or assemble, especially for a formal meeting *If we _____ the meeting at 9:00, we can be finished by noon.*	convene interact demonstrate imply justify locate
52. something which controls what you do by keeping you within particular limits *Her injuries will _____ her to a wheelchair for a few months.* 53. to cause something to be ineffective and probably useless *Her words _____ everything I just said. Now, no one will believe me.* 54. to find, put or establish something in a place or position *General Motors wants to _____ their new factory in our little town.*	negate constrain deduce compensate alternate locate

Parts of Speech

Write the parts of speech (noun, verb, adjective or adverb form).
Word Forms: Be careful with nouns and verbs:
Some *nouns* might need to be plural (~s).
Some *verbs* might need ~s, ~ed, ~ing.

alternative　1. There is an _____ solution to this problem.

You have no _____ but to pay back your loan.

circumstance　2. In certain _____, some birds do not migrate.

The jury cannot convict her based solely on _____ evidence.

comment　3. Don made several _____ about me that I didn't like.

Let's get started, without further _____.

compensate　4. Because I caused the accident, I have to pay _____.

Elaine was a poor reader, but she could use a _____ strategy to get through a novel.

component　5. Most of the engine's _____ are available locally.

Cream is a key _____ in this recipe.

consent　6. Yesterday, Carl _____ to become the new chairman.

We must _____ to follow the rules.

considerable　7. The weather is _____ warmer today.

There is a _____ amount of snow on the roof.

constant　8. Korey is liked for his _____ and his loyalty.

Jen is _____ looking for new ways to decorate the house.

constrain　9. You should not let the children run around without _____.

Our travel plans are _____ by our lack of money.

contribute　10. The Democratic Party is asking me for a _____.

Industrial pollution _____ to global warming.

convene　11. We have been _____ every morning at 10:00.

Last week, the meeting _____ at 9:00.

Unit 3

coordinate   12. We worked in close _____ with our neighbors.

Alison usually _____ the program very well.

core   13. It won't take long to get to the _____ of the problem.

Justin has strong _____ values.

corporate   14. Community outreach is an important part of our _____ responsibility.

The new CEO really knows how to run a _____.

correspond   15. One meter _____ approximately to one yard.

I still maintain _____ with my old high school friends.

criteria   16. You need to meet certain _____ in order to work here.

One important _____ to consider when buying a new car is fuel efficiency.

deduce   17. We didn't know what to _____ from his statement.

Sherlock's brilliant _____ amazed everyone.

demonstrate   18. Ted gave us a _____ of the speed of his computer.

We will give money to people who have clearly _____ needs.

document   19. Irene printed out twelve _____ to read on the train.

You need to provide _____ of your disability.

dominate   20. One player clearly _____ last night's game.

How can he have total _____ over those people?

emphasis   21. She's putting too much _____ on her role as a mother.

We want to _____ the importance of being on time.

ensure   22. Hard work _____ success more than luck does.

Can the hotel _____ that we will have a non-smoking room?

Unit 3

exclude   23. Gerald was _____ from the discussion.

Bart focused on winning, to the _____ of everything else.

framework   24. You need to work within the established _____.

Marvin came up with an interesting theoretical _____ for solving the physics problem.

fund   25. The new housing project is _____ by local banks.

The CEO will set up a _____ for employees with small children.

illustrate   26. Daniel offered an _____ of how the fabric of space-time could be warped.

Arlene always _____ her books with her own drawings.

immigrate   27. Thousands of _____ arrived in Texas last year.

Illegal _____ is a serious problem in the US.

imply   28. I don't mean to _____ that you are lazy, but … .

Interest rates are very low. By _____, bonds are not a good investment right now.

initial   29. My _____ response was not positive.

_____ , I thought it was not a good idea.

instance   30. In most _____, children can be taught good manners.

This looks like an _____ of foul play.

interact   31. The two groups had a negative _____ with each other.

Aaron _____ well with other teen-agers.

justify   32. Nothing _____ cheating on your taxes.

There is no _____ for being mean to your neighbors.

layer   33. They put a new _____ of paint on their house.

There were several _____ of newspapers stuck to the walls of the old home.

Unit 3

link 34. In 1988, explorers _____ the ancient temple to the Egyptian god Isis.

Several roads _____ the major cities.

locate 35. This looks like a good _____ for our picnic.

More companies are now _____ their businesses here.

maximize 36. Some corporations can _____ their profits and take care of the environment at the same time.

The _____ amount of time we have is two hours.

minor 37. Beethoven made _____ variations to his sonata.

The _____ were not allowed into the night club.

negate 38. The poor economy is having a _____ impact on local businesses.

Bright sun light _____ affects good outdoor photography.

outcome 39. One of the _____ of the war was the economic boom.

We can evaluate the _____ by observing temperature variations.

philosophy 40. Dad loves to _____ about everything.

You should be more _____ about what is happening right now.

physical 41. Getting to the top of the mountain will require quite a bit of _____ effort.

Lilly is very _____ fit. She exercises every day.

proportion 42. Think carefully. Don't blow things out of _____.

Two quantities y and x are said to be inversely _____ if y is given by a constant multiple of 1/x.

react 43. It's interesting how Anthony _____ against everything that I suggest.

My forgetfulness set off a chain _____ of events.

rely 44. The car is old, but it is _____ safe.

Ralph _____ on his GPS too much. He doesn't look around to see where he is.

- 77 -

Unit 3

scheme   45. We think that her fake kidnapping was just some sort of publicity
_____.

What are you two guys _____ about?

sequence   46. The books on this shelf are not arranged _____. They need to be placed in alphabetical order.

No one could have predicted the _____ of events.

shift   47. The discovery of many planets outside our solar system has caused a major _____ in the way we think about the universe.

We watched the nervous girl as she _____ from one foot to the other.

specify   48. The camera's lenses are made to Sony's exact _____.

A good teacher always _____ exactly what she wants in the way of homework assignments.

sufficient   49. There wasn't _____ reason to fire Wanda.

I think this new coat will keep you _____ warm.

task   50. Trying to keep our tents dry during the storm was a hopeless _____.

Some _____ are more important than others.

technical   51. It's a great computer. Don't worry about the _____ details. Just buy it.

_____, you are not old enough to watch this film.

technique   52. Melinda uses several different _____ to help her students learn new vocabulary words.

The engineers worked out a new _____ for manufacturing solar panels cheaply.

valid   53. If your passport is not _____, you cannot enter the country.

Do you have a _____ reason for quitting your job?

volume   54. I can't hear the TV. Would you please turn up the _____?

The complete works of Shakespeare are available in a new set containing three _____ .

Unit 3

Collocations

In each group of sentences, write *one* word from the list which goes with the **highlighted collocations**. You may have to change the form of the word.

Exercise 1	framework dominance alternative compensate deduce
	circumstance imply document comment initial justify consent

1. **By mutual** _____, we agreed to remove the advertisement.

   My neighbor **gave me her** _____ to park in her driveway.

   Yesterday, father _____ **to** letting Ollie get his driver's license.

2. **In certain** _____ , passengers can get a refund on their tickets.

   Due to _____ beyond our control, the program is cancelled.

   The jury's decision was not **based on** _____ **evidence**.

3. The victims were _____ **for damages** to their home.

   The company fired its employees **without adequate** _____.

   I lost my job, so I'll have to live on **unemployment** _____.

4. The enemy **has no** _____ **but to** stop fighting.

   This medication makes me _____ **between** being sleepy **and** being hungry.

   If Plan A doesn't work, you can **fall back on an** _____ plan.

5. My job is boring. All I do is **sign** _____ all day long.

   She **provided appropriate** _____ **for** her claim.

   Birth certificates and driver's licenses are **legal** _____.

6. Parents naturally **have** _____ **over** their children.

   Every day, Harold's work **totally** _____ his life.

   Poland **came under foreign** _____ in the 20th century.

7. The researchers **came up with a theoretical** _____ to explain the expansion of the universe.

   We are limited because we must **work within a certain** _____.

8. Does anyone **have any** _____ **to make** about the new proposal?

   Audrey **made a passing** _____ about her sister.

   Without further _____, let's get down to business.

9. Uncle Cent fired his nephew **without the slightest** _____.

   Nothing _____ cheating.

10. My _____ **impression** was that Martine would be a great instructor.

    The _____ **impact** of the new tax was that the city was able to hire more police.

Unit 3

Collocations

Exercise 2	scheme emphasis core layer philosophy location
	illustration fund convene valid criteria correspond

1. She put two **protective** _____ on the valuable painting.

   Straw formed **the bottom** _____ of the bed.

   Scientists think **the ozone** _____ buffers against global warming.

2. Her **homespun** _____ drew heavily from the agricultural practices of her village.

   That's a **purely** _____ question, if you ask me.

3. We have an **emergency** _____ to use if we need it.

   Owen invested most of his money in a **mutual** _____ .

   Mr. Hope is _____ **a new venture** called "Vistas."

4. I'm going to talk about Russia, **with special** _____ **on** its contribution to world literature.

   The professor **put considerable** _____ **on** string theory.

   In your paper, be sure **to place the** _____ **on** your own research.

5. He didn't have **a** _____ **excuse** for missing class today.

   I hope you have **a** _____ **reason** for coming late.

6. Some trees produce better fruit than others. **By way of** _____, take a look at this particular tree.

   First, I will **give** two _____ of what I mean by *imperialism*.

   This stonework **provides an** _____ of how the Incas mastered hydrology.

7. The producers wanted **to shoot the film on** _____ .

   The weapons are kept at several **undisclosed** _____ .

   The exact _____ of the original tomb is still unknown.

8. A desire to increase profits is **at the** _____ **of** the proposal.

   She's a terrible child. She's **rotten to the** _____ .

   Stop talking so much. **Get to the** _____ **of the matter**.

9. There is a very **close** _____ **between** the your essay and the information in Wikipedia, so I think your essay is plagiarized.

   Line up the dials so the two arrows _____ **exactly** to each other.

   In Spanish, *embarazada* _____ **to** the word *pregnant* in English.

10. Student essays must **meet the** _____ listed in the syllabus.

    We **apply certain** _____ **to** each oral presentation.

    The test was well-written and it had **reliable** grading _____ .

Unit 3

Collocations

Exercise 3	constant proportion exclusive link maximum alternative minor implications reaction scheme considerable instances

1. The news about the mayor has been **blown out of** _____.

   A good journalist should **have a sense of** _____ about what is important and what is not.

   Her earnings were **directly** _____ **to** the effort she made.

2. **With** _____ **modifications**, the new engine ran perfectly.

   I agree with your ideas, **with** _____ a few **exceptions**.

   Don't worry about the _____ **details**. They are not important.

3. My **initial** _____ was one of amazement.

   His error **set off a chain** _____ of events that affected everyone.

   At yesterday's event, we _____ **with alarm** to the news.

4. My uncle **came up with a get-rich-quick** _____ that made everyone laugh.

   We need **to cook up a** _____ to get Kevin back on the team.

   The police **foiled a** _____ by the criminals to launder money.

5. **The** _____ **amount** they are willing to pay is $25.

   Banks do everything they can to _____ **their profits**.

   This room will **accommodate a** _____ **of** 100 people.

6. There is **a strong** _____ **between** smoking and cancer.

   The money missing from the bank account is **somehow** _____ **to** Danny's disappearance.

   Our organization wants to **establish a** _____ **with** other organizations in our effort to provide better services.

7. The restructuring **has serious** _____ **on** the world economy.

   Please **consider the** _____ your decision has on your family.

   The court's ruling will have **far-reaching** _____ for businesses in our community.

8. The US **wields** _____ **power over** world markets.

   Apparently, your brother **has** _____ **power over** you.

9. Some areas of religious and scientific thought are **mutually** _____.

   The lottery winner was **offered** _____ **membership** in the club.

   We didn't think it was right for the mayor to **belong to an** _____ **organization**.

10. Our tenants _____ **complain** about everything.

    After the accident, Kay was **in** _____ **pain** for weeks.

Unit 3

Collocations

Exercise 4	technical sufficient volume instance exclusive contribute
	shift coordinate negative outcome interaction illustrate

1. That music is too loud. Please turn **down the** _____.

   The saleswoman was rewarded for her **increased sales** _____.

   The **storage** _____ of this box is not adequate.

2. Certain _____ **aspects** were difficult to understand.

   The camera will have **to meet certain** _____ **requirements** before I will buy it.

   The judge threw out the case on **a legal** _____.

3. More tests were done, but all of them **proved** _____.

   Her decision **has potentially** _____ **consequences** on everyone.

   The word *skinny* **has a** _____ **connotation** for most people.

4. We hope that the new policy will improve **social** _____ among the employees.

   After the accident, Jake had trouble with **human** _____.

   We need more **face-to-face** _____ and less Facebooking.

5. **In most** _____ , clients can manage their accounts on line.

   In rare _____ , the medication can cause sleepiness.

   A mother gorilla may not bond with her new infant. **In this** _____ , we will take the infant way.

6. She **asked** us **for a** _____ to United Way.

   Bill and Melinda Gates _____ **substantially** to universities.

   My wife _____ **to charities** and volunteers at the church.

7. Jim worked in **close** _____ **with** his wife to make sure that the party would be a success.

   _____ **among** the various tribes will be difficult.

8. She tried to _____ **the blame from** herself to someone else.

   Don't expect a **dramatic** _____ **away from** the current policy.

   Recently, there has been **a gradual** _____ **away from** relying on scientific evidence.

9. The delegates **welcomed the positive** _____ of the conference.

   The judges will **decide the final** _____ later today.

   Our efforts did not **have the desired** _____.

10. The money was **barely** _____ **for** them to pay their rent.

    The expired license plate **provided** the officer **with** _____ **reason** to stop the motorist.

    Police cannot enter your home **without** _____ cause.

Unit 3

Synonyms Use the synonym clues to solve this crossword puzzle.

Across
1. regular, steady, stable
3. spell out, define, indicate, establish
5. agree, match, resemble
6. move, relocate
8. small, unimportant, slight
9. hint, suggest
10. stress, importance, focus, highlight
12. job, duty, work, chore, assignment
17. thought, belief, ideology
18. result, conclusion, consequence
19. leave out, omit, keep out, skip
20. control, rule, govern
21. make up for, offset, balance, equal
22. depend on, trust, count on
24. first, prime, original
25. observation, remark, statement
26. illustrate, show, describe, tell
27. choice, option

Down
2. cancel, destroy, deny, nullify
4. big, great, substantial, ample
7. demonstrate, show, illuminate
11. mix, ratio, balance, relationship
13. plot, deal, plan, tactic
14. agree, approve, comply
15. center, heart, nucleus, foundation
16. arrange, organize, harmonize
20. conclude, infer, determine
21. gather together, meet, assemble
23. connection, bond, tie

Unit 3

Review

Write the correct word in each sentence.

1.	My _____ impression was that she was telling the truth.	deductive
		sufficient
2.	There was not _____ evidence to prove he was wrong.	initial
		considerable
3.	We went to _____ lengths to get more information from her.	physical
		technical
4.	The coach put _____ pressure on his players to perform better.	constant
		core
5.	His _____ strength is incredible. He can lift 150 kilos over his head.	circumstantial
		alternative
6.	If you want to make up the exam, you need a _____ excuse.	valid
		physical
7.	To put a man on the moon, the Space Agency had to overcome considerable _____ difficulties.	valid
		corporate
8.	There was a _____ problem with his schedule, but he was easily able to fix it.	specific
		minor
9.	We made a _____ decision to work together to rebuild our community.	technical
		domineering
10.	Too much _____ is placed on accuracy; it's OK to make mistakes once in a while.	core
		criteria
11.	There was no _____ to his plan. We had to do it his way.	emphasis
		framework
12.	By his careful questioning, he was able to get to the very _____ of my argument.	volume
		alternative
13.	Can you name one _____ in which I ever lied?	instance
		outcome
14.	Costs seem to vary in direct _____ to workers' output.	proportion
		compensation
15.	We had to consider the worst possible _____ if our plan didn't work.	coordination
		technique
16.	The program is cancelled due to _____ beyond our control.	reactions
		components
17.	There is a set of _____ for judging the best dogs in the show.	criteria
		circumstances
18.	Your _____ will be difficult, but I'm sure you can do them.	tasks
		locations

Unit 3

Review

19. Money will be distributed within the _____ of the state plan.		interaction
		layer
20. The leaders came up with a _____ for making more money.		outcome
		scheme
21. He put one _____ upon another, until the cake was nearly 30 cm. high.		emphasis
		framework

22. My college _____ is nearly gone. I need to get a job.		fund
		illustration
23. They found the _____ useful for improving their reading skills.		technique
		volume
24. One _____ of a good marriage is trust.		component
		shift

25. An odd _____ of events led up to the discovery of the new planet.		philosophy
		sequence
26. Every year at Christmas, the _____ of mail increases.		emphasis
		location
27. Many people agree with the President's educational _____ .		volume
		implication

28. His _____ about my new shirt puzzled me.		link
		comment
29. The lawyer produced a _____ which proved his client was innocent.		document
		deduction
30. Scientists have found a _____ between vitamin B and certain health benefits.		illustration
		contribution

31. He thinks that rigid policies _____ his imagination.		shift
		imply
32. If we _____ our efforts, we can get the work done quite rapidly.		immigrate
		constrain
33. Some people do not like American culture, but others like it and want to _____ to this country.		dominate
		coordinate

34. Harry always _____ the conversation. No one else gets a chance to speak.		relies
		interacts
35. Sally usually _____ on her mother whenever she needs advice.		documents
		dominates
36. SmartMart usually _____ its newest store in suburban malls.		locates
		constrains

Unit 3

Review

37. Her father would not _____ to her marriage to a poor artist.	consent
38. Low interest rates roughly _____ to low rates of inflation.	rely
39. If we _____ John, there will be only ten on our team.	correspond convene exclude link
40. Students should _____ with each other in the classroom.	exclude
41. We need to _____ our focus from expanding our business to just trying to maintain what we have so far.	negate imply interact
42. The extra business expenses will _____ our profits this year.	specify shift
43. He had to _____ his sister for the damage he did to her car.	maximize
44. You need more data before you can _____ what really happened.	dominate deduce compensate
45. A hypothetical example will _____ this point.	illustrate correspond
46. It was difficult for the ruler to _____ war on the neighboring country. He had no good reasons.	contribute
47. Architects must _____ the materials to be used in construction of buildings they design.	specify negate fund
48. Corporations are allowed to _____ millions of dollars to political campaigns.	justify convene
49. Research can _____ that animals have the ability to think.	alternate
50. Airlines must take steps to _____ that passengers will be safe.	imply ensure comment
51. I don't mean to _____ that you are wrong. I just don't understand you.	contribute demonstrate
52. To _____ our profits, we need to increase productivity.	react
53. People _____ to colors in different ways.	correspond shift convene
54. The meeting will _____ in the library at 5:00.	maximize consent

Unit 3

Definitions ○ Parts of Speech ○ Collocations

alternative (n) one of two or more things, offering the possibility of choice
    to propose an alternative, to fall back on an alternative
    to have no alternative but to: *They have no alternative but to surrender.*
    to leave ~ with no (other) alternative (but): *Your decision to raise my rent leaves me with no alternative but to find another place to live. I just have no other alternative.*
    to provide an alternative, to seek an alternative, to find an alternative
    an attractive alternative, constructive alternative, acceptable alternative: *If you don't have your original document, a photocopy is an acceptable alternative.*
    safe alternative, healthy alternative: *Some people think that tea is a healthy alternative to coffee.*
    satisfactory alternative, realistic alternative, reasonable alternative, credible alternative [= acceptable alternative]: *Community service is sometimes seen as a credible alternative to imprisonment.*
    a viable alternative: *It's expensive to fly to Springfield, but since it's not far, going there by train is a viable alternative.*
alternate (v)
    alternate between (x and y): *Winter weather alternates between rainy days and mild sunny days.*
alternative (adj)
alternatively (adv)
circumstance (n) [usually plural] an event associated with or having an impact on a situation
    favorable circumstances, exceptional circumstances, special circumstances
    difficult circumstances, unfavorable circumstances, suspicious circumstances, adverse circumstances
    unusual circumstances, tragic circumstances, extenuating circumstances [= circumstances that reduce the seriousness]: *Because of these extenuating circumstances, you will not have to take the final exam.*
    mysterious circumstances, suspicious circumstances
    economic circumstances, financial circumstances, political circumstances, social circumstances
    due to circumstances beyond our control: *We are unable to bring you tonight's program due to circumstances beyond our control.*
    a combination of circumstances, a victim of circumstances [= someone who suffers due to events that he or she cannot control] *You should stop being a victim of circumstances and start taking control of your life.*
    in such a circumstance
    in any circumstance: *It might rain tomorrow, or it might even snow. In any circumstance, we have to leave for the airport by 8:00.*
    in certain circumstances
    in light of these circumstances
    circumstances change, circumstances dictate
circumstantial (adj) based on unproven facts associated with or having an impact on a situation
    (based on) circumstantial evidence: *The jury cannot convict you based solely on circumstantial evidence.*
circumstantially (adv)
comment (n) a written or spoken observation or opinion
    to invite comment, to welcome comment
    to have a comment, to make a comment; to have a comment to make
    an appropriate comment, fitting comment, favorable comment
    helpful comment, constructive comment
    a casual comment, passing comment, off-the-cuff comment [= casual comment]: *His off-the-cuff comment seemed innocent enough, but it really made me worry.*
    a critical comment, nasty comment, sarcastic comment, hostile comment
    derogatory comment, disparaging comment [= comment that insults someone]: *The teacher's disparaging comment made the student angry.*
    editorial comment, official comment, public comment
    a comment from: *After that comment from Jim, I'm not sure what to think about the elections.*
    without further comment: *Let's get started, without further comment.*
comment (v)
    to comment on, to comment about: *I just wanted to comment on your speech. It was terrific!*
    to decline to comment, to refuse to comment
compensate (v) to offset; to be exchanged for something of equal or better value
    to compensate for a loss: *Your brother was a wonderful person. Nothing can compensate for your loss.*
    to compensate for damages: *If you win the court case, you will be compensated for damages.*
    fully compensate, adequately compensate
compensation (n)
    to authorize, grant, make or pay compensation
    to deny or refuse compensation: *The judge ruled in favor of the defendant and denied compensation to his accuser.*

adequate compensation, appropriate compensation; financial compensation

to live on/to file for unemployment compensation: *When I lost my job, I had to file for unemployment compensation so that I could have money to live on until I found another job.*

in compensation for: *She should loan you her car in compensation for the damage she did to yours.*

compensatory (adj)

compensatory strategy: *The poor student used compensatory strategies to get through the novel.*

component (n) a part or element which combines with other parts to form a whole

a basic component, key component, essential component, main component, principal component

individual component, separate component

minor component, common component: *The cell phones look entirely different, but they share common components.*

component of

consent (n) permission, agreement or approval

to give one's consent: *I did not give you my consent to use my home for your graduation party.*

to withhold consent, to require consent, to imply consent

mutual consent, full consent, general consent

mutual consent: *The two leaders agreed to rule the country together by mutual consent.*

by consent: *In a free country, the citizens are governed by consent.*

the age of consent: *In some states, eighteen is the age of consent for sexual relations.*

with the consent of

consent (v) to give your permission, your agreement or your approval

freely consent, kindly consent: *Frederic kindly consented to take Marna to the dance.*

to consent to: *Charles will never consent to living in Salem.*

considerable (adj) of noticeable importance; proportionally large

considerable power; considerable influence

to have considerable power, to have considerable influence over: *My father has considerable power over my educational choices.*

to wield considerable power, to wield considerable influence over: *The lawyer wielded considerable power over his clients.*

considerably (adv)

constant (adj) staying the same; uniform

to remain constant*: In an expanding universe, the entropy of the cosmic background radiation remains constant.*

to stay constant, to keep constant

relatively constant, reasonably constant, remarkably constant

in constant pain, constant sorrow, constant noise; (to hear) constant complaints

constant across

constantly (adv) continually; never stopping

constancy (n)

constrain (v) something which controls what you do by keeping you physically or morally limited

to constrain someone to do something; to be constrained to do something

to feel constrained

tightly constrained, severely constrained

constraint (n) [often plural]

to place constraints, to impose constraints, to remove constraints

tight constraints, severe constraints

without constraint

contribute (v) to give money, support, or help towards a particular aim or purpose

to be asked to contribute, to be encouraged to contribute

to have a lot to contribute, to have much to contribute: *Thomas had much to contribute to the discussion, but he had trouble making himself heard.*

to contribute greatly, to contribute substantially, to contribute significantly, to contribute enormously

regularly contribute

to contribute to one's success: *Certainly, hard work contributed to Sam's success as a football player.*

to contribute to a charity; to contribute financially

contribution (n)

ask for a contribution; make a contribution: *Erin made a $10 contribution to our charity.*

to make a contribution

generous contribution, significant contribution, important contribution, enormous contribution

modest contribution, minor contribution, small contribution

valuable contribution, useful contribution, positive contribution

contributor (n)

a regular contributor: *She is a regular contributor to the radio station.*

convene (v) to gather or assemble, especially for a formal meeting

to convene a meeting: *It's time to begin, so let's convene the meeting.*

Unit 3

convention (n) a formal gathering

coordinate (v) to make various things work harmoniously as a whole

    to coordinate carefully, to coordinate closely

    to coordinate with: *We can use Twitter to coordinate our plans with each other.*

coordination (n)

    to ensure coordination, to facilitate coordination [= to make coordination easier]: *Because Karen facilitated the coordination of the dinner party, it was a huge success.*

    international coordination, economic coordination

    a lack of coordination: *It took forever to get the hall ready for the party because of a lack of coordination among the volunteers.*

    in close coordination with: *We were successful because the members of the committee worked in close coordination with each other.*

    coordination among, coordination between: *Coordination among team members is essential for the success of the marketing plan.*

core (n) the central, basic and most important part of something

    to form a core, to make up a core: *There are 29 muscles that make up the core of your body.*

    to get to the core of a matter: *Stop talking about unimportant things. Just get to the core of the matter.*

    at the core of: *At the core of our proposal is the fact that we will save a great deal of money.*

    rotten to the core: *I knew he would end up in jail. He's rotten to the core.*

    the hard core [= the most active, committed, uncompromising]: *The hard core Republicans will insist on lowering taxes for the wealthy.*

    hollow core, solid core, inner core

    core activity, core curriculum, core belief, core value

core (v) to remove the center of something, especially fruit

    to core an apple

corporate (adj) shared or united as a whole group of individuals

    the corporate mind; corporate taxes; corporate responsibility

corporation (n)

    to establish a corporation, to form a corporation, to set up a corporation

    to manage a corporation, to run a corporation

    a public corporation; a multinational corporation

correspond (v) to match, be similar to, be equal to or in agreement with

    to correspond approximately, to correspond roughly

    to closely correspond, to exactly correspond, to roughly correspond, to broadly correspond

    to correspond to: *The Russian letter "P" corresponds to the English letter "R."*

    to correspond with: *Your conclusion does not seem to correspond with your thesis.*

correspond (v) to communicate in writing

    to regularly correspond: *Diane and I regularly correspond by email.*

correspondence (n) match or connection

    to enter into correspondence

    close correspondence, one-on-one correspondence, direct correspondence, exact correspondence

    a correspondence between: *I'm happy when there is a close correspondence between theory and practice.*

correspondence (n) written exchanges

    to enter into correspondence, to carry on correspondence, to keep up correspondence

    to receive correspondence, to read correspondence, to handle correspondence

    to intercept correspondence: *During the Cold War, the US regularly intercepted the correspondence of Russians who traveled to the West.*

    personal correspondence, private correspondence, confidential correspondence

    business correspondence, official correspondence, diplomatic correspondence

    correspondence concerning, correspondence relating to, correspondence regarding

criteria (n pl) [criterion = n. sing.] tests or standards by which to judge or deal with something

    to adopt criteria, to establish criteria; to meet the criteria

    to satisfy the criteria: *You will be issued the permit when you satisfy all of the criteria.*

    apply (certain) criteria to: *Certain investment criteria are applied to every company that we are interested in acquiring.*

    reliable criteria, valid criteria; reliability criteria: *This Technical Bulletin provides reliability design criteria for wastewater treatment works projects seeking Federal financial assistance.*

    sole criterion, main criterion

    according to the criteria, criteria for: *What are the criteria for being accepted into the program?*

deduce (v) to reach an answer or draw a conclusion by careful reasoning about the known facts

    to easily deduce, to logically deduce: *Since the measurement of angle A is greater than 90°, we can logically deduce that A is an obtuse angle.*

    to deduce from: *We can deduce from the temperature of the body that he died about 12 hours ago.*

    to deduce that: *We deduced that she was lying.*

deduction (n)
deductive (adj)
deductively (adv)
demonstrate (v) to show; to make clear; to explain or describe in detail using many examples
>   to convincingly demonstrate, to clearly demonstrate, to conclusively demonstrate
>   to demonstrate beyond (any) doubt: *We will demonstrate beyond doubt that Martin could not have stolen the money.*
>   to further demonstrate, to neatly demonstrate, to elegantly demonstrate
>   to graphically demonstrate, to vividly demonstrate, to empirically demonstrate [= demonstrate based on experiment and/or objective observation]
demonstrate (v) protest
>   to peacefully demonstrate, to violently demonstrate
demonstration (n) explaining, showing or making clear
>   to give a demonstration
>   practical demonstration, clear demonstration, dramatic demonstration, impressive demonstration
demonstration (n) protest
>   to hold a demonstration, to organize a demonstration, to stage a demonstration
>   to join a demonstration, to participate in a demonstration, to take part in a demonstration
>   to put down a demonstration, to suppress a demonstration
>   a demonstration erupts [= grows suddenly]: *When the value of the peso fell suddenly, a demonstration erupted in the main square.*
>   a public demonstration, a massive demonstration, a popular demonstration
>   a hostile demonstration, a violent demonstration
>   a peaceful demonstration, a spontaneous demonstration [= a demonstration that happens without being planned beforehand]: *No one was sure if the gathering in front of the embassy was a planned or a spontaneous demonstration.*
>   at a demonstration, during a demonstration
>   a demonstration for, a demonstration in favor of, a demonstration against
demonstrator (n)
>   to disperse demonstrators [= to make demonstrators spread out]: *The police quickly dispersed the demonstrators and the streets became quiet once again.*
>   to open fire on demonstrators [= to use weapons on demonstrators]: *When the soldiers opened fire on the demonstrators, two people were killed.*
>   demonstrators gather, demonstrators march, demonstrators demand, demonstrators attack
>   angry demonstrator: *The angry demonstrators built fires in the streets and broke windows.*
>   a crowd of demonstrators, a group of demonstrators
>   clashes between police and demonstrators
demonstrable (adj)
>   clearly demonstrable
demonstrably (adv)
document (n) written or printed information, usually official, that provides information, evidence, or proof of something
>   to sign a document, to draw up a document, to draft a document
>   to issue a document, to submit a document, to present a document
>   to file a document, to store a document
>   to classify a document, to falsify a document, to shred a document
>   to revise a document, to examine a document, to consider a document, to study a document
>   to attach a document, to enclose a document, to address a document
>   a lengthy document, a detailed document
>   a brief document, a single document
>   a classified document, a confidential document, a legal document, an official document
>   an authentic document, a genuine document
>   a forged document, a fake document [= not real, not genuine]: *The customs officer quickly realized that the passport was a fake document.*
>   an historic document, a secret document, an authentic document
>   travel document: *Your passport is your most important travel document.*
>   document is concerned with, document states, document focusses on, document covers
>   document details, document explains, document indicates, document notes
>   document shows, document reveals, document says
>   a document about, a document concerning
documentation (n)
>   to provide documentation for
>   adequate documentation, appropriate documentation, proper documentation
document (v)
dominate (v) to have control over or govern by rule or by power

to dominate someone; to dominate a game; to dominate a conversation or discussion

increasingly dominate, largely dominate: *Questions about the role of neighborhood watchmen largely dominated our conversation.*

domination (n)

to have domination (over), to establish domination, to maintain domination

to be/come/fall under someone's domination

world domination, total domination, complete domination

dominance (n)

world dominance

dominant (adj)

emphasis (n. sing) [emphases = n. pl.] a stress or special importance for something

to put emphasis on, to lay emphasis on, to place emphasis on

emphasis shifts, emphasis moves: *Recently, emphasis has been moving more toward individual freedom rather than mutual social benefit.*

strong emphasis, heavy emphasis, great emphasis, considerable emphasis

particular emphasis, special emphasis

a change of emphasis

emphasis (n) stress on a syllable, word or phrase

to put emphasis on: *Some English speakers put the emphasis on the second syllable of the word "controversy."*

emphasize (v)

to strongly emphasize, to clearly emphasize

it is important to emphasize: *Before I begin, it is important to emphasize that this is a discussion, not a lecture, so feel free to join in whenever you have something to say.*

emphatic (adj)

emphatically (adv)

ensure (v) to make certain something happens

must ensure: *Before we agree to rent the cabin, you must ensure us that it is equipped with a stove and running water.*

take steps to ensure, take care to ensure

designed to ensure, help to ensure

(it is) important to ensure: *At the beginning of the course, it is important to ensure that all the students have the proper books and supplies.*

to ensure success

to ensure someone something: *We can ensure you a position on the staff.*

exclude (v) to leave out, keep out or omit something or someone

to try to exclude, to attempt to exclude

to feel excluded: *When the family gets together to discuss financial matters, I feel excluded.*

to be designed to exclude, to tend to exclude: *I like many flowering shrubs, but I tend to exclude roses from my garden.*

to completely exclude, to automatically exclude, to unfairly exclude

to exclude from

exclusion (n)

social exclusion, virtual exclusion

to the exclusion of: *He focused on the book, to the exclusion of everything around him.*

exclusive (adj)

to remain exclusive, to keep exclusive

mutually exclusive: *Some people believe that serving God and being wealthy are mutually exclusive.*

to make an exclusive offer

to offer an exclusive membership or benefits

to belong to an exclusive organization or club: *Being a member of Congress is like belonging to an exclusive club.*

exclusively (adv)

framework (n) a supporting structure, enclosure or idea

to establish a framework, to work within a framework, to provide a framework

a theoretical framework; a conceptual framework

a broad framework, a basic framework, a general framework

within (a certain) framework: *If we want to accomplish our goal without spending too much money, we will have to work within a certain framework.*

outside the framework

fund (n) a sum of money saved, collected or provided for a particular purpose

to establish a fund, to set up a fund, to start a fund, to administer a fund, to manage a fund

an emergency fund: *When our car broke down, we bought a new one with our emergency fund.*

a charitable fund: *Many people contribute to charitable funds, such as the Pew Foundation.*

a trust fund, a mutual fund: *Investing in mutual funds has been popular since the 1970s.*

funds (n. pl.) money available to be spent
    to have funds, to borrow funds, to raise funds, to allocate funds, to provide funds
    to make funds available, to have access to funds
    to be out of funds [= to lack funds] *I can't buy the TV I wanted because I am out of funds.*
    sufficient funds, insufficient funds
    limited funds, unlimited funds
fund (v) to provide money
    to agree to fund, to refuse to fund: *The angry father refused to fund his daughter's college education.*
    to fund a project; to fund a new venture
    to be entirely funded by, to be largely funded by
    to be adequately funded by, to be partially funded by
illustrate (v) to clarify or show the meaning or truth of something, especially with examples or pictures
    vividly illustrate, lavishly illustrate, richly illustrate, handsomely illustrate
    perfectly illustrate: *The film perfectly illustrates what students can accomplish with limited funds.*
    merely illustrate, simply illustrate: *Her comments simply illustrate that she hasn't been listening.*
    to illustrate with, to illustrate by
illustration (n)
    to give an illustration, to offer an illustration, to provide an illustration, to serve as an illustration
    a clear illustration, an apt illustration, a dramatic illustration, a vivid illustration
    by way of illustration: *Some apple trees produce better fruit than others. By way of illustration, take a look at this particular tree.*
illustrative (adj)
immigrate (v) to come into a country to which you are not native in order to live there permanently
    to immigrate from, to immigrate to
immigration (n)
    to control immigration, to restrict immigration
    legal immigration, illegal immigration, mass immigration, large-scale immigration
    immigration law, immigration measures, immigration policy, immigration officer
immigrant (n)
    to welcome immigrants, to deport immigrants, to return immigrants
    legal immigrant, illegal immigrant, foreign immigrant
    first generation immigrant, second-generation immigrant
    a flood of immigrants, an influx of immigrants [= the arrival of a large number of immigrants]: *Due to the sudden influx of immigrants, the people of the border town were alarmed.*
    a wave of immigrants: *A wave of immigration to the United States followed bad economic conditions in Europe.*
    an immigrant community, immigrant population
    immigrant labor: *Much of the agricultural work in the US is done by immigrant labor.*
imply (v) to communicate an idea or feeling indirectly
    seem to imply: *The test results seem to imply that the infection is nearly gone.*
    clearly imply, strongly imply, heavily imply
    in no way imply: *My agreeing no way implies that I have no reservations.*
    not mean to imply that: *When I yawned, I didn't mean to imply that I'm bored. I'm just tired.*
implication (n)
    to have an implication, to carry an implication
    to understand the implication, to grasp the implication, to examine the implication
    important implications, enormous implications, far-reaching implications, wide implications
    clear implication, obvious implication, long-term implication, serious implication
    practical implication, potential implication; frightening implication, disturbing implication
    implications arise: *A few important implications arise now that the wedding has been called off.*
    by implication: *The writer lied by implication. That is, he suggested an untruth without actually coming out and stating it.*
    to have implications on
    to consider the implications (of/for); discuss the implications
    serious implications, practical implications, profound implications [= very great] *The school board's decision has profound implications for both teachers and students.*
initial (adj) of or at the beginning; first
    the initial impact, initial impression
initially (adv)
initial (n) first letter of a name
    first initial, middle initial, last initial
    initials stand for: *The initials P. J. in my name stand for Paula Jean.*
initial (v) to carry the initials, to be known by the initials
    Please initial each line to acknowledge that you understand and agree.

Unit 3

instance (n) a particular situation, occasion or fact, especially an example of something that happens generally
    to contain instances of, to provide an instance, to cite an instance, to recall an instance
    occasional instance, rare instance, numerous instances
    an isolated instance: *We hope that the attack on the shopkeepers is just an isolated incidence.*
    for an instance: *Professors on this campus generally wear casual clothes. For an instance, just take a look at what Dr. Magoto wears every day: blue jeans and a tee shirt.*
    at a certain instance
    in most instances
    in this instance: *The two chemicals may fail to react. In this instance, make sure the temperature is correct.*

interact (v) to communicate with or react to one another in a social situation
    closely interact, directly interact
    to interact with: *During group work, I expect all students to interact with each other politely.*
interaction (n)
    a negative interaction, a positive interaction
    complex interaction; classroom interaction
    social interaction, face-to-face interaction, human interaction
    to foster interaction
interactive (adj)
interactively (adv)

justify (v) to give or to demonstrate a good reason for something
    to justify one's actions
    nothing justifies: *Nothing justifies that kind of behavior. Nothing justifies cheating.*
justification (n)
    considerable justification, the slightest justification
    ethical justification, moral justification, legal justification, intellectual justification
    justification for
    in justification, with justification, without justification
justifiable (adj)
    justifiable homicide [= justifiable killing of a human]
    justifiable on the grounds that: *Some extremists believe that terrorism is justifiable on the grounds that there is no peaceful way to achieve their aims.*
justifiably (adv)

layer (n) a thickness of material or a thin sheet of a substance spread over a surface
    bottom layer, base layer, middle layer, top layer
    even layer, uneven layer, fine layer, thin layer, thick layer: *A fine layer of dust lay on the old desk.*
    generous layer: *Marsha put a generous layer of leaves over the entire garden.*
    outer layer, inner layer, bottom layer, top layer, upper layer, double layer
    protective layer: *Put a protective layer of plastic over the LCD display.*
    ozone layer
    in layers: *They applied the paint in layers.*
    beneath a layer, under a layer: *An amazing fresco was hidden under a layer of newer paint.*
    layer cake [= a cake that has two or more layers]
    layer after layer, layer upon layer: *She built her compost pile with layer after layer of leaves and grass.*
    layer by layer: *She gradually built her compost pile layer by layer.*
layer (v)

link (n) a bond or connection between two things
    to establish a link, to foster a link, to forge a link [= to make a strong link]: *The Prime Minister tried to forge a link with America's new leader.*
    to provide a link, to maintain a link, to preserve a link
    to break a link, to cut a link, to sever a link [= to break a link]: *In Excel, the easiest way to sever a link is to remove the formula and replace it with its resulting value.*
    a direct link, a close link, a strong link, a weak link, a useful link
    a connecting link, a rail link, a road link, a link in a chain
    a missing link, a broken link
    a link between, a link to, a link with: *She has links with the Mafia.*
link (v)
    closely linked, strongly linked, tightly linked, loosely linked, directly linked, indirectly linked
    linked in some way, linked somehow: *The paranoid blogger thought that Houston's death was linked somehow to a "Black Sabbath" performance by another singer.*
    to link together, to link up, to link into

locate (v) to find, put or establish something in a place or position
    to try to locate, to fail to locate, to be difficult to locate, to be easy to locate: *The hotel is close to the airport, just off the main highway, and is easy to locate.*

location (n)
>a good location, an excellent location, a poor location, a central location
>the exact location: *Sheldon has gone away to work on his new book, but his exact location is unknown.*
>at a location, at an undisclosed location
>to shoot a film on location: *The movie "The Descendants" was filmed on location in Hawaii.*

maximize (v) to increase something in as great an amount, size or importance as possible
>to maximize profits: *One way to maximize profits is to increase worker efficiency and output.*

maximum (n)
>to reach the maximum, to exceed the maximum
>the maximum allowed; to allow a maximum: *The maximum allowed time for this test is 25 minutes.*
>to make a maximum effort
>to accommodate a maximum of: *The elevator can only accommodate a maximum of four people.*
>the maximum penalty, maximum amount
>a maximum of; above the maximum, below the maximum

maximization (n)
maximal (adj)
maximally (adv)

minor (adj) having lesser importance, influence or seriousness than other things of the same type
>a minor problem
>with minor exceptions
>minor modifications, minor details, minor variations

minor (n) a person who is less than 21 years old.
>to serve a minor [to sell alcohol to a minor]: *Sorry, we are not allowed to serve minors here.*

minor (v) to have a secondary course of study [to major = to have a primary course of study]: *When Mary goes to college, she wants to major in French and minor in Art History.*

negate (v) to cause something to be ineffective and probably useless
>to have the power to negate: *A properly prepared will has the power to negate all previous wills.*

negation (n)
negative (n) denial
>in the negative: The witness answered every question in the negative.

negative (n) photographic film
>to develop a negative: *Before digital photography, developing negatives was sometimes a fine art.*

negative (adj) something that says "no"; the opposite of positive
>to prove negative, to test negative: *Jim was happy to find that he tested negative for Hepatitis B.*
>to have a negative impact on
>to have potentially negative consequences
>to have a negative connotation [= to have a negative feeling]: *The term "young woman" is acceptable, but the term "babe" has a negative connotation.*

negatively (adv)

outcome (n) a result or consequence of an action, situation, etc.
>to decide the final outcome of: *Ironically, a coin toss decided the final outcome of the game.*
>to evaluate the outcome, to measure the outcome
>a probable outcome, a negative outcome, a positive outcome

philosophy (n) system of belief; ideas about knowledge, truth, values
>to have a philosophy, to embrace/espouse a philosophy [= to be committed to a philosophy]: *Our members espouse a philosophy of being of sevice to the weakest members of our community.*
>to develop a philosophy, to formulate a philosophy
>ancient philosophy, classical philosophy, Eastern philosophy, Western philosophy
>moral philosophy, natural philosophy; political philosophy, social philosophy, religious philosophy
>economic philosophy, market philosophy
>homespun philosophy, moral philosophy, political philosophy
>philosophy that: *It was his philosophy that children should be seen but not heard.*

philosophize (v)
philosophical (adj)
>purely philosophical, rather philosophical
>to get philosophical, to wax philosophical: *The painter waxed philosophical about his childhood home.*

philosophically (adv)

physical (adj) of the body or material things that can be seen or felt; not spiritual or mental
>to have a physical examination (exam)
>to give a physical examination (exam)
>purely physical: *Shin's attraction to Maiko was purely physical.*

physical (n) a medical examination
>a complete physical: *Every year, I go to my doctor for a complete physical checkup.*

physically (adv)
>physically fit: Surprisingly, many young soldiers are not physically fit enough to meet army standards.

Unit 3

proportion (n) the relative part of a whole
    large proportion, sizeable proportion, considerable proportion, significant proportion: *A significant proportion of the population is overweight.*
    small proportion, tiny proportion
    minute proportion [= very small proportion], negligible proportion [= insignificant proportion]: *A negligible proportion of my investments are in real estate.*
    fixed proportion [= proportion that does not change]
    exact proportion, varying proportion, growing proportion, increasing proportion
proportion (n) the relationship of one thing when compared to another
    to put things in proportion; to blow things out of proportion [= to over react; to treat too seriously]: *Harold was extremely angry and blew everything I said out of proportion.*
    (in) correct proportion), direct proportion, inverse proportion: *The human population increased in inverse proportion to the population of lions: as the number of humans increased, the number of lions decreased.*
    out of proportion, in proportion
    a sense of proportion
proportion (n) the size or shape of something
    to take on proportions, to reach proportions
    alarming proportions, crisis proportions, epidemic proportions: *The spread of dysentery reached crisis proportions in the most of the villages affected by the flood.*
    epic proportions, gigantic proportions, staggering proportions, monumental proportions
    modest proportions, manageable proportions
proportion (v) to adjust something so that it is in a good relationship to something else
proportional (adj)
    directly proportional to, roughly proportional; inversely proportional
react (v) to act in a particular way in response to something else
    to calmly react, to favorably react, to cautiously react, to coolly react: *The crowd reacted favorably to the speaker's announcement that one of their demands had been met.*
    to strongly react, to violently react, to sharply react
    to automatically react, to instinctively react, to physically react
    to react against, to react to: *It's interesting how some people react to snakes.*
    to react with (alarm, disgust, horror): *He reacted with alarm when I said I was moving to Mexico.*
reaction (n)
    to have a reaction, to meet with a reaction
    to produce a reaction, to spark a reaction, to set off a reaction, to trigger a reaction
    to judge by a reaction, to gauge by a reaction [= to estimate by a reaction]: *To gauge by Tina's reaction to the offer, you would think that she had never been more insulted in her life.*
    a negative reaction, an adverse reaction; an allergic reaction, an emotional reaction, a critical reaction
    an initial reaction, an immediate reaction, a first reaction
    a natural reaction, a normal reaction, a common reaction, a general reaction
    an automatic reaction, an instinctive reaction, a spontaneous reaction [= a reaction that happens without any planning or thought]: *Her laughter was just a spontaneous reaction to what I said.*
    a chemical reaction, a nuclear reaction
    to set off or to start a chain reaction
reactive (adj)
reactively (adv)
rely (v) to depend on
    to heavily rely, to strongly rely, to rely a lot
    to entirely rely, to solely rely, to mainly rely, to exclusively rely
    rely on, rely upon: *We'll help you move into your new apartment. You can rely on us.*
rely (v) to trust
    to safely rely, to simply rely: *Lazy students simply rely on Wikipedia for most of the information they need for their research papers.*
reliance (n)
reliable (adj)
reliably (adv)
scheme (n) a devious plan for obtaining an advantage
    to devise a scheme, to think up a scheme, to design a scheme, to dream up a scheme
    to concoct a scheme, to cook up a scheme [= to devise a scheme]: *The students cooked up a scheme whereby they would be able to get the answers to the exam beforehand.*
    to thwart a scheme, foil (stop) a scheme: *The police foiled the thieves' scheme to rob the bank.*
    to announce a scheme, to introduce a scheme, to launch a scheme [= to start a scheme]: *The three young musicians launched a scheme for marketing their music.*
    to go ahead with a scheme, to proceed with a scheme
    crazy scheme, hare-brained scheme [= stupid, foolish scheme]: *It would be a hare-brained scheme to hike on that trail now that bears have been spotted on it.*

Unit 3

grand scheme, ambitious scheme, grandiose scheme [= an overly complicated scheme]: *Harold came up with a grandiose scheme for building a new church on his farm.*
a diabolical scheme [= very evil scheme]: *The corporation came up with a diabolical scheme for getting the government to pay them to build private prisons.*
a fantastic scheme, a get-rich-quick scheme; a publicity scheme
in the grand scheme of things: *In the grand scheme of things, we are lucky to have our good health and loving family.*

scheme (v)
to scheme against, to scheme for
to scheme to: *The group were arrested for scheming to take over the government.*

sequence (n) a process or series of related things or events which follow each other
to follow a sequence
to complete a sequence: *The math instructor asked us to complete the following sequence: 2, 5, 11, 23.*
correct sequence, complex sequence, alphabetical sequence, chronological sequence
logical sequence, natural sequence, random sequence
sequence of events
in sequence, out of sequence

sequential (adj)
sequentially (adv)

shift (v) to switch, move or change slightly from one place or direction to another
to shift slightly: *A phenomenon called parallax causes the apparent position of stars to shift slightly.*
to shift uncomfortably, to shift restlessly, to shift nervously
to shift the emphasis; to shift the burden (from ~ to ~); to shift the blame
to shift from foot to foot: *As the clerk stared at me, I began to nervously shift from foot to foot.*

shift (v) to change
gradually shift, slowly shift, begin to shift: *As I learned more about Napoleon, my ideas about him gradually began to shift.*
shift dramatically, shift markedly
shift suddenly, shift rabidly, shift constantly

shift (n)
to bring about a shift in, to produce a shift in: *The new evidence was enough to bring about a shift in the jury's opinion about the case.*
a sudden shift, an abrupt shift
a major shift, a dramatic shift, a marked shift, a fundamental shift, a profound shift, a pronounced shift
a slight shift, a small shift, a gradual shift: *Over the years, there has been a gradual shift from liberalism to conservatism.*
a policy shift
a paradigm shift [= a change from one way of thinking to another way of thinking]: *The discovery of germs caused a major paradigm shift in the way doctors thought about illness.*
a shift in one's perceptions
a shift away from: The new rules are a shift away from the conservative policy that we started with.

shift (n) a work period
night shift, day shift, swing shift [= evening shift, between morning shift and night shift]: *Nancy can't join us for dinner tonight because she has to work the swing shift.*
early shift, late shift

specify (v) to state or name clearly and exactly
clearly specify, carefully specify, precisely specify
explicitly specify, correctly specify; uniquely specify

specification (n)
to draw up specifications, to draft specifications, to lay down specification
to meet specifications: *These machines meet every specification drawn up by the engineers.*
detailed specification, exact specification, complete specification
technical specification, design specification, customer specification
according to specifications: *Each home is custom-designed according to the client's specifications.*

specific (adj)
highly specific, fairly specific, rather specific, quite specific: *Margaret was quite specific about the kind of wedding she wanted.*
specific about: *You need to be more specific about how you intend to spend the money.*
specific to [= located in a specific place or time]: *This bird is specific to a small region in Tanzania.*
be more specific: *Just how many times have you skipped class? Can you be more specific?*

specifically (adv)

sufficient (adj) enough or adequate for a particular purpose
to prove sufficient, to sound sufficient, to consider something sufficient, to deem something sufficient
to regard as sufficient
(to provide) sufficient proof, sufficient reason, sufficient justification, sufficient cause

barely sufficient, hardly sufficient, far from sufficient; quite sufficient

sufficient for; sufficient unto oneself

suffice (v)

sufficiently (adv)

task (n) a specific piece of work done regularly, unwillingly or with difficulty

to carry out a task, to fulfill a task, to perform a task, to take on a task, to undertake a task

an enviable task, a pleasant task, a welcome task; a delicate task, a tricky task

a hopeless task: *We need to grade over 200 papers this weekend, and it looks like a hopeless task.*

a difficult task, a thankless task, an unpleasant task: *Taking care of children is sometimes a thankless task, but it's one of the most important jobs we can do.*

a daunting task, a monumental task, an arduous task [= a very difficult task]: *It would be an arduous task to create sample sentences for every collocation in this book.*

to take someone to task: *We had to take her to task for not getting her work finished on time.*

to be faced with a task: *Lottie was faced with the task of forming a committee that could solve the company's financial problems.*

technical (adj) concerned with specialized skills or knowledge, especially in science and engineering

technical aspects, technical college, technical education, technical expertise, technical guidance, technical requirements, technical details

(to require) technical skill, technical training

technically (adv)

technicality (n)

a legal technicality

to win (lose) on a technicality: *We all knew she was guilty, but she won the case on a legal technicality.*

technique (n) a specific way of performing an activity requiring skill in the arts, sports, science, etc.

to acquire a technique, to develop a technique, to devise a technique, to work out a technique

to apply a technique to

an acting technique, a dance technique, a teaching technique

a relaxation technique: *My favorite relaxation technique is to do yoga.*

valid (adj) based on truth, fact, logic or reason; able to be accepted

a valid excuse: *If you want to be excused from class, you will need a valid excuse, such as a note from your doctor.*

a valid reason; valid for: Your bus ticket is valid for one month.

volume (n) the number or amount of something

sales volume: *The latest report shows that sales volume has increased since January.*

volume of imports: *US companies are worried because the volume of imports from other countries is increasing rapidly.*

volume (n) the amount of space that something occupies

volume of air, volume of water; molecular volume

storage volume: *The storage volume of this rectangular box is equal to the storage area of that square one.*

volume (n) one book in a series of books

first volume, second volume, etc.: *Volumes One and Two of Sandberg's biography of Lincoln deals with his youth, while the remaining volumes deal with his presidency and the Civil War.*

volume (n) the degree of loudness of sound

turn down the volume, turn up the volume

increase the volume, decrease the volume

Synonyms

alternative:	choice, option
circumstance:	condition, situation, detail
comment:	observation, remark, statement
compensate:	make up for, offset, balance, equal
component:	part, element, member, element
consent:	agree, approve, comply
considerable:	big, great, substantial, ample
constant:	regular, steady, stable
constrain:	bind, compel, require, oblige
contribute:	give, donate, provide, supply
convene:	gather together, meet, assemble
coordinate:	arrange, organize, harmonize
core:	center, heart, nucleus, foundation
corporate:	business, joint, united
correspond:	agree, match, resemble
criteria:	standards, norms, bench marks, guides
deduce:	conclude, infer, determine
demonstrate:	illustrate, show, describe, tell
document:	paper, record
dominate:	control, rule, govern
emphasis:	stress, importance, focus, highlight
ensure:	assure, guarantee, insure
exclude:	leave out, omit, keep out, skip
framework:	form, outline
fund:	supply, stock, budget
illustrate:	demonstrate, show, illuminate
immigrate:	migrate, move
imply:	hint, suggest, connote
initial:	first, prime, original
instance:	example, time, model, sample
interact:	relate, deal with
justify:	support, uphold, legitimize, explain
layer:	coating, sheet, overlay, shell
link:	connection, bond, tie
location:	place, scene, site, spot, setting
maximum:	most, greatest, utmost
minor:	small, unimportant, slight
negate:	cancel, destroy, deny, nullify
outcome:	result, conclusion, consequence
philosophy:	thought, belief, ideology
physical:	bodily, concrete, material
proportion:	mix, ratio, balance, relationship
react:	respond, answer, reply
rely:	depend on, trust, count on
scheme:	plot, deal, plan, tactic
sequence:	chain, series, progression, succession
shift:	move, relocate, change
specify:	spell out, define, indicate, establish
sufficient:	adequate, enough, ample
task:	job, duty, work, chore, assignment
technical:	specialized, mechanical, industrial
technique:	method, mode, way, manner
valid:	legitimate, in effect, authentic
volume:	book; capacity; amount; loudness

Unit 3

Answers

<table>
<tr><td colspan="4">Definitions</td></tr>
<tr><td>

1. alternative
2. considerable
3. corporate
4. instance
5. outcome
6. emphasis
7. dominate
8. justify
9. coordinate
10. valid
11. technical
12. sufficient
13. circumstances
14. documents
15. criteria

</td><td>

16. immigrated
17. illustrated
18. implied
19. constantly
20. physically
21. Initially
22. comment
23. scheme
24. link
25. ensures
26. specifies
27. contributes
28. layer
29. task
30. component

</td><td>

31. compensate
32. deduce
33. rely
34. minor
35. core
36. framework
37. react
38. maximize
39. shift
40. volume
41. philosophy
42. technique
43. consent
44. correspond
45. exclude

</td><td>

46. fund
47. sequence
48. proportion
49. interact
50. demonstrate
51. convene
52. constrain
53. negate
54. locate

</td></tr>
</table>

<table>
<tr><td colspan="4">Parts of Speech</td></tr>
<tr><td>

1. alternative
   alternative
2. circumstances
   circumstantial
3. comments
   comment
4. compensation
   compensatory
5. components
   component
6. consented
   consent
7. considerably
   considerable
8. constancy
   constantly
9. constraint
   constrained
10. contribution
    contributes
11. convening
    convened

</td><td>

12. coordination
    coordinates
13. core
    core
14. corporate
    corporation
15. corresponds
    correspondence
16. criteria
    criterion
17. deduce
    deduction
18. demonstration
    demonstrated
19. documents
    documentation
20. dominated
    domination
21. emphasis
    emphasizes
22. ensures
    ensure

</td><td>

23. excluded
    exclusion
24. framework
    framework
25. funded
    fund
26. illustration
    illustrates
27. immigrants
    immigration
28. imply
    implication
29. initial
    Initially
30. instances
    instance
31. interaction
    interacts
32. justifies
    justification
33. layer
    layers

</td><td>

34. linked
    link
35. location
    locating
36. maximize
    maximum
37. minor
    minors
38. negative
    negatively
39. outcomes
    outcome
40. philosophize
    philosophical
41. physical
    physically
42. proportion
    proportional
43. reacts
    reaction
44. reliably
    relies

</td></tr>
<tr><td>

45. scheme
    scheming
46. sequentially
    sequence
47. shift
    shifted
48. specifications
    specifies

</td><td>

49. sufficient
    sufficiently
50. task
    tasks
51. technical
    Technically
52. techniques
    technique

</td><td>

53. valid
    valid
54. volume
    volumes

</td><td></td></tr>
</table>

Unit 3

Answers

Collocations

Exercise 1	Exercise 2	Exercise 3	Exercise 4
1. consent consent consented	1. layers layer layer	1. proportion proportion proportional	1. volume volume volume
2. circumstances circumstances circumstantial	2. philosophy philosophical	2. minor minor minor	2. technical technical technicality
3. compensated compensation compensation	3. fund fund funding	3. reaction reaction reacted	3. negative negative negative
4. alternative alternate alternative	4. emphasis emphasis emphasis	4. scheme scheme scheme	4. interaction interaction interaction
5. documents documentation documents	5. valid valid	5. maximum maximize maximum	5. instances instances instance
6. domination dominates domination	6. illustration illustrations illustration	6. link linked link	6. contributed contribute contributes
7. framework framework	7. location locations location	7. implications implications implications	7. coordinates Coordination/ Coordinating
8. comments comment comment	8. core core core	8. considerable considerable	8. shift shift shift
9. justification justifies	9. corresponds correspond corresponds	9. exclusive exclusive exclusive	9. outcome/~s outcome outcome/~s
10. initial initial	10. criteria criteria criteria	10. constantly constant	10. sufficient sufficient sufficient

Unit 3

Answers

Synonyms (Crossword)

Across	Down
1. constant	2. negate
3. specify	4. considerable
5. correspond	7. illustrate
6. shift	11. proportion
8. minor	13. scheme
9. imply	14. consent
10. emphasis	15. core
12. task	16. coordinate
17. philosophy	20. deduce
18. outcome	21. convene
19. exclude	23. link
20. dominate	
21. compensate	
22. rely	
24. initial	
25. comment	
26. demonstrate	
27. alternative	

Review

1. initial	19. framework	37. consent
2. sufficient	20. scheme	38. correspond
3. considerable	21. layer	39. exclude
4. constant	22. fund	40. interact
5. physical	23. technique	41. shift
6. valid	24. component	42. negate
7. technical	25. sequence	43. compensate
8. minor	26. volume	44. deduce
9. corporate	27. philosophy	45. illustrate
10. emphasis	28. comment	46. justify
11. alternative	29. document	47. specify
12. core	30. link	48. contribute
13. instance	31. constrain	49. demonstrate
14. proportion	32. coordinate	50. ensure
15. outcome	33. immigrate	51. imply
16. circumstances	34. dominates	52. maximize
17. criteria	35. relies	53. react
18. tasks	36. locates	54. convene

Unit 4

Word List

n = noun   **v** = verb   **adj** = adjective   **adv** = adverb   **prep** = preposition

access (n)	**error (n)**	**parameter (n)**
access (v)	err (v)	**phase (n)**
accessible (adj)	erroneous (adj)	phase (v)
accessibly (adv)	erroneously (adv)	**predict (v)**
adequate (adj)	**goal (n)**	prediction (n)
adequately (adv)	**grant (n)**	**principal (n)**
annual (adj)	grant (v)	principal (adj)
annually (adv)	**hence (adv)**	principally (adv)
annual (n)	**hypothetical (adj)**	**prior (adj)**
apparent (adj)	hypothetically (adv)	prior (n)
apparently (adv)	hypothesis (n)	priority (n)
attitude (n)	hypothesize (v)	**project (n)**
attribute (n)	**implement (n)**	project (v)
attribute (v)	implement (v)	projection (n)
civil (adj)	implementation (n)	**promote (v)**
civilly (adv)	**implicate (v)**	promotion (n)
code (n)	implication (n)	promotional (adj)
code (v)	**impose (v)**	promotionally (v)
commit (v)	imposition (n)	**regime (n)**
commitment (n)	**integrate (v)**	**resolve (n)**
concentrate (n)	integration (n)	resolve (v)
concentrate (v)	**internal (adj)**	resolution (n)
concentration (n)	internally (adj)	**retain (v)**
concentrated (adj)	internalize (n)	retention (n)
conference (n)	**investigate (v)**	**series (n. singular)**
confer (v)	investigation (n)	**statistic (n)**
contrast (n)	investigatory (adj)	statistics (n. singular)
contrast (v)	**label (n)**	**status (n)**
contrastive (adj)	label (v)	**stress (n)**
cycle (n)	**mechanism (n)**	stress (v)
cycle (v)	mechanic (n)	stressful (adj)
debate (n)	mechanical (adj)	stressfully (adv)
debate (v)	mechanically (adv)	**subsequent (adj)**
debatable (adj)	**obvious (adj)**	subsequently (adv)
debatably (adv)	obviously (adv)	**sum (n)**
despite (prep)	**occupy (v)**	sum (v)
dimension (n)	occupation (n)	**summarize (v)**
dimensional (adj)	occupied (adj)	summarily (adv)
dimensionally (adv)	**optional (n)**	**undertake (v)**
domestic (adj)	optional (adj)	undertaking (n)
domestically (adv)	optionally (adv)	
domestic (n)	**output (n)**	
domesticate (v)	output (v)	
domesticated (adj)	**parallel (n)**	
emerge (v)	parallel (v)	
emergence (n)	parallel (adj)	
emerging (adj)	parallel (adv)	
	parallelism (n)	

Unit 4

Definitions Use the definition clues to write the correct words in the blanks.

1.	to promise or be obliged to do something *Everyone was* _____ *to winning the game.*	implicated occupied imposed committed emerged
2.	to show that someone is involved in an affair, situation or crime or is partly responsible for something bad that has happened *Kevin was at the party where the theft occurred, so he was* _____ *in the crime.*	
3.	to fill up or live in *Ten people* _____ *the two-room apartment.*	
4.	a feeling, opinion or mental state in regard to something or someone *Amy always has a positive* _____ *, even when she is tired.*	regime attitude parallel error sum
5.	a particular government or administration *The people tried to fight against the new* _____ *.*	
6.	a mistake *It would be a serious* _____ *to drop out of college.*	
7.	to systematically examine in order to discover the truth *The police were called in to* _____ *the crime.*	attribute debate investigate predict retain emerge
8.	to appear from, rise up from or come out from behind something *We hope that the truth will eventually* _____ *.*	
9.	to keep or continue to possess *She tried to* _____ *control of the meeting.*	
10.	a number of similar or related events or things, one following another *There's a new documentary* _____ *about faith in America.*	statistics series parameters errors codes grants
11.	a set of facts or a boundary which limits how something can be done *The agency must act within the* _____ *of the existing laws.*	
12.	numerical information *Based on these* _____ *, the recession is now over.*	
13.	therefore; for this reason *We had no money;* _____ *we could not buy the house.*	status hence despite parallel undertake subsequent
14.	happening after or following *There were* _____ *reports that the free fix was not adequate.*	
15.	regardless of, in spite of; without being prevented by something *She lost the match* _____ *her best effort.*	

Unit 4

16.	to restate in a short and clear form *The whole report was _____ in one sentence.*	resolved summarized occupied imposed contrasted predicted
17.	to say what will happen in the future *Mark _____ that it would rain today, and it did!*	
18.	to establish something as a rule to be obeyed or accepted *The European Union _____ sanctions on Iran.*	
19.	clear, obvious *It became increasingly _____ that Sam had to go.*	internal adequate civil optional subsequent apparent
20.	enough or satisfactory for a particular situation or need *The hotel room was small but _____ for our needs.*	
21.	located inside a person, object, organization, place or country *We do not want to interfere in Turkey's _____ affairs.*	
22.	a position, rank or condition, especially in a social group *Because of their financial _____, they were not invited to membership in the Country Club.*	conference status output mechanism dimension parameter
23.	a meeting for the exchange of ideas on a particular subject *At the news _____, the mayor announced her proposal for renovating the city center.*	
24.	a process or an amount of something produced *Industrial _____ declined in 2008.*	
25.	to decide or begin to do something or a promise to do something *They agreed to _____ the building of the new bridge.*	project undertake integrate promote contrast label
26.	to mix with or blend together *They wanted to_____ the third graders with the fourth graders.*	
27.	to support or encourage *The policy is designed to _____ economic growth.*	
28.	the way of approaching a place or person *As a student, you have _____ to over 7,000,000 books in the university's library.*	access cycle stress conference dimension mechanism
29.	a group of events that are often repeated *The children were amazed when the learned about the life _____ of butterflies*	
30.	a structure or a set of parts of a machine or device *The locking _____ for this gun does not work properly.*	

Unit 4

31. of the home, household or family *All families have the right to have* _____ *peace.* 32. clear; easy to see, recognize or understand *Pam's illness soon became* _____ *to everyone.* 33. first in value, status or order of importance *My* _____ *objection to driving there is that it would take twenty hours.*	hypothetical parallel obvious resolved principal domestic
34. a strong focus on particular activity, subject or problem *That loud music is disrupting my* _____. 35. a description used to classify or describe the contents of something *Didn't you read the warning* _____ *on the bottle?* 36. a characteristic feature *Being a team player is a desirable* _____ *for all employees who work here.*	label concentration prediction access attribute cycle
37. an aim or purpose *Ten new words a day is a realistic* _____. 38. putting a plan into operation *Geri will oversee the* _____ *of the plan.* 39. a measurement or a feature or way of considering something *Time, the fourth* _____, *is finite.*	phase code goal implementation dimension conference
40. being very polite and well-behaved in society *Winston is a remarkably* _____ *human being.* 41. happening once every year, or relating to a period of one year *We take our* _____ *vacation in August.* 42. having the same character or tendency *The twins, separated at birth, still led* _____ *lives.*	civil parallel annual apparent committed principal
43. to discuss a subject in which there are two opposing points of view *Abortion is a hotly* _____ *topic in America.* 44. to agree to give or do something that someone has requested *The Queen* _____ *the old man his wish.* 45. to reach the solution to or end of a problem or difficulty *The problem was finally* _____ *after days of discussions.*	predicted debated granted resolved promoted implicated

46. a set of rules, laws or regulations which are accepted as general principles *You can't wear jeans here. We have a strict dress _____.* 47. a distinct stage in a process or in a cycle of development *We are entering the final _____ of the discussions.* 48. the total amount of something when things have been added together *She has a considerable _____ of money in the bank.*	code sum attitude conference output phase
49. earlier or before something or before a particular time *I can't go to your party. I have a _____ engagement.* 50. based on a proposed idea or explanation for something *Some people believe that global warming is just _____.* 51. not required *The extra grammar class is entirely _____. You don't have to take it.*	hypothetical optional prior civil domestic subsequent
52. to give emphasis or extra importance to something *She was careful to _____ that gift-giving was optional.* 53. to show a clear difference *Native Americans' version of history can often _____ with Europeans' version.* 54. to guess or plan about the future *Scientists _____ that the average global temperature will rise over the next several decades.*	occupy promote contrast project stress debate

Unit 4

Parts of Speech

Write the parts of speech (noun, verb, adjective or adverb form).
Word Forms: Be careful with nouns and verbs:
    Some *nouns* might need to be plural (~**s**).
    Some *verbs* might need ~**s**, ~**ed**, ~**ing**.

access
1. My wife always _____ my bank account without my permission.

    Last night, the thieves _____ the house through an unlocked door.

adequate
2. Are you _____ prepared for tomorrow's test?

    We didn't have _____ time to finish our project.

annual
3. Hundreds of orangutans are killed _____ for meat.

    Only ten people showed up for our _____ meeting.

apparent
4. It looked like an _____ suicide attempt.

    Chris didn't come to work. _____, he's sick today.

attitude
5. Iris has a good _____ about everything she does.

    When the team loses, _____ change among fans.

attribute
6. The increase in cancer cases can be _____ to pollution of the drinking water.

    Laziness and a bad attitude are _____ of a poor worker.

civil
7. Laughing at disabled people is no way to act in _____ society.

    There must be a more _____ way to discuss this.

code
8. The army uses various _____ to send secret messages.

    The lock was _____ so that only Mr. Hobbs could open it.

commit
9. Larivière was very _____ to making the university a great place.

    Before you _____, you need to read the fine print.

concentrate
10. They made a _____ effort to find a better solution.

    She _____ better when she listens to music.

conference
11. Our organization holds two _____ every year.

    At the end of the _____ there was a lottery.

Unit 4

contrast
12. The 19th Century Impressionists' techniques _____ greatly with the techniques of classical artists of their times.

The second movement of Beethoven's seventh symphony provides an interesting _____ to the first movement.

cycle
13. After the computer _____ through the boot-up, it still failed to start properly.

No one has found a solution for breaking the _____ of unemployment, poverty and crime.

debate
14. Yesterday, we _____ the issue of capital punishment.

Which of the two _____ did you like better?

despite
15. More than 100 people came _____ the heavy rain.

_____ her age, 87, Maria ran the marathon race.

dimension
16. Some mathematicians believe there are eleven _____ in hyperspace.

We need to know the _____ of the room before we buy the new furniture.

domestic
17. Last year, _____ manufacturing rose sharply.

The economy is growing, both _____ and internationally.

emerge
18. Now is not a good time to invest in _____ markets.

By morning, it was clear that Sal had _____ as the winner.

error
19. Erin mistakenly sent an _____ report to me.

There are several major _____ in this document.

goal
20. One of my _____ is to master French grammar.

Nick's short-term _____ is to graduate from high school.

grant
21. The federal government awarded _____ to five different universities.

You can apply for the _____ on line.

hence
22. Our new dog escaped injury from a car accident and a house fire, _____ the name "Lucky."

She lived in Bali for many years, _____ her interest in *batik*.

Unit 4

hypothesis 23. That's an interesting _____, but I don't believe it.

Think about a _____ situation in which you are alone in a desert. How could you survive without a cell phone?

implement 24. If the plan is widely _____, it will be successful.

Immediate _____ of the law is required.

implicate 25. Doris was _____ in the scheme along with two of her friends.

The court rules against the individual man, and by _____ the rest of society.

impose 26. Before the holiday arrived, the City _____ a ban on fireworks.

My neighbor always _____ on me to help her do something around her house.

integrate 27. Currently, the countries of Europe are working on closer economic _____.

Many of Microsoft's programs are fully _____ with each other.

internal 28. I don't want Zoe to interfere with our _____ affairs.

It took a long time, but Grace finally _____ the poem that she had been reading.

investigate 29. The Board of Directors carefully _____ the claims.

The police promised a full _____ .

label 30. No one could attach a _____ to Ruby.

All of the little bottles were carefully _____ .

mechanism 31. The surgeon used a _____ device to aid in the surgery.

The steering _____ of the drone is controlled remotely.

obvious 32. If you are looking for a great partner, Bethany is an _____ choice.

You don't have a library card, so _____ you can't borrow books.

occupy 33. We've been _____ with caring for our elderly parents.

option   34. The coach had no _____ but to take Jones out of the game.

We seem to be running out of _____. What shall we do now?

output   35. The factory reduced its _____ because of the economic slowdown.

Daily _____ varies.

parallel   36. Line up the dots in rows until they are roughly _____.

Researchers found several _____ in the lives of the two scientists.

parameter   37. This document explains how to embed a *YouTube* player in your application and also defines the _____ that are available in the *YouTube*.

Math expressions operate within specific _____ .

phase   38. Quentin was going through a rough _____ in his life.

The trial entered a new _____ when the judge threw out some critical evidence.

predict   39. It was hard to _____ what would happen next.

From time to time, people come up with _____ about the end of the world.

principal   40. One of our _____ concerns is the safety of our students.

I'm trying to pay down the _____ on my loan.

prior   41. Helen had plenty of _____ experience working with small children.

Because seating is limited, _____ is given to seniors.

project   42. She walked up on the stage and _____ an image of supreme confidence.

According to current _____ , we are on course to increase our profits by more than 15% this year.

promote   43. The clever marketers came up with a _____ scheme.

I hope my wife gets the _____ she has earned.

regime   44. The military _____ in Egypt resisted change.

No one thought the _____ in Myanmar could be overthrown.

resolve   45. The issue was peacefully _____ when Mom gave both children equal pieces of the birthday cake.

The UN issued a formal _____ concerning the status of the Occupied Territories.

retain   46. It was difficult to _____ control of the border.

They left the building but they _____ the right to return at any time.

series   47. A _____ of earthquakes struck north of Tokyo.

Professor Stout will give a lecture _____ on the migratory habits of African swallows.

statistic   48. Your research paper would be stronger if you would cite more _____ .

According to these _____, the gap between the rich and the poor is becoming larger.

status   49. Rene had trouble adjusting to her new celebrity _____ .

On this form, you have to indicate whether or not there is a change in your legal _____ .

stress   50. Her new job was not as emotionally _____ as her old job.

By the time Christmas arrived, everyone in the house was _____ out.

subsequent   51. A _____ investigation revealed that Arthur had traveled to Switzerland more than ten times.

We are restructuring the administrative offices. _____, your new office will be on the second floor.

sum   52. It seemed a vast _____, but it was only about $100.

No food, no water, no medicine. That just about _____ it up.

summarize   53. "Boring" rather neatly _____ what I think about the film.

You need to provide a brief _____ of your arguments.

undertake   54. After we found a buyer for our home, we _____ to buy a new house.

I think Habitat for Humanity is a worthwhile _____ .

Collocations

In each group of sentences, write *one* word from the list which goes with the **highlighted collocations**. Be careful with word forms.

Exercise 1	despite cycle access adequate apparent label
	debate project prior internal annual investigation

1. The children **gained** _____ **to** the cellar through an outside door.

    My phone plan **provides unlimited** _____ to the Internet.

    Few people know that RAM refers to **random** _____ **memory**.

2. When the washer **completes a full** _____ you can open the door.

    It's important to understand **business** _____ and their effects on sales.

    It was difficult to **end the** _____ **of poverty** and unemployment.

3. The committee will **carry out an** _____ to see if there has been any wrongdoing.

    We can't speak to you during the **ongoing** _____.

    Upon further _____, it was discovered that no money was missing.

4. No one will hire you since you don't have _____ **experience**.

    We **give top** _____ **to** candidates with masters degrees.

    Before working on the project, we **drew up a list of** _____.

5. Jason wasn't _____ **prepared for** the difficulty of the exam.

    Her salary was **barely** _____ to pay the rent.

    I think this will be **more than** _____. Thank you.

6. Suddenly, Tom **entered into a** _____ with his best friend.

    Everyone should own a gun? **That's a matter of** _____.

    The issue of the safety of nuclear energy is **widely** _____.

7. Two of the children **were** _____ **as** trouble-makers.

    When you **attach a** _____ **to** a foreigner without getting to know him, you are just making a stereotype.

    Don't **remove the** _____ from your new shirts and pants.

8. We are ready to **launch our new** _____.

    Regina _____ **an image of** superiority when she conducts a meeting.

9. My car stopped running **for no** _____ **reason**.

    It is **all too** _____ that you don't want to give us a hand.

10. She stayed outside _____ **the fact that** it was raining cats and dogs.

    We didn't meet our deadline _____ **our best efforts**.

Unit 4

Collocations

Exercise 2	regime obvious attribute code domestic series
	promote emerge integrate occupy attitude dimension

1. It didn't take much for her to **adopt an** _____ **of** concern.

    Sue Ann **has a bad** _____, so just ignore her.

    They weren't sure that the business would be successful, so they **took a wait-and-see** _____.

2. With the new information, this situation **takes on a new** _____.

    The financial problem of Europe is now a problem **of international** _____.

    The **physical** _____ of the jail cell were hard to estimate.

3. I **hate to state the** _____, but this movie is really boring.

    It **has become increasingly** _____ **that** we will need more time.

    It should be **perfectly** _____ why we should get married.

4. After working at Exxon for two years, Yolanda **put in for a** _____.

    The two presidents teamed up **to actively** _____ AIDS awareness.

    What are the chances that you will actually **get a** _____ this year?

5. Getting the flu **is commonly** _____ **to** exposure to cold weather.

    Being a team player is **a desirable** _____ for this job.

    Carla _____ **her success to** her excellent education.

6. Pigs are not usually considered to be _____ **pets**.

    Dogs became _____ **animals** thousands of years ago.

7. Mothering can be **a full-time** _____.

    Let's get rid of the old car. It's **just** _____ **space** in the driveway.

    The **military** _____ ended after many years of fighting.

8. The opposition forces tried to **overthrow the** _____.

    Many people think that now is the time for _____ **change**.

9. **A** _____ **of events** led to my decision to move to France.

    Kendal is enjoying a **documentary** _____ on cable TV.

10. After many hours of interrogation, the true picture of what happened that morning **slowly** _____.

    Luckily, everyone _____ **unscathed** after the earthquake destroyed the house.

Unit 4

Collocations

Exercise 3	concentration code error predict commit resolve
	output hypothesis option parallel phase goal statistic

1. We have a _____ **of honor** that everyone must follow.

    They could not **decipher the** _____ I invented to send secret messages.

    Computer programs operate on the **binary** _____.

2. The CEO made **a costly** _____ that resulted in a huge loss for the quarter.

    Nice paper! It doesn't have very many **grammatical** _____.

    I think Ophelia is making **an** _____ **in judgment** about you.

3. The movie is sold out. We **don't even have the** _____ to catch the last showing.

    Remember **to keep your** _____ **open** when you look for a new job.

    We **explored all available** _____ before we made our decision.

4. Shouting is no way to _____ **a problem**.

    The UN **issued a formal** _____ condemning Israel for the attacks.

    I think your problem **can be easily** _____.

5. Jean's death **become just another** _____ in the history of the city.

    You need to do more than **quote** _____ in your paper.

6. Mara seems **to lack** _____ to her relationship with Kim.

    Many **crimes have been** _____ in the name of religion.

    Dr. Adams was able to _____ **to memory** 200 new words every day.

7. First, **set a** _____.

    Make sure it is **a worthwhile** _____.

    Then do everything in your power **to achieve that** _____.

8. I'm not interested in discussing **purely** _____ **questions**.

    Well, that's **an interesting** _____, but no one will believe it.

    _____ **speaking**, we could retire early and go live in Mexico.

9. They thought he was **just going through a** _____, but he was serious about joining the marines.

    The discussions are **entering a critical** _____ right now.

10. Dr. Tomlin has **incredible powers of** _____.

    I found Vincent alone in his room, in **deep** _____.

Unit 4

Collocations

Exercise 4	apparent contrast predict status undertake retain
	stress implement grant impose investigate sum

1. Only a few teachers will **achieve the** _____ of senior instructor.

    The lottery winner **enjoyed celebrity** _____ for a day.

    You must not lie about your **legal** _____.

2. Who is able _____ **the future** accurately?

    I'm going **to make a** _____ **about** today's game.

    It's **impossible to** _____ what Theo will do next.

3. You need to **briefly** _____ the main points of your essay.

    They found **a small** _____ **of money** under the old woman's bed.

    It looks like more hot humid weather and no air conditioning. **That just about** _____ **it up.**

4. Fred's kindness **stands in sharp** _____ **with** his brother's meanness.

    In this essay, you will **compare and** _____ capitalism and socialism.

5. The new rules were **widely** _____ all over the land.

    How can we _____ **our plan** to win back the people's confidence?

    Moses was charged with **overseeing the** _____ of pharaoh's orders.

6. Unfortunately, we could not _____ **control of the situation** for long.

    I insist on _____ **the right** to visit the children twice a month.

7. Why are you so _____ **out**? Do you have an exam coming up?

    Be sure **to place the** _____ **on** the correct syllable.

    If you **suffer from emotional** _____, avoid drinking alcohol.

8. I'm sorry I can't _____ **a wish** to everyone who asks.

    The university will receive **a federal** _____ of $1,000,000.

9. We **hate to** _____ **upon you**, but can we borrow your car?

    The authorities _____ **a ban on** smoking on campus.

10. Darwin _____ **a journey** of discovery that would lead to the theory of evolution.

    Helping poor people find shelter is **a worthwhile** _____.

Unit 4

Synonyms Use the synonym clues to solve this crossword puzzle.

Across
1. device, tool, instrument
3. pledge, promise, do
7. supposed, theoretical
13. major, main, chief
14. sequence, chain, string
16. previous, earlier, former
18. period, circle
20. mistake, fault, blunder
22. argument, discussion
23. settle, decide, conclude
25. following, next
26. differentiate, differ
27. research, examine, explore
28. inside, within, interior

Down
2. limit, boundary
4. alternative, elective
5. machine, device, instrument
6. clear, apparent, evident
8. public; polite, courteous
9. therefore, thus, accordingly
10. in spite of, although
11. unite, blend, assimilate
12. visible, noticeable
15. enough, sufficient
17. meeting, discussion
18. focus; gather, collect
19. size, scope, extent
21. foretell, forecast, foresee
24. period, chapter, stage

Unit 4

Review

1. We didn't have _____ time to finish painting the house.	internal
	obvious
	domestic
2. Some Americans prefer to buy _____ rather than foreign cars.	parallel
	adequate
3. It was _____ that he did not know the answer.	principal
4. She quit working for no _____ reason.	alternative
	considerable
5. The machine is broken, and _____ useless.	prior
6. I can't join you tonight. I have a _____ engagement.	apparent
	initial
	hence
7. The new symphony is a close _____ to one that Bartok wrote a century ago. It sounds the same in many ways.	physical
	subsequent
	parallel
8. Every year at this time, the employees get nervous about the upcoming _____ review.	sufficient
	annual
9. We were surprised by his illness and _____ decision to retire.	technical
10. The _____ cause of the crash was the bad weather; the pilot's condition was only a small factor.	internal
	civil
	potential
11. We need to safeguard the _____ and political rights of everyone.	normal
	appropriate
12. The US should leave other countries alone when they have their own _____ problems to solve.	principal
13. If you are suffering from too much _____ , you need to take a vacation.	stress
	dimension
	access
14. The nuclear weapons added a new _____ to the peace talks.	code
	error
15. He is not an easy man to classify or put a _____ on.	label
16. All societies have _____ of right and wrong.	codes
	regimes
17. In military _____ , there is great respect for authority.	parameters
	mechanisms
18. We had the freedom to innovate, within certain _____ .	phases
	sums

Review

19. The factory is capable of a daily _____ of ten tons of plastic.	attitude conference dimension cycle access output
20. We were lucky to get _____ to his private collection.	
21. He couldn't escape the _____ of fear, relief, and more fear.	
22. We finished the job by operating the _____ by hand.	grant label phase mechanism error parameter
23. Tomorrow, we begin the final _____ of the project.	
24. He only made one _____ on the test, but it was a big one.	
25. She started to enjoy her new _____ as full professor.	attitude status project debate output statistic
26. Because of his bad _____ , we decided to not invite him.	
27. Campaign finance reform is the subject of current public _____ .	
28. The school's most interesting _____ is the number of students who go on to college.	stress option regime statistic project attitude
29. You have only one _____ . You have to sell your motorcycle.	
30. His latest _____ is to build a new garage.	
31. A _____ of events led to the disaster.	series code sum dimension status contrast
32. She spent a large _____ of money on new clothes.	
33. In _____ to his earlier paintings, he started to use dark colors instead of light ones.	
34. The university's _____ is to increase enrollment to 20,000.	emergence conference hypothesis occupation cycle goal
35. According to your _____ , there could be an infinite number of universes.	
36. While attending a _____ , I met several researchers who were interested in collaborating with me.	

Unit 4

Review

37. I can't _____ on what I'm reading when you are so noisy.	implement
38. We started walking _____ not knowing where we were going.	retain
39. The governor will _____ his new plan next year.	attribute
	concentrate
	despite
	emerge

40. My parents _____ to visit me more often.	occupy
41. We need to _____ the causes of the crash.	resolve
42. Irene will _____ several new projects this month.	investigate
	undertake
	label
	hypothesize

43. Good students can _____ their success to hard work.	emerge
44. Only one player will _____ as the winner.	resolve
45. Overly-protective parents sometimes _____ too many restrictions on their teen-agers.	stress
	summarize
	attribute
	impose

46. The president wants to _____ $1,000,000,000 to education.	undertake
47. We _____ that the climate will become much warmer.	retain
48. The company wants to attract and _____ new talent.	occupy
	predict
	promote
	commit

49. The king will _____ favors to those who obey him.	grant
50. Everything was done to _____ a new image.	access
51. How can we help immigrants _____ into our society?	promote
	attribute
	integrate
	concentrate

52. Now, I will _____ my main points.	emerge
53. I have enough work to _____ myself for several hours.	integrate
54. The butler did his best to _____ someone else as the real murderer.	summarize
	occupy
	resolve
	implicate

Unit 4

Definitions ◦ Parts of Speech ◦ Collocations

access (n) the way of approaching a place or person, or the right to use or look at something
  to gain access, to get access, to have access, to seek access, to offer access, to allow access
  to deny access, to refuse access, to restrict access
  to give access, to grant access to: *She gained access to her father's library.*
  direct access, easy access, free access, unlimited access, quick access, random access
  access to: *Many rural communities do not have access to good libraries.*
access (v)
accessible (adj)
  readily accessible, immediately accessible, easily accessible
  accessible by, accessible from, accessible for
accessibly (adv)
adequate (adj) enough or satisfactory for a particular situation or need
  to be considered adequate, to prove adequate, to seem adequate, to remain adequate
  adequate for; barely adequate: *Your grades are barely adequate for passing your chemistry course.*
  perfectly adequate, totally adequate, more than adequate; more or less adequate
  adequate for: *The office is small, but it is adequate for our needs.*
adequately (adv)
  adequately prepared for: *Make sure you are adequately prepared for winter weather.*
annual (adj) happening once every year, or relating to a period of one year
  annual review [= a review that employers do once a year]: *Every spring, the employees work hard in preparation for their annual review.*
  annual rainfall, annual precipitation
annually (adv)
annual (n) a plant that grows for only one year or one season
annual (n) a special book that is published at the end of the school year with pictures and stories about the year's students and activities
apparent (adj) clear; obvious
  to become (increasingly/more and more) apparent (that): *It has become increasingly apparent that people are driving more and flying less these days.*
  for no apparent reason: *He got up and walked out of the meeting for no apparent reason.*
  clearly apparent: *That you love your new car is clearly apparent.*
  glaringly apparent [= very obviously apparent]: *It is glaringly apparent that Jonas is too sick to work with us today.*
  all too apparent, painfully apparent: *Her lack of social skills was painfully apparent to everyone.*
apparently (adv)
attitude (n) a feeling, opinion or mental state in regard to something or someone
  to adopt an attitude, to strike an attitude, to take an attitude, to have an attitude
  to change an attitude: *You have been angry all day. It's time for you to change your attitude.*
  to assume an attitude of defiance: *I was about to pick up the dog when it suddenly assumed an attitude of defiance.*
  a cheerful attitude, a positive attitude, a realistic attitude
  a respectful attitude, a casual attitude,(to take) a wait-and-see attitude: *We're going to take a wait-and-see attitude before we decide whether or not to vote for the amendment.*
  a bad attitude, a negative attitude; a change in attitude
  with attitude [= aggressively challenging the normal ways]: *The chef prepared a fantastic meal using Indian spices. Now that's cooking with attitude!*
attribute (v) to say or think that something is the result or a characteristic of
  to directly attribute, to solely attribute, to mainly attribute: *The failure of the house to sell quickly can be directly attributed to its poor location.*
  to commonly attribute, to generally attribute, to widely attribute
  to attribute one's success to: *Ted attributes his success to the fact that he graduated from one of the best universities in the nation.*

to attribute to: *Her promotion was attributed to her hard work.*

attribute (n) a characteristic feature

chief attribute, main attribute, great attribute, key attribute: *Motivation is the key attribute we look for when we hire new employees.*

useful attribute, desirable attribute, essential attribute, positive attribute

divine attribute, human attribute, cultural attribute

personal attribute, physical attribute: *A recent survey showed that women are more attracted to a man's character more than to his physical attributes.*

civil (adj) being very polite and well-behaved in society

to be civil to; to be civil of someone: *It was civil of you to be concerned about my health.*

remarkably civil, perfectly civil

civilly (adv)

civil (adj) relating to the ordinary citizens of a country, not military or religious

a civil servant; civil law, civil lawsuit

civil disobedience [= civilians disobeying the government]: *Civil disobedience will not be tolerated.*

civil war [= a war fought between citizens of the same nation]

code (n) a set of rules, laws or regulations which are accepted as general principles

to establish a code, to lay down a code, to formulate a code

to break a code, to violate a code, to infringe a code [= to break a code]

an ethical code, a moral code

civil code, criminal code; a building code, a dress code; a code of honor

code (n) a system of numbers, letters or symbols for information

to design a code, to make up a code, to invent a code

to break a code, to crack a code, to decipher a code

a binary code; a secret code

barcode [a code which shows data about an object, such as its price]

an area code [= code for a telephone region], zip code [= postal code]

in code

code (v) to change a message into a secret

commitment (n) being obligated or willing

to make a commitment; to show commitment, to demonstrate commitment; to lack commitment

life-long commitment: *Marriage is a life-long commitment.*

genuine commitment, continued commitment, increased commitment

full commitment, total commitment, strong commitment

passionate commitment: *We remember Trish's passionate commitment to teaching.*

commitment (n) a responsibility

to take on a commitment (to), to fulfill a commitment, to meet a commitment

a social commitment, a work commitment, a military commitment, a teaching commitment

a domestic commitment, a family commitment; a financial commitment

commit (v) to promise or give in trust to a certain principle, person or plan of action

to commit to: *He committed himself to helping disabled students succeed in their studies.*

to commit something to memory: *I try to commit ten new words to memory each week.*

commit (v) to do something bad or perform a bad act

to commit a crime, to commit suicide, to commit murder, to commit sins

concentration (n) a strong focus on particular activity, subject or problem

to disrupt concentration, to disturb someone's concentration: *I tried to finish reading the book, but the children playing noisily in the schoolyard next door disrupted my concentration.*

demand concentration, require concentration

deep concentration, intense concentration: *Being a good poker player requires intense concentration.*

in concentration: *He has been in deep concentration for more than an hour.*

powers of concentration: *Due to her strong powers of concentration, she is able to remain focused on a single problem for a long time until she can solve it.*

concentration (n) a large amount of something in a (small) space

heavy concentration: *There is a heavy concentration of Hispanics living in parts of Miami.*

high concentration, low concentration, great concentration, geographical concentration

concentration rises, concentration increases

concentrate (v) to focus on or draw together towards a particular activity, subject or problem

hard to concentrate, difficult to concentrate, impossible to concentrate

concentrate intently, concentrate hard: *If you concentrate hard, you can get your work done.*

to concentrate on, to concentrate upon

concentrated (adj) made more intense or pure

highly concentrated

concentrated juice: *This frozen concentrated orange juice tastes almost as good as fresh juice.*

concentrated (adj) drawn together into a space

heavily concentrated: *Enemy troops are heavily concentrated in the hills above the town.*

highly concentrated, largely concentrated, mainly concentrated

conference (n) a meeting for the exchange of ideas on a particular subject, often with the intention of reaching a decision about what action to take

to convene a conference, organize a conference, to have a conference, to hold a conference

to attend a conference, to go to a conference

an annual conference, yearly conference, quarterly conference [= a conference held four times a year]

regional conference, state conference, national conference, international conference

private conference, video conference, student–teacher conference

a news conference, a peace conference, trade conference, industrial conference

education conference, environmental conference

a conference devoted to, a conference examines, a conference focuses on: *This year's conference focuses on the needs of immigrant children.*

conference site, conference center, conference building, conference facilities

conference hall, conference chamber, conference room

conference speaker, conference chairperson, conference participant

conference delegate [= someone elected to attend a conference]

conference program, conference theme, conference session

a conference between: *We need to have a conference between the teachers and the parents.*

to be in conference; at a conference

confer (v) to hold a discussion

confer (v) to give in a formal way

to confer an award, to confer a medal: *The Prime Minister conferred the Medal of Valor upon the brave young police woman.*

contrast (n) a clear difference between two or more things

to provide a contrast, to make a contrast, to offer a contrast

to stand in contrast with/against

in contrast, by contrast

in sharp contrast, in stark contrast, in marked contrast: *The President favored a peaceful solution. In marked contrast, the Prime Minister was in favor of war.*

a contrast between, a contrast with

contrast (v)

to contrast with

to contrast favorably, to contrast unfavorably, to contrast sharply

to compare and contrast [= to show the similarities and differences]

contrastive (adj)

contrastive analysis

cycle (n) a group or sequence of events which are often repeated

to go through a cycle, to complete a cycle, to repeat a cycle

to be caught (up) in a cycle: *Lately, Congress has been caught in a cycle of political showdowns.*

cycle begins again: *The lottery ended, the winner was chosen, and the cycle began again.*

a daily cycle, a weekly cycle, a monthly cycle, a seasonal cycle, an annual cycle

to complete a (full) cycle; to go through a cycle, to pass through a cycle

a business cycle, an economic cycle; a life cycle

cycle of poverty, cycle of crime, cycle of drug use

vicious cycle [= a cycle that is extremely difficult to break]: *Many poor working families are caught up in a vicious cycle of having to borrowing money and then not being able to repay it.*

lunar cycle [= moon cycle], solar cycle [= sun cycle]

breeding cycle, menstrual cycle, reproductive cycle

a cycle of poverty, a cycle of despair: *Many inhabitants of the ghetto suffered from the cycle of despair: lack of education, few jobs, little money for schools.*

cycle (v)

to cycle through

cycle (n) a small vehicle with one or more wheels (unicycle, bicycle, motorcycle)

to ride a ~cycle: *Kurt rides a unicycle to work every day.*

a ~cycle tour, ~cycle helmet: *Alan's motorcycle helmet saved his life.*

~cycle lane, ~cycle path, ~cycle route, ~cycle track: *There are hundreds of kilometers of bicycle paths all over this city.*

debate (n) a serious discussion of a subject in which there are two opposing points of view

to conduct a debate, to hold a debate, to have a debate, to enter into a debate (with)

to chair a debate, to moderate a debate [= to guide or preside over a debate]

to encourage debate, to spark (off) debate, to provoke debate

to win a debate, to lose a debate; to close a debate

a bitter debate, a heated debate, sharp debate, pointed debate, stormy debate

a lively debate, a spirited debate, a healthy debate

a public debate, political debate, congressional debate, parliamentary debate

formal debate, lengthy debate

a debate about, a debate over, a debate between, a debate with: *They were debating over whether to build a park or a new subdivision on the land.*

that's a matter for debate

debate (v)

to hotly debate, fiercely debate

to openly debate, publically debate

to seriously debate, fully debate, to widely debate, thoroughly debate

to debate with

debatable (adj)

debatably (adv)

despite (prep) regardless of, in spite of; without being prevented by something

despite objections, despite (best) efforts, despite rumors

despite rumors to the contrary: *Despite rumors to the contrary, Steve was not interested in the head coaching job at Rutgers.*

despite the fact that : *Congress refused to raise tax despite the fact that many people thought it was necessary.*

despite (n) the feeling of contempt or strong dislike

out of despite: *He stopped going to the baseball games out of despite for the team.*

dimension (n) a feature or way of considering something

to add a dimension of, to take on a new dimension, to take to a new dimension: *New technology takes cancer research to a new dimension.*

global dimensions, national dimensions, regional dimensions

cultural dimensions, historical dimensions

a problem of international dimensions

dimension (n) a measurement, usually of height, length, or width

to check dimension: *Before we buy the new bookshelves, let's check the dimensions of the room to make sure it will fit.*

physical dimension, spatial dimension; horizontal dimension, vertical dimension

second dimension, third dimension, fourth dimension: *The fourth dimension, time, is finite.*

in two dimensions, in three dimensions

dimensional (adj)

one dimensional, two dimensional, multi-dimensional

dimensionally (adv)

domestic (adj) of the home, household or family

domestic tranquility, domestic security

domestic help; a domestic animal , a domestic pet

domestically (adv)

domestic (n) a person who is paid to do housework

domesticate (v)

to domesticate animals; to domesticate livestock

domesticated (adj)

domesticated animals; domesticated livestock

emerge (v) to appear from, rise up from or come out from behind something

slowly emerge, suddenly emerge, finally emerge

eventually emerge: *Rick's supporters believed he would eventually emerge as the favorite.*

subsequently emerge, ultimately emerge

to emerge as: *It looks as though Thurgood will emerge as the new mayor.*

to emerge from: *In the spring, tiny plants emerge from the earth after their winter rest.*

to emerge unscathed: *The tornado destroyed the building, but all of the inhabitants emerged unscathed.*

emerge from, emerge into, emerge out of

emergence (n)

to mark the emergence of, to signal the emergence of, to witness the emergence of

to encourage the emergence of: *Antibiotics encourage the emergence of "super bugs."*

gradual emergence, sudden emergence, rapid emergence

emerging (adj)

emerging markets: *Investors should keep an eye on emerging markets, especially in South Africa, Malaysia and Turkey.*

error (n) mistake

to make an error, to commit an error, to compound an error [= to make an error worse]

to correct an error, to admit to an error

to point out an error, to show an error, to find an error, to spot an error

a costly error, a glaring error, a major error, a serious error, a fatal error, a fundamental error

a minor error, a slight error

human error, pilot error; a grammatical error, a typographical error

error detection, error message, error correction

a comedy of errors: *My whole day has been a comedy of errors. First, I was late to work, then I forgot my dentist appointment, an finally I ripped my pants at the gym.*

an error in/of judgment

in error/by error: *Lawrence was sent a check for $10,000 by error. It should have been $100.*

err (v)

to err is human: *"To err is human, to forgive, divine" is a quote from Alexander Pope's "An Essay on Criticism," published in 1711.*

erroneous (adj)

erroneously (adv)

goal (n) an aim or purpose

to set a goal, to work towards a goal, to pursue a goal, to strive for a goal

to achieve a goal, to attain a goal, to reach a goal, to realize a goal

a main goal, primary goal, major goal

an ambitious goal, a worthwhile goal, an unattainable goal, an unrealistic goal

a modest goal, a desirable goal, an achievable goal

a realistic goal, the ultimate goal

an immediate goal, a short-term goal, a long-term goal

goal (n) the scoring of a point or points in a game

to score a goal, to allow a goal

a well-taken goal, a brilliant goal, a scrappy goal, a soft goal

a field goal [= in US football, a three-point goal made by kicking the ball; in basketball, a goal made while the ball is in play]

grant (v) to present or agree to give or do something that someone has been requested

to agree to grant, to refuse to grant, to decide to grant, to be willing to grant to grant one's wishes: *The wealthy woman was able to grant the girl's wishes.*

to grant a pardon [= to officially cancel punishment for a crime]

to be willing to grant, to refuse to grant

grant (n)

to apply for a grant, to qualify for a grant, to be eligible for a grant

to obtain a grant, to receive a grant, to award a grant,

to write a grant proposal

a federal grant, an EU grant, a government grant

a substantial grant, a small grant

hence (adv) that is the reason or explanation for; therefore

We have run out of time. Hence, we must stop now.

It's freezing cold outside, hence the heavy jacket and gloves.

hypothesis (n) a proposed idea or explanation for something that is based on known facts and is used to guide further research

an interesting hypothesis, an acceptable hypothesis, a plausible hypothesis, a bold hypothesis

to formulate a hypothesis, to construct a hypothesis, to form a hypothesis

to advance a hypothesis, to suggest a hypothesis, to propose hypothesis

to put forth a hypothesis, to put forward a hypothesis: *In 1954, Niels Jerne put forward a hypothesis which stated that there is already a vast array of lymphocytes in the body prior to any infection.*

to confirm a hypothesis, to prove a hypothesis, to test a hypothesis

to accept a hypothesis, to reject a hypothesis

a working hypothesis, an untenable hypothesis [= a hypothesis that cannot be supported]: *Gopnik's bold hypothesis is untenable because it neglects the many important ways in which human minds are designed to operate within a social environment.*

(based) on the hypothesis that: *His assumption is based on the hypothesis that the universe will expand forever.*

hypothesize (v)

to hypothesize about; to hypothesize that

hypothetical (adj)

totally hypothetical, entirely hypothetical, purely hypothetical

a hypothetical example: *Let me give you a hypothetical example.*

a hypothetical situation

hypothetically (adv)

hypothetically speaking

implement (v) to carry out a plan or put something into operation

to try to implement, to attempt to implement, to agree to implement, to promise to implement

to fully implement, to partially implement, to adequately implement

to successfully implement, to effectively implement

to be widely implemented, to be effectively implemented, to be quickly implemented

to implement a plan, implement a policy, implement a program

implementation (n)

to oversee implementation, to monitor implementation, to supervise implementation

to achieve implementation, to ensure implementation

practical implementation: *You must do everything possible to ensure the practical implementation of the discussion process.*

effective implementation, successful implementation, detailed implementation

early implementation, immediate implementation

the implementation process

implicate (v) to show that someone is involved in an affair, situation or crime or is partly responsible for something bad that has happened

heavily implicate, strongly implicate, deeply implicate

to implicate someone in; to directly implicate

implication (n)

to grasp the implications, to realize the implications, to understand the implications

to consider implications, to examine implications, to study implications, to explore implications

to carry implications, to have implications

to explain implications, to discuss implications, to accept implications

to digest implications [= to study and understand implications]: *Trading on the stock market slowed as investors tried to digest the implications of the Fed's newest monetary tightening.*

major implications, fundamental implication, main implication, enormous implication

far-reaching implications, long-term implication, wider implication

practical implication, general implication, cost implication, safety implication, security implication

health implication, psychological implication

legal implication(s), social implication(s), economic implication(s), political implication(s): *The president's decision to raise the minimum wages of federal workers will have enormous political implications in an election year.*

by implication: *Warren was guilty of leaving the cage unlocked, and, by implication, should be punished for letting the cats get away.*

impose (v) to establish something as a rule to be obeyed or accepted

to effectively impose, artificially impose

(hate) to impose upon [= to bother or ask for a favor]: *I hate to impose on you, but could you please come over and help me move some furniture?*

to impose a ban (on): *The NRA does not want the government to impose a ban on hand guns.*

to impose sanctions on: *The EU imposed sanctions on Iran in an effort to prevent them from developing nuclear weapons.*

imposition (n)

unacceptable imposition, rude imposition: *We thought that her insistence on serving only vegetarian food was a rude imposition on us.*

integrate (v) to mix with or blend together

closely integrate, fully integrate, tightly integrate, completely integrate, thoroughly integrate

properly integrate, successfully integrate, smoothly integrate, seamlessly integrate [= to integrate smoothly]: *Our software is capable of integrating seamlessly into any network topology, and with virtually any third-party firewall.*

to integrate into, to integrate with

poorly integrated, highly integrated

integration (n)

to facilitate integration, to achieve integration, to speed up integration, to promote integration

to bring about integration: *The new policies are designed to bring about greater economic integration of the member countries.*

economic integration, monetary integration, social integration, racial integration, political integration

greater integration, increased integration, seamless integration, rapid integration

integrity (n) [see Unit 10]

internal (adj) located inside a person, object, organization, place or country

internal affairs; internal revenue

internal combustion (engine), internal losses, internal markets, internal pressure

internalize (v)

to internalize emotions, to internalize (social) norms: *When children fail to internalize accepted social norms, they run the risk of getting into trouble with the law.*

internally (adv)

investigate (v) to systematically examine especially to discover the truth

to call in to investigate, to promise to investigate

investigate carefully, investigate thoroughly

investigation (n)

to carry out an investigation, to conduct an investigation, to make an investigation

to launch an investigation [= to start an investigation]: *The National Consumer Council will launch an investigation of the cost of prisoners' phone calls.*

a cursory investigation: *After a cursory investigation, the police decided to drop the charges.*

a full investigation, a thorough investigation; an ongoing investigation; pending investigation

a criminal investigation, police investigation

upon further investigation: *Upon further investigation, we discovered that the books were not stolen after all. They were merely misplaced.*

under investigation: *Several senators are under investigation for accepting bribes.*

investigatory (adj)

label (n) a description used to classify or describe the contents of something

to attach a label to, to put a label on, to stick a label on

to carry a label, to remove a label, to take off a label

a warning label; a designer label, a price label

label (v)

to falsely label, to wrongly label

carefully label, neatly label, clearly label

to label someone as: *During the war, many innocent citizens were falsely labeled as unpatriotic.*

mechanism (n) a structure or a set of parts of a machine or device

to activate a mechanism, to trigger a mechanism

a firing mechanism, a locking mechanism, a steering mechanism

underlying mechanism, complex mechanism, social mechanism

avoidance mechanism, control mechanism, defense mechanism, escape mechanism, survival mechanism

mechanic (n) someone who works skillfully with machinery

mechanical (adj)

mechanically (adv)

obvious (adj) clear; easy to see, recognize or understand

to appear obvious, to seem obvious, to sound obvious, to become obvious

(hate) to state the obvious: *I hate to state the obvious, but it's raining, so why don't you take an umbrella?*

perfectly obvious, completely obvious, increasingly obvious

blatantly obvious, glaringly obvious [= extremely obvious]: *Tad's efforts to cover up his mistake were glaringly obvious. No one was fooled.*

far from obvious, not at all obvious, not entirely obvious, by no means obvious, less than obvious

rather obvious, pretty obvious, fairly obvious

obvious to, obvious that: *It was obvious to everyone that Jane was angry.*

an obvious reference to: *Her remark about the restaurant was an obvious reference to the bad experience she had there last week.*

the obvious conclusion

obviously (adv)

occupy (v) to fill up, live in, or exist in a place or a time, sometimes by force

to occupy space: *We don't really need the piano in the living room. It's just occupying space.*

to occupy Wall Street

occupation (n) controlling another country

a military occupation; during the occupation; under occupation

occupy (v) to be busy

occupied (adj) busy

to stay occupied, to keep occupied: *Can you keep the children occupied while I run to the store?*

to be occupied with: *We can't help you move as we are occupied with painting our house right now.*

happily occupied, fully occupied

occupied (adj) being used

densely occupied, entirely occupied, permanently occupied, illegally occupied

occupation (n) job

a full-time occupation, a dangerous or hazardous occupation

to choose an occupation, to follow an occupation, to provide (someone) with an occupation

occupation (n) living in a place

illegal/legal occupation; ready for occupation, unfit for occupation

option (n) the right, power, or freedom to choose from a set of possibilities

to exercise the option of; to have an option: *If you don't like living in this apartment, you always have the option to move to a different one.*

to choose an option, to take an option, to select an option

to have no option but: *We had no option but to sell our house.*

to keep one's options open: *We don't want to take him off the team. We need to keep our options open.*
an exclusive option, the first option
(to explore) all available options: *Before we shut down the business, let's explore all available options for keeping it open.*
a possible option, viable option, realistic option; attractive option

optional (adj) not required
entirely optional, purely optional
clothing optional [= not required to wear clothes]: *This area of the beach is clothing optional.*

optionally (adv)

output (n) a process or an amount of something produced by a person, machine, factory, country, etc.
to increase output, to step up output; to double output, to expand output
to cut output, to decrease output, to reduce output, to curtail output [= to reduce output]
industrial output, manufacturing output
daily output, annual output, monthly output, steady output
a fall in output, an increase in output

output (v)

parallel (n) having the same character or tendency
to draw a parallel between (with): *When we examine the works of Mallory, we can sometimes draw parallels with Shakespeare.*
to find parallels among (between): *Even high school students are able to find parallels between these two stories.*
a striking parallel, direct parallel, obvious parallel
without parallel; to have no parallel: *These chocolates are the best. They are without parallel.*

parallel (v) to go in the same direction
A row of small houses parallel the road from the church to the farm.

parallel (adj) going in the same direction without touching
parallel to, parallel with; nearly parallel, exactly parallel, roughly parallel

parallel (adv)
to run parallel: *The two roads run parallel for ten miles, then they diverge.*

parallelism (n)

parameter (n) a set of facts or a boundary which limits how something can be done
to know the parameters
to operate within certain parameters: *The Operations Integrity Management System (OIMS) calls for key procedures to ensure ExxonMobil's facilities are operated within established parameters.*
operating parameters, established parameters

phase (n) a distinct stage in a process or in a cycle of development
to begin a phase, to end a phase, enter the final phase, to reach a phase
to enter a (new) phase: *The negotiators entered a new phase in their discussions.*
to go through a phase: *Don't be mad at him. I think he's just going through a phase.*
a critical phase, a crucial phase, a rough phase: *You'll have to excuse Sally's rudeness. She's going through a rough phase at this time.*
an early phase, initial phase, new phase: *The recent agreements between Israel and Tajikistan begin a new phase in commercial trade between the two countries.*

phase (v)
to phase in [= to gradually start]: *The new regulations will be phased in starting in January.*
to phase out [= to gradually end]: *They decided to gradually phase out the old curriculum.*

predict (v) to say what will happen in the future
to predict the future, to make a prediction
to use something to predict, to allow to predict: *The software allows doctors to predict which patients will need surgery.*
accurately predict, confidently predict; difficult to predict, impossible to predict

prediction (n)
an unfavorable prediction, a gloomy prediction [= a prediction that something bad will happen]: *After looking at the economic report, the committee made a gloomy prediction for the upcoming quarter.*
a favorable prediction

a prediction comes true

principal (adj) [Do not confuse this word with "principle"] first in value, status or order of importance

principal actor, principal theme, principal objection, principal source

principally (adv)

principal (n) an amount of borrowed money, separate from interest on the loan

to pay down the principal, to pay off the principal

principal (n) a person who is primarily in charge of an educational institution

a school principal, a high school principal, a college principal

prior (adj) earlier or before something or before a particular time

prior experience; a prior engagement

prior to: *You need to remove all of the old paint prior to putting on the new paint.*

a prior conviction: *Because if her prior conviction, the judge was not inclined to be lenient.*

prior (n) a previous arrest: *The police found out that Evan had had two priors.*

priority (n) coming earlier or being of more importance

to sort out one's priorities, to decide on priorities, to determine priorities: *Health officials need to determine the needs that are of the highest priority.*

to give priority (to); to have priority over

top priority, major priority, immediate priority, number one priority: *Customer service is our number one priority.*

low priority

a list of priorities, in order of priority

project (n) a piece of planned work or activity intended to achieve a particular goal

to conceive a project, to draw up a project

to launch a project, to take on a project; to carry out a project

to do a project on: *The students are doing a project on Martin Luther King.*

a pilot project; a research project, community project, joint project

to shelve a project: *Because of a lack of funds, NASA decided to shelve the Mars project.*

project (v) to throw forward

to project an image: *He projects the image of a great hero, though he is far from being one.*

project (v) to guess or plan about the future: *It will be hard to project what next year's profits will be.*

projection (n) something that sticks out

projection (n) an estimation of a future situation

current projection, latest projection, financial projection, profit projection, sales projection

promotion (n) to a higher position

to approve a promotion, to recommend for promotion, to deserve a promotion

to get a promotion: *After two years, he finally got his promotion.*

to put (someone) in for a promotion: *Because Michelle accomplished so much in her first three months on the job, she decided to put in for a promotion.*

rapid promotion, internal promotion

promote (v) to support or encourage something

to serve to promote: *The Kindle Fire will serve to promote sales of physical as well as electronic items.*

to promote from, to promote to

to actively promote, intentionally promote, deliberately promote

promotional (adj)

promotionally (adv)

regime (n) a particular government or administration

military regime, totalitarian regime, communist regime, dictatorial regime; a puppet regime

a democratic regime, a liberal regime, old regime, established regime

oppressive regime, brutal regime, harsh regime, repressive regime: *The brutal regime was replace by a parliamentary regime that took much better care of the citizens.*

under a regime: *Certain wealthy people suffered under Stalin's regime.*

to establish a regime, to bring down a regime, to overthrow a regime

(time for) regime change: *Some observers think it is time for regime change in Iran.*

regime (n) a set of rules or procedures

to follow a regime (of), to be subjected to a regime of, to impose a regime of

a strict regime (of), a rigid regime, a strenuous regime
a health regime, fitness regime, training regime, dietary regime
a drug regime, therapeutic regime [= a regime that promotes health]
a financial regime, a fiscal regime, a legal regime, a regulatory regime

resolve (v) to reach the solution to or end of a problem or difficulty
to take steps to resolve, to try to resolve, to attempt to resolve
to resolve a problem, to resolve an issue, to resolve a crisis
to be easily resolved, to be readily resolved, to be successfully resolved,
to be peacefully resolved, to be amicably resolved [= resolved in a friendly way]: *The diplomats hoped that the border issues could be amicably resolved.*
to resolve differences: *They resolved their differences after weeks of discussions.*
a method of resolving, a means of resolving
through resolve, by resolve

resolution (n) a decision taken after a vote
to draw up a resolution, to draft a resolution, to propose a resolution: *The UN delegate proposed a resolution to ban the sale of weapons to Sudan.*
adopt a resolution, to approve a resolution
to consider a resolution, to vote on a resolution, to pass a resolution, to issue a resolution
a draft resolution, a formal resolution, a joint resolution, an emergency resolution
a resolution aimed at, a resolution authorizing

resolve (v) to made a strong decision
resolve to: *We resolved to get more exercise every day.*

resolution (n) a decision to do (or not do) something
New Year's resolution: *We don't always keep our New Year's resolutions.*

retain (v) to keep or continue to possess
to be allowed to retain, to have the right to retain, to be entitled to retain
to struggle to retain, to manage to retain, to wish to retain, to try to retain
to retain control (of the situation), to retain the right to

retention (n)

series (n) a number of similar or related events or things, one following another
a series of events
in a series, an unbroken series, a whole series of, an endless series of, a long series of
a TV series, a radio series, a comedy series, a crime series, a documentary series
a concert series, a lecture series, a test series

statistic (n) numerical information based on the number of times something happens or is present
to become just another statistic: *The people who lost their jobs became just another statistic.*
to collect/gather statistics: *Researchers must collect statistics before they test their hypotheses.*
to cite/quote statistics: *He thought he could win his argument by citing statistics.*
cold, hard statistics: *It's hard to beat cold, hard statistics.*
vital statistics [= basic information about the health of the body]: *Before the doctor sees you, the nurse will record your vital statistics, such as height, weight, age, etc.*
latest statistics, reliable statistics, valid statistics: *Make sure the statistics are reliable before you cite them in your research paper.*

statistics (n. singular) a branch of mathematics dealing with the analysis of great amounts of numerical data
Brian had to master statistics before he could complete his Ph. D. dissertation.

status (n) a position, rank or condition, especially in a social group
to achieve (the) status (of); to confer status, give status, grant status; to recognize status
to enjoy status; to have status, to acquire status, to grant status
financial status, marital status, social status, celebrity status
privileged status, professional status, employment status
equal status, high status, superior status; low status, inferior status
legal status; diplomatic status, immigrant status
(enjoy) the status quo [= the way things are now]
a status symbol: *Their six-bedroom house is quite a status symbol.*

a change in status

stress (n) great worry caused by a difficult situation, or something which causes this condition

to shift the stress from ~ to, to place the stress on; to be under stress

to cause stress, to create stress, to generate stress

to increase stress; to alleviate stress, to decrease stress

to manage stress, to avoid stress, to remove stress, to stand stress [= to tolerate stress]

to be stressed out; to stress out (over): *The test will be difficult, but don't stress out over it.*

(to suffer from) emotional stress, mental stress, physical stress

high stress, acute stress, considerable stress, severe stress

stress (v)

to heavily stress, to strongly stress, to constantly stress, to repeatedly stress

to be anxious to stress, to be careful to stress

stressful (adj)

to find stressful, to prove stressful

emotionally stressful

stressfully (adv)

stress (v) to give emphasis, importance or significance to something

to stress that: *I want to stress that I will help you if you just ask me to.*

it's worth stressing that; be at pains to stress; be careful to stress

stress (n) emphasis

to put the stress on; to carry the stress, to take the stress: *Pay attention to which syllables take the stress.*

subsequent (adj) happening after or following

subsequent to; subsequent effort, subsequent discussion, subsequent investigation

subsequently (adv)

sum (n) the total when two or more numbers or amounts have been added together

to raise a sum, to borrow a sum, to lend a sum, to repay a sum

a considerable sum, a large sum, a substantial sum, a handsome sum, a tidy sum, a lump sum

an astronomical sum, a staggering sum

a princely sum [= used ironically to indicate a small sum]: *Sara paid the princely sum of $3.00 for her lunch at the café.*

a sum of money

sum (v) to get the total amount; to summarize

that just about sums it up [= that more or less summarizes it]

summarize (v) to restate in a short and clear form

to attempt to summarize, to concisely summarize [= to summarize very briefly]

to summarize as: *The gist of the argument may be summarized as follows.*

to briefly summarize, neatly summarize, attempt to summarize

summary (n)

an accurate summary, a brief summary, a clear summary, a useful summary, a quick summary

a short summary, a concise summary [= very short summary]

news summary, financial summary, plot summary

write a summary, prepare a summary, provide (someone) with a summary

summarily (adv) briefly; in a short form

summarily rejected: *Her request was summarily rejected because she did not provide documents.*

undertake (v) [past= undertook] to decide or begin to do something, or a formal to promise that you will do something

to undertake a project; undertake a journey; undertake to do something

undertaking (n)

a hazardous undertaking, a risky undertaking

a worthwhile undertaking, a major undertaking, a considerable undertaking

Unit 4

Synonyms

access:	approach, entry, admittance
adequate:	enough, sufficient, satisfactory
annual:	yearly
apparent:	visible, observable, clear, noticeable
attitude:	feeling, viewpoint, opinion
attribute:	accredit, ascribe, relate, connect
civil:	public, communal; courteous, polite
code:	law, rules; cipher
commit:	pledge, promise; do, perform
concentrate:	focus, centralize; gather, collect
conference:	meeting, convention, discussion
contrast:	differentiate, differ, distinguish
cycle:	circle, period, alternate
debate:	argument, discussion, deliberation
despite:	in spite of, although
dimension:	size, scope, extent
domestic:	family, home, native
emerge:	appear, arise, transpire
error:	mistake, fault, blunder
goal:	aim, purpose, objective, intention
grant:	pay, award, give, provide
hence:	therefore, thus, accordingly
hypothetical:	supposed, theoretical, speculative
implement:	device, tool, instrument
implicate:	accuse, incriminate, involve
impose:	force, bother, inflict
integrate:	assimilate, unite, blend, bring together
internal:	inside, interior, within
investigate:	research, examine, explore
label:	tag, sticker; name, designation
mechanism:	machine, instrument, device
obvious:	apparent, clear, evident
occupy:	reside in; possess; utilize
optional:	alternative, elective, voluntary
output:	production, yield, achievement
parallel:	corresponding, same, equivalent
parameter:	limit, boundary, restriction
phase:	period, chapter, stage
predict:	foretell, foresee, forecast
principal:	major, main, chief
prior:	former, earlier, previous
project:	assignment, task; plan, propose
promote:	cultivate, encourage, support
regime:	rule, government, system
resolve:	settle, decide, conclude
retain:	keep, hold, store
series:	sequence, chain, string
statistic:	datum, information, measurement
status:	grade, level, rank, standing
stress:	emphasis; pressure, strain, tension
subsequent:	following, next, consequent
sum:	amount, total, quantity
summarize:	sum up, review, condense
undertake:	set about, begin, attempt, try

Unit 4

Answers

Definitions

1. committed	16. summarized	31. domestic	46. code
2. implicated	17. predicted	32. obvious	47. phase
3. occupied	18. imposed	33. principal	48. sum
4. attitude	19. apparent	34. concentration	49. prior
5. regime	20. adequate	35. label	50. hypothetical
6. error	21. internal	36. attribute	51. optional
7. investigate	22. status	37. goal	52. stress
8. emerge	23. conference	38. implementation	53. contrast
9. retain	24. output	39. dimension	54. project
10. series	25. undertake	40. civil	
11. parameters	26. integrate	41. annual	
12. statistics	27. promote	42. parallel	
13. hence	28. access	43. debated	
14. subsequent	29. cycle	44. granted	
15. despite	30. mechanism	45. resolved	

Parts of Speech

1. accesses / accessed	12. contrasted / contrast	23. hypothesis / hypothetical	34. option / options
2. adequately / adequate	13. cycled / cycle	24. implemented / implementation	35. output / output
3. annually / annual	14. debated / debates	25. implicated / implication	36. parallel / parallels
4. apparent / Apparently	15. despite / Despite	26. imposed / imposes	37. parameters / parameters
5. attitude / attitudes	16. dimensions / dimensions	27. integration / integrated	38. phase / phase
6. attributed / attributes	17. domestic / domestically	28. internal / internalized	39. predict / prediction
7. civil / civil	18. emerging / emerged	29. investigated / investigates / investigation	40. principal / principal
8. codes / coded	19. erroneous / errors	30. label / labeled	41. prior / priority
9. committed / commit	20. goals / goal	31. mechanical / mechanism	42. projected / projections
10. concentrated / concentrates	21. grants / grant /grants	32. obvious / obviously	43. promotional / promotion
11. conferences / conference	22. hence / hence	33. occupied	44. regime / regime

45. resolved / resolution	49. status / status	53. summarizes / summary
46. retain / retained	50. stressful / stressed	54. undertook / undertaking
47. series / series	51. subsequent / Subsequently	
48. statistics / statistics	52. sum / sums	

Unit 4

Answers

<table>
<tr><td colspan="4">Collocations</td></tr>
<tr><td>Exercise 1</td><td>Exercise 2</td><td>Exercise 3</td><td>Exercise 4</td></tr>
<tr>
<td>

1. access
   access
   access
2. cycle
   cycles
   cycle
3. investigation
   investigation
   investigation
4. prior
   priority
   priorities
5. adequately
   adequate
   adequate
6. debate
   debate
   debated
   / debatable
7. labeled
   label
   labels
8. project
   projects
9. apparent
   apparent
10. despite
    despite

</td>
<td>

1. attitude
   attitude
   attitude
2. dimension
   dimensions
   dimensions
3. obvious
   obvious
   obvious
4. promotion
   promote
   promotion
5. attributed
   attribute
   attributes
   / attributed
6. domestic
   domesticated
   / domestic
7. occupation
   occupying
   occupation
8. regime
   regime
9. series
   series
10. emerged
    emerged

</td>
<td>

1. code
   code/codes
   code
2. error
   errors
   error
3. option
   options
   options
4. resolve
   resolution
   resolved
5. statistic
   statistics
6. commitment
   committed
   commit
7. goal
   goal
   goal
8. hypothetical
   hypothesis
   Hypothetically
9. phase
   phase
10. concentration
    concentration

</td>
<td>

1. status
   status
   status
2. predict
   prediction
   predict
3. summarize
   sum
   sums
4. contrast
   contrast
5. implemented
   implement
   implementation
6. retain
   retaining
7. stressed
   stress
   stress
8. grant
   grant
9. impose
   imposed
10. undertook
    undertaking

</td>
</tr>
</table>

Unit 4

Answers

Synonyms (Crossword)

Across
1. implement
3. commit
7. hypothetical
13. principal
14. series
16. prior
18. cycle
20. error
22. debate
23. resolve
25. subsequent
26. contrast
27. investigate
28. internal

Down
2. parameter
4. optional
5. mechanism
6. obvious
8. civil
9. hence
10. despite
11. integrate
12. apparent
15. adequate
17. conference
18. concentrate
19. dimension
21. predict
24. phase

Review

1. adequate
2. domestic
3. obvious
4. apparent
5. hence
6. prior
7. parallel
8. annual
9. subsequent
10. principal
11. civil
12. internal
13. stress
14. dimension
15. label
16. codes
17. regimes
18. parameters
19. output
20. access
21. cycle
22. mechanism
23. phase
24. error
25. status
26. attitude
27. debate
28. statistic
29. option
30. project
31. series
32. sum
33. contrast
34. goal
35. hypothesis
36. conference
37. concentrate
38. despite
39. implement
40. resolve
41. investigate
42. undertake
43. attribute
44. emerge
45. impose
46. commit
47. predict
48. retain
49. grant
50. promote
51. integrate
52. summarize
53. occupy
54. implicate

Unit 5

Word List

n = noun   **v** = verb   **adj** = adjective   **adv** = adverb   **prep** = preposition

academy (n)
  academic (adj)
  academically (adv)
  academic (n)
adjust (v)
  adjustment (n)
  adjusted (adj)
  adjustable (adj)
alter (v)
  alteration (n)
  alterable (adj)
amend (v)
  amendment (n)
  amendable (adj)
aware (adj)
  awareness (n)
capacity (n)
challenge (n)
  challenge (v)
  challenger (n)
compound (n)
  compound (v)
conflict (n)
  conflict (v)
consult (v)
  consultation (n)
  consultant (n)
contact (n)
  contact (v)
decline (n)
  decline (v)
discrete (adj)
  discretely
  discreteness (n)
draft (n)
  draft (v)
enable (v)
  enabler (n)
energy (n)
  energize (v)
  energized (adj)
enforce (v)
  enforcement (n)
  enforceable (adj)
entity (n)
equivalent (n)
  equivalent (adj)
  equivalently (adv)
  equivalency (n)
expose (v)
  exposure (n)
  exposed (adj)

evolve (v)
  evolvement (n)
  evolved (adj)
  evolution (n)
  evolutionist (n0
  evolutional (adj)
  evolutionally (adv)
facilitate (v)
  facility (n)
  facilitation (n)
  facilitator (n)
fundamental (adj)
  fundamentally (adv)
  fundamental (n)
  fundamentals (n. pl.)
generate (v)
  generation (n)
generation (n)
  generational (adj)
image (n)
  image (v)
  imagery (n)
liberal (adj)
  liberally (adv)
  liberalize (v)
  liberalism (n)
license (n)
  license (v)
  licensed (adj)
logic (n)
  logical (adj)
  logically (adv)
margin (n)
  marginal (adj)
  marginally (adv)
mental (adj)
  mentally (adv)
  mentality (adj)
monitor (n)
  monitor (v)
network (n)
  network (v)
notion (n)
  notional (n)
objective (n)
  objective (adj)
  objectively (adv)
  objectivity (n)
orient (v)
  orientation (n)
  oriented (adj)
  Orient (n)

perspective (n)
precise (adj)
  precisely (adv)
  precision (n)
  preciseness (n)
prime (adj)
  prime (n)
  prime (v)
psychology (n)
  psychological (adj)
  psychologically (adv)
  psychologist (n)
pursue (v)
  pursuit (n)
  pursuer (n)
  pursuant (adv)
ratio (n)
reject (v)
  reject (n)
  rejection (n)
revenue (n)
stable (adj)
  stably (adv)
  stabilize (v)
  stability (n)
style (n)
  style (v)
  stylize (v)
  stylized (adj)
substitute (n)
  substitute (v)
  substitution (n)
sustain (v)
  sustainable (adj)
  sustainably (adv)
  sustainability (n)
symbol (n)
  symbolize (v)
  symbolic (adj)
  symbolically (adv)
  symbolism (n)
target (n)
  target (v)
  targetable (adj)
transit (n)
  transit (v)
trend (n)
  trend (v)
  trendy (adj)
version (n)
welfare (n)

Unit 5

Definitions Use the definition clues to write the correct words in the blanks.

1.	the scientific study of the mind and behavior *My wife knows much about children's behavior. She is an expert in child* _____ .	psychology style academy ratio draft conflict
2.	a relationship which shows how much more one thing is than another *A* _____ *of 1:5 says that the second number is five times as large as the first.*	
3.	a piece of text which has undergone or needs revision *The final* _____ *of the essay was much better than the previous ones.*	
4.	to make it possible for someone to achieve an aim *The federal grants* _____ *us to further our research.*	enforce enable monitor contact sustain generate
5.	to cause to exist; to produce *Great sports teams* _____ *much enthusiasm among students.*	
6.	to carefully watch or keep track of something *Good teachers constantly* _____ *every student's progress.*	
7.	a touch or a connection *He left home and avoided all* _____ *with his family.*	contact equivalent welfare version transit target
8.	doing well physically, mentally and emotionally *Religious organizations promote the* _____ *of the poor, the elderly, and the sick.*	
9.	the movement of people or things from one place to another *Astronomers follow the* _____ *of planets in front of distant stars.*	
10.	to double or increase *They got angry at the child who was misbehaving, but that just* _____ *the problem.*	oriented consulted licensed amended facilitated compounded
11.	to give permission or freedom to act or own something *The film maker* _____ *the movies to movie theaters.*	
12.	to acquaint something to the surrounding situation *As soon as we moved to the new house, we* _____ *ourselves to our new neighborhood.*	
13.	something that exists apart from other things *A corporation is a separate legal* _____ *from its owners.*	energy entity capacity generation alteration objective
14.	a slight change *After a slight* _____ *, the jacket fit much better.*	
15.	all the people of a similar age within a society *Few soldiers of the World War II* _____ *are still alive today.*	

16. knowing, perceiving or realizing that something exists *I wasn't _____ that you were an expert on Russian grammar.* 17. of or about the mind, involving emotional and intellectual response *She relaxed her mind and went into a _____ state known as "flow."* 18. steady or firmly fixed; not likely to move or change Businesses benefit from _____ economic policies.	mental precise liberal marginal aware stable
19. to make something more fitting or more correct; to change or alter *It didn't take long for the cats to _____ to their new home.* 20. to cause to be obeyed or accepted, especially when people are unwilling to accept it *I have to _____ the rules for everyone equally.* 21. to refuse to accept, consider, use, submit to or believe *We hope they don't _____ the offer we made on their house.*	substitute enforce reject orient adjust evolve
22. the chief or most important, or of the very best quality *At 50, she was in the _____ of her life.* 23. exactly stated; sharply defined in form, time, detail or description *"About 200 guests?" Can you please be more _____ ?* 24. having the same amount, force, value, purpose, qualities, etc. *A terabyte is the _____ of one thousand gigabytes.*	equivalent precise discrete prime exposed liberal
25. a formal way of thinking or reasoning *It was hard to argue with the formal _____ of her argument.* 26. the capacity to be physically and mentally active *Sam finished writing the last chapter in a burst of _____ .* 27. a way of doing something or expressing oneself *This coat is beautiful, and it will never go out of _____ .*	monitor capacity notion logic style energy
28. to put right; to make a change for the better *It is difficult to _____ the Constitution.* 29. to develop, achieve or make gradually *New forms of bacteria rapidly _____ in nature.* 30. to keep something in existence; to give support or relief to *Let's slow down! I can't _____ running at this speed.*	amend prime evolve target sustain enforce

Unit 5

31.	having a clearly independent, individual or distinct shape or form *Some mathematical structures are _____ rather than continuous.*	precise discrete liberal marginal evolutional fundamental
32.	forming the base, from which everything else originates; of central importance *Food, clothing and shelter are the _____ needs of humans.*	
33.	respecting and allowing many different types of beliefs or behavior *Giving women the right to vote was a _____ idea.*	
34.	a sign, shape or object which is used to suggest or stand for something else *The rattlesnake was the _____ for the 13 American Colonies who were beginning their war with England in 1775.*	perspective symbol energy generation revenue orientation
35.	a particular way of considering something based on true relationships or relative importance *After Larry lost his job, he began to look at homeless people from a whole new _____ .*	
36.	the total income that a government or company receives regularly *The city's monthly _____ from parking meters is just over $80,000.*	
37.	to get information, opinion or advice from *You should _____ with your parents before you make a major decision about your career.*	pursue facilitate consult contact trend amend
38.	to make possible or easier; to help bring about *A GPS device can _____ driving in a strange city.*	
39.	to chase after something *Alan wants to _____ his goal of becoming an artist.*	
40.	the total amount that can be contained, produced or accomplished *The _____ of this room is 35 people.*	draft license image objective capacity
41.	a picture in the mind of the form of something *I can't get that _____ out of my mind.*	
42.	something which you plan to do or achieve *Our primary _____ is to save more money this year.*	
43.	a general development or change in a situation or in the way that people are behaving; a current style or preference *Chocolate diamonds are the latest _____ in jewelry.*	trend notion version capacity generation equivalent
44.	an individual's belief, idea or conception of something known, experienced, or imagined *I don't have the slightest _____ what they are talking about.*	
45.	a particular account of something which varies from and contrasts with other forms of the same thing *She downloaded the newest _____ of iTunes.*	

46.	to require great mental or physical effort in order to be done successfully *The students accepted the* _____ *to finish their project in less than one week.* 47. to form a system of interconnected parts *Facebook makes it easy to* _____ *with your friends.* 48. to show or reveal *Political campaigns* _____ *the weaknesses of the politicians who are running for office.*	adjust challenge network orient reject expose
49.	the outer edge or limit of an area or action *Warren Buffett practices investing with a* _____ *of safety.* 50. a level or situation which you intend to achieve *We missed our* _____ *of raising $500,000.* 51. a school, usually private, which teaches a particular subject or trains people for a particular job above the elementary level *Marvin benefitted from attending a military* _____ *when he graduated from high school.*	ratio academy target image challenge margin
52.	to actively disagree with people who have opposing opinions *When two opposing ideas* _____ *, it is wise to seek the advice of a judge.* 53. to go, often slowly, from a higher or better position to a lower or worse one *The Swiss franc may* _____ *if the Euro weakens.* 54. something or someone that takes the place of another *In many recipes, you can* _____ *margarine for butter.*	conflict sustain decline draft generate substitute

Unit 5

Parts of Speech

Write the parts of speech (noun, verb, adjective or adverb form).
Word Forms: Be careful with nouns and verbs:
      Some *nouns* might need to be plural (~s).
      Some *verbs* might need ~s, ~ed, ~ing.

academy
1. Susan spends more time on sports than she does on her _____ work.

   He's a student who does well _____ but not socially.

adjust
2. This chair has an _____ head rest.

   They had trouble _____ to the new neighborhood.

alteration
3. The waist on this jacket is not _____, but we can change the length of the sleeves.

   After listening to your advice, I decided to _____ my plans for visiting France this summer.

amend
4. We need to make an _____ to our governing rules.

   The speaker _____ her speech to make it shorter.

aware
5. Because of her medication, she had no _____ of what was going on around her.

   Are you _____ that there are more than three million millionaires in the United States?

capacity
6. Nora certainly has the _____ to become a senator.

   It's beyond my _____ to finish the project by Friday.

challenge
7. The loser _____ the winner to a rematch.

   He _____ every remark that I make.

compound
8. Frank attempted to help us, but he just _____ the problem.

   There are two residential _____ next to the campus.

conflict
9. The witness's story _____ with the known facts.

   A good coach tries to prevent _____ among teammates.

consult
10. Oren _____ with his doctor before he decided to have the operation.

   After the _____, he felt relieved.

contact
11. Sheldon thinks he has made _____ with aliens.

   Before the announcement, the bride _____ her best friends.

Unit 5

decline   12. Crime in New York City _____ during the 1990s.

Bond prices are on the _____.

discrete   13. X is _____ from Y if they have no part in common.

Sentences are made of _____ units called *words*.

draft   14. A new constitution for the USSR was _____ in 1935.

The student gave the final _____ of his essay to his teacher, then hoped for the best.

enable   15. These glasses _____ you to see better at night.

Social Security _____ many disabled people to live normal lives.

energy   16. We were _____ when we heard the good news.

The children seem to have boundless _____ today.

enforce   17. I don't think the new laws are going to be _____.

The immigration laws need to be better _____ .

entity   18. A corporation is a business _____ that is legally considered to be a person.

We have a list of all the _____ involved in the case.

equivalent   19. Some people wonder if home schooling is the _____ of classroom schooling.

It is said that one human year is the _____ of seven dog years.

evolve   20. New ways of political and social thinking _____ after the coal mine disasters.

Technology influences the _____ of military weapons.

expose   21. Mistakes were _____ during the investigation.

The film was ruined when it was _____ to light.

facilitate   22. Janine _____ yesterday's meeting.

Paul will be the _____ at the next meeting.

Unit 5

fundamental 23. You need a _____ understanding of mathematics before you can study physics.

These conclusions are _____ untrue because they are based on incorrect data.

generate 24. Natural gas is used for the _____ of electricity.

The announcement _____ excitement.

generation 25. The new _____ of thinkers is a threat to the status quo.

Future _____ will thank us for our foresight.

image 26. He had no trouble putting his mental _____ into his paintings.

I still have _____ of our Cuban vacation in my mind.

liberal 27. The judge seems to be interpreting the law too _____.

She was sorry that she had joined the _____ group.

license 28. The doctor's medical _____ was taken away.

The county office _____ all new construction in the county.

logic 29. We didn't understand the _____ of his decision.

It's cheaper to buy the laptop computer, so _____ that's what we should do.

margin 30. Support for the plan was _____ at best.

The _____ of profit on printed books is very small.

mental 31. Ursula seems to be _____ healthy, but sometimes I wonder about the illogical things she says.

They might build a new _____ hospital near here.

monitor 32. Every day last week, the doctors _____ the patient.

Fran closely _____ everything her children do.

network 33. When I was on LinkedIn, I _____ with dozens of professional colleagues.

I miss _____ with my former colleagues.

Unit 5

notion
34. Sometimes, a great _____ comes to my mind.

Stan has only a slight _____ about how Twitter works.

objective
35. They had no trouble reaching both of their _____.

You need to look at the situation more _____.

orient
36. When the students arrive, they first go to an _____ meeting.

At first, the hikers were lost, but then they _____ themselves by facing the sun.

perspective
37. From the _____ of the villagers, the king was almost a god.

Before we get too angry with each other, let's try to put things into _____ .

precise
38. Daniela's answers were usually _____ and clear.

The tickets cost _____ what I thought they would.

prime
39. The _____ cause of winter accidents is icy roads.

You have to pay more for _____ cuts of beef.

psychology
40. The field of _____ provides information about human behavior that marketers can and do use.

His teachers think she needs a _____ evaluation.

pursue
41. The fans _____ the singer all the way to the airport.

I'm no longer interested in _____ a career in the fast food industry.

ratio
42. What is the _____ of Hispanics to Blacks in this school?

Inverse _____ is the opposite of the original ratio.

reject
43. Aaron was so afraid of _____ that he started to cling too closely to his girlfriend.

Toni _____ the manager's offer.

revenue
44. We can use the _____ from the sale of our business to take a trip around the world.

The great weather resulted in a huge increase in crop _____ this year.

Unit 5

stable   45. The _____ of their marriage enabled them to raise five children who turned out to be fine citizens.

Travis is in _____ condition in the hospital.

style   46. Carla has an interesting _____ of speaking.

Felicia hasn't changed her hair _____ in decades.

substitute   47. You should not _____ rye flour for wheat flour in this recipe.

Who _____ for the sick actress last night?

sustain   48. The poor painter _____ himself by selling newspapers.

Margot was no longer interested in _____ her relationship with Paolo.

symbol   49. The plus sign and the minus sign are mathematical _____.

A diamond ring is _____ of love.

target   50. The charity drive reached its _____.

The Prime Minister was _____ by her enemies.

transit   51. The astronomers were able to observe Mercury as it _____ across the face of the sun.

My trip was excellent, but I lost one suitcase in _____.

trend   52. In general, bond prices _____ gradually upwards while stock prices rise and fall.

Quentin lives in a very _____ neighborhood.

version   53. So far, I have heard three different _____ of the story.

The film _____ was not nearly as interesting as the book.

welfare   54. A kind, gentle government should be more concerned about the _____ of its citizens.

Brendan thought he might have to go on _____.

Unit 5

Collocations

In each group of sentences, write *one* word from the list which goes with the **highlighted collocations**. Be careful with word forms.

Exercise 1	liberal psychology margin alter energy amend draft sustain orient welfare academic adjustment

1. The difference between the two theories is **purely** _____ .

    You must **attend the police** _____ before you can become a policeman.

    Half of the cadets at the **naval** _____ were women.

2. He threw away the **poorly** _____ **letter** and started over.

    The **working** _____ **of the essay** sat on the desk for weeks.

    The lawyers _____ a new **contract** and gave it to us to sign.

3. Mike is conservative in most things, but he **holds** _____ **attitudes** about education.

    We were shocked by our elderly uncle's **remarkably** _____ **attitude**.

    The Democrats want to _____ the **economic policies**.

4. We had to **make a slight** _____ to the time table.

    Penny is a **well-**_____ girl.

    The estimates had been _____ **downward**.

5. I just **don't have the** _____ **to** keep working on this project.

    Politician who are running for office need to _____ **their base** of supporters.

    The children were too **full of** _____ to settle down and take a nap.

6. We were not impressed by Annette's _____ **performance**.

    Don't **write in the** _____ of your **books**.

    Dirk won the election **by a wide** _____ .

7. The US was accused of **conducting** _____ **warfare**.

    Devin became interested in **abnormal** _____ after reading the biography of Vincent Van Gogh.

8. She returned the stolen money, but that **does not** _____ **the fact that** she committed a crime in the first place.

    Our friends had to **make a slight** _____ to their plans to visit us.

    My old suit doesn't fit any more. It needs a few **slight** _____ .

9. It was **hard to** _____ **interest in** the terribly long speech.

    Luckily, Pierre _____ only minor **injuries** in the crash.

10. The senator doesn't seem to care much about **public** _____ .

    The city is making cuts to **social** _____ **programs**.

Unit 5

Collocations

Exercise 2	entity stable enforce revenue notion contact image aware monitor version ratio capacity logic

1. It was hard **to make** the protesters _____ **of** the danger.

   They **have a much greater** _____ **of** the problems of inner city children.

   We were **painfully** _____ that Mark's illness was terminal.

2. The ban against guns cannot be **legally** _____ .

   Law _____ in Guatemala is sometimes weak.

   It might **be impossible to** _____ **the law** requiring everyone to have health insurance.

3. Kirk **projects a positive** _____ **of** himself wherever he goes.

   O'Neill's **use of vivid** _____ in his plays raised theater to a high art form respected around the world.

4. I **don't have the foggiest** _____ why she called me.

   Belinda **has a vague** _____ that people will support her at the meeting.

   It's not wise **to entertain the** _____ that women in Saudi Arabia will soon have the right to drive cars.

5. If _____ **drop** this year, we'll have to replace them from our cash reserves.

   Tax fraud costs the government millions in **lost** _____ .

   Hopefully, this year's budget will be _____ **neutral**.

6. The **unofficial** _____ of Bruno's biography is not very flattering.

   The **uncut** _____ **of the film** is three hours long.

   Ron told us what happened, but **let's hear your** _____ .

7. Children have **a remarkable** _____ for learning languages.

   Hiking to the top of Mt. Fuji is not **within the** _____ **of** most people.

   Some people believe that dogs share **the human** _____ for love.

8. After Doug bought a guitar, it didn't take him long **to learn the** _____ **of** chord progressions.

   The whole idea **seems rather** _____ to me.

9. The nurses _____ **the progress** of their patient for several hours.

   The new **computer** _____ shows pictures in 3-D.

10. Dorothy has a hard time staying in **a** _____ **relationship**.

    With luck, prices will **remain** _____ for the rest of the year.

Unit 5

Collocations

Exercise 3	expose precise objective contact evolve orientation reject challenge style generate perspective symbol

1. Helen and Bob remodeled their home in a more **contemporary** _____.

    The _____ **version** of the video game became popular.

    For some reason, Gibson's **formal** _____ of writing appealed to me.

2. Complex life forms **gradually** _____ **from** simple organisms.

    In the 19th Century, social equality **slowly** _____ **over time**.

    This book **traces the** _____ of the English language.

3. They _____ **the offer out of hand**.

    Linda's design was _____ **in favor of** Luann's design.

    For his entire life, the artist **suffered from feelings of** _____.

4. The players **responded to the** _____ by playing even harder.

    Every day, engineers **face enormous** _____.

    How dare you _____ my **authority**!

5. These plants will die if they are _____ **to** direct sunlight.

    When the Americans left the village, the residents were **dangerously** _____ to the Taliban.

    Traveling gives people **greater** _____ **to** other cultures.

6. The Berlin wall was **a powerful** _____ **of** the Cold War.

    It was clear that the arrest would **come to** _____ resistance to authority.

    The Senate's vote on the budget is **purely** _____ and not at all intended to pass.

7. Carol likes **to keep in close** _____ **with** her former colleagues.

    Please **don't hesitate to** _____ us if you have any questions.

    Pat **immediately** _____ **the police** when he saw the broken window.

8. The new policies were designed to _____ **revenue**.

    Yesterday's announcement _____ **excitement** among the students.

    The computer program is good at **randomly** _____ numbers.

9. Our **short-term** _____ are not as important as our long-term goals.

    Janet was successful in **achieving** her _____ of finding a boyfriend.

    Let's try to **look at the situation** more _____.

10. These data **put a new** _____ **on** the crisis.

    Try **to look at** this **from** my _____.

    The president tried **to put things into** _____ for the reporters.

Unit 5

Collocations

Exercise 4	generation entity target license transit consult pursue discrete conflict decline substitute precise

1. Memorizing ten new words a day is **a realistic** _____ for anyone.

    Most of Joe's earnings **were** _____ **for** his college fund.

    Everything went smoothly and we were **right on** _____ .

2. Iran tried to **provoke a** _____ between Syria and Israel.

    When a _____ **arises**, the Secretary of State flies to the region.

    The time of tomorrow's party _____ **with** my work schedule.

3. Farmers have worked in these fields **for** _____ .

    Future _____ will look back and think we were so primitive.

    Steve Jobs invented **a new** _____ of hand-held devices.

4. We can predict the phases of the moon **with a high degree of** _____ .

    The team worked together with **military** _____ .

    The accountant's task **calls for a high level of** _____ .

5. The **mass** _____ **system** in New York could be better.

    The computers are **in** _____ **from** Seattle **to** Portland.

    Unfortunately, the goods were damaged **in** _____ .

6. Ken's interest in the project _____ **dramatically** when he found out that he would not be paid.

    Her **health** has been **in a gradual** _____ for weeks.

    We **are** _____ **your offer** because we found a better one.

7. In the US, the church and the state are considered **separate** _____ .

    The independent committees were joined **to create a single** _____ .

    A **legal** _____ , such as a corporation, has the right to enter into a contract.

8. **There's no** _____ **for** careful preparation.

    Ryan often _____ olive oil **for** butter in his recipes.

    Who will be our _____ **teacher** today?

9. After she graduated, Kitty was **free to** _____ her **dreams**.

    A career in farming **is not worth** _____ .

    We **intend to** _____ **the matter** further.

10. We _____ **with** our **lawyer about** the contract before we signed it.

    Josie's parents **felt** they had not **been properly** _____ before she quit her job.

    You shouldn't take that medicine **without first** _____ your **doctor**.

Unit 5

Synonyms Use the synonym clues to solve this crossword puzzle.

Across
2. income, profit, earning
5. proportion, fraction
9. goal, aim, objective
10. develop, change, adapt
11. enable, assist, help
14. main, principal, chief
15. ask, check, confer
16. empower, allow, facilitate
17. thing, object
19. exact, specific, clear
20. border, frame, edge
24. ability, volume, role
28. activity, force, power
29. mindful, conscious, knowing
31. fashion, design, trend
33. tendency, direction, inclination

Down
1. generous, tolerant, open
2. refuse, decline, disapprove
3. idea, view, thought
4. alike, identical, same
6. exchange, alternate, replace
7. dare, problem, provocation
8. descend, decrease, refuse
12. fixed, firm, steady
13. institute, school
18. locate, situate, familiarize
21. develop, create, produce
22. separate, distinct, different
23. benefit, assistance, relief
25. alter, change, adapt
26. picture, likeness, depiction
30. plan, outline, sketch
32. argument, reasoning, thought

Unit 5

Review

1. The _____ reason for their errors was that they were overworked.	aware
	stable
2. After deducting expenses, our _____ taxable income was less than $44,000 this year.	adjusted
	discrete
	fundamental
3. He found it difficult to maintain a _____ relationship with his girlfriend.	psychological
4. The psychologist was successful in treating her _____ disorder.	mental
	equivalent
5. At one time, it was thought that 'mind' could be analyzed into _____ bits called 'sensations.'	marginal
	discrete
	objective
6. He eventually became _____ of his own shortcomings.	aware
7. The _____ newspapers tend to favor Democrats, whereas the conservative newspapers favor the Republicans.	stable
	precise
	prime
8. His definition was so _____ that we had no doubt as to what the word meant.	liberal
	aware
9. That's a _____ example of what happens when you don't pay attention to details.	trendy
10. The _____ will be to get everyone to agree with us.	challenge
	transit
11. We imagine there will always be _____ in the Middle East.	compound
	license
	entity
12. They combined the companies into a single _____ .	conflict
13. I have some _____ of how engines work.	logic
	notion
14. Little is being done to promote a new _____ for the senator.	network
	image
15. He wrote a brilliant article on the _____ of great sportsmen highlighting the importance of mind over matter.	psychology
	generation
16. Lately, there has been a _____ towards downsizing.	trend
	alteration
17. Fidel Castro had become a _____ of defiance in Latin America.	symbol
	contact
	welfare
18. I think we can use your classroom just as it is, without any _____ at all.	alteration

Unit 5

Review

19. I sometimes feel I am the _____ at which their anger is directed. 20. He brings a wonderful historical _____ to the analysis of the crisis. 21. Government _____ is expected to drop considerably this year.	perspective revenue trend ratio pursuit target
22. They have moved with the times just as much as the younger _____ has. 23. It was interesting to monitor the _____ of the simple essay into a longer, more complex paper. 24. After all the expenses are considered, there will not be a very great _____ of profit.	perspective orientation margin generation evolution challenge
25. He left the university to attend a military _____ . 26. These things improved her _____ for creative thinking. 27. Water is a _____ of hydrogen and oxygen.	academy image capacity compound notion revenue
28. Two women were at the center of a _____ of political activity. 29. The _____ of teachers to students is about 1 to 45. 30. The villagers earn the _____ of three US dollars a week.	ratio decline image equivalent network perspective
31. The _____ of the people is the main objective of law. 32. We have received one shipment. The other is still in _____ . 33. His _____ of the events did not match hers.	compound welfare generation transit revenue version
34. They worked on the new regulations until the final _____ was approved. 35. I don't understand the _____ of your argument. 36. She stayed in bed to conserve her _____ .	notion target energy draft logic contact

Unit 5

Review

37. Her writing _____ is simple, yet delightful.	style
38. He was arrested for driving without a _____ .	license
39. The long-range _____ is to limit the damage caused by flooding.	capacity awareness objective academy

40. He removed the new paint to _____ the original painting beneath.	reject
41. I have to _____ her to give her the message before she leaves for Chicago.	sustain expose consult
42. The industry wants to _____ itself towards the export market.	orient contact

43. We must cooperate in order to _____ the expanding economy.	sustain
44. She tried to _____ every person to take part in the local government.	amend network monitor
45. We will need to _____ the law to reflect the new situation.	enable compound

46. It is feared that conservatives will _____ the peace proposal.	orient expose
47. She tried to _____ a lot of enthusiasm for her new plan.	generate reject
48. He forgot to _____ his boss, so he really got into trouble.	generate consult

49. Developed countries have a duty to _____ international trade.	expose decline
50. A brilliant battle is no _____ for a sound policy.	license substitute
51. There has been a _____ in the value of the currency.	compound facilitate

52. They wanted to _____ their higher education.	pursue decline
53. She can be trusted with the power to make and _____ decisions.	monitor enable
54. This machine will _____ the amount of oxygen you are using.	enforce challenge

Unit 5

Definitions ○ Parts of Speech ○ Collocations

academy (n) a school, usually private, which teaches a particular subject or trains people for a particular job above the elementary level

    military academy, naval academy, police academy, riding academy

    an academy for: *They decided to put him in an academy for boys.*

academic (adj) related to a school or university

    academic freedom: *The academic freedom in this university allows professors to do research in areas that really interest them.*

    purely academic, merely academic, strictly academic

    largely academic, somewhat academic, rather academic

academic (adj) hypothetical or without practical value: *This debate is merely academic.*

academically (adv)

academic (n) someone who works at a school: *Dr. Nation has been an academic for over thirty years.*

adjust (v) to make something more fitting or more correct; to change or alter

    to try to adjust (to), to take time to adjust (to), to need to adjust (to)

    to adjust quickly, to adjust gradually, to adjust slowly

    to adjust upward, to adjust downward: *The estimates for this year's profits need to be adjusted downward.*

adjustment (n)

    to make an adjustment: *We made a small adjustment to the fuel mixture which really improved the car's performance.*

    a slight adjustment, a fine adjustment, a small adjustment

    a necessary adjustment, an appropriate adjustment

    a major adjustment, a significant adjustment, an important adjustment

adjusted (adj)

    well-adjusted, finely adjusted, automatically adjusted

adjustable (adj)

alteration (n) a slight change

    to make an alteration (to/in): *Because of the weather, we need to make an alteration in our plans.*

    a minor alteration, a slight alteration; a major alteration

alter (v)

    not alter the fact that: *She returned the stolen money, but that does not alter the fact that she committed a crime in the first place.*

alterable (adj)

amend (v) to put right; to make a change for the better

    to amend a speech

    to amend your ways: *You are always getting into trouble. You must amend your ways.*

amends (n. pl.)

    to make amends: *You have offended her, so you will have to make amends.*

amendable (adj)

amendment (n)

    to make an amendment to the Constitution

aware (adj) knowing, perceiving or realizing that something exists, or having knowledge or experience of a particular thing

    to become aware, to seem aware, to make someone aware

    well aware, very much aware, painfully aware,

    acutely aware, keenly aware [= extremely aware]: *We are keenly aware that our decision will cost us a great deal of money.*

    aware of (the difficulties, etc.)

    aware that: *We were aware that we were late.*

awareness (n)

    a sudden awareness, a greater awareness, a dawning awareness

    a growing awareness, a heightened awareness, a much greater awareness

    a general awareness: *There is a general awareness that the economy is getting better.*

capacity (n) the ability to do something

beyond one's capacity; within one's capacity: *She can't read all those books by next week. It's beyond her capacity.*

(to work in) an administrative, supervisory, professional capacity

official capacity, voluntary capacity, advisory capacity: *For the next two weeks, Charles is working in an advisory capacity to the director.*

an amazing capacity, an enormous capacity, a remarkable capacity, human capacity

capacity (n) the total amount or potential that can be contained or produced or accomplished

to fill to capacity: *The auditorium was filled to capacity, and many people were still waiting to get in.*

seating or storage capacity; a capacity for: *She has a capacity for getting the work done quickly.*

capacity (n) the position in which someone works

in one's capacity as: *In my capacity as captain, I must ask you to come to practice on time.*

challenge (n) something which requires or deserves great mental or physical effort in order to be done successfully

to issue a challenge: *The president issued a challenge to the dictator: destroy weapons of mass destruction or face war.*

to mount a challenge, to pose a challenge (to): *The steep incline posed a challenge to the bicyclists.*

to accept or respond to a challenge; to face or meet a challenge

a direct challenge, real challenge, serious challenge; legal challenge

a challenge to do something: *They challenged us to swim across the lake.*

considerable challenge, enormous challenge, huge challenge, tough challenge

challenge (v)

to challenge the status quo; to challenge authority

to challenge ~ on the grounds of: *Georgiana challenged the court's ruling on the grounds that it put an undue burden of proof on her client.*

to challenge to a duel [= to challenge another person to a formal gun fight]

seriously challenge, effectively challenge, successfully challenge

challenger (n)

compound (n) something consisting of two or more different elements or parts

chemical compound; an organic compound

compound fracture, compound leaf, compound microscope, compound sentence

compound fraction, compound number, compound interest

compound (v) to double or increase

to compound a problem: *It was bad enough that we were losing the game, but the problem was compounded when John was injured.*

compound (n) an enclosed area: *We live in a residential compound next to the campus.*

conflict (n) an active disagreement between people with opposing opinions or principles

to provoke a conflict: *The president tried to provoke a conflict with congress.*

to avert/avoid a conflict: *Good negotiators try to avert conflict between those who disagree.*

to resolve a conflict: *It's difficult to resolve conflicts when both parties refuse to talk to each other.*

a conflict about/over: *They were involved in the conflict between Iraq and Iran.*

a conflict among, between: *There was a serious conflict among the four teammates.*

to be involved in a conflict: *I always find myself involved in a conflict between my wife and her sister over how to raise kids.*

conflict arises, conflict occurs, conflict erupts [= conflict suddenly arises]: *When the two men finally met face-to-face, a conflict erupted.*

a major conflict, a serious conflict, growing conflict, increasing conflict

global conflict, regional conflict

cultural conflict; ethnic or religious conflict

conflict (v)

to conflict with: *The two virus protection software programs conflict with each other.*

conflict (n) a battle or a war

military conflict

conflict (n) a situation in which two or more things do not go together

in conflict with: *My class schedule is in conflict with my work schedule.*

Unit 5

consult (v) to get information, opinion or advice from

should consult, need to consult: *If the pain continues, you should consult a doctor.*

to consult about, to consult on, to consult with: *Before you decide on your major, you should probably consult with your advisor.*

to consult a lawyer, to consult a doctor, to consult an expert

to be/to feel properly consulted: *The parents felt they had not been properly consulted .*

without first consulting: *You shouldn't take that medicine without first consulting your doctor.*

consultation (n)

consultant (n) a person who gives information, opinion or advice

to bring in a consultant, to employ a consultant

to act as a consultant, to hire a consultant

tax consultant, legal consultant, business consultant, financial consultant, management consultant

public relations consultant, independent consultant, outside consultant

contact (n) a touch or a connection

to come into contact with: *These knives will rust if they come into contact with water.*

to break contact

(to make) eye contact, face-to-face contact

direct contact: *The batteries are activated when they come into direct contact with air.*

contact between, on contact (with): *The plane was destroyed on contact with the ground.*

a contact print, a contact lens

physical contact, sexual contact

contact (v) to get in touch with someone by speaking or writing

to put someone in contact with: *If you need a repair person, I can put you in contact with my sister.*

to keep in contact, to establish contact (with)

to get in contact with, to make contact with: *As governor, Mr. Kitzhaber makes contact with people from all over the state.*to contact immediately, to contact directly, to contact personally

to avoid (all) contact, to lose contact

regular contact, direct contact

in close contact: *Are you still in close contact with Dr. Shih?*

to contact by e-mail, to contact by phone

to contact the police, to contact the hospital, to contact the office

do not hesitate to contact someone

decline (n) a falling off, a loss; a decrease; a downward movement

to be on the decline, to go into a decline, to sink into a decline, to suffer a decline

a gradual decline, a steep decline, a sharp decline, a steady decline

in a decline, on the decline: *Crime is on the decline now that there are more police in the city.*

decline (v) to go from a higher or better position to a lower or worse one

to decline considerably, to decline dramatically, to decline sharply

to decline gradually, to decline slowly, to decline steadily

health declines, condition declines: *After the accident, her heath declined steadily.*

decline (v) to refuse

politely decline, absolutely decline

discrete (adj) having a clearly independent, individual or distinct shape or form

discrete from: *The psychologist's job is to try to make the fear-producing events discrete from ordinary events in the patient's mind.*

discrete mathematics, discrete variable, discrete methods

discretely (adv)

discreteness (n)

[Watch out! The word "discreet" (adjective) has the same sound, but a different meaning. "Discreet" means cautious, reserved or modest: *The actress was loved for her discreet behavior off screen.* The noun form is "discretion."]

draft (n) a piece of text which has undergone or needs further development

to make a draft, to prepare a draft, to draw up a draft: *The first step in writing a long research paper is to draw up a preliminary draft which will be extended and modified later.*

a final draft, a polished draft, a preliminary draft, a rough draft, a working draft

Unit 5

draft (v) to prepare a text; to put into writing
   to draft a letter, to draft a proposal, to draft a contract, to draft an essay
   carefully drafted, poorly drafted
draft (v) to choose from a group (military or sports)
draft (n) the selection of someone to serve a duty, such as military or sports.
   draft dodger [= a person who avoids being drafted for military duty]: *During the Vietnam War, many draft dodgers left the US to live in Canada.*
draft (n) a current of air that flows through an area such as a room
   to feel a draft: *It's cold in here. Do you feel a draft?*
enable (v) to make it possible for someone to achieve an aim
   to enable someone to do something: *The new computer software enables us to build web sites easily.*
enabler (n)
energy (n) the capacity to be physically and mentally active
   to dissipate one's energy; to sap someone's energy [= to take away energy]: *It is too hot today. The heat really saps my energy. I just can't work.*
   to be bursting with energy, to be full of energy
   to devote one's energy (to), to channel one's energy (to), to direct one's energy (to)
   to have the energy (to); to harness energy [= to control and make use of energy]: *It has been the dream of many scientists to learn how to harness the energy of the atom through fusion.*
   to waste energy, to save energy
   boundless energy, limitless energy; latent energy, youthful energy, creative energy
   (in) a burst of energy
energy (n) power or heat
   solar energy, atomic energy, nuclear energy
   conservation of energy; radiant energy, kinetic energy
   high-energy, high-energy particle
   an energy crisis, an energy shortage
   energy production, energy consumption
   energy needs, energy supply, energy demands
energize (v) to make something more active; to supply an electric current to something
   to energize the base [= to make members of a political party more active]: *Mr. Obama was very skillful at energizing the liberal base prior to the election.*
energized (adj)
enforce (v) to cause to be obeyed or accepted, especially when people are unwilling to accept it
   to rigidly enforce, to strictly enforce, to legally enforce
   to enforce the rules, to enforce the law
   difficult to enforce, impossible to enforce
enforcement (n)
   law enforcement
   strict enforcement, vigorous enforcement
enforceable (adj)
entity (n) something which exists apart from other things, having its own separate, self-contained existence
   to create an entity; to form an entity: *The two departments will combine to form a new entity.*
   a single entity, a separate entity, a discrete entity
   a political entity, a legal entity, a business entity
equivalent (adj) having the same amount, force, value, purpose, qualities, etc.
   equivalent to: *Synonyms are only approximately equivalent to each other.*
   equivalent in: *The two computers are equivalent in many of their features.*
equivalently (adv)
equivalent (n)
   an approximate equivalent, an exact equivalent
equivalency (n)
evolve (v) to develop, achieve or make gradually
   to evolve gradually, to evolve slowly, to evolve rapidly, to evolve over time

to continue to evolve
to evolve from
evolved (adj)
highly evolved, fully evolved
evolvement (n)
evolution (n)
to trace the evolution of
gradual evolution, rapid evolution, continuous evolution, natural evolution, peaceful evolution
cultural evolution, historical evolution, political evolution, social evolution
animal evolution, human evolution
evolution takes place, evolution occurs, evolution proceeds
evolutionist (n)
evolutional (adj)
evolutionary (adj)
expose (v) to show or reveal; to leave without protection
to expose as: *They intend to expose the wizard as a fraud.*
to expose to: *We were exposed to a great deal of interesting Middle East culture.*
exposed (adj)
to feel exposed, to become exposed, to some something exposed
completely exposed, fully exposed, increasingly exposed
exposed to: *The colors will fade if they are exposed to the sunlight.*
exposure (n) the act of showing or revealing; opening up to the light (in photography)
excessive exposure, low level exposure; great exposure, brief exposure, limited exposure
sun exposure
to reduce exposure, to limit exposure; to increase exposure, to maximize exposure
facilitate (v) to make possible or easier; to help bring about
to facilitate greatly, to further facilitate
to facilitate a meeting
designed to facilitate; help to facilitate
facility (n) a space or equipment for doing something
The university is interested in building a new basketball facility next year.
facility (n) the ability to learn something easily and well
(to have a) facility with: *She was hired because she has a facility with languages.*
facilitation (n)
facilitator (n)
fundamental (adj) forming the base, from which everything else originates; of central importance
to remain fundamental, to seem fundamental
truly fundamental, fairly fundamental, rather fundamental
fundamental to
fundamental (n) a basic principle
fundamentally (adv)
fundamentals (n. pl.) basics
let's get down to fundamentals
to teach the fundamentals, to learn the fundamentals: *Young German workers take classes at the same time that they work for companies where they learn the fundamentals of their trade.*
to go back to fundamentals, to return to fundamentals
one of the fundamentals of
generate (v) to cause to exist; to produce
to generate excitement, to generate enthusiasm
to generate wealth, to generate jobs, to generate revenue
to generate electricity, to generate energy
to randomly generate, to automatically generate
generation (n) something that has been produced
gas generation, energy generation, power generation; income generation

Unit 5

generation (n) all the people of a similar age within a society; all the offspring (in one step) of one ancestor within a particular family

a new generation (of); the coming generation, the future generation, the next generation

the former generation, the past generation, the preceding generation, the previous generation

a generation gap [= a space between generations]: *Businesses are working to bridge the generation gap in hopes of selling more products to older folks in addition to young people.*

Generation X, Generation Y, Millennial Generation, Generation Next, Net Generation

the baby boomer generation

from generation to generation; for a generation, for generations

generational (adj) of or relating to a particular generation

Government policies have shifted due to generational changes.

image (n) a picture in the mind of the form of something

to keep up an image, to live up to an image, to project an image: *In his new suit, he projects the image of a very important person.*

to clean up one's image, to polish one's image, to improve one's image: *You'll improve your image if you wear nicer clothes.*

public image: *Her public is image is of a woman who has no cares or worries.*

mirror image: *The letter b is the mirror image of the letter d.*

the spitting image [= appearing to be exactly the same]: *Eli is the spitting image of his dad.*

a positive image, a negative image, a clean-cut image

imagery (n)

powerful imagery, vivid imagery, popular imagery

to draw on imagery, to use imagery: *Shakespeare drew on imagery that was familiar to the common folks of his time.*

image (v)

liberal (adj) respecting and allowing many different types of beliefs or behavior

to hold liberal views, a liberal attitude

a liberal interpretation; a liberal education

remarkably liberal, relatively liberal, comparatively liberal

Liberal Democrats, Liberal Party

liberally (adv)

to apply liberally: *Apply this lotion to your skin liberally every morning and evening.*

liberalize (v)

to liberalize a policy, to liberalize the markets

liberalism (n)

liberal (adj) in a large amount; generous

a liberal dose of, liberal advice: *Rita gives liberal advice, even when no one really wants it.*

to be liberal with

license (n) [British: licence] permission or freedom to act or to own something

to grant a license, to issue a license, to renew a license

to apply for a license, to receive a license

to revoke a license, to suspend a license: *The judge wants to suspend her driver's license because she has had too many traffic tickets.*

a driver's license, a hunting license, a dog license, a marriage license; a license plate

license (v) [British licence] to give permission or freedom to act or to own something

licensed (adj)

licensed driver, licensed nurse, licensed plumber, licensed electrician

logic (n) a formal way of thinking or reasoning

to apply logic, to use logic

clear logic, cold logic, simple logic, false logic

deductive logic, inductive logic, formal logic

symbolic logic

logic in: *At first, their idea seems crazy, but there really is a logic in their plan.*

logical (adj)

it is logical to assume (that): *When you see dark, heavy clouds overhead, it is logical to assume that it is going to rain.*

logically (adv)

margin (n) the outer edge or limit of an area or action

(to win/to lose) by a narrow margin

to write in the margin(s): *I like to write notes in the margins of my books.*

at the margin, in the margin(s)

(by) a close margin, a slim margin, a wide margin, a clear margin, a narrow margin: *He won the election by a narrow margin.*

a margin of error, a margin of safety

a profit margin

marginal (adj)

a marginal performance

marginally (adv)

mental (adj) of or about the mind, involving emotional and intellectual response

to perform mental gymnastics [= to do difficult and complex thinking]: *I had to perform mental gymnastics to convince myself that Ivan was not really an idiot.*

to make a mental note [= to remember]: *That's an interesting idea. I'll make a mental note of it.*

one's mental state, mental age

mental illness, mental health, mental hospital, mental retardation

a mental block [= difficulty in thinking or remembering]: *I can't remember your name. I'm having a mental block.*

mentally (adv)

mentality (n)

monitor (v) to carefully watch or keep track of something

to closely monitor: *We will monitor the situation closely.*

to monitor the progress of

monitor (n) a device for observing, checking, or keeping records

heart monitor

computer monitor, video monitor

monitor shows, monitor detects

network (n) a large system of interconnected parts

communications network, road network, computer network, national network, local network

a network of friends, an old-boy network, an old-girl network: [= a network of the "insiders" who are support each other]: *After graduating from Yale, Caroline took advantage of the old-girl network in her search for a good-paying job.*

network (v) to form a system of interconnected parts

to network with each other

to network with the right people

notion (n) an individual's belief, idea or conception of something known, experienced, or imagined

to have a notion that, to entertain a notion, to dispel a notion. *I have a notion that it's going to rain.*

to have no notion, not have the faintest notion, not have the foggiest notion [= to have no notion]: *We do not have the foggiest notion of how the penguins got here.*

an abstract notion, a concrete notion

a vague notion, hazy notion: *I have only a hazy notion of how quantum mechanics works.*

odd notion, strange notion, an absurd notion

a slight notion, a preconceived notion, a widespread notion , a general notion

notional (adj)

objective (n) something which you plan to do or achieve

to meet an objective, to achieve an objective, to attain an objective, to gain an objective: *After many years of hard work, Hilary gained her objective of being elected to the school board.*

to formulate an objective, to set an objective, to state an objective

major objective, primary objective, realistic objective, worthy objective: *Improving the efficiency of government operations is a worthy objective, but we worry that the President has other motives.*

key objective, stated objective, clear objective, specific objective

Unit 5

an economic objective, a military objective, a political objective

a long-range objective, a short-range objective

the ultimate objective: *The ultimate objective in sports is to win.*

objective (adj) based on facts or conditions; not influenced by personal beliefs or feelings

to seem objective, (try) to remain objective

truly objective, completely objective, totally objective, as objective as possible

objective approach, objective assessment, objective criterion: A*n objective criterion for an educational app might be "includes feedback for correct answers." A subjective criterion, conversely, might be "is fun and engaging."*

objectively (adv)

to look at something objectively: *We need to look at the situation objectively before we make a decision.*

objectivity (n) the quality of being uninfluenced by personal beliefs or feelings

orient (v) to acquaint something to the surrounding situation or environment

to orient oneself to: *It will take us a while to orient ourselves to our new office.*

orientation (n)

oriented (adj) [British: orientated]

profit-oriented, career-oriented

Orient (n) the East (Asia)

Lionel plans to spend three months traveling throughout the Orient.

perspective (n) a particular way of considering something based on true relationships or relative importance

to put something into perspective; to put a new perspective on something: *When we found out that Mrs. Anazi was a silent partner in the company, that put a whole new perspective on the contract.*

the proper perspective, the right perspective, the true perspective

the wrong perspective, to have a distorted perspective, to lose perspective

new perspective, wider perspective, broader perspective

historical perspective, social perspective, political perspective, theoretical perspective

from a perspective of

in/into perspective: *I know we disagree, but let's try to put things into perspective.*

precise (adj) exactly stated; sharply defined in form, time, detail or description

precise about, precise in

extremely precise, fairly precise, reasonably precise, increasingly precise; precise enough

precisely (adv)

precision (n)

to demand precision, to call for precision, to require precision

(with) absolute precision, surgical precision, military precision

a high degree of precision, a high level of precision; a lack of precision

preciseness (n)

prime (adj) the chief or most important, or of the very best quality

prime time, prime real estate, prime rib

in the prime of one's life

prime minister

prime (n) the best part or best time of something

to come into one's prime, to reach one's prime: *The vineyard was planted twenty years ago and is just now coming into its prime.*

to be cut down in one's prime [= to be stopped in one's prime]

to be at your prime

the prime of one's life [= the time in one's life when one has the greatest power]: *Malcom was in the prime of his life when he met Harriet.*

prime (v) to make ready; to prepare

to prime the pump [= to make a well ready for use]: *You need to pour water into the pipes in order to prime the pump if you haven't used the well for a long time.*

to prime the pump [= to make an event ready for use]: *The goal of this partnership is to "prime the pump" for global social entrepreneurship, according to USAID.*

Unit 5

psychology (n) the scientific study of the mind and behavior
   use psychology on someone
   abnormal psychology, applied psychology, behavioral psychology, child psychology, developmental psychology, educational psychology, social psychology
psychological (adj)
   (to conduct) psychological warfare
psychologically (adv)
psychologist (n)
pursue (v) to chase after something
   to pursue a dream, to pursue a matter
   to pursue aggressively, pursue relentlessly, pursue doggedly; pursue patiently, pursue further
   to decide to pursue, intend to pursue, wish to pursue: *Do you wish to pursue this matter further?*
   to be able to pursue, to be at liberty to pursue, to be free to pursue
   not worth pursuing: *If you are not completely excited about your new idea, then it is not worth pursuing.*
pursuit (n)
   in hot pursuit [= chasing with the intent of not letting someone escape]: *The police do not need a search warrant if they are in hot pursuit of a suspected criminal.*
pursuer (n)
pursuant (adv) in accordance with a law; consistent
   pursuant to: *Pursuant to our agreement, you are required to remove the empty cardboard boxes.*
ratio (n) the relationship in quantity, amount or size which expresses how much more one thing is than the another
   at a ratio of ~ to ~: *Mix the ingredients at a ratio of one cup of solid to one gallon of liquid.*
   a direct ratio, an inverse ratio [= a relation between two quantities such that one increases in proportion as the other decreases]: *The volume of a gas is in inverse ratio to its pressure.*
   a ratio between: *We need to know the ratio between correct answers and incorrect answers.*
reject (v) to refuse to accept, consider, use, submit to or believe
   to reject completely, reject out of hand: *They didn't even listen to our proposal. They just rejected it out of hand.*
   to have the right to reject: *You have the right to reject my offer.*
   to reject on ~ grounds: *The legislation was rejected on economic grounds.*
   to reject ~ in favor of: *Cristo's design was rejected in favor of Monte's design.*
   firmly reject, emphatically reject, roundly reject, strongly reject, flatly reject
   reject demands, reject an offer
reject (n)
rejection (n)
   to fear rejection; to have a fear of rejection, (to suffer from) feelings of rejection
   to cope with rejection [= deal effectively with rejection]: *Teenagers often have difficulty coping with rejection and sometimes consider suicide as a result.*
   blanket rejection, outright rejection
revenue (n) the total income that a government or company receives regularly
   to generate revenue, to produce revenue, to raise revenue, to increase revenue
   annual revenue, weekly revenue, monthly revenue
   expected revenue, projected revenue, potential revenue; lost revenue
   revenue neutral [= income equals expenses]: *Congress will not pass the bill unless it is revenue neutral.*
   revenues drop, revenues rise, revenues hold steady
stable (adj) steady or firmly fixed; not likely to move or change
   to remain stable, to keep something stable, to feel stable, to look stable
   to be in stable condition: *The accident victim is in the hospital now and he is in stable condition.*
   a stable relationship: *They have been in a stable relationship for 15 years.*
   a stable marriage: *A stable marriage is good for raising children.*
   stable prices: *The economy benefits from stable prices.*
   a stable foundation: *You should build your life on a stable foundation.*
   perfectly stable, pretty stable, reasonably stable, remarkably stable

stably (adv)

stabilize (v)

stability (n)

style (n) a way of doing something or expressing oneself

to develop one's style, to polish one's style, to refine one's style

to lack style

to cramp someone's style [= to make it difficult for someone to do what they normally do]: *Don't get so close to me. You're cramping my style.*

to live in a grand style: *They are not as rich as they seem, but they live in a grand style.*

an affected style, classic style, elegant style, formal style, informal style, plain style, vigorous style

an aggressive style, an abrasive style: *He's loud and rude. In short, he has an abrasive style.*

high style; in style, out of style: *This leather jacket will never go out of style.*

classical style, traditional style, contemporary style

personal style, individual style, original style, distinctive style

a touch of style

style (v)

stylize (v)

stylized (adj)

a stylized version

substitute (n) something or someone that takes the place of another

to serve as a substitute for, to provide a substitute, to act as a substitute

an acceptable substitute, and adequate substitute

a good substitute, a satisfactory substitute, a reasonable substitute

a poor substitute: *Cramming for a test is a poor substitute for regular study.*

no substitute for: *There's no substitute for careful planning.*

substitute teacher: *Your substitute teacher for today is Mr. Burgess.*

substitution (n)

to make a substitution for

substitute (v) to put or use someone or something in the place of another

sustain (v) to keep something in existence; to give support or relief to

unable to sustain, able to sustain

no longer sustain: *The troops could no longer sustain the enemy's pounding.*

difficult to sustain, impossible to sustain, hard to sustain

sustain interest, sustain a relationship

to sustain an injury [= to get an injury]: *Amy sustained an injury to her shoulder during the volleyball game.*

sustainable (adj)

sustainable pace, sustainable future

sustainably (adv)

sustainability (n)

symbol (n) a sign, shape or object which is used to suggest or stand for something else

a chemical symbol, a religious symbol, a political symbol

a status symbol, a sex symbol

powerful symbol, clear symbol, universal symbol

linguistic symbol, geometric symbol, mathematical symbol, musical symbol, chemical symbol

a symbol of: *Please take this ring as a symbol of my love for you.*

symbolize (n)

to come to symbolize

symbolic (adj)

purely symbolic, highly symbolic, largely symbolic (of)

symbolically (adv)

symbolism (n)

full of symbolism: *This painting is full of religious symbolism.*

rich in symbolism

pagan symbolism, religious symbolism, political symbolism

Unit 5

target (n) a level or situation which you intend to achieve; something to shoot at or for
    to aim at a target, to hit a target, to shoot at a target, to destroy a target
    to miss a target, to overshoot a target
    a moving target; an easy target, an inviting target; a favorite target, a perfect target
    a sitting target [= not having protection]: *Alex had no chance to escape blame. He was a sitting target.*
    on target, off target, right on target
    an achievable target, a realistic target, a difficult target, an immediate target
target (v) to select as an object of attention or attack
    to target someone as; to carefully target, to deliberately target
    to be targeted for [= to be the object of attention]: *Most of our profits are targeted for capital improvements.*
targetable (adj)
transit (n) the movement of people or goods from one place to another
    mass transit, rapid transit; air transit, rail transit, road transit, sea transit
    in transit: *The goods were damaged in transit.*
    in transit between, in transit from, in transit from ~ to ~.
transit (v)
trend (n) a general development or change in a situation or in the way that people are behaving; a current style or preference
    to start a trend, to create a trend, to follow a trend
    to reverse a trend, to buck a trend [= to do the opposite of what is trendy]: *Pauline decided to buck the trend, so she deleted her Facebook page.*
    a noticeable trend, a general trend
    upward trend, downward trend
    a welcome trend, an unwelcome trend
    an economic trend, a political trend
    a trend towards
trend (v)
trendy (adj)
version (n) a particular account of something which varies from and contrasts with other forms of the same thing
    to give one's version; let's hear your version: *They told us what happened from their point of view, but let's hear your version.*
    a watered-down version; an uncut version
    latest version, current version, updated version, original version, final version
    the (un)official version; the (un)authorized version
    an oral version, a written version
    paper version, electronic version, interactive version, 3-D version
    a film version, movie version: *I didn't like the film version of that book.*
welfare (n) doing well physically, mentally and emotionally
    (to go, to be) on welfare
    to promote the general welfare, to improve the welfare, to lookout for the welfare (of)
    public welfare, child welfare, social welfare, animal welfare
    welfare state, welfare program, welfare services
    welfare spending, welfare benefits

Synonyms

adjust:	alter, change, adapt
academy:	institute, school
alter:	amend, revise, transform
amend:	revise, modify, change
aware:	mindful, conscious, knowing
capacity:	ability; volume; role
challenge:	dare, problem, provocation
compound:	combined, multiple, complex
conflict:	clash, fight, battle, struggle
consult:	ask, check, confer
contact:	meeting, touching, connecting
decline:	refuse; descend, decrease
discrete:	separate, different, distinct
draft:	plan, outline, sketch
enable:	empower, allow, facilitate
energy:	activity, force, power
enforce:	impose, pressure, administer
entity:	thing, object
equivalent:	alike, identical, same
evolve:	develop, change, adapt
expose:	uncover, show, reveal
facilitate:	enable, assist, help
fundamental:	basic, central, essential
generate:	develop, create, produce
generation:	life period
image:	picture, likeness, depiction
liberal:	generous, tolerant, open
license:	permission, approval, authorization
logic:	argument, reasoning, thought
margin:	border, frame, edge
mental:	intellectual, psychological, cerebral
monitor:	oversee, track, observe
network:	organization, system, web
notion:	idea, view, thought
objective:	unbiased, fair, neutral
orient:	locate, situate, familiarize
perspective:	viewpoint, angle, outlook
precise:	exact, specific, clear
prime:	main, principal, chief
psychology:	mind, mindset, mentality
pursue:	chase, follow, hunt
ratio:	proportion, fraction
reject:	refuse, decline, disapprove
revenue:	income, profit, earning
stable:	fixed, firm, steady, solid
style:	fashion; design; trend
substitute:	exchange, alternate, replace
sustain:	support, maintain, encourage
symbol:	sign, mark, token
target:	goal, aim, objective
transit:	transport, passage, travel
trend:	tendency, direction, inclination
version:	variation, arrangement, rendition
welfare:	benefit, assistance, relief

Unit 5

Answers

Definitions

1.	psychology	16.	aware	31.	discrete	46.	challenge
2.	ratio	17.	mental	32.	fundamental	47.	network
3.	draft	18.	stable	33.	liberal	48.	expose
4.	enable	19.	adjust	34.	symbol	49.	margin
5.	generate	20.	enforce	35.	perspective	50.	target
6.	monitor	21.	reject	36.	revenue	51.	academy
7.	contact	22.	prime	37.	consult	52.	conflict
8.	welfare	23.	precise	38.	facilitate	53.	decline
9.	transit	24.	equivalent	39.	pursue	54.	substitute
10.	compounded	25.	logic	40.	capacity		
11.	licensed	26.	energy	41.	image		
12.	oriented	27.	style	42.	objective		
13.	entity	28.	amend	43.	trend		
14.	alteration	29.	evolve	44.	notion		
15.	generation	30.	sustain	45.	version		

Parts of Speech

1. academic / academically	12. declined / decline	23. fundamental / fundamentally	34. notion / notion
2. adjustable / adjusting	13. discrete / discrete	24. generation / generated	35. objectives / objectively
3. alterable / alter	14. drafted / draft	25. generation / generation	36. orientation / oriented
4. amendment / amended	15. enable / enables	26. images / images	37. perspective / perspective
5. awareness / aware	16. energized / energy	27. liberally / liberal	38. precise / precisely
6. capacity / capacity	17. enforced / enforced	28. license / licenses	39. prime / prime
7. challenged / challenges challenges	18. entity / entities	29. logic / logically	40. psychology / psychological
8. compounded / compounds	19. equivalent / equivalent	30. marginal / margin	41. pursued / pursuing
9. conflicts / conflicts	20. evolved / evolution	31. mentally / mental	42. ratio / ratio
10. consulted / consultation	21. exposed / exposed	32. monitored / monitors	43. rejection / rejected
11. contact / contacted	22. facilitated / facilitator	33. networked / networking	44. revenue / revenues

45. stability / stable	49. symbols / symbolic	53. versions / version
46. style / style	50. target / targeted	54. welfare / welfare
47. substitute / substituted	51. transits / transit	
48. sustains / sustaining	52. trend / trendy	

Unit 5

Answers

<table>
<tr><td colspan="2">Collocations</td></tr>
<tr><td>Exercise 1</td><td>Exercise 2</td><td>Exercise 3</td><td>Exercise 4</td></tr>
<tr>
<td>

1. academic
   academy
   academy
2. drafted
   draft
   drafted
3. liberal
   liberal
   liberalize
4. adjustment
   adjusted
   adjusted
5. energy
   energize
   energy
6. marginal
   margins
   margin
7. psychological
   psychology
8. alter
   alteration
   alterations
9. sustain
   sustained
10. welfare
    welfare

</td>
<td>

1. aware
   awareness
   aware
2. enforced
   enforcement
   enforce
3. image
   imagery
4. notion
   notion
   notion
5. revenue/~s
   revenue/~s
   revenue
6. version
   version
   version
7. capacity
   capacity
   capacity
8. logic
   logical
9. monitored
   monitor
10. stable
    stable

</td>
<td>

1. style
   stylized/stylish
   style
2. evolved
   evolved
   evolution
3. rejected
   rejected
   rejection
4. challenge
   challenges
   challenge
5. exposed
   exposed
   exposure
6. symbol
   symbolize
   symbols
   / symbolic
7. contact
   contact
   contacted
8. generate
   generated
   generating
9. objectives
   objective
   objectively
10. perspective
    perspective
    perspective

</td>
<td>

1. target
   targeted
   target
2. conflict
   conflict
   conflicts
3. generations
   generations
   generation
4. precision
   precision
   precision
5. transit
   transit
   transit
6. declined
   decline
   declining
7. entities
   entity
   entity
8. substitute
   substitutes/~ed
   substitute
9. pursue
   pursuing
   pursue
10. consulted
    consulted
    consulting

</td>
</tr>
</table>

Unit 5

Answers

<table>
<tr><td colspan="2">Synonyms (Crossword)</td></tr>
<tr><td>Across</td><td>Down</td></tr>
<tr><td>

2. revenue
5. ratio
9. target
10. evolve
11. facilitate
14. prime
15. consult
16. enable
17. entity
19. precise
20. margin
24. capacity
27. license
28. energy
29. aware
31. style
33. trend
34. enforce
35. monitor

</td><td>

1. liberal
2. reject
3. notion
4. equivalent
6. substitute
7. challenge
8. decline
12. stable
13. academy
18. orient
21. generate
22. discrete
23. welfare
25. adjust
26. image
30. draft
32. logic

</td></tr>
</table>

<table>
<tr><td colspan="3">Review</td></tr>
<tr><td>

1. fundamental
2. adjusted
3. stable
4. mental
5. discrete
6. aware
7. liberal
8. precise
9. prime
10. challenge
11. conflict
12. entity
13. notion
14. image
15. psychology
16. trend
17. symbol
18. alteration

</td><td>

19. target
20. perspective
21. revenue
22. generation
23. evolution
24. margin
25. academy
26. capacity
27. compound
28. network
29. ratio
30. equivalent
31. welfare
32. transit
33. version
34. draft
35. logic
36. energy

</td><td>

37. style
38. license
39. objective
40. expose
41. contact
42. orient
43. sustain
44. enable
45. amend
46. reject
47. generate
48. consult
49. facilitate
50. substitute
51. decline
52. pursue
53. enforce
54. monitor

</td></tr>
</table>

Unit 6

Word List

n = noun   **v** = verb   **adj** = adjective   **adv** = adverb   **prep** = preposition

abstract (n)
- abstract (v)
- abstract (adj)
- abstractly (adv)

accurate (adj)
- accurately (adv)
- accuracy (n)

acknowledge (v)
- acknowledgement (n)

aggregate (n)
- aggregate (v)
- aggregate (adj)
- aggregation (n)

allocate (v)
- allocation (n)

assign (v)
- assignment (n)
- assignable (adj)

attach (v)
- attachment (n)
- attached (adj)

bond (n)
- bond (v)

brief (adj)
- briefly (adv)
- brief (n)
- briefing (n)
- brevity (n)
- brief (v)

capable (adj)
- capably (adv)
- cabability (n)

cite (v)
- citation (n)

cooperate (v)
- cooperation (n)
- cooperative (adj)
- cooperatively (adv)

discriminate (v)
- discrimination (n)
- discriminatory (adj)
- discriminate (adj)
- discriminative (adj)
- discriminatively (adv)
- discriminately (adv)

display (n)
- display (v)

diverse (adj)
- diversely (adv)
- diversify (v)
- diversity (n)

domain (n)

edit (v)
- edit (n)
- edition (n)
- editor (n)

enhance (v)
- enhancement (n)

exceed (v)
- exceeding (adj)
- exceedingly (adv)

expert (adj)
- expertly (adv)
- expert (n)
- expertise (n)

explicit (adj)
- explicitly (adv)
- explicitness (n)

federal (adj)
- federally (adv)

fee (n)

flexible (adj)
- flexibly (adv)
- flexibility (n)
- flex (v)
- flex (n)

furthermore (adv)

ignorant (adj)
- ignorantly (adv)
- ignore (v)
- ignorance (n)

incorporate (v)
- incorporation (n)

index (n)
- index (v)

inhibit (v)
- inhibition (n)
- inhibitor (n)
- inhibited (adj)
- inhibitory (adj)

initiate (v)
- initiation (n)
- initiation (n)
- initiative (n)

input (n)
- input (v)
- input (adj)

instruct (v)
- instruction (n)
- instructive (adj)

intelligence (n)
- intelligent (adj)
- intelligently (ad)
- intelligible (adj)
- intelligibly (adv)

interval (n)

lecture (n)
- lecture (v)
- lecturer (n)

migrate (v)
- migration (n)
- migratory (adj)

minimum (adj)
- minimal (adj)
- minimally (adj)
- minimum (n)
- minimalize (v)

ministry (n)
- minister (n)
- ministerial (adj)
- minister (v)

motive (n)
- motivate (v)
- motivated (adj)
- motivation (n)
- motivational (adj)
- motivationally (adv)

neutral (adj)
- neutrally (adv)
- neutrality (n)
- neutralize (v)

nevertheless (adv)

precede (v)
- precedence (n)
- precedent (n)

presume (v)
- presumption (n)
- presumable (adj)
- presumably (adv)
- presumptuous (adj)

rational (adj)
- rationally (adv)
- rationalize (v)
- rationalization (n)
- rationale (n)

recover (v)
- recovery (n)
- recoverable (adj)

reveal (v)
- revelation (n)
- revealing (adv)

scope (n)
- scope (v)

subsidy (n)
- subsidize (v)

tape (n)
- tape (v)

trace (n)
- trace (v)

transform (v)
- transformation (n)
- transformational (adj)
- transformative (adj)

transport (n)
- transport (v)

underlie (v)
- underlying (adj)

utilize (v)
- utility (n)

Unit 6

Definitions Use the definition clues to write the correct words in the blanks.

1.	to give out as a task *The teacher _____ every student a new book to read.*	presumed assigned instructed migrated utilized exceeded
2.	to be greater or superior *The fund-raiser _____ its target of raising $10,000.*	
3.	to give instruction in a methodical way *The technician _____ everyone on how to use the new copy machine.*	
4.	the range or area covered by a given activity or thought *The _____ of Hugo's knowledge of history was vast.*	input fee scope interval motive bond
5.	something that unites or holds things together *The soldiers formed a strong _____ with each other.*	
6.	an amount of money paid for a service or privilege *We paid a small _____ to buy our tickets on line.*	
7.	formed in the mind, not in the physical world; theoretical *"Equal opportunity" is an _____ idea that has real-world consequences.*	inhibited diverse flexible federal minimum abstract
8.	a form of government in which individual states are united under a central authority *According to _____ regulations, certain industries are required to limit the amount of pollution they create.*	
9.	representing the smallest amount or degree *The _____ delivery charge is $5.00.*	
10.	to move from one region or country to another *Birds _____ to warm regions in the winter.*	migrate incorporate acknowledge motivate instruct allocate
11.	to unite or blend something with something else that already exists *As he writes, he likes to _____ poetry into his prose.*	
12.	to set something apart for a specific purpose *You should _____ about $30 per person for the wedding dinner.*	
13.	something that makes reference easy; a list of alphabetized items *The author was not listed in the _____ .*	expert index display trace domain ministry
14.	an area, especially one over which rule or control is exercised *The Congo was once part of the _____ of Belgium.*	
15.	something that is presented or held up to view or made evident *There is a beautiful _____ of Korean art at the museum.*	

Unit 6

16. however; in spite of that *We ran out of food and water. _____, we continued to climb the mountain.* 17. in addition; moreover *She locked herself in her study and refused to answer her phone. _____, she told the butler that she was not to be disturbed.* 18. taking a short amount of time *Do you want to know what I thought of the movie? _____, it was awesome!*	Briefly Diversely Federally Minimum Nevertheless Furthermore
19. to recognize the existence or, reality of, rights, authority, or status of *First, I want to _____ that I received your email.* 20. to modify, adapt or alter in order to make suitable or acceptable *As you _____ your paper, check it for spelling.* 21. to start something going by taking the first step *If we _____ the work of cleaning up the park, I'm sure others will follow us.*	initiate precede acknowledge transform display edit
22. having or exercising the ability to reason or understand; sane *It is sometimes hard to make a _____ decision when it comes to buying a new car.* 23. very skilled or very knowledgeable *You can trust her _____ advice buying clothes.* 24. belonging to neither side in a controversy *Teachers should stay _____ when they listen to students' arguments during the debates.*	rational revealing brief abstract expert neutral
25. to hold back, restrain or discourage from freely doing something *Nothing _____ her from saying what she thinks.* 26. to assume as being true in the absence of proof to the contrary *Henry doesn't ask if he can talk with me. He simply _____ that I have the time and the desire.* 27. to put to use, especially in a practical way *Thornton always _____ all of the data I give him to make good decisions.*	presumes inhibits exceeds cites utilizes migrates
28. a visible mark or evidence left by something that has passed *There was a _____ of gunpowder on her fingers.* 29. a space of time between two objects, points, events or states *Everyone went to get a refreshment during the _____ between Act 1 and Act 2.* 30. something put into a system to achieve output or a result *The city council will receive _____ from interested parties before it makes its decision.*	tape input interval display trace bond

Unit 6

31. exact in performance or amount; free from error *We need a reasonably _____ estimate as to the cost.* 32. differing one from another *Typically, ESL classes are culturally _____.* 33. having capacity or ability *Jan is _____ of running the marathon.*	abstract diverse capable minimum ignorant accurate
34. to carry from one place to another; to carry away *Ships _____ goods more cheaply than trains do.* 35. to improve the value, beauty or desirability of something *Usually, frames _____ the beauty of pictures.* 36. to quote as an authority or example *Don't forget to _____ the source of every quote that you use in your essay.*	reveal incorporate discriminate transport cite enhance
37. a speech given to an audience or a class for the purpose of instruction *Did you enjoy Professor Delaney's _____ on the search for the Higgs boson?* 38. a continuous, narrow band or strip of material *Chaz put a _____ around the cut on his hand.* 39. a person, thing or act through which something is served or accomplished, especially in a religious or governmental capacity *Marna worked for the health _____ before getting a job in the private sector.*	tape lecture motive ministry display bond
40. capable of changing; yielding to influence *You need to be more _____ and willing to listen to the other side of the story.* 41. having the ability to acquire and apply knowledge and understanding *Many _____ people go to college to prepare themselves for a better life.* 42. without knowledge, awareness or education *People who are _____ of Islam incorrectly assume that many Muslims are terrorists.*	intelligent transformed flexible diverse ignorant allocated
43. to come, exist or occur before or in front of *Let me _____ my lecture with a little story.* 44. to work together for a common purpose *More work gets done when we _____ well.* 45. to be the support, foundation or basis of *The reasons that _____ your argument are interesting but not very convincing.*	precede tape input underlie cooperate enhance

46. a gift of money, usually from a government, to support a person or group *Thanks to the generous _____, the banks were able to stay in business.*	motive subsidy recovery index subsidy display
47. getting back to an original position or state *The doctors said Eva should make a complete _____ within a few days.*	
48. the reason for acting in a particular way *What was Peggy's _____ for wanting us to hire Sal?*	
49. to greatly change the appearance or structure of something *It didn't take long to _____ the little mountain town into a popular ski village.*	discriminate motivate cooperate enhance transform reveal
50. to make something known which has been hidden or kept secret *Tonight, we will _____ the super hero's true identity.*	
51. to make a clear distinction; to make a difference in treatment *Most well-educated people know that it is wrong to _____ against minority groups.*	
52. fully revealed and clearly expressed, leaving nothing implied *Rachel gave us _____ instructions on how to write our research papers.*	explicit attached aggregate discriminated diverse federal
53. joined to, fastened to or secured to *I couldn't open up the files that were _____ to the email.*	
54. combined; considered as a whole *Lara worked at three jobs. Her _____ income was still not enough for her to buy a house.*	

Unit 6

Parts of Speech

Write the parts of speech (noun, verb, adjective or adverb form).
Word Forms: Be careful with nouns and verbs:
      Some *nouns* might need to be plural (~s).
      Some *verbs* might need ~s, ~ed, ~ing.

abstract
1. I want you to give me a concrete example rather than an _____ .

    Let's talk about actual events. Let's not talk _____.

accurate
2. Before you hand in your quiz, check it for _____.

    Amy can _____ name all of the countries of Africa.

acknowledge
3. Beth was grateful for the _____ of her hard work.

    Finally, Erwin _____ that Ursula had helped him.

aggregate
4. No one wanted the _____ of the independent departments into one centralized office.

    Before she died, Quinn _____ a fortune in rare coins.

allocate
5. The _____ of representatives to the congress is based on the population in each region of the country.

    How much money has been _____ for research?

assign
6. You can finish your new _____ in less than a week.

    Yesterday, the instructor _____ more work than usual.

attach
7. Claudia felt a strong _____ to her nieces and nephews.

    Two blank pages were _____ to the document.

bond
8. It is healthy to have strong family _____.

    Over the years, the brothers _____ over their mutual interest in baseball.

brief
9. At the end of your speech, you should _____ summarize your main points.

    During her visit, she _____ mentioned her new job.

capable
10. The new captain quite _____ took over leadership of the team.

    Young Henry has the _____ to become a great engineer one of these days.

cite
11. Lionel _____ more than twenty sources in his essay.

    In the "works cited" section of your research paper, every _____ must be listed in alphabetical order.

cooperate   12. The witnesses are _____ with the police in every way.

The US worked in full _____ with the United Nations.

discriminate   13. In some areas, Blacks are still _____ against.

It is against the law to practice _____ when hiring new employees.

display   14. Some Americans advertise their patriotism by _____ the flag in front of their homes.

The department store puts many different _____ in its windows throughout the year.

diverse   15. London has a _____ population.

Cultural _____ does not exist in some countries.

domain   16. Barbara is an expert in the _____ of literature and art.

The Pope helped Spain expand its _____ in the New World.

edit   17. In today's _____ of the New York Times, there is a story about religion in sports.

Todd _____ his paper carefully before he handed it in.

enhance   18. A beautiful garden can _____ the value of a home.

Dr. Li said that gingko is good for memory _____.

exceed   19. Karen could not carry her suitcase on to the plane because it _____ the size limitation.

Last night's sunset was _____ beautiful.

expert   20. We talked to several _____ before we made our final decision.

The small company is famous for its _____ designed and perfectly constructed furniture.

explicit   21. They gave us _____ directions on how to get to their house, but we still got lost.

I _____ told you not to invite Helen to the party.

federal   22. _____ law requires us to collect sales tax.

Should health insurance be _____ mandated for all citizens?

Unit 6

fee 23. Yuki charges different _____ to different students for her tutoring them.

The accountant charged only a small _____ to seniors who needed help with their income taxes.

flexible 24. You can get cheap airline tickets if your dates are _____ .

It would be easier to work with you if you would show a little more _____ .

furthermore 25. Please take me off your phone list, and _____ , stop sending me email.

Religious sentiments can spread beyond the church. For example, even some non-church members share the values of Christianity. _____ religion tends to integrate a whole range of values of God.

ignorant 26. People who work in the public sector sometimes have to put up with rude and _____ customers.

_____ of the law is not an excuse.

incorporate 27. Mr. Li noted that Shenzhen's bid to _____ the nearby Bao'an County had been supported by the Guangdong authorities.

Bremer did not believe that the _____ of the Baath party into mainstream government would be a good idea.

index 28. The Hang Seng _____ fell by 250 points.

One of the best parts of the book is the thorough _____ .

inhibit 29. Radiation _____ the spoilage of vegetables.

He recounted all the details of his youthful days in California without _____ .

initiate 30. Lumumba complicated the UN's mission by _____ small "wars" with the secessionist province of Katanga.

Social workers should take the _____ rather than be passive when dealing with certain cases.

input 31. We would like to hear your _____ on this matter.

Public _____ influenced the council's decision.

instruct 32. Mr. Deng gave _____ that certain items be discussed.

It is _____ to recall what happened in 1987.

intelligent 33. Kendra is admired for her beauty and her _____ .

He surrounded himself with highly _____ men.

Unit 6

interval 34. We'll check back with you at regular _____.

Miami and Kansas City were tied 17-17 at the _____.

lecture 35. Dr. Soelberg is a senior _____ at Harvard Law School.

All three _____ will be recorded and put on line.

migrate 36. The family had _____ to Canada several years earlier.

In summer, _____ workers lived five and six to a room.

minimum 37. If you only pay the _____ amount on your credit card bill, you will end up paying an extra $50 for this purchase.

I don't mean to _____ the problem, but do we really need to deal with it right now?

ministry 38. Which _____ does your mother work for?

One of the foreign _____ was caught spying.

motive 39. We think their offer is politically _____.

Candidates will be chosen based on previous experience and demonstrated _____.

neutral 40. Judges are required to remain _____ as they listen to lawyers on both sides.

We tried without success to _____ the effects of the overdose.

nevertheless 41. it may seem difficult to envision any definitive resolution of the problem of ownership and control, there are _____ certain suggestions which seem to be in order.

The temperature dropped to below zero. _____, the soldiers marched on towards Moscow.

precede 42. The CEO's actions set a very bad _____.

From the _____ remarks, it is clear that there can be no agreement on this issue.

presume 43. Solar activity could _____ bring periods of flood or drought.

The _____ proved to be false.

rational 44. Mr. Patten reacted calmly and _____ to our proposal.

Even _____ people can get emotional sometimes.

Unit 6

recover   45. Jim's wife is _____ nicely after the operation.

The _____ rate for recyclable paper is quite high.

reveal   46. Officials _____ that there were 890 wounded soldiers.

The police do not want to _____ the identity of the suspect at this time.

scope   47. It is not within the _____ of this report to explain the consequences in great detail.

There is plenty of _____ for expansion of mining operations in this region.

subsidy   48. The corporation has refused to continue _____ fresh fruit brought in from South America.

We can no longer afford heavy _____ for many hospital services.

tape   49. The show was _____ and will be shown later this month.

We found a box of old audio and video _____ in the garage.

trace   50. His new approach to painting was directly _____ to his visit, in 1885, to the Rijksmuseum in Amsterdam.

The drug test turned up _____ of cannabis.

transform   51. Advances in artificial intelligence will _____ medical diagnosis when computers begin to assist doctors in the exam room.

Jenkins made a remarkable _____ from an ordinary gardener to an extraordinary landscape designer.

transport   52. Trucks need a special license for _____ hazardous materials on interstate highways.

Unfortunately, air _____ is too expensive, so we will have to settle for rail.

underlie   53. Researchers have come to assume that the neuronal changes which _____ the neurosis are functional and reversible.

There was no challenge to the _____ principles upon which our argument rested.

utilize   54. The new arrangement led to a better _____ of our time and resources.

Wise people _____ the expertise of the people who surround them.

Unit 6

Collocations

In each group of sentences, write *one* word from the list which goes with the **highlighted collocations**. Be careful with word forms.

Exercise 1	edit presume diverse precede domain enhance
	accurate inhibit index allocation acknowledge aggregate

1. All of the guesses were **reasonably** _____.

   Maria writes in English with **a high degree of** grammatical _____.

   We have come **to question the** _____ of Judd's statement.

2. The US is a very **culturally** _____ country.

   To be safe, you should _____ **your investment portfolio.**

   Wolves need to be protected **to maintain their genetic** _____.

3. The **cost-of-living** _____ is starting to rise again.

   All of the **titles are** _____ at the back of the book.

   The librarians are **compiling an** _____ of the rare manuscripts.

4. In the months that **immediately** _____ the war, tensions mounted.

   I know you are busy, but your school work should **take** _____.

   This court case could **set an important** _____ for similar cases that may follow.

5. The unhappy losers **privately** _____ that they had made mistakes.

   We finally **received an** _____ of our application letter.

   Last night, the mayor **publically** _____ that she had misappropriated the funds.

6. Be sure to _____ **the draft** before you hand it in.

   When will they **publish the next** _____ **of your book**?

   The **managing** _____ will retire next year.

7. His fear of heights _____ him **from** hiking in the mountains.

   She **feels rather** _____ **about** having her picture taken.

   He tried **to get over his** _____ **about** voicing his opinions.

8. I don't _____ **to know** everything about teaching grammar.

   People forget that the accused person is _____ **innocent until proven guilty**.

   Our actions are **based on the** _____ **that** we will have enough money to last through the end of the month.

9. The **budget** _____ **was reduced** by 10%.

   More money was _____ **for** local charities.

10. Book sales were **greatly** _____ **by** Oprah's recommendation.

    These reforms are **designed to** _____ operations of the market.

- 179 -

Unit 6

Collocations

Exercise 2	initiate rational assign recover input expert
	exceed instruction attach subsidy intelligence reveal

1. The students were _____ **homework** over the weekend.

   They raced **to finish the** _____ before the football game started.

   The socialist experiment in Malaysia has been _____ **to the dustbin of history**.

2. The donations have already _____ **our expectations**.

   Around here, high winter temperatures **rarely** _____ 5° C.

   Quentin is writing a novel that is **likely to** _____ 500 pages.

3. Don't forget to _____ **the file** before you send the email.

   Brendan is more **emotionally** _____ **to** his dogs than to his children.

   Patrice **developed a romantic** _____ **to** Will.

4. It would be better if we **called in an** _____ to fix the problem for us.

   They gave us some _____ **advice** on how to paint our house.

   Jason **lacks** _____ in using a word processor.

5. The tutor **provided advanced** _____ in algebra.

   Stay here and **wait for further** _____.

   She was good at **carrying out** _____ **to the letter**.

6. Ned **never fully** _____ **from** his financial losses.

   It's going **to take a long time to** _____ **from** the marathon run.

   I think we are **on the road to** _____ now.

7. Einstein was a man of **considerable** _____.

   Someday, **artificial** _____ will surpass that of humans.

   She spoke so softly that her words were **barely** _____.

8. No one could _____ **the identity of** the Secret Santa.

   His sly remarks were **rather** _____.

   The WikiLleaks documents were full of **embarrassing** _____.

9. There must be **a perfectly** _____ **explanation** for Ben's behavior.

   That **seems quite** _____ **to** me.

10. Suddenly, I was _____ **into the world of** glamor.

    The _____ **ceremony** lasted more than one hour.

Unit 6

Collocations

Exercise 3	ministry fee brief bond tape lecture
	flexible migrate trace scope interval motive

1. It is important that the legislation **have a narrow** _____.

    Several techniques can be used **to broaden your** _____.

    The police decided **to widen the** _____ of the investigation.

2. There was peace in the kingdom, except **during a brief** _____.

    After a short _____, the buzzing sound started again.

    We generally meet at **monthly** _____.

3. Thomas felt **a strong spiritual** _____ with the rabbi.

    Athletes often **form** _____ **of friendship** with their team mates.

    The sisters were **linked by an emotional** _____.

4. Is it OK if I _____ **this interview**?

    Listen to the sentence, then **pause the** _____ and write as much as you can remember.

    We know you are lying because we **have everything on** _____.

5. **During the boring** _____, many students fell asleep.

    As Dan was growing up, his parents often _____ him **about** the evils of drinking and smoking.

    Today, our **visiting** _____ is Dr. Ruth Harris.

6. **For a small** _____, members' guests may use the swimming pool.

    The accountant **charged a modest** _____ to do our taxes.

    The **membership** _____ are $50.00.

7. Our aunt **is fairly** _____ **about** when we can visit her.

    Next week, I **have a completely** _____ **schedule**.

    They did not **demonstrate sufficient** _____ during the meeting.

8. When you speak at the meeting, please **keep it** _____.

    The President **received a detailed** _____ before traveling to Korea.

    The key information is _____ **summarized** in this report.

9. The explosion **left faint** _____ **of** various agricultural chemicals.

    Georgiana packed her bags and **left without a** _____.

    Luckily, the investigators **were able to** _____ **the phone call**.

10. The Ruby-Throated Hummingbird _____ **from** North America **to** as far south as Panama **for the winter**.

    The **seasonal** _____ of some whales is poorly understood.

Unit 6

Collocations

Exercise 4	motive ignorant minimum cooperate input display capable explicit cite neutral discriminate transform

1. It is illegal to _____ **against** gays and lesbians at this university.

    In the past, African Americans **faced racial** _____ in the US.

    The present law _____ **unfairly against** women.

2. The neighbors **appeared blissfully** _____ **about** the burglary next door.

    The huge billboard on our street is **difficult to** _____.

    It was foolish to think that the warning signs **could be safely** _____.

3. Personally, I would **question** Marissa's _____ for wanting to housesit for you.

    Alex seems **to lack the** _____ to go look for a job.

    The coach **made a** _____ **speech** that helped the team win the game.

4. Haussmann's efforts **radically** _____ Paris within a few years.

    Teenagers can't **be** _____ **overnight** into rational adults.

    After winning the lottery, Janet **underwent an amazing** _____.

5. General Motors **agreed to fully** _____ **with** the government on the restructuring.

    Mexico is **willing to** _____ **with** the US to stop drug trafficking.

    With Turkey's **full** _____, the UN was able to help the refugees.

6. The "sold" sign was **clearly** _____ in the window.

    In the parade, the army **put on an impressive** _____ of its power.

    My car **is beginning to** _____ signs of old age.

7. While Jo and Tony fought, I tried **to take a** _____ **position**.

    It was difficult for Switzerland **to maintain** _____ during the war.

    This acid will **effectively** _____ **the effects of** the alkaline in the concrete.

8. A lack of interest **was** _____ **as the reason** for closing the park.

    All of the **previously** _____ studies have one thing in common.

    She didn't realize she had to _____ every **source** that she used in her paper.

9. Roger **seems perfectly** _____ **of** taking care of the children.

    Vernon **demonstrated** his _____ of running the business.

10. We tried **to keep** our energy consumption **to a bare** _____.

    Mr. Larkin was not happy earning _____ **wages** at the fast food restaurant.

Unit 6

Synonyms Use the synonym clues to solve this crossword puzzle.

Across
4. suppose, assume, guess
9. begin, start, activate
10. however, nonetheless, still
11. bendable, changeable
14. prejudge, discern, distinguish
16. least, smallest, lowest
17. improve, enrich, better
19. able, competent, effectual
22. exhibit, show, demonstrate
24. talk, speech, address
25. join, bind, cement
27. logical, sensible, reasonable
28. smart, knowing, thinking
29. use, apply, employ
30. direct, well-defined

Down
1. show, uncover, expose
2. range, extent, reach
3. change, convert, alter
5. short, concise, fleeting
6. gap, break, pause
7. varied, mixed, assorted
8. reason, purpose, inspiration
12. teach, inform, tutor
13. go beyond, outdo, surpass
15. prevent, restrain, suppress
18. designate, assign, allot
20. collect, combine, assemble
21. master, specialist, authority
23. theoretical, conceptual, hypothetical
26. mention, quote, refer to

Unit 6

Review

1. We don't think he was _____ of acting alone.		explicit
		neutral
2. In an effort to be strictly _____ , we listened to both sides carefully.		minimum
		capable
		dangerous
3. He gave us directions, but he wasn't _____ enough. We got lost!		diverse

4. There must be a _____ explanation for her behavior.		ignorant
		neutral
		rational
5. We need to be more _____ in our demands, and know that we might have to give up something if we have to.		instructional
		minimum
6. There are _____ requirements for joining the military.		flexible

7. She does a fairly _____ job of reporting on the Middle East.		rational
		accurate
		abstract
8. The law limits the use of _____ funds in this situation.		federal
		diverse
9. Professor Jones enjoys lecturing to _____ audiences.		brief

10. Professor Langston was more comfortable working with concrete, solid materials than with _____ mental images.		abstract
		nevertheless
		capable
11. You have to pay back the money; _____ , you must apologize.		furthermore
		rational
12. He's somewhat greedy. He is, _____ , very kind to everyone.		dangerous

13. There was a _____ of lipstick on his collar.		attachment
		trace
14. He was admired for his great _____ and wisdom.		intelligence
		abstract
15. Over the years, they formed a _____ of friendship.		bond
		display

16. They need to be liberated from poverty, _____ and hunger.		ignorance
		display
		edition
17. Just after sunset, there was a huge _____ of fireworks at the stadium.		input
		fee
18. We asked for everyone's _____ so that we would be able to make the right decision.		incentive

Unit 6

Review

19. The clerk put a big piece of _____ around the package to make it more secure.	bond
20. She gave us a lengthy _____ on how to behave properly.	expert
	ministry
	display
	tape
21. They demolished the defense _____ , then proceeded to attack the President's palace.	lecture

22. He considers himself to be an _____ on wine.	input
	expert
23. The government reported that the _____ of prices reported by farmers rose by ten percent.	index
	lecture
24. Concrete is an _____ of stone, sand and cement.	inhibition
	aggregate

25. The elderly doctor saw patients for a nominal _____ .	scope
	abstract
26. They changed their minds during the brief _____ between the first and second meetings.	allocation
	interval
	fee
27. The size and _____ of the programs have been limited.	display

28. The school has been encouraged to make better use of its _____ of outside funds.	intelligence
	allocation
	attachment
29. They sent it as an _____ to the e-mail.	ministry
30. The king has full _____ over all the lands north of here.	subsidy
	domain

31. We will not _____ to speak for all Americans on this topic.	inhibit
	transport
32. With an eye to the future, several principles should _____ the new regional policy.	cooperate
	underlie
	presume
33. Fear of embarrassment can _____ a student's willingness to speak up in class.	transform

34. Every winter, millions of birds _____ to Mexico.	assign
	migrate
35. Success in a career in architecture depends on the ability to _____ visual imagery.	enhance
	utilize
	aggregate
36. By working harder, they tried to materially _____ their lives.	enhance

Unit 6

Review

37. Economists _____ consumer confidence as being the most important factor for the stability of the economy.		cite presume initiate incorporate discriminate brief
38. We need to _____ the newly arrived committee members on what we have done so far.		
39. It is unfair to _____ against individuals because they are old.		
40. The judge asked the lawyer to _____ the source of his information.		recover motivate migrate reveal transform initiate
41. They wanted to _____ new legislation governing the use of land in that region.		
42. Ford wants to _____ the image of its electric cars.		
43. They didn't know which tasks to _____ to which people.		instruct utilize edit assign bond subsidize
44. A word-processor makes it easy to _____ your essay before you hand it in.		
45. He will hold a seminar next month to _____ others how to use his new method.		
46. He was honest enough to _____ that he had made a mistake.		exceed cooperate acknowledge underlie trace motivate
47. Police are not kind to those who fail to _____ fully.		
48. In many professions in America, men's incomes _____ the incomes of most women.		
49. You certainly should try to _____ the money you lost.		migrate precede reveal transport recover precede
50. Huge dark clouds _____ heavy rain.		
51. In some countries, trains _____ more goods than planes do.		
52. Microsoft intends to _____ some of the new technology into its latest operating system.		incorporate assign subsidize discriminate motivate presume
53. Some people wonder why the government should _____ art at all.		
54. She is known for her ability to _____ people to take better care of their health.		

Unit 6

Definitions ○ Parts of Speech ○ Collocations

abstract (adj) formed in the mind, not in the physical world; theoretical
   abstract concept, abstract idea
   abstract expressionism [= a form of art in which expresses the artist's feeling rather than an accurate representation of any object in particular]: *The American painter, Jackson Pollack, was a master of abstract expressionism.*
   completely abstract, purely abstract, increasingly abstract
abstractly (adv)
abstract (v) consider a concept theoretically without connection to a particular instance
   to abstract from: *We can abstract certain concepts from his presentation.*
abstract (n)
   in the abstract: *That sounds fine in the abstract, but in the real world, it might be problematic.*
abstraction (n)
accurate (adj) exact in performance or amount; free from error
   fairly accurate, reasonably accurate, pretty accurate, entirely accurate, deadly accurate
   historically accurate: *It is historically accurate to note that Jefferson owned slaves.*
   accurate in: *Her portrait is accurate in every detail.*
   in an accurate way
   accurate to: *These measurements are accurate to a micrometer.*
accurately (adv)
   accurately portray
accuracy (n)
   to check for accuracy
   to improve accuracy, to increase accuracy
   to question the accuracy of, to doubt the accuracy of: *It is tempting to doubt the accuracy of the Gospels when they mention camels at a time when camels were not domesticated.*
   complete accuracy, absolute accuracy, pinpoint accuracy: *He hit the target with pinpoint accuracy.*
   (a high) degree of accuracy, level of accuracy
acknowledge (v) to recognize the existence or, reality of, rights, authority, or status of
   to openly acknowledge, to gratefully acknowledge, to fully acknowledge
   to frankly acknowledge [= to honestly acknowledge]: *Ben frankly acknowledged that he had been having an affair with one of his students.*
   to readily acknowledge, to clearly acknowledge, to explicitly acknowledge
   to privately acknowledge, to publicly acknowledge; to refuse to acknowledge
   to acknowledge as: *We reluctantly acknowledged him as our leader.*
acknowledgement (n)
   to make an acknowledgement, to get an acknowledgement, to receive an acknowledgement
   a frank acknowledgement, a brief acknowledgement
   an explicit acknowledgement [= a very clear acknowledgement]: *A quarterly report filed yesterday contained the first explicit acknowledgment that Time Warner's relationship with AOL.*
   a public acknowledgement, an official acknowledgement, a welcome acknowledgement
   in acknowledgement of: *In acknowledgement of you recent letter, I would like to inform you that . . .*
aggregate (n) units or parts collected together into a whole
   in (the) aggregate: *The fees amounted, in aggregate, to just over $500.*
aggregate (n) a material or structure formed from a loosely compacted mass of fragments or particles.
aggregate (v) to collect together into one sum or group: *Seagulls usually aggregate on the beach in spots where people go to have picnics.*
aggregate (adj) combined; considered as a whole
   aggregate demand, aggregate sales: *This year's aggregate housing sales exceeded last year's by 17%.*
aggregation (n) a collection, or the gathering of things together.
   Phil's coin collection represents the aggregation of different types of coins from around the world.
allocation (n) something set apart for a specific purpose
   to make an allocation; to increase an allocation, to cut an allocation, to reduce an allocation
   a budget allocation

allocate (v)
    to allocate something to/for: *We allocated $100 for the party, but it wasn't enough.*

assign (v) to give out
    to assign (something) to (someone): *We wanted cabins in the woods, but we were assigned the cabins by the lake.*
    to assign a task, to assign a name
    [computers] to assign a drive letter, to assign a network address, to assign an IP address

assign (v) to give as a task
    to assign homework, to assign a paper: *The teacher assigned us a ten-page paper, due by Friday.*
    assigned to do something: *We were assigned to clean the bathrooms.*
    to assign to the dustbin of history [= to let something go; to end something]: *Now that eBooks are becoming popular, some readers fear that "dead tree" books will be assigned to the dustbin of history.*

assignment (n) a task; a piece of school work
    to give an assignment, to hand out an assignment
    to complete an assignment, to hand in an assignment, to do an assignment
    to take on an assignment, to accept an assignment

assignable (adj)

attachment (n) something that is fastened, secured, or joined to something else
    to feel an attachment: *We felt a certain attachment to the villagers.*
    to develop an attachment, to form an attachment to: *It didn't take long for us to form an attachment to our new home.*
    a deep attachment, a strong attachment, a close attachment, a passionate attachment [= a strongly emotional attachment]: *George Washington advised the new nation to avoid having a passionate attachment to other nations.*
    a lasting attachment, a lifelong attachment
    an emotional attachment, a romantic attachment, a sentimental attachment [= an attachment based on tender feelings, such as love, sadness, pity or nostalgia]: *The author felt a sentimental attachment to his hometown and often wrote about it in his novels.*

attach (v)
    attach a file, attach a document
    firmly attach (to), securely attach, loosely attach

attached (adj)
    to become attached (to), to grow attached
    deeply attached, firmly attached, securely attached

attachment (n)

bond (n) something that unites or binds things together
    to feel a bond, to be linked by a bond, to create a bond, to develop a bond
    to forge a bond [= to create a strong bond]: *The United States has forged a bond with Israel.*
    to form a bond of (friendship, etc.), to strengthen a bond with
    a firm bond, a strong bond, a close bond
    a common bond, a natural bond, an emotional bond, a spiritual bond
    strong family bonds

bond (v) to unite or bind things together
    to bond over: *The two housewives bonded over a cup of coffee.*

bond (n) a financial instrument representing a debt that must be repaid with interest
    to invest in bonds, to put money in bonds; to cash in a bond, to redeem a bond
    bond market; stocks and bonds
    government bond, savings bond, treasury bond

brief (adj) short in time, duration, extent or length
    to keep it brief: *It's your turn to speak, but please keep it brief. We don't have much time.*
    fairly brief, quite brief, rather brief
    mercifully brief [= thankfully brief]: *It was a terribly hot morning, but the preacher's sermon was mercifully brief so that we could leave the church and find relief from the heat.*
    tantalizingly brief [= brief, but desirable and out of reach]: *After listening to Melinda Stocker's tantalizingly brief violin sample, we wanted to hear more.*

Unit 6

briefly (adv)
>briefly stated, briefly mentioned

briefing (n) a meeting at which essential information or precise instructions are given
>to attend a briefing, to go to a briefing, to hold a briefing, to receive a briefing: *Before flying to Iraq, the Secretary received a briefing on the latest developments.*
>a detailed briefing, a full briefing, a thorough briefing; a formal briefing, an informal briefing
>a press briefing

brevity (n) *We enjoyed the brevity of the speech. If it had been longer, it might have become boring.*

brief (n) a short summary; a formal outline used in a legal case
>to file a brief; to write a brief, to prepare a brief
>to be part of someone's brief: *It wasn't part of John's brief to advise on divorce issues.*
>a legal brief, a technical brief

brief (v) to give a short report: *The secretary briefed us on what to expect in the meeting.*

capable (adj) having capacity or ability
>to seem capable, to appear capable, to become capable
>to prove capable [= to be shown to be truly capable]: *Kaepernick proved capable of leading the team to the championship.*
>physically capable, clearly capable, more than capable, quite capable
>to be perfectly capable of, to be truly capable of: *You don't have to worry about him. He is perfectly capable of doing it himself.*

capably (adv)

capability (n)
>to demonstrate, display or show one's capability: *She showed her leadership capability by conducting the meeting in a very businesslike manner.*
>a defense or military capability

cite (v) to quote as an authority or example
>to cite a source [= to indicate the person or text quoted in a paper]: *If you do not cite the sources that you quote in your research paper, you will be guilty of plagiarism.*
>to cite something to someone: *To prove out point, we cited our research results to the audience.*
>cited above, previously cited, cited earlier, already cited
>commonly cited, frequently cited, widely cited

cite (v) to compliment or point out as a great example
>to cite as: *Her recent behavior was cited as an example of her inability to follow directions.*

cite (v) to mention or point out the reason for something
>to cite ~ as the reason: *The authorities cited bad weather as the reason for closing the airport.*

citation (n) the act of citing or quoting; an item in a list of texts that have been cited

citation (n) an official notice, or summons, to appear in court
>to issue a citation: *The policewoman issued a citation to the drivers of the illegally parked cars.*

cooperate (v) to work together for a common purpose
>to cooperate closely, to cooperate fully
>to agree to cooperate, to be willing to cooperate
>(it would) be wise to cooperate: *If we are going to win this competition, it would be wise for us to cooperate with each other, don't you think?*
>cooperate on, cooperate with, cooperate in

cooperation (n)
>close cooperation, full cooperation
>increased cooperation, greater cooperation
>to get someone's cooperation, to enlist someone's cooperation: *In order to make sure we could finish the work on time, we enlisted Tom's cooperation.*
>to encourage cooperation, to promote cooperation, to ensure cooperation
>cooperation between, cooperation in, cooperation on, cooperation with
>without someone's cooperation, with someone's cooperation
>in cooperation with: *The United States, in cooperation with the United Nations, is sending aid to the flood victims.*
>with ~ cooperation: *With your cooperation, I'd like to set up a new committee.*

Unit 6

cooperative (n) an organization consisting of people who work together for a common good
> to set up a cooperative; a consumer cooperative, a farmer cooperative, a worker cooperative

cooperative (adj) *The neighbors were being very cooperative with the police.*

cooperatively (adv) *Johnny works cooperatively with his classmates.*

discriminate (v) making an unfair or prejudicial distinction between different categories of people or things
> to discriminate against: *For many years, gays have been discriminated against by conservative Christian groups.*
> to discriminate in favor of: *The chairman always discriminates in favor of his friends' suggestions.*

discrimination (n)
> to practice discrimination, to subject someone to discrimination: *In some countries, disabled people are subjected to discrimination by government policies.*
> to amount to discrimination, to constitute discrimination: *The Congressmen have very different theories as to what exactly constitutes job discrimination.*
> to experience discrimination, to face discrimination, to suffer discrimination
> age discrimination, racial discrimination, sex discrimination, religious discrimination
> unlawful discrimination, illegal discrimination, institutionalized discrimination
> job discrimination, employment discrimination

discriminatory (adj) an unfair or prejudicial distinction between different categories of people or things
> discriminatory behavior, discriminatory hiring practices

discriminate (v) to make a fine or clear distinction
> to discriminate among, to discriminate between: *Sometimes, you have to discriminate between what you want and what you need.*
> to discriminate right from wrong: *Children do not always discriminate right from wrong.*
> unfairly discriminate (against)
> to discriminate on the grounds of

discriminate/discriminative (adj) making nice distinctions
> *We enjoy inviting discriminate people to our dinner parties. We know they will enjoy the fine food, wine and stimulating conversation.*

discriminately (adv)

discriminatively (adv)

display (n) something that is presented or held up to view or made evident
> to make a display (of): *Our neighbors like to make a display of their wealth by parking their Rolls Royce in the driveway instead of in the garage.*
> to put on a display, to have a display, to mount a display
> a dazzling display, an impressive display, a lavish display: *The huge department store on Fifth Avenue puts on an impressive display in its windows during the holidays.*
> a modest display, a disappointing display, a lackluster display; a public display
> an impressive display, an astonishing display, a breathtaking display
> a brief display, a rare display
> a display of power
> the display shows, the display illustrates

display (v) to present or hold up to view; to make evident
> (beginning) to display signs of: *My old leather coat is beginning to display signs of wear and tear.*
> clearly display, proudly display: *My uncle proudly displays the American flag every Fourth of July.*

diverse (adj) differing one from another
> culturally diverse, ethnically diverse, religiously diverse
> exceptionally diverse, highly diverse, remarkably diverse

diversely (adv)

diversity (n)
> cultural diversity, multicultural diversity, ethnic diversity, religious diversity
> considerable diversity, great diversity, rich diversity, wide diversity, greater diversity
> growing diversity, increasing diversity
> genetic diversity
> to maintain diversity, to preserve diversity, to protect diversity

diversify (v)
to diversity one's portfolio

diversification (n)

domain (n) an area, especially an area over which rule or control is exercised
(in) the private domain, (in) the public domain: *They followed certain rules of etiquette, both in the private domain and in the public domain.*
outside the domain, within the domain
[Internet] domain name
[math] domain and range; domain of a function

edit (v) to modify, adapt or alter in order to make suitable or acceptable for a particular purpose
to edit a draft, to edit a newspaper, to edit an article

edition (n) an issue of a newspaper, book, magazine, etc.
to publish an edition, to bring out an edition (of a book)
an abridged edition; an annotated an edition, the first edition, limited edition
morning edition, evening edition: *Nowadays, most newspapers no longer publish an evening edition.*

editor (n)
a copy editor, a fashion editor, a news editor
the chief editor, the executive editor, the managing editor
letter(s) to the editor

edit (n)
to give something an edit: *She gave her essay a careful edit before she handed it in.*

enhance (v) to increase or improve in value, beauty, desirability or effectiveness
to enhance the value of: *To enhance its value, we added two new rooms to our house.*
to enhance one's chances, to enhance efficiency, to enhance quality
to enhance and improve: *The new engine enhances and improves the performance of the new Cadillac.*
considerably enhance, dramatically enhance, greatly enhance
designed to enhance, serve to enhance

enhancement (n)

exceed (v) to extend beyond or outside of; to be greater than or superior to
to exceed in; to exceed someone in: *She exceeds me only in laziness.*
to exceed expectations: *When they finished the race in less than four minutes, they exceeded our expectations.*
to comfortably exceed, to far exceed, to greatly exceed, to easily exceed, to rarely exceed
expected to exceed, likely to exceed

exceeding (adj)

exceedingly (adv)

expert (n) a person with a great amount of skill or mastery in or knowledge of a certain subject
to call in an expert, to consult an expert
an acknowledged expert, a recognized expert, a leading expert, a qualified expert, a recognized expert
a so-called expert, a self-styled expert, a self-proclaimed expert: *Don't believe everything that Greta tells you. She's a self-proclaimed expert on every subject that you can imagine.*
a panel of experts, a committee of experts, a team of experts
an expert at ~ing: *She's an expert at telling great stories.*
an expert in: *He's an expert in math.*
an expert on: *They are experts on anti-matter.*

expert (adj) very skilled, very knowledgeable
expert advice, expert opinion: *We asked Luke his expert opinion on which stocks to invest in.*

expertly (adv)

expertise (n) expert skill or knowledge
to have expertise, to lack expertise, to require expertise, to develop expertise, to gain expertise
to provide expertise, to bring expertise (to)
to bring expertise to bear (on), to draw on expertise
considerable expertise, extensive expertise, great expertise;
limited expertise, relevant expertise: *Why is Allison on this committee? She brings limited expertise to the table.*

Unit 6

explicit (adj) fully revealed and clearly expressed, leaving nothing implied; not vague

   to make something explicit, to render something explicit

   highly explicit, quite explicit

   sexually explicit: *Those web sites have sexually explicit content.*

   explicit as to: *She was quite explicit as to what she expected of her students.*

   explicit about: *Can you be more explicit about what it is you want us to do?*

explicitly (adv)

explicitness (n)

federal (adj) a form of government in which individual states unite under a central authority

   (to make a) federal case [= to make something seem a lot more serious than it really is]: *I know I need to fix the plumbing. Don't make a federal case out of it.*

   federal budget, federal court, federal government, federal regulations, federal taxes

federally (adv)

   federally mandated [= required by the federal government]: *Health insurance for all employees is federally mandated.*

fee (n) a fixed sum of money paid for a privilege or service

   to charge a fee, to pay a fee, to split a fee, to waive fees [= to not require fees]: *Because the couple were so poor, the doctor waived her normal fees.*

   a large fee, a fat fee [= large fee], a hefty fee [= large fee],

   a substantial fee [= very large fee], an exorbitant fee [= a too large fee]: *We decided not to hire the lawyer because she wanted to charge us an exorbitant fee.*

   a low fee, a small fee, a modest fee, a reasonable fee, a flat fee, a nominal fee: *The lawyer charged only a nominal fee for her services in the child abuse case.*

   the appropriate fee, the usual fee, the standard fee: *Send in your application with the appropriate fee.*

   monthly fee, annual fee

   [usually plural:] legal fees, professional fees, membership fees, subscription fees

   booking fee, handling fee, cancellation fee, registration fee

   college fee, course fee, student fee, tuition fee

   for a small fee: *I'll help you with your homework for a small fee.*

flexible (adj) capable of being bent; yielding to influence

   to be flexible about, to be flexible in, to be flexible towards

   to seem flexible, to become flexible; to keep something flexible, to remain flexible

   highly flexible, extremely flexible, completely flexible

   fairly flexible, reasonably flexible, relatively flexible

   flexible schedule

flexibly (adv)

flexibility (n)

   to restore flexibility, to permit flexibility

   to demonstrate flexibility, to show flexibility: *If you really want to cooperate, you'll need to show some flexibility in your demands.*

   to have the flexibility to: *They will succeed because they have the flexibility to change when the situation calls for it.*

   considerable flexibility, enormous flexibility, great flexibility; sufficient flexibility

   added flexibility, additional flexibility, increased flexibility

   maximum flexibility, total flexibility; financial flexibility

flex (v) to bend

   to flex one's muscles

flex (n) [British] an electric cord or cable

   long flex, trailing flex; electrical flex, kettle flex, telephone flex

furthermore (adv) in addition; moreover

ignorant (adj) without knowledge, awareness or education

   to appear ignorant, to seem ignorant; to keep someone ignorant

   to remain ignorant (of/about)

   completely ignorant, totally ignorant, woefully ignorant [= extremely ignorant]: *It's impossible to discuss climate change with people who remain woefully ignorant of the facts.*

Unit 6

blissfully ignorant [= happily ignorant]: *Safe and warm in our mountain cabin, we were blissfully ignorant of the fact that snow had blocked all the roads.*

ignorantly (v)

We ignorantly assumed that we could enter the monastery without buying tickets.

ignore (v)

to ignore altogether, to ignore completely, to ignore entirely, to ignore totally

to ignore the fact that ~, something can be safely ignored: *Most of the folks on Wall Street thought that the protestors could be safely ignored.*

almost ignore, practically ignore, virtually ignore, largely ignore, just ignore, simply ignore

(not) easily ignored

deliberately ignore, pointedly ignore, cheerfully ignore

difficult to ignore, impossible to ignore, try to ignore, choose to ignore

ignorance (n) the condition of being uneducated, unaware, or uninformed

to demonstrate ignorance, to display ignorance, to show ignorance, to betray ignorance

to remain in ignorance, to keep someone in ignorance

to admit ignorance, to confess ignorance, to plead ignorance

ignorance about, ignorance of

in (total) ignorance of: *We were in total ignorance of what had happened.*

incentive (n) something that motivate action or effort

to give an incentive, to offer an incentive, to provide an incentive, to have an incentive

a powerful incentive, a strong incentive: *The boss offered me a powerful incentive to finish writing up the contract over the holiday weekend.*

a tax incentive

incorporate (v) to unite or blend something with something else that already exists

to incorporate into

fully incorporate, largely incorporate, clearly incorporate, expressly incorporate

gradually incorporate, quickly incorporate, eventually incorporate

easily incorporate, readily incorporate

satisfactorily incorporate, effectively incorporate, successfully incorporate

forcibly incorporate: *The dictator forcibly incorporated several countries into the Soviet Union.*

incorporation (n)

articles of incorporation [= primary rules governing the management of a corporation]: *We will be able to do business in California as soon as we file our articles of incorporation with the state.*

index (n) something that makes reference easy, especially a list of alphabetized items

to make an index, to create an index, to compile an index [= to assemble an index]: *After writing the cookbook, Dale compiled an index arranged by ingredients.*

to look (something up) in the index, to consult the index

an author index, a subject index, a title index

an index to: *There is an index to all the journals that the library subscribes to.*

index (n) a sign, indication or measure that shows the level of something

a cost-of-living index, a consumer-price index, Hang Seng Index, Dow Jones Index

a good index, a reliable index, a sensitive index

index (v)

inhibit (v) to hold back, restrain or discourage from freely doing something

to inhibit from: *Nothing seems to inhibit him from smoking.*

seriously inhibit, severely inhibit, significantly inhibit

inhibition (n)

to have (no) inhibitions, to lose one's inhibitions, to get over one's inhibitions: *When Sheila got over her inhibitions, she was able to sing solo in front of a large audience.*

without inhibition

inhibitor (n) a substance that slows a chemical reaction

Serotonin re-uptake inhibitors are often used as anti-depression medications.

inhibited (adj)

to feel inhibited, to become inhibited: *When she is at party where she doesn't know many people, Hilda becomes inhibited and doesn't say much.*

rather inhibited, slightly inhibited, emotionally inhibited
inhibited by, inhibited from, inhibited about

inhibitory (adj)

Some neurotransmitters have inhibitory effects on the neuron; they decrease the likelihood that the neuron will fire.

initiate (v) to start something going by taking the first step

to initiate into; initiate a discussion

to initiate proceedings [= to begin a legal trial]: *There was sufficient evidence to initiate proceedings against the dentist and his wife.*

to formally initiate

initiation (n)

to conduct an initiation, to hold an initiation

an initiation ceremony, an initiation rite, an initiation ritual; a rite of initiation [= a ceremony marking a passage marking entrance or acceptance into a group or society]. *Baptism, the Christian rite of initiation, is a ritual cleansing with water.*

an initiation into (the world of): *My success in New York was my initiation into the world of acting.*

initiative (n) the initial or leading action in a process

to take the initiative: *The new web site won't get launched unless I take the initiative to design and program it.*

to demonstrate initiative, to show (some) initiative: *If you want to join the team, you'll have to show some initiative.*

to lose the initiative; a private initiative

on one's own initiative: *We don't know why she decided to volunteer her services. She just did it on her own initiative.*

input (n) something put into a system to achieve output or a result

to receive input, to hear input

to want someone's input: *If I'd wanted your input into the matter, I would have asked.*

technical input, major input, additional input: *Before we make our final decision, we wish to ask for additional input from members of the audience.*

input (v)

to input data

input (adj)

an input valve

instruction (n) knowledge that is learned in methodical way

to conduct instruction, to give instruction, to provide instruction

advanced instruction, beginning instruction, elementary instruction

bilingual instruction, computer-assisted instruction

instructions (n. pl.)

to wait for instructions, to await instructions; to follow instructions, to comply with instructions

to accept instructions, to ignore instructions

according to the instructions, in accordance with the instructions, to be under instructions

to carry out instructions to the letter [= to do exactly as told]: *If we don't carry out Dr. Young's instructions to the letter, she will be very angry with us.*

clear instructions, explicit instructions, fresh instructions, further instructions

final instructions, written instructions

instruct (v) to give knowledge to, especially in a methodical way

to instruct in: *The father decided to instruct his son in the fine art of building bird houses.*

to be instructed to: *We were instructed to leave the money in a suitcase near the bus station.*

carefully instruct, explicitly instruct

as instructed: *You must take the medicine as instructed by your doctor.*

instruct (v) to give an order: *The fire fighters instructed us to stay away from the burning building.*

instructive (adj)

intelligence (n) the ability to acquire and apply knowledge and understanding

to have the intelligence of: *Sometimes, I think he doesn't have the intelligence of a block of wood.*

considerable intelligence, great intelligence, high intelligence (of) average intelligence, normal intelligence, limited intelligence, low intelligence

human intelligence, artificial intelligence; innate intelligence [= intelligence that you are born with]

native intelligence [= common sense]: *Vera seems to lack native intelligence. She makes stupid mistakes all the time.*

intelligent (adj) having the ability to acquire and apply knowledge and understanding

intelligently (adv)

intelligible (adj) easily understood

to become intelligible, to make something intelligible: *The writer the ability to make complex concepts intelligible to the average reader.*

barely intelligible, scarcely intelligible

immediately intelligible, readily intelligible; mutually intelligible: *To some extent, Spanish and Italian are mutually intelligible.*

intelligibly (adv)

intelligence (n) information of military or political value

to gather intelligence, to collect intelligence: *The spies were able to gather enough intelligence to show that the enemy were planning an attack at dawn.*

military intelligence, reliable intelligence

intelligence officer, intelligence service, intelligence operation, intelligence report

interval (n) a space of time between two objects, points, events or states

(to maintain) an interval between

a brief interval, a long interval, a wide interval, an irregular interval; at regular intervals

after a short interval, during the interval: *During the interval between World War I and World War II, many countries experienced economic depression.*

interval training [= an exercise program consisting of high intensity work alternating with periods of rest]: *Jim's interval training caused him to increase his strength and lose weight at the same time.*

at intervals, at fixed intervals, at frequent intervals, at periodic intervals, at regular intervals

at hourly intervals, at daily intervals, at weekly intervals, at monthly intervals, at yearly intervals

lecture (n) a speech given to an audience or a class, as for the purpose of instruction

to give a lecture, to deliver a lecture; to get a lecture on

to lecture about, to lecture on

a brief lecture, fascinating lecture, boring lecture, formal lecture, guest lecture

public lecture, popular lecture; keynote lecture, plenary lecture; memorial lecture

lecture course, lecture program, lecture series: *This semester, we are planning a lecture series featuring distinguished national and international experts.*

lecture hall, lecture room, lecture theater; lecture notes, lecture tour, lecture circuit

at a lecture, during a lecture, in a lecture

a lecture on, a lecture entitled ~, a lecture on the subject of ~

lecturer (n)

to be a lecturer in

senior lecturer, principle lecturer, assistant lecturer, junior lecturer, college lecturer, university lecturer

guest lecturer, visiting lecturer

lecture (v) to speak to an audience or a class

lecture (v) to warn or scold for a long time

to lecture someone for: *They lectured us for being lazy.*

to be lectured to [= to be scolded or disapproved]: *We were always lectured to by Mother because we hated to eat our vegetables.*

don't lecture to me: *I know I have to finish the report tonight. Don't lecture to me!*

migrate (v) to move from one country or region and go to live in another

to migrate towards, to migrate to, to migrate between

to migrate north, to migrate south; to migrate for the winter: *Many birds in North America migrate to Mexico for the winter.*

migration (n)

seasonal migration, annual migration

migration route, migration path, migration pattern

a wave of migration; mass migration

Unit 6

migratory (adj)

minimum (n) the least possible amount or degree
    to keep something to a minimum
    a bare minimum; the irreducible minimum, the absolute minimum: *The CEO is working hard to keep costs to the absolute minimum without sacrificing quality.*
    the legal minimum, mandatory minimum, required minimum
    at a minimum, above the minimum, below the minimum

minimum (adj) representing the least possible amount or degree
    minimum wages
    the minimum acceptable, the minimum needed, the minimum required, the minimum allowable
    minimum risk, minimum discomfort, minimum effort, minimum fuss [= minimum effort]: *We were able to set up for the party with minimum fuss.*

minimally (adv)
    minimally invasive surgery

minimalize (v)

ministry (n) a person, thing or act through which something is served or accomplished, especially in a religious or governmental capacity
    to enter the ministry [= join a religious organization]
    defense ministry, foreign ministry, health ministry; ministry of defense

minister (n)
    defense minister, foreign minister, health minister, defense minister

ministerial (adj)

minister (v) to serve in a religious or medical capacity: *Nurses minister to the needs of their patients.*

motive (n) the reason for acting in a particular way
    to understand the motive, to establish a motive
    to be suspicious of someone's motives, to examine someone's motives, to question someone's motives
    the motive behind something, the motive for something: *It was hard to understand the prime motive behind his poor business decision.*
    a hidden motive, a good motive, a clear motive, a strong motive
    an ulterior motive [= a secret motive]: *Jason suspected that Martin had an ulterior motive for wanting to spend the afternoon at the movies.*
    base motive, selfish motive, prime motive, underlying motive

motivate (v) to cause action based on emotion, desire, physiological need, or desire
    to motivate someone to do something

motivation (n)
    to have the motivation to, to lack motivation, to improve motivation, to strengthen motivation
    strong motivation, main motivation, primary motivation, real motivation, underlying motivation
    low motivation, poor motivation
    the motivation behind, the motivation for, the motivation in

motivated (adj)
    strongly motivated; highly motivated

motivational (adj)
    a motivational speech

motivationally (adv)

neutral (adj) belonging to neither side in a controversy
    to stay neutral, to remain neutral: *I tried to remain neutral in the dispute.*
    to take a neutral position
    strictly neutral, completely neutral; fairly neutral, relatively neutral
    gender neutral

neutrally (adv)

neutrality (n)
    to declare neutrality, to maintain neutrality, to preserve neutrality
    political neutrality, armed neutrality

neutralize (v)
    to effectively neutralize

Unit 6

nevertheless (adv) however; in spite of that; nonetheless
> *It started to rain heavily. Nevertheless, the boys continued their football game.*

precede (v) to come, exist or occur before or in front of
> immediately preceded by; directly preceded by

precedence (n) being considered more important; priority in importance, order, or rank
> to take precedence over: *The needs of our children should take precedence over our own needs.*
> historical precedence: *Frankel looks to historical precedence as a guide in determining the renminbi's chances of becoming an international currency.*
> in order of precedence: *We will send the books in order of precedence. Those that were ordered first will be sent first.*

precedent (n) an earlier event or action that is regarded as an example or guide to be considered in subsequent similar circumstances
> (to set) a dangerous precedent, a bad precedent, an unfortunate precedent
> to serve as a precedent (for)
> a necessary precedent, a good precedent, an important precedent
> without precedent: *Bush's decision to invade Iraq was without precedent.*

presume (v) to assume as being true in the absence of proof to the contrary
> to presume to know, presume to have, to presume that
> presumed innocent (until proved guilty): *News reporters must always remember that suspects are presumed innocent until they are proven guilty.*
> to presume upon [= to bother, to ask for]: *May I presume upon you for another cup of tea?*

presumable (adj)

presumably (adv)

presumption (n)
> to act on the presumption, to be based on the presumption that: *The invasion was based on the presumption that the enemy was getting ready to attack us.*
> a false presumption, a strong presumption, a general presumption
> presumption of innocence

presumptuous (v)
> presumptuous of someone: *It's presumptuous of you to think that you will automatically get the job.*

rational (adj) having or exercising the ability to reason or understand; sane
> to seem rational
> highly rational, perfectly rational, quite rational
> (there must be) a rational explanation (for)

rationally (adv)

rationalize (v) to account for one's actions apparently based on a good reason
> to rationalize one's way out of something: *He knew he should not have bought the new car, but then he tried to rationalize his way out of his decision.*

rationalization (n)
> to make a rationalization: *You don't really need to eat chocolate for your health. You are just making a rationalization.*

rationale (n) a fundamental reason; a basis

recover (v) to get back again or go back to an original position or condition; regain
> to completely recover, to fully recover; not quite recovered, never really recovered (from)
> to help someone recover, to struggle to recover (from)
> (to take a long time) to recover from

recovery (n)
> to make a recovery, to stage a recovery; to stimulate a recovery, to speed up a recovery
> a complete recovery, an amazing recovery, a dramatic recovery, a remarkable recovery
> a satisfactory recovery, a limited recovery, a modest recovery
> a long-term recovery, a lasting recovery
> a sustained recovery [= a recovery that can be maintained]: *Due to the President's economic policies, the economy is in a period of sustained recovery.*
> an economic recovery, a political recovery; post-war recovery
> to recover from a recession, to recover from a depression; to recover from an illness

to be on the road to recovery; to have prospects of recovery

a sign of recovery: *The garden was badly damaged by the ice and snow, but it is beginning to show signs of recovery now that spring is here.*

recovery is on the way

beyond recovery; recovery from

recoverable (adj)

The computer crashed, but fortunately, the data was recoverable from the hard drive.

reveal (v) to make something known which has been hidden or kept secret

to reveal a secret, to reveal the identity (of); to reveal that

revealing (adj)

deeply revealing, quite revealing, rather revealing

(to offer/to make) revealing insights, revealing remarks

revelation (n) a surprising and previously unknown fact, esp. one that is made known in a dramatic way

to prove a revelation, to come as a revelation

an astonishing revelation, an amazing revelation, an embarrassing revelation, a sudden revelation

a shocking revelation, a sensational revelation, a startling revelation

(according to/by) divine revelation [= a revelation given by a god]

scope (n) the area or opportunity covered by a given activity or subject, usually without being limited

to allow scope, to give someone scope: *A liberal education gives students a broad scope for developing their outlook on life.*

to broaden one's scope, to expand one's scope

to widen the scope: *The police want to widen the scope of the investigation.*

narrow scope, broad scope, full scope, ample scope [= full scope], sheer scope [= complete, thorough scope]: *We were amazed at the sheer scope of the army's efforts to find the missing soldiers.*

the scope of; within the scope of; outside the scope of

in scope: *This survey of South American literature is too narrow in scope.*

beyond the scope of, outside the scope of, within the scope of: *These issues are within the scope of the federal court's jurisdiction.*

scope out (v) to examine or look over

scope (n) an instrument used to view something

gun scope, rifle scope, microscope, telescope

subsidize (v) to make a gift of money, usually from a government to a person or group in support of an enterprise which is in the public interest

to subsidize heavily

subsidy (n)

to provide a subsidy (for/to), to grant a subsidy, to provide a subsidy

a reduction in subsidies, a cut in subsidies

a big subsidy, a heavy subsidy, a generous subsidy, a massive subsidy

a small subsidy, a direct subsidy

a farm subsidy, government subsidy, public subsidy, state subsidy

tape (n) a continuous narrow, flexible strip or band

adhesive tape, sticky tape, friction tape, magnetic tape, measuring tape

Scotch™ Tape, masking tape, double-sided tape

a piece of tape, a strip of tape, a roll of tape

tape (n) a band on which video and/or audio can be recorded

to make a tape; to play a tape, to listen to a tape, to watch a tape

to start a tape, to pause a tape, to replay a tape, to rewind a tape, to fast forward a tape

to have something on tape: *The police knew that she had been working for the drug dealers. They had her conversations with the gang members on tape.*

video tape, audio tape; blank tape, recorded tape

a tape recording

tape (v) to make a recording

to tape a movie, to tape a program, to tape a show, to tape an interview

trace (n) a visible mark or other evidence left by something that has passed

to leave a trace: *When the gun was fired, it left a trace of gunpowder on his fingers.*

to show a trace: *This special light shows traces of blood on various surfaces.*
to leave a trace behind
a faint trace, a minute trace [= a very small trace], a slight trace, a tiny trace
a slight trace of: *She didn't show the slightest trace of regret.*

trace (n) evidence of a past event
to lose all trace: *I've lost all trace of the friends I used to have in high school.*
to disappear without a trace: *The stranger helped us pick up the spilled groceries, then disappeared without a trace.*

trace (v) to find out where something comes from
to trace something to something: *The pollution in this river can be directly traced to the factories upstream.*
to be able to trace, to be unable to trace; to trace back to: *The English word* castle *can be traced back to the Arabic word* al-qasr.
to trace a phone call

trace (v) to mark with a line
to lightly trace, to trace an outline, to trace with a finger

traceable (adj)

transform (v) to greatly change the appearance, form, composition or structure
to transform from; to transform into; to transform to
completely transform, considerably transform, fundamentally transform, radically transform
slowly transform, suddenly transform; miraculously transform
transform overnight
(to have) the power to transform

transformation (n)
to undergo a transformation, to carry out a transformation, to bring about a transformation
to effect a transformation, to lead to a transformation
a complete transformation, a radical transformation, a total transformation
an amazing transformation: *Davis underwent an amazing transformation from an average player to one of the league's top performers.*
a dramatic transformation, a fundamental transformation, a profound transformation
a slow transformation, a sudden transformation, a miraculous transformation

transformational (adj)

transformative (adj)

transport (v) to carry from one place to another; to carry away
to transport bodily, to transport from; to transport to

transport (n) [primarily British usage]
to arrange transport, to provide transport
mass transport, public transport
air transport, river transport; passenger transport, freight transport
a means of transport: *Bicycles are a popular means of transport for many college students.*
oxygen transport

transportation (n) [primarily American usage]
to arrange transportation, to provide transportation
mass transportation, public transportation
air transportation, river transportation; passenger transportation, freight transportation
a means of trans transportation

transportation (n)

underlie (v) to be the support, foundation or basis of

underlying (adj)
underlying conditions, underlying assumption

utilize (v) to put to use, especially in a practical way
to utilize for; to utilize fully
heavily utilized, effectively utilized

utility (n)
(to have) great utility; high utility, low utility, social utility

Unit 6

Synonyms

abstract:	theoretical, hypothetical, conceptual
accurate:	precise, exact, right
acknowledge:	admit, recognize, accept
aggregate:	collect, combine, assemble
allocate:	designate, assign, allot
assign:	appoint, designate, give
attach:	join, bond, fasten, link
bond:	unite, bind, cement
brief:	short, concise, fleeting
capable:	able, competent, effectual
cite:	mention, quote, refer to
cooperate:	join in, team up, collaborate
discriminate:	prejudge, discern, distinguish
display:	exhibit, show, demonstrate
diverse:	varied, mixed, assorted
domain:	territory, area, region
edit:	rewrite, review, amend
enhance:	improve, enrich, better
exceed:	go beyond, outdo, surpass
expert:	master, specialist, authority
explicit:	direct, well-defined, straightforward
federal:	central authority
fee:	payment, bill, charge, price
flexible:	bendable, accommodating, changeable
furthermore:	moreover, besides, also
ignorant:	unlearned, untaught, uninformed
incorporate:	blend in, combine, consolidate
index:	list, listing, catalog
inhibit:	prevent, restrain, suppress
initiate:	begin, start, activate
input:	data, information, advice
instruct:	teach, inform, tutor
intelligent:	smart, knowing, thinking
interval:	gap, break, pause
lecture:	talk, address, speech
migrate:	move, relocate, travel
minimum:	least, smallest, lowest
ministry:	administrative department
motive:	reason, purpose, inspiration
neutral:	unbiased, impartial, objective
nevertheless:	however, nonetheless, still
precede:	antecede, predate, come before
presume:	suppose, assume, guess
rational:	logical, sensible, reasonable
recover:	regain, revive, recuperate
reveal:	show, expose, uncover
scope:	range, reach, size
subsidy:	grant, support, assistance
tape:	strip, band
trace:	mark, track, evidence
transform:	change, convert, alter
transport:	carry away, move, haul
underlie:	under, beneath, bottom
utilize:	use, apply, employ

Unit 6

Answers

Definitions

1. assigned	16. Nevertheless	31. accurate	46. subsidy
2. exceeded	17. Furthermore	32. diverse	47. recovery
3. instructed	18. Briefly	33. capable	48. motive
4. scope	19. acknowledge	34. transport	49. transform
5. bond	20. edit	35. enhance	50. reveal
6. fee	21. initiate	36. cite	51. discriminate
7. abstract	22. rational	37. lecture	52. explicit
8. federal	23. expert	38. tape	53. attached
9. minimum	24. neutral	39. ministry	54. aggregate
10. migrate	25. inhibits	40. flexible	
11. incorporate	26. presumes	41. intelligent	
12. allocate	27. utilizes	42. ignorant	
13. index	28. trace	43. precede	
14. domain	29. interval	44. cooperate	
15. display	30. input	45. underlie	

Parts of Speech

1. abstraction / abstractly	12. cooperating / cooperation	23. fees / fee	34. intervals / interval
2. accuracy / accurately	13. discriminated / discrimination	24. flexible / flexibility	35. lecturer / lectures
3. acknowledgment / acknowledged	14. displaying / displays	25. furthermore / Furthermore,	36. migrated / migrant
4. aggregation / aggregated	15. diverse / diversity	26. ignorant / Ignorance	37. minimum / minimize
5. allocation / allocated	16. domains / domain	27. incorporate / incorporation	38. ministry / ministers
6. assignment / assigned	17. edition / edited	28. Index / index	39. motivated / motivation
7. attachment / attached	18. enhance / enhancement	29. inhibits / inhibition	40. neutral / neutralize
8. bonds / bonded	19. exceeded / exceedingly	30. initiating / initiative	41. nevertheless / Nevertheless
9. briefly / briefly	20. experts / expertly	31. input / input	42. precedence / preceding
10. capably / capacity/capability	21. explicit / explicitly	32. instructions / instructional / instructive	43. presumably / presumption
11. cited/cites / citation	22. Federal / federally	33. intelligence / intelligent	44. rationally / rational

45. recovering / recovery	49. taped / tapes	53. underlie / underlying
46. revealed / reveal	50. traced / traces	54. utilization / utilize
47. scope / scope	51. transform / transformation	
48. subsidizing / subsidies	52. transporting / transport/transportation	

Unit 6

Answers

Collocations			
Exercise 1	**Exercise 2**	**Exercise 3**	**Exercise 4**

1. accurate
  accuracy
  accuracy
	1. assigned
	  assignment
	  assigned
		1. scope
		  scope
		  scope
			1. discriminate
			  discrimination
			  discriminates

2. diverse
  diversify
  diversity
	2. exceeded
	  exceed
	  exceed
		2. interval
		  interval
		  intervals
			2. ignorant
			  ignore
			  ignored

3. index
  indexed
  index
	3. attach
	  attached
	  attachment
		3. bond
		  bonds
		  bond
			3. motivation
			  motivation
			  motivational

4. preceded
  precedence
  precedence
	4. expert
	  expert
	  expertise
		4. tape
		  tape
		  tape
			4. transformed
			  transformed
			  transformation

5. acknowledged
  acknowledgement
  acknowledged
	5. instruction
	  instruction/~s
	  instructions
		5. lecture
		  lectured
		  lecturer
			5. cooperate
			  cooperate
			  cooperation

6. edit
  edition
  editor
	6. recovered
	  recover
	  recovery
		6. fee
		  fee
		  fees
			6. displayed
			  display
			  display

7. inhibits
  inhibited
  inhibition
	7. intelligence
	  intelligence
	  intelligible
		7. flexible
		  flexible
		  flexibility
			7. neutral
			  neutrality
			  neutralize

8. presume
  presumed
  presumption
	8. reveal
	  revealing
	  revelations
		8. brief
		  briefing
		  briefly
			8. cited
			  cited
			  cite

9. allocation
  allocated
	9. rational
	  rational
		9. traces
		  trace
		  trace
			9. capable
			  capability

10. enhanced
  enhance
	10. initiated
	  initiation
		10. migrates
		  migration
			10. minimum
			  minimum

Unit 6

Answers

Synonyms (Crossword)	
Across	**Down**
4. presume	1. reveal
9. initiate	2. scope
10. nevertheless	3. transform
11. flexible	5. brief
14. discriminate	6. interval
16. minimum	7. diverse
17. enhance	8. motive
19. capable	12. instruct
22. display	13. exceed
24. lecture	15. inhibit
25. attach	18. allocate
27. rational	20. aggregate
28. intelligent	21. expert
29. utilize	23. abstract
30. explicit	26. cite

Review

1. capable	19. tape	37. cite
2. neutral	20. lecture	38. brief
3. explicit	21. ministry	39. discriminate
4. rational	22. expert	40. reveal
5. flexible	23. index	41. initiate
6. minimum	24. aggregate	42. transform
7. accurate	25. fee	43. assign
8. federal	26. interval	44. edit
9. diverse	27. scope	45. instruct
10. abstract	28. allocation	46. acknowledge
11. furthermore	29. attachment	47. cooperate
12. nevertheless	30. domain	48. exceed
13. trace	31. presume	49. recover
14. intelligence	32. underlie	50. precede
15. bond	33. inhibit	51. transport
16. ignorance	34. migrate	52. incorporate
17. display	35. utilize	53. subsidize
18. input	36. enhance	54. motivate

Word List

n = noun   **v** = verb   **adj** = adjective   **adv** = adverb   **prep** = preposition

adapt (v)
  adaptation (n)
  adaptable (adj)
  adaptive (adj)
  adaptively (adv)
  adapter (n)
adult (n)
  adulthood (n)
advocate (n)
  advocate (v)
  advocacy (n)
aid (n)
  aid (v)
channel (n)
  channel (v)
chemical (n)
  chemical (adj)
  chemically (adv)
  chemistry (n)
  chemist (n)
classic (adj)
  classical (adj)
  classically (adv)
  classic (n)
  classics (n. pl)
comprehensive (adj)
  comprehensively (adv)
  comprehensiveness (n)
  comprehensives (n. pl.)
comprise (v)
confirm (v)
  confirmation (n)
  confirmable (adj)
  confirmative (adj)
contrary (adj)
  contrary (n)
  contrarily (adv)
  contrariness (n)
convert (v)
  convert (n)
couple (n)
  couple (v)
decade (n)
  decadal (adj)
definite (adj)
  definitely (adv)
  definiteness (n)
deny (v)
  denial (n)
differentiate (v)
  differentiation (n)
  differential (adj)
  differential (n)

dispose (v)
  disposal (n)
  disposable (adj)
  disposed (adj)
eliminate (v)
  elimination (n)
empirical (adj)
  empirically (adv)
  empiricism (n)
equip (v)
  equipment (n)
extract (v)
  extract (n)
  extraction (n)
file (n)
  file (v)
finite (adj)
  finitely (adv)
  finite (n)
  finiteness (n)
foundation (n)
  foundational (adj)
globe (n)
  global (adj)
  globally (adv)
guarantee (n)
  guarantee (v)
hierarchy (n)
  hierarchical (adj)
  hierarchically (adv)
identical (adj)
  identically (adv)
ideology (n)
  ideological (adj)
  ideologically (adv)
infer (v)
  inference (n)
  inferable (adj)
  inferential (adj)
innovate (v)
  innovation (n)
  innovative (adj)
  innovator (n)
insert (v)
  insert (n)
  insertion (n)
  insertable (adj)
intervene (v)
  intervention (n)
isolate (n)
  isolation (n)
  isolationist (n)
  isolationism (n)

media (n. pl.)
  medium (n. sing.)
mode (n)
paradigm (n)
  paradigmatic (adj)
  paradigmatically (adv)
phenomenon (n. sing.)
  phenomena (n. pl.)
  phenomenal (adj)
  phenomenally (adv)
priority (n)
  prioritize (v)
  prioritization (n)
prohibit (v)
  prohibition (n)
  prohibited (adj)
  prohibitive (adv)
  prohibitively (adv)
release (n)
  release (v)
reverse (n)
  reverse (v)
  reverse (adj)
  reversal (n)
  reversible (adj)
simulate (v)
  simulation (n)
sole (adj)
  sole (n)
somewhat (adv)
submit (v)
  submission (n)
  submittal (n)
  submissible (adj)
succeed (v)
  succession (n)
  successor (n)
thesis (n. sing.)
  theses (n. pl.)
topic (n)
  topical (adj)
transmit (v)
  transmission (n)
  transmitter (n)
ultimate (adj)
  ultimately (adv)
  ultimate (n)
unique (adj)
  uniquely (adv)
visible (adj)
  visibly (adv)
  visibility (n)
  vision (n)

Unit 7

Definitions Use the definition clues to write the correct words in the blanks.

1.	to change a form, function or measure *The students learned how to* _____ *kilos to pounds.*	equip adapt convert infer aid confirm
2.	to provide with the necessary tools, supplies, etc. *Habitat for Humanity will* _____ *each worker with all the necessary tools for building the new houses.*	
3.	to conclude from facts, evidence, observation, deduction *From what you have just said, may I* _____ *that you would be willing to work for free?*	
4.	a person who follows another and takes that person's job *As I end my term as president of this organization, I wish good luck to my* _____ *.*	successor mode adult channel decade globe
5.	a way of doing something *When Jason is in work* _____ *, he gets a lot done.*	
6.	a ball-shaped object; the world *Around the* _____ *, people celebrated the New Year.*	
7.	opposed, opposite or quite different, as in character or purpose *They are both moderate Republicans,* _____ *to what they claim.*	priority contrary somewhat classically solely media
8.	alone; single; without others *The CEO is* _____ *responsible for the corporation's losses this year. There is no need to blame anyone else.*	
9.	a little; to some extent *It seems complicated, but actually it is* _____ *simple.*	
10.	to set free or let go *Inserting the key* _____ *the locking mechanism.*	extracts releases intervenes couples denies infers
11.	to come between two things; to involve oneself or interfere in a dispute *You can't see the hills from this window because the garage* _____ *.*	
12.	to draw, pull out or separate an object, a substance or an idea *This software* _____ *images from .pdf files.*	
13.	a period of ten years *The past* _____ *has seen an increase in flooding.*	hierarchy denial decade reversal topic ideology
14.	the body of ideas and beliefs which serve as the foundation for a social, economic or political system *We need an open debate on the role of religious* _____ *in American politics.*	
15.	the subject of a talk or of a written text *The* _____ *index allows you to search the book's content by subject area.*	

Unit 7

16. exactly the same *We laughed when we saw Bill and his brother wearing* _____ *shirts.* 17. certain, sure *Pippa had a very* _____ *theory about the murder.* 18. fully grown, mature or of legal age *Children under 16 must have* _____ *supervision.*	adult visible isolated empirical definite identical
19. to get rid of or throw away; to finish using *There are few ways to safely* _____ *of nuclear waste.* 20. to separate; to keep apart *Mountains tend to* _____ *small villages from each other.* 21. to convey or pass on; to send from one place to another *Satellites* _____ *phone signals all over the globe.*	transmit isolate dispose submit release infer
22. model or pattern or example *Java language turned the existing computing* _____ *upside down. Programmers had to change their pattern of thinking.* 23. a course or pathway; a route of communication or access *The first goal is to open a new* _____ *of communication between the Palestinians and the Israelis.* 24. an idea or proposition to be supported or maintained by argument *Pinker's doctoral* _____ *touched on the roots of modern secularism.*	innovation successor foundation channel paradigm thesis
25. one of a kind; no others are equal to it *The recent supernova has given astronomers a* _____ *opportunity to study star deaths.* 26. able to be seen *The hills of the Lake District became* _____ *when the fog lifted.* 27. having a definite limit or end *We had to limit our spending due to our* _____ *resources.*	chemical unique contrary classic visible finite
28. to imitate or to appear to be like something else *The computer model can* _____ *the dynamics of space flight.* 29. to put something inside something else *First,* _____ *a recordable disk into the DVD drive.* 30. to establish a difference or distinction between things *It is important to* _____ *between the two types of muscle cells.*	differentiate comprehend simulate convert insert deny

Unit 7

31. any system of persons or things ranked one above another *When new pigs are introduced to the herd, they fight to establish a* _____ *in which the heaviest pigs are dominant.* 32. a perceptible occurrence, circumstance, or fact *Audio programming has become cheap and easy to make and has led* *to the rapid spread of the podcasting* _____. 33. something that needs attention before other things *High* _____ *has been given to the teaching of reading.*	hierarchy phenomenon chemical topic mode priority
34. to give something so that it will be considered by others *Please* _____ *your request in writing before Friday.* 35. to contain, include, consist of or be composed of something specified *The gardens* _____ *two acres which are tastefully* *enclosed and planted with a variety of trees and shrubs.* 36. to make suitable to or fit for a new situation *It might be possible to* _____ *the existing buildings to* *accommodate the influx of new students.*	transmit simulate isolate comprise adapt submit
37. derived from or relying on experience, observation or experiment *Accepting (or rejecting) a naturalistic theory requires only* _____*observation and analysis.* 38. serving as an outstanding or established model or example *Marshall's essay is a* _____ *example of post-modern* *thinking.* 39. last or final in a series or process; fundamental or basic; most important or greatest *After the long train ride, you still need to take a bus to your* _____ *destination.*	sole classic unique empirical ultimate identical
40. to support or try to get others to accept something *Pauline likes to* _____ *on the behalf of poor children.* 41. to forbid, especially by law or other authority *The authors* _____ *the use of their materials without* *their written consent.* 42. to introduce something new; make changes in anything that is already established *The best corporations are those that constantly* _____ *to keep ahead of their competitors.*	advocate prohibit channel confirm dispose innovate
43. help or assistance *Flash cards can be used as an* _____ *to learning.* 44. the means by which information and entertainment are communicated *Some autistic children communicate well through the* _____ *of art.* 45. the act of getting rid of something *Through the* _____ *of fat from his diet, he was able to* *lose more than twenty pounds.*	elimination foundation medium decade release aid

Unit 7

46. relating to substances such as elements or molecular compounds *Dopamine is a brain* _____ *that plays a role in communication.* 47. opposite in direction, position or movement *The housing market has been terrible for years, but now we are seeing a* _____ *trend. Things are getting better.* 48. covering or including a large area or scope *Our* _____ *guide to Osaka gave us an enormous amount of information about the city and its history.*	reverse chemical identical empirical ideological comprehensive
49. to support or establish the certainty or validity of; to finalize or make definite *Ten passengers were* _____ *dead while another sixteen were missing.* 50. to promise that something will happen *To get me to sign the lease agreement, they* _____ *me free parking.* 51. to declare something not to be true; to refuse to believe *Mr. Bell* _____ *any knowledge of the cover up.*	confirmed adapted converted equipped denied guaranteed
52. two of something *The newly-married* _____ *traveled to Guatemala for their honeymoon.* 53. the basic structure that supports a theory, idea or a building *Because the house is built on a solid* _____ *, it should last for centuries.* 54. a collection of paper or records or other materials *The downloadable* _____ *is in .pdf format.*	file globe decade channel couple foundation

Unit 7

Parts of Speech

Write the parts of speech (noun, verb, adjective or adverb form).
Word Forms: Be careful with nouns and verbs:
   Some *nouns* might need to be plural (~s). Some *verbs* might need ~s, ~ed, ~ing.

adapt
1. The film _____ of Doctor Zhivago accurately portrays Pasternak's novel.

   This chair is _____ for use as a small bed.

adult
2. When young bears reach _____ they leave their mothers.

   Let's sit down and have an _____ conversation.

advocate
3. Alisha and her sister are strong _____ for women's rights.

   Dr. King was known for his _____ of civil rights.

aid
4. Dogs _____ police in last night's search.

   Tom wears two hearing _____.

channel
5. Last year, Apple _____ more money into its advertising budget.

   Two deep _____ in the river lead to the safe harbor.

chemical
6. There are many _____ in ordinary drinking water.

   Linda wants to study _____ engineering at Yale.

classic
7. The _____ music period lasted for 70 years following the baroque period.

   Don collects and restores _____ cars.

comprehensive 8. Dr. Henfield answered our questions _____.

   Kathleen finished her _____ faster than the other students and received the highest grades on all of them.

comprise
9. The art survey book is _____ almost entirely of text but very few illustrations.

   Older people _____ a large proportion of those living in poverty.

confirm
10. Yesterday's experiment _____ our initial theory.

   Be sure to immediately send _____ when you receive the money.

contrary
11. Mr. Bush's opponents held _____ views about the state of the economy.

   We thought that the parents would be bored by the simplicity of the film, but on the _____, that was what they liked most.

Unit 7

convert | 12. To save money, Ted _____ his dining room table into a work desk.

The Islamic community welcomed the ten new _____ to Islam.

couple | 13. A strong quarterback _____ with fast receivers can win games.

After a _____ of hours, we grew tired of the journey.

decade | 14. for more than six _____, North Korea has been separate from South Korea.

Personal computer ownership skyrocketed during the last _____ of the 20th Century.

definite | 15. At the moment, I can't tell you if I can join you tomorrow, but I will give you a _____ answer later this evening.

Siri _____ has a pleasing voice.

deny | 16. Wellington _____ victory to Napoleon in 1815.

She said she did not know the prisoner, but no one believed her _____.

differentiate | 17. During cellular _____, the less specialized cells become more specialized.

Critical thinkers know how to _____ fact from opinion.

dispose | 18. Langston's love of poetry _____ him to read poetry books late into the night.

One day, reusable plastic chopsticks will replace _____ wooden chopsticks.

eliminate | 19. Malek gained more power after the _____ of his enemies.

Plain soap _____ most germs.

empirical | 20. Some therapies, such as acupuncture, have not been _____ supported.

The existence of supernatural beings cannot be proved based on _____ observation.

equip | 21. The sedan comes _____ with heated seats.

Usually, the army _____ its soldiers with the latest weapons.

extract | 22. Last week, our teacher _____ a paragraph from a long essay and asked us to write our opinions about it.

This oil is actually an almond _____ that gives flavor to cakes and cookies.

Unit 7

file   23. Have you _____ all of the necessary paperwork?

None of her _____ were in any kind of order.

finite   24. Some people do not believe that we live in a _____ universe.

Because of our _____ natural resources, we cannot expect to expand the economy forever.

foundation   25. Some new research results undermine the _____ of our original theory.

Rockefeller contributed greatly to a _____ for the arts.

globe   26. The news traveled quickly all around the _____.

The president headed a _____ initiative to provide clean drinking water for poor people.

guarantee   27. Current earnings are no _____ of future earnings.

This computer is _____ against defects.

hierarchy   28. The pope stands at the top of the church _____.

The army is structured _____, with generals at the top and privates at the bottom.

identical   29. It was hard to differentiate between the _____ dressed brothers.

The latest earthquake struck at almost the _____ location as last week's earthquake.

ideology   30. The neighbors argued over their two different _____.

The economists engaged in an _____ debate.

infer   31. Chad's position on same-sex marriage is _____ from his negative comments.

Although we do not have all of the facts, we are able to make the reasonable _____ that the water pollution is caused by industrial activity in the area.

innovate   32. An interesting _____ for digital cameras is 3D photography.

Traditional thinkers often resist the efforts of _____.

insert   33. With the _____ of tab dividers, it is easier to organize your papers in the binder.

He puts _____ into his shoes to make him look taller.

Unit 7

intervene   34. Dr. Buckley runs a drug _____ program.

If Ursula had not _____, we would be in serious trouble by now.

isolate   35. The _____ villagers had not heard about the king's death.

Some people fear _____ more than others do.

media   36. The _____ were fascinated by the murder at the Queen's Sandringham estate.

The printed newspaper is losing its popularity as a news _____.

mode   37. People living in the 18th Century would be amazed at modern _____ of transportation and communication.

The President ended his vacation in campaign _____.

paradigm   38. Throughout history, authority figures have tended to dismiss new _____ because they threatened their authority.

When we are faced with a _____ of 'being' rather than 'doing,' suddenly the rules shift.

phenomenon   39. A tsunami is an incredibly destructive natural _____.

Mirages and green flashes are two _____ caused by refraction in the Earth's atmosphere.

priority   40. Poor workers are often unable to _____ their tasks.

New Year's Eve is a good time to establish your _____ for the upcoming year.

prohibit   41. Hunting is _____ in this region.

Some farmers are in favor of the _____ of genetically modified farm crops.

release   42. Gerry caught several fish, but she _____ all of them.

Diane is working hard for Jeff's _____ from prison.

reverse   43. It's hard to work with Jill because she often _____ her decisions about important matters.

The senator suffered several _____ in her attempt to be the first woman nominated for the presidency.

simulate   44. In the science fiction movie, the "humans" were merely computer _____ being run by a post-human society.

The _____ diamonds were hard to distinguish from the real ones.

- 212 -

Unit 7

sole

45. I didn't want to buy the entire CD just to get the _____ song that I liked.

I am _____ responsible for the decline in our company's profits this year.

somewhat

46. The students were _____ relieved that the teacher had decided to grade on a curve.

The movie was _____ more exciting than I thought it would be.

submit

47. Kendal _____ his report two days before the deadline.

In the photo contest, only one _____ per person is allowed.

successor

48. William will probably _____ his father as king of England.

General Allen has proved to be a worthy _____ to General Petraeus in Afghanistan.

thesis

49. Brian's doctoral _____ is on the grammar of definite articles in English.

A _____ statement declares what you believe and what you intend to prove in your essay.

topic

50. The issue of gun control is a common _____ in ESL writing classes.

No one was interested in any of the _____ that the teacher suggested.

transmit

51. Fortunately, AIDS cannot be _____ by mere touching.

Somehow, the message became garbled during _____.

ultimate

52. Dali's _____ achievement was probably his painting called "Hallucinogenic Toreador."

We don't mind stopping over in New York, but _____ we need to go to Boston.

unique

53. The platypus is _____ to Australia.

Norman is _____ qualified for the position of lab director.

visible

54. Because of the low clouds, _____ is poor today.

Warren was _____ shaken by the news.

Unit 7

Collocations

In each group of sentences, write *one* word from the list which goes with the **highlighted collocations**. Be careful with word forms.

Exercise 1	chemical	decade	infer	adult	differentiate	definite
	hierarchy	visible	deny	channel	adapt	prohibit

1. Let's **have an** _____ **conversation** about your college plans.

   _____ **education** classes are being given in the evenings.

   Few chicks **survive into** _____ due to harsh environmental conditions.

2. The government continues to _____ **the existence of** secret prisons.

   Dr. Patterson **issued a** _____ that he had received funds from gangs.

   Gerald is **in** _____ about his gambling problem.

3. It is difficult for non-royal family members to **rise up in the political** _____ of Bahrain.

   Eichmann **moved to a high status in the ruling** _____ of Nazi Germany.

   The island's society seems to be both **rigidly** _____ and egalitarian.

4. Even young children can _____ **between right and wrong**.

   It is important to _____ assessment **from** testing.

   The students worked hard to solve the _____ **equations**.

5. The office has been **specially** _____ to accommodate people with disabilities.

   The old factory is not **readily** _____ to manufacturing the new electric vehicles.

   The **process of** _____ to colder weather **occurs** gradually.

6. Smoking inside this building is **strictly** _____.

   Some areas of the US still have _____ **laws** against selling alcohol.

   Building a new bridge would be _____ **expensive**.

7. The senator is **a highly** _____ **public figure**.

   Ban Ki-moon was _____ **shaken** after visiting the worst-hit areas of flooded Pakistan.

   Grandma Jones still has **20/20** _____.

8. The ability **to draw** _____ is an important reading skill.

   You should **make an** _____ **based on** specific evidence.

   What can you _____ **from** Kevin's remarks?

9. Karzai tried **to open a** _____ **of communication** with the Taliban.

   Teachers try to _____ children's **energy towards** learning.

   The reporter **went through the proper** _____ and was able to interview the president.

10. Many **organic** _____ are harmful to one's health.

    Salt is a _____ **compound** consisting of sodium and chlorine.

Unit 7

Collocations

Exercise 2	paradigm intervene dispose classic simulate guarantee eliminate comprehensive reverse sole confirm innovate

1. Be sure to sign your name **on the** _____ **side** of the card.

   The rebels **suffered a** _____ in their efforts to capture the capital.

   A well-made _____ **jacket** can add versatility to your wardrobe.

2. Apple is **constantly** _____ to keep ahead of the competition.

   Government subsidies sometimes **stifle** _____.

   The chancellor's ultimate aim is to develop a workable model for sharing knowledge and **stimulating** _____ in development projects.

3. The city now has the problem of **waste** _____ at the old landfill.

   The pharaoh was **favorably** _____ **toward** the Israelites.

   _____ chop sticks are cheap but they harm the environment.

4. The study is **a** _____ **example of** scientific reductionism.

   A degree in _____ **literature** is not practical in today's job market.

   Forster's book is one of the **contemporary** _____ that you must read.

5. First, we need **to run a computer** _____.

   These models are **designed to** _____ biological functions.

   The reporters are taking a flight which _____ **weightlessness**.

6. Use **the process of** _____ to narrow the possible answer choices.

   The charity works to _____ **hunger** in rural America.

   Marcus became healthier **by** _____ salt **from** his diet.

7. NATO refused **to sign a written** _____ concerning the missiles.

   Our products are _____ **against defects** for a period of one year.

   You have my _____ that you will be promoted to manager.

8. David _____ **our suspicion** that his son had been arrested.

   She can **neither** _____ **nor deny** whether these allegations are true.

   In the meantime, we **await further** _____ of the results.

9. NATO is **reluctant to** _____ in Chad's **internal affairs**.

   Some senators criticized US **military** _____ in Libya.

   Should the state _____ **on behalf of** morbidly obese children?

10. Zeta was the _____ **survivor** of the crash.

    This website is published by ARGOS which **is** _____ **responsible for its contents**.

Unit 7

Collocations

Exercise 3	aid convert foundation mode successor empirical
	submit unique comprise contrary topic equip

1. That is not Paul's **normal** _____ **of operation**.

   When Fran is **in work** _____ , she doesn't like being interrupted.

   Visitors have several _____ **of transportation** from which to choose.

2. Khadafi had **designated a** _____ : his son.

   Bernard will be **a worthy** _____ to follow in the footsteps of his mentor.

   William is next **in line of** _____ after his father, Prince Charles.

3. The treatment of lung cancer is one of the most **controversial** _____ in oncology.

   Unemployment benefits remain **a hot** _____ in Michigan.

   In your essay, you must **expand on your** _____ without being repetitive.

4. The team is conducting _____ **studies** to assess the quality of health care information on the Web.

   _____ **validated** treatments are those that have been studied in clinical trials and demonstrated effectiveness with specific disorders

   Nowell, and Kerkvliet (2006), in an _____ **investigation**, indicated that academic dishonesty in online classes is no more pervasive than in traditional education.

5. "Short selling" is a risky technique that involves **going** _____ **to** the overall direction of the market.

   Despite claims to the _____ , air travel is safer than ever.

   Occupy Wall Street, _____ **to popular opinion**, had its leaders.

6. The discredited coach was forced to _____ **his resignation**.

   We refuse to _____ **to threats** or other forms of intimidation.

   NATO's plan was **to bomb** the dictator **into** _____ .

7. "The British nation is _____ **in this respect**. They are the only people who like to be told how bad things are." Churchill, 1941.

   The region's claims for political autonomy, rooted in a strong sense of ethnic and linguistic identity, are **by no means** _____ .

8. He cleverly _____ his armchair **into** a motorized vehicle.

   It is hoped that the new Windows program will **win** _____ .

   Arnold is **a recent** _____ **to** Catholicism.

9. The grant allows us to **install state-of-the-art** _____ in each room.

   The gym is **well-** _____ with everything a body-builder would want.

10. The type of preliminary evidence necessary **to lay the proper** _____ depends on the form and type of material evidence offered.

    I am sure that the 'Magnitsky list' won't **undermine the** _____ of Russia-US relations.

Unit 7

Collocations

Exercise 4	transmit file advocate aid finite insert isolation ultimate globe priority phenomenon release

1. Only female **mosquitoes** _____ **malaria**.

   There are hundreds of known **genetically** _____ **diseases**.

   Engineers have developed a **one-way** _____ system for sound waves.

2. If they don't pay you, you can _____ **a lawsuit**.

   The reporters rushed to _____ their **reports**.

   The director **keeps** _____ **on** all the employees.

3. **Consumer** _____ support the rights of the consumer to obtain safe goods and services at fair prices.

   My role in the campaign is **to play the devil's** _____ to each new policy before it's introduced to the public.

   Betty Ford was an **outspoken** _____ for the Equal Rights Amendment.

4. The world **came to** Haiti's _____ after the earthquake.

   If you need help, you can **enlist the** _____ of a librarian.

   Congress acted **to extend** _____ **to** the jobless.

5. Many people don't realize that water is a _____ **resource**.

   Only a _____ **number of possibilities** need to be considered to determine the complete list of solutions.

6. Sometimes it's not a good idea **to look at** certain statistics **in** _____.

   The stigma of stuttering can make you feel **socially** _____.

   Animal rights activists tried to stop the **total** _____ experiments on monkeys.

7. Nationwide celebrations marking the All Blacks _____ **achievement** in winning the Rugby World Cup continued for many days.

   If you **take** atheism **to its** _____ **conclusion**, you get nihilism.

   My _____ **goal** is to convince you.

8. **In all corners of the** _____, people yearn for freedom.

   Today, the term _____ **village** is mostly used as a metaphor to describe the Internet.

9. Sports programs sometimes **take** _____ **over** academic programs.

   We need to **rethink** our _____.

   The war against terror was the **top** _____ of the Delhi police.

10. The protest in New York was not an **isolated** _____.

    Known as the Northern Lights, this **natural** _____ is both beautiful and mysterious.

Unit 7

Synonyms Use the synonym clues to solve this crossword puzzle.

Across
3. opposite, conflicting, reverse
6. validate, affirm, verify
10. pair, twosome, duo
11. liberate, let go, free
12. course, bed, waterway
14. seen, observable
17. grown-up, mature, big
18. furnish, outfit, supply
25. disallow, negate, forbid
26. issue, subject, point
27. abolish, remove, dispose
28. final, last, utmost

30. accommodate, arrange
Down
1. rather, fairly, pretty
2. discard, eliminate
3. contain, include, consist
4. conclude, guess, determine
5. help, assist, serve
7. lone, only, solitary
8. same, alike, equal
9. pattern, model, example
12. thorough, complete, extensive

13. rank, level, status
15. assurance, promise
16. earth, world, sphere
19. base, support, groundwork
20. disallow, forbid, ban
21. transform, change, remake
22. separate, seclude
23. sole, singular, individual
24. exact, precise, specific
29. method, way, approach

Unit 7

Review

1. They developed a _____ plan for dealing with the waste.
2. The _____ number of solutions to this math problem made it easier to solve.
3. Our _____ goal is to raise one million dollars.

| contrary |
| comprehensive |
| identical |
| ultimate |
| finite |
| adult |

4. Our plans are not _____ yet. We have a few more decisions to make before we are sure.
5. We thought she would be angry, so her happy reaction was _____ surprising.
6. His landscape design was almost _____ to mine. There were hardly any differences.

| identical |
| contrary |
| definite |
| isolated |
| visible |
| somewhat |

7. That's a _____ example of how to win a game; everyone should follow that model.
8. Their _____ aim was to become as rich as possible; they had no other goals.
9. Her conclusion is based on _____ findings.

| empirical |
| global |
| classic |
| contrary |
| sole |
| finite |

10. This health care system is _____ to Britain. No other European country has a system exactly like it.
11. There was no _____ evidence that the brakes had been damaged in any way. We did not see any broken parts.
12. The new survey shows that most people support higher taxes, _____ to previous evidence.

| contrary |
| adult |
| unique |
| sole |
| visible |
| priority |

13. That TV program is more suitable for an _____ than it is for a child. Grown-ups would enjoy it more.
14. We thought it would take more than ten years, but within a _____ , we were able to rebuild the entire city.
15. There is no _____ that she will ever be able to walk again. We just can't be that positive.

| guarantee |
| channel |
| convert |
| decade |
| adult |
| mode |

16. Mass _____ , especially the Internet, influence the way children think.
17. He made it his first _____ to gather as much information as possible.
18. Khalid's essay is very convincing. In his _____ , he states that the death does not stop most violent crimes.

| disposal |
| media |
| thesis |
| file |
| globe |
| priority |

Unit 7

Review

19. Each of the subjects used a different _____ of responding to the stimulus.	advocate mode decade hierarchy adult channel
20. Maslow noted that humans have a _____ of needs ranging from basic biological needs to self-actualization.	
21. The small boat could easily sail through the narrow _____.	
22. She is a devoted _____ of fresh air and plenty of exercise.	file extraction aid foundation advocate channel
23. They work hard but have little money. They need less sympathy and more financial _____.	
24. He looked in every _____ in the cabinet, but could not find the memo.	
25. Her individualism reflects her political _____. She has strong beliefs about government interference in our personal lives.	adaptation denial ideology globe foundation paradigm
26. The results of his experiments resulted in a _____ shift that led to a revolution in scientific thinking.	
27. People all around the _____ will be watching the Olympics.	
28. Education provides a solid _____ for your future career.	phenomenon foundation successor media paradigm couple
29. A new _____, called "road rage," is starting to alarm us.	
30. When she resigned from her position as program coordinator, her _____ decided to cancel all the projects she had initiated.	
31. The sales figures _____ what we have suspected all along.	comprise dispose transmit confirm deny equip
32. The Taliban tried to _____ the US troops the ability to re-supply themselves.	
33. Airbus wants to _____ their airliners with Rolls Royce engines.	
34. She wondered if she should _____ one more paragraph into her essay.	insert isolate infer differentiate transmit release
35. The government is planning to _____ five prisoners.	
36. Cutting the antenna in half will decrease its ability to _____ a signal.	

Unit 7

Review

37. The government should _____ further building on the island. It's already too crowded there now.	adapt
	isolate
38. The researchers should be allowed to _____ rather than use the same methods over and over again.	innovate
	prohibit
39. It is difficult to _____ diet from other factors which affect health.	couple
	equip
40. If we _____ the horses together, they can pull the wagon faster.	extract
	guarantee
41. Irish families _____ more than 20% of the population of my hometown.	comprise
	couple
42. It doesn't take me long to _____ to a new living environment.	transmit
	adapt
43. Our bodies can't _____ fat to energy easily. We change sugar to usable energy much more quickly.	dispose
	infer
44. We need to find a way to _____ of nuclear waste.	innovate
	equip
45. It was difficult to _____ what she really meant because she did not tell us directly.	convert
	file
46. Let them work it out for themselves. We must not _____.	advocate
	couple
47. If you do not _____ your paperwork on time, your application cannot be considered.	intervene
	submit
48. After considering the new evidence, the judge agreed to _____ his decision.	prohibit
	reverse
49. Scientists are now able to _____ tiny bits of DNA from dinosaur fossils.	extract
	adapt
50. She found it difficult to _____ between the real and the unreal.	confirm
	eliminate
51. They tried to _____ any possibility that the students could cheat.	differentiate
	reverse
52. Toluene and acetone are two _____ used in the manufacture of illegal drugs.	inferences
	chemicals
53. New computer _____ help astronomers find habitable moons around alien planets.	simulations
	prohibitions
54. For your essay, choose one of the _____ that we discussed in class last week.	releases
	topics

Unit 7

Definitions ∘ Parts of Speech ∘ Collocations

adapt (v) to make suitable to or fit for a new situation
> to adapt oneself to: *It didn't take Ken long to adapt himself to the cold weather.*
> to be adapted from: *This movie is adapted from the book.*
> to adapt to: *To help you adapt to your new job, we have prepared a series of orientation programs.*
> to be able to adapt, to be unable to adapt: *Organisms that are unable to adapt to climate change may gradually die out.*
> to be specially adapted: *This kitchen is specially adapted for people who are in wheelchairs.*
> quickly adapt, easily adapt, readily adapt; difficult to adapt, hard to adapt

adaptation (n)
> (to undergo) a process of adaptation
> an adaptation of: *We really enjoyed John's film adaptation of Shakespeare's Hamlet.*
> an adaptation for: *Their adaptation of the web site for commercial purposes is going to be very successful.*
> a special adaptation, a successful adaptation
> adaptation occurs

adaptable (adj)
> to prove adaptable [= to show or demonstrate adaptability]: *These binoculars proved adaptable for use with a camera.*
> fairly adaptable, easily adaptable, readily adaptable

adaptive (adj) *The orchid's adaptive ability guarantees its continued survival.*

adaptively (adv)

adapter (n) [also spelled: adaptor] *When you use electronic equipment in different countries, you need to use an adapter in order to plug it into the wall socket.*

adult (n) fully grown, mature or of legal age
> adult education, adult literacy, adult conversation, adult behavior
> young adult
> single adult [= unmarried adult]: *As the only single adult at the party, Jen felt uncomfortable with all the talk about children, schools and other family concerns.*

adulthood (n)
> to attain adulthood, to make it to adulthood, to survive into adulthood
> to reach adulthood: *Soon after Thelma reached adulthood, she moved out of her parents' house.*
> early adulthood, young adulthood

advocate (n) someone who supports, recommends or argues for an idea, proposal or cause
> an aggressive advocate, a strong advocate, an outspoken advocate, an enthusiastic advocate
> an ardent advocate, a staunch advocate [= a strong advocate]: *The senator is a strong advocate for raising the minimum wage.*
> a consumer advocate
> (to play) the devil's advocate [= to pretend to take the opposite side in an argument]: *Don't be angry with Alex. He doesn't really disagree with you. He's just playing the devil's advocate.*

advocate (v)
> to strongly advocate
> to advocate for, to advocate against

advocacy (n) the giving of support to someone or some idea
> political advocacy

aid (n) help or assistance
> to offer aid, to extend aid, to provide aid, to come to someone's aid, to increase aid
> to cut aid, to reduce aid, to withdraw aid, to withhold aid, to suspend aid [= to stop giving aid]: *The UN decided to suspend aid to the rebels until the situation on the ground becomes clearer.*
> to enlist someone's aid; to aid in: *The dogs can aid us in our search.*
> a teaching aid [= a devise that helps teachers teach better]: *Nowadays, the computer has become an important teaching aid in many school rooms.*

a hearing aid [= a devise that helps someone hear better]: *If you continue to listen to such loud music, you will have to wear hearing aids one of these days.*

a walking aid, a memory aid, a visual aid

economic aid, foreign aid, federal aid, humanitarian aid, military aid, legal aid, emergency aid

a call for aid, an appeal for aid [= asking for aid]: *Doctors without Borders issued an appeal for aid to help the victims of the tsunami.*

an aid for; an aid to: *Music can be used as an aid to memorization.*

with/without (the) aid (of): *She walks with the aid of a cane.*

first-aid kit [= a box or bag containing emergency supplies for treating injuries or illnesses]: *We never go for long hikes without taking a small first-aid kit with us.*

aid (v)

channel (n) a course or pathway; a route of communication or access

to open or close a channel

to go through the proper channels [= to work through the correct people and/or offices to get something done]: *The CEO won't listen to your ideas unless you go through the proper channels.*

to establish a channel, to open up a channel

a channel of communication: *Though several channels of communication are available to our customers who wish more information, we prefer that you email rather than phone.*

a radio channel, a TV channel, a cable channel, a satellite channel

a commercial channel, a movie channel, a sports channel

an indirect channel, an appropriate channel, a normal channel

a back channel [= an unofficial or secret means of communication]: *The news reporter is famous for her ability to gather information through back channels.*

channel (n) a water route

a river channel, a drainage channel, a deep channel, a narrow channel, a shipping channel

channel (v)

to channel into: *The criminals were channeling money into offshore accounts.*

to channel towards

to channel one's energy [= to focus one's energy in order to get better results]: *After the accident, the Olympic skier channeled her energy into helping people with disabilities become better athletes.*

to channel money: *The tycoon was effective at channeling money to her favorite candidates.*

chemical (n) a substance such as an element or molecular compound

to be exposed to chemicals, to dump chemicals

chemical-free; chemical warfare; chemical engineering

organic chemical, inorganic chemical

hazardous chemical, harmful chemical, toxic chemical [= a chemical that may cause harm or death]: *Many common garden plants actually produce toxic chemicals.*

agricultural chemical, industrial chemical, household chemical

chemical (adj)

chemical compound, chemical reaction, chemical substance

chemically (adv)

chemistry (n) the study of chemicals

chemist (n) [American: a person who studies chemistry]

a research chemist, an analytical chemist, an organic chemist, an inorganic chemist

chemist (n) [British: a person who prepares and sells medicines]

a local chemist, a dispensing chemist; a chemist's shop, the chemist's

classic (adj) serving as an outstanding or established model or example

a classic example (of): *That's a classic example of how not to get on a horse!*

a classic case (of): *The parliament's action was a classic example of Thatcherism.*

classic car, classic motorcycle

a minor classic, a great classic, a contemporary classic, an all-time classic, a pop/popular classic

classical (adj) relating to ancient Greece or Rome

classical architecture, classical style, classical poetry, classical drama, classical literature

classical (adj) relating to European concert music from the 17th and 18th centuries

classical music, classical guitar

classically (adv)

classic (n) a work of art having well-established value; something known as the best of its kind
To some car lovers, the 1964 Thunderbird is a real classic.

classics (n. pl.) writings of ancient Greece or Rome

comprehensive (adj) covering or including a large area or scope
comprehensive (medical) examination: *The doctor will give you a comprehensive physical examination once every year.*
a comprehensive response, a comprehensive list
extremely comprehensive, fully comprehensive, totally comprehensive
increasingly comprehensive, pretty comprehensive, reasonably comprehensive, fairly comprehensive

comprehensively (adv)

comprehensiveness (n)

comprehensives (n. pl.) exams that cover an entire year and/or field of study
to pass the comprehensives, to study for the comprehensives

comprise (v) to contain, include, consist of or be composed of something specified
comprised of : *This particular garden is comprised mostly of roses.*

confirm (v) to support or establish the certainty or validity of; to finalize or make definite
to confirm one's suspicion
to be able to confirm, to be unable to confirm, to be unwilling to confirm, seem to confirm
neither confirm nor deny: *We could neither confirm nor deny reports that the program would be cut next year.*
merely confirm, only confirm, simply confirm: *The tests merely confirmed our suspicion that there was alcohol in the drinks.*

confirmation (n)
to ask for confirmation, to need confirmation, to require confirmation, to seek confirmation [= to look for or try to get confirmation]: *Before you buy that software, you should seek confirmation from the supplier that it is compatible with your other programs.*
to await confirmation, to wait for confirmation, to receive confirmation, to obtain confirmation
further confirmation, independent confirmation, direct confirmation, final confirmation
official confirmation
confirmation bias [= the tendency of people to favor information that confirms what they already believe]: *It is difficult for some scientists to conduct fair, objective experiments due to their unconscious confirmation bias.*
confirmation in writing: *Thank you for agreeing to do business with us. I'll send you a confirmation of our agreement in writing.*

confirmable (adj) able to be verified or confirmed

confirmatory (adj) giving confirmation or supporting information

contrary (adj) opposed, opposite or quite different, as in character or purpose
contrary views
contrary to
contrary to one's expectations: *The results of the experiment ran totally contrary to our expectations.*
contrary to public opinion: *Contrary to public opinion, Mr. Beech will not run for office next year.*
contrary to popular myth: *Contrary to popular myth, the Great Wall of China is not visible from space.*
contrary to popular belief, contrary to popular opinion
completely contrary, entirely contrary, totally contrary

contrary (adv)
to run contrary to, to seem contrary to, to go contrary to

contrary (n)
on the contrary, to the contrary
despite claims to the contrary: *The Internal Revenue Service continues to target conservative groups for audits, despite claims to the contrary.*

contrarily (adv)

contrariness (n)

convert (v) to change a form, function or measure
to convert from: *Ben converted from Protestantism to Catholicism to please his new wife.*

to convert into: *Helen converted her kitchen table into a work desk.*

convert (n) a person who has changed his or her beliefs to a new system or religion

to win converts, to gain converts

recent convert, enthusiastic convert, reluctant convert

a convert to: *I'll never be a convert to your way of thinking.*

couple (v) to join together; connect

to couple to: *If you couple the wagon to the cart, you can pull them both at the same time.*

to couple with: *High prices coupled with unemployment can cause economic disaster.*

couple (n) a pair of people

a handsome couple, a beautiful couple, a lovely couple

an elderly couple, a young couple, a middle-aged couple

a bridal couple, a newly-married couple, a newly-wed couple

couple (n) two or three things or two or three times

a couple of minutes, a couple of hours, a couple of weeks, a couple of months, a couple of years

a couple of guys, a couple of beers, a couple of ideas

decade (n) a period of ten years

a decade ago, a decade later, the last decade, the preceding decade, the previous decade

the present decade, the current decade, the next decade, the coming decade, the new decade

a decade of: *The 1960s was a decade of civil disobedience.*

during the decade, throughout the decade, over the decade

decadal (adj) relating to a decade or to the number ten

definite (adj) certain, sure

definite about: *She wasn't definite about what color to paint this room.*

(it is) definite that: *It is definite that grandfather will arrive tomorrow.*

a definite advantage, a definite disadvantage

definitely (adv)

definiteness (n)

deny (v) to declare something not to be true; to refuse to believe

to deny the existence of, to deny the reports, to deny the accusations, to deny the allegations [= to deny the things that people say without proof]: *The investment banker denied the allegations that he had bribed several members of Congress.*

to deny angrily, categorically, emphatically, fervently, flatly, strongly, vehemently

denial (n)

to issue a denial: *The mayor issued a denial that she had used drugs.*

to be in denial [= refuse to believe that something is true]: *Although it was obvious to us that she had a drinking problem, she was in denial.*

deny (v) to prevent someone from having something

deny nothing: *Frank gives his wife everything; he denies her nothing.*

deny admittance: *Because they were too young, the teenagers were denied admittance to the movie.*

deny a goal: *The football team were denied a goal when the goalie deflected the ball.*

deny a victory: *The enemy were denied a victory when they ran out of ammunition.*

differentiate (v) to establish a difference or distinction between things

to differentiate between: *It's almost impossible to differentiate between Josh and Jake because they are identical twins.*

to differentiate from: *It is said that night begins when it is too dark to differentiate a black thread from a white thread.*

to differentiate right from wrong: *Education is sometimes of process of learning how to differentiate right from wrong.*

(it is) important to differentiate, (it is) possible to differentiate, (it is) difficult to differentiate

differentiation (n) the act of differentiating

product differentiation, instructional differentiation

differentiation (n) the way biological structures or processes become increasingly specialized

cell differentiation

differentiation (n) [mathematics] the process of finding a derivative

differentiation calculus, differentiation rule, differentiation formula differential (adj) being, causing or indicating a difference

differential (n) a difference between things that can be compared; a margin

  salary differential: *The salary differential between men and women in the US is growing smaller, but it is still a problem.*

differential (n) [machines] a system of gears that allow something to turn at different speeds

  differential gears

differential (n) [mathematics] a mathematical equation for an unknown function of one or several variables that relates the values of the function itself and its derivatives of various orders.

  differential equation, differential calculus

differential (n) [physics] the amount of difference between two or more forces or rates.

dispose (v) to get rid of or throw away

  to dispose of the rubbish, the garbage, the sewage, the waste

dispose (v) to finish using so that the matter is ended

  to dispose of the opposition

  to dispose of one's enemies: [= to defeat or vanquish one's enemies]: *The whole world was shocked when a video surfaced showing how the terrorists disposed of the enemies.*

disposal (n)

  garbage disposal, rubbish disposal, sewage disposal, waste disposal

disposal (n) availability; for use

  at someone's disposal: *We have two computers at your disposal in the lobby.*

  at someone's disposal [= to be ready to help]: *If you need help moving into your new house, I am at your disposal.*

disposable (adj)

  disposable plates, disposable cups, disposable spoons

  disposable diapers, disposable contact lenses

disposed (v) to be inclined to, to tend to

  well-disposed, naturally disposed, agreeably disposed, kindly disposed

  favorably disposed, generally disposed: *Oren is generally disposed to let his apartment become a mess.*

eliminate (v) to get rid of, exclude, or remove

  to eliminate altogether, to eliminate completely, to eliminate entirely, to eliminate totally

  to eliminate waste, to eliminate fraud, to eliminate corruption

  to seek to eliminate, to take steps to eliminate: *Elliot Ness took steps to eliminate corruption.*

  to eliminate from: *Because of his allergies, he had to eliminate peanuts from his diet.*

  designed to eliminate, impossible to eliminate

elimination (n)

  by the process of elimination: *Mark didn't borrow the book, Judy didn't borrow it, nor did I. Therefore, by the process of elimination, Bob must have borrowed it.*

empirical (adj) derived from or relying on experience, observation or experiment

  empirical studies, empirical evidence, empirical investigation, empirical observation, empirical findings

empirically (adv)

  empirically supported treatment

  empirically validated treatment

empiricism (n) a philosophy or belief that all knowledge is based on experience or observation

equip (v) to provide with the necessary tools, supplies, etc.

  to come equipped with: *The hotel room comes equipped with a microwave, a mini-refrigerator and a coffee maker.*

  to equip for: *With our new wood-burning stove, I think we are well-equipped for winter.*

  to equip with: *This new computer comes equipped with a DVD burner.*

  well-equipped, lavishly equipped, superbly equipped

equipment (n) tools or supplies that are used for a particular task

  to install equipment, to use equipment, to provide (the necessary) equipment

  modern equipment, the latest equipment, state-of-the-art equipment [= the most recent, modern equipment]: *The music studio contains state-of-the-art recording equipment.*

  outdated equipment

piece of equipment

faulty equipment, defective equipment [= broken equipment]: *It took the workers several days to replace the defective piece of equipment with a new one.*

office equipment, business equipment, medical equipment, military equipment

communication equipment, navigation equipment, radar equipment, radio equipment

camera equipment, video equipment

safety equipment, security equipment, protective equipment

extract (v) to draw, pull out or separate a substance or idea

to extract from: *We have ways to extract the truth from anyone.*

to extract a tooth, to extract a price

extract (v) to pull out a passage from a piece of writing: *The professor extracted several paragraphs from the long essay and had the students discuss them.*

extraction (n)

of ~ extraction [= the ethnic origin of one's family]: *Many of the people who live in Wisconsin are of German extraction.*

extractable (adj)

extract (n) a part of a written passage that is taken from the original

extract (n) a condensed and concentrated substance

an herbal extract, vanilla extract, plant extract

file (n) a collection of paper or records or other materials

to start a file, to open a file, to lose a file, to close a file

an official file, a confidential file, a secret file

to keep something on file; to keep a file on someone: *The CIA is keeping a file on the students and faculty who marched in the protest.*

to access a file, to copy a file, to delete a file, to erase a file

to upload a file, to download a file

a data file, a text file

file (v) to submit an application

to file for divorce, to file for bankruptcy; to file a lawsuit, to file a peace order

to file a report: *Our correspondent in Beirut has filed this report.*

file (v) to walk in a line

to file past, to file into, to file through, to file along: *The children filed along the sidewalk until they reached the church.*

finite (adj) having a definite limit or end

finite resources, finite number of possibilities, finite number of elements

finite verb, finite calculus

finite universe

finitely (adv)

[mathematics] finitely generated group: *Every finitely generated abelian group is isomorphic to a direct sum of cyclic groups.*

finitely generated algebra, finite set

finite (n)

finiteness (n)

foundation (n) the basic structure that supports a theory, idea or a building

to lay a foundation

to undermine the foundation

a firm foundation, a solid foundation, a sound foundation, a proper foundation: *Many parents believe that pre-school can lay a proper foundation for a child's future academic success.*

a shaky foundation, a weak foundation

the foundation of: *The foundation of a good life is a good education.*

foundational (adj)

found (v) [see Unit 9]

globe (n) a ball-shaped object; the world

to circle the globe

around the globe

in all corners of the globe: *McDonald's restaurants are located in all corners of the globe.*

global (adj)
    global initiative, global finances
    global village; global warming

globally (adv)

guarantee (n) a promise that something will happen
    to offer a guarantee, to give a guarantee, to sign a guarantee
    a written guarantee: *To make you feel more confident, I'll give you a written guarantee.*
    you have my guarantee: *You have my personal guarantee that these pills will make you smarter.*

guarantee (v)
    to guarantee for: *These tires are guaranteed for 40,000 miles.*
    to guarantee against (defects): *This TV is guaranteed against defects or your money back.*
    to fully guarantee, absolutely guarantee, personally guarantee, virtually guarantee: *When the heavy rains began, the English were virtually guaranteed victory.*
    by no means guaranteed, not necessarily guaranteed

hierarchy (n) any system of persons or things ranked one above another
    to rise (up) in the hierarchy, to move up in the hierarchy
    to create a hierarchy, to establish a hierarchy
    an academic hierarchy, a church hierarchy, a military hierarchy, a corporate hierarchy, the ruling hierarchy
    complex hierarchy, strict hierarchy, established hierarchy, rigid hierarchy [= a hierarchy that never changes]: *For centuries, the Catholic church has had a rigid hierarchy with the Pope at the top.*
    within the hierarchy
    position in the hierarchy, status in the hierarchy, level in the hierarchy

hierarchical (adj)
    extremely hierarchical, rigidly hierarchical, strictly hierarchical, extremely hierarchical
    fairly hierarchical, essentially hierarchical

hierarchically (adv)

identical (adj) exactly the same
    to appear identical, to seem identical, to look identical, to remain identical
    nearly identical, virtually identical, practically identical, basically identical, essentially identical
    almost identical: *Your paragraph and the paragraph in this article are almost identical. That's plagiarism!*
    identical with, identical to: *This necklace is identical to the one I lost last year.*
    identical twins

identically (adv)

ideology (n) the body of ideas and beliefs which serve as the foundation for a social, economic or political system

    to embrace an ideology, to espouse an ideology, to adopt an ideology; to reject an ideology
    religious ideology, political ideology, communist ideology, capitalist ideology
    dominant ideology, official ideology, coherent ideology [= a logical, consistent ideology]: *It does not seem to be a real political movement as it does not have a coherent ideology or specific goals.*
    strong ideology, cultural ideology, economic ideology

ideological (adj)

ideologically (adv)

infer (v) to conclude from facts, evidence, observation, deduction
    to infer from: *I think we can infer from Kevin's silence that he is dissatisfied with his role.*
    to logically infer: *If your dinner guests ask for seconds, you can logically infer that they think the food is good.*

inference (n)
    to draw an inference, to make an inference (about)
    a valid inference, a reasonable inference, a fair inference, a logical inference
    an inference based on: *We made some inferences based on how the children reacted to our questions.*
    by inference: *He is critical of modern serious music. Therefore, by inference, he is not fond of Takemitsu's latest work.*

inferable (adj)

inferential (adj)

innovate (v) to introduce something new; make changes in anything that is already established
constantly innovate, continually innovate

innovation (n)
to encourage innovation, to foster innovation, to facilitate innovation, to stimulate innovation
to stifle innovation, to thwart innovation [= to try to stop innovation]: *For some reason, the director tried to stifle innovation by not allowing faculty members to meet to discuss the curriculum.*
educational innovation, industrial innovation, technical innovation, scientific innovation
a daring innovation, a major innovation, a radical innovation
constant innovation, continuous innovation

innovative (adj)

innovator (n)

insert (v) to put something inside something else
to insert into; insert gently
to insert a key into a lock
to insert between, to insert through

insert (n)

insertion (n)

insertable (adj)

intervene (v) to come between two things; to involve oneself or interfere in a dispute
to intervene in (someone's affairs)
to intervene to: *We will try to intervene to help the Bosnians recover from the war.*
to actively intervene, to directly intervene; to personally intervene, to intervene militarily
to be reluctant to intervene, to be powerless to intervene: *We were horrified that the two dogs were fighting, but we were powerless to intervene.*
intervene on behalf of: *Mr. Costner intervened personally on behalf of the other actors.*

intervention (n)
to call for intervention, to demand intervention, to resist intervention
direct intervention, active intervention, decisive intervention, forceful intervention
early intervention, childhood intervention, timely intervention
personal intervention, government intervention, official intervention, ministerial intervention
external intervention, foreign intervention, armed intervention, military intervention

isolate (v) to separate; to keep apart
to isolate from

isolation (n)
to live in isolation, to experience isolation, to suffer from isolation
to look at something in isolation: *You shouldn't look at his behavior in isolation, but as a part of an on-going pattern.*
total isolation, complete isolation
emotional isolation, social isolation
international isolation, diplomatic isolation, political isolation
isolation hospital, isolation ward [= a section of a hospital that is separated from other sections] :
in splendid isolation

isolated (adj)
to appear isolated, to feel isolated, to become isolated, to remain isolated, to leave isolated
completely isolated, entirely isolated, totally isolated
rather isolated, somewhat isolated, largely isolated, relatively isolated

isolate (n) something that has been separated from others in the same group [This term is used in psychology, biology, linguistics and chemisty.]

isolationism (n) the belief that a nation should not get involved with other countries

isolationist (n)
culturally isolated, politically isolated, socially isolated, physically isolated

media (n. pl.) [medium = n. sing.] the means by which information and entertainment are communicated

mass media, electronic media, news media, local media, national media
audio-visual media, broadcast media
foreign media, international media, local media, national media, mainstream media
(to focus) media attention (on), media coverage, media interest, media reporting
media circus [= sensational news coverage that is out of proportion to the actual news itself]
media mogul, media magnate, media tycoon, media baron [= a rich and powerful person who controls the media]: *Within two decades, Pierre-Karl Péladeau had become a well-known media mogul in Quebec.*
in the media: *Don't believe everything you see and read in the media.*

mode (n) a way of doing something
to change to a mode, to switch to a mode
normal mode, traditional mode, usual mode
in playback mode, in recording mode, in work mode
mode of operation, mode of address, mode of communication, mode of expression, mode of transport

paradigm (n) model or pattern or example
to serve as a paradigm; to generate a paradigm
a paradigm shift; the prevailing paradigm
paradigmatic (adj)
paradigmatic association
paradigmatically (adv)

phenomenon (n) [pl: phenomena] a perceptible occurrence, circumstance, or fact
a natural phenomenon, a rare phenomenon, an isolated phenomenon
an urban phenomenon, a cultural phenomenon, a social phenomenon
a common phenomenon, a new phenomenon, a universal phenomenon, a widespread phenomenon
a psychic phenomenon, a supernatural phenomenon
phenomenal (adj)
phenomenally (adv)

priority (n) something that needs attention before other things
to have priority over, to set priorities
to establish priorities: *New Year's Eve is an excellent time to establish your priorities for the upcoming year.*
to take priority (over): *Students' needs should take priority over administrative procedures.*
high priority, low priority; first priority, top priority
to reexamine priorities, rethink priorities; to determine priority, to sort out priorities
to sort out one's priorities: *I agree that you could drop out of school and get a job. However, I think you had better sort out your priorities.*
high priority, main priority, number one priority, top priority, first priority, immediate priority; low priority
prioritize (v) to put or do according to priority
If you have too many things to do in one day, you need to prioritize your tasks.
prioritization (n)

prohibit (v) to forbid, especially by law or other authority
to prohibit from: *We were prohibited from attending the lecture.*
strictly prohibit, expressly prohibit, specifically prohibit, constitutionally prohibit
prohibition (n)
to impose prohibition, to order prohibition
alcohol prohibition, drug prohibition; prohibition of alcohol, prohibition of drugs
absolute prohibition, total prohibition
prohibited (adj)
strictly prohibited: *Smoking is strictly prohibited in public spaces.*
prohibitive (adj)
prohibitively (adv) excessively
prohibitively expensive, prohibitively costly, prohibitively difficult

release (v) to set free or let go
to release prisoners, to release one's grip

to catch and release (fish)

release (v) to make available

  newly released, recently released; originally released

  officially release: *The government officially released the latest economic data.*

release (n)

  news release, press release, release time

  prerelease [pre-release]: *The new Amazon Kindle pre-release is somewhat buggy.*

reverse (v) to turn in the opposite direction

  to reverse a position

reverse (n)

  to suffer a reverse, to sustain a reverse; (to suffer) a financial reverse

  reverse psychology

  a reverse in fortunes; the exact reverse

  reverse discrimination [= discrimination against previously favored groups]: *Some people think that hiring members of minority groups when members of the majority group are better qualified is an example of reverse discrimination.*

  on the reverse; on the reverse page, on the reverse side: *George Washington is on one side of the coin and an eagle is on the reverse.*

reversal (n) a setback, a loss, or an end to progress

  to suffer a reversal, to amount to a reversal, to mark a reversal, to represent a reversal

  a complete reversal, total reversal, dramatic reversal, sudden reversal, apparent reversal

reverse (adj)

  reverse phone book, reverse mortgage, reverse trend

reversible (adj)

  reversible sweater, reversible jacket

  easily reversible, readily reversible

simulate (v) to imitate or to appear to be like something else

  to simulate weightlessness

  to be designed to simulate, to be used to simulate

simulation (n)

  to run a simulation, to carry out a simulation

  computer simulation, laboratory simulation, real-time simulation

  accident simulation, flight simulation, design simulation

  simulation program, simulation game, simulation exercise

sole (adj) alone; single; without others

  sole survivor, sole reason

  [business] sole proprietorship

solely (adv)

  solely responsible for: *Betty was solely responsible for the education of her students.*

sole (n) the bottom surface of shoes or feet

  thin sole, thick sole, leather sole, rubber sole

  to have blisters on the soles of one's feet

sole (n) a type of fish

somewhat (adv) a little; to some extent: *It was somewhat warm yesterday.*

submit (v) to offer (oneself) as a subject

  submit to an examination: *The athletes were required to submit to a physical examination.*

  submit to treatment: *The prisoners were required to submit to treatment for drug abuse.*

submit (v) to give something so that it will be considered by others

  to invite to submit, to require to submit

  to submit a resignation: *Dr. Li submitted her resignation and will retire in two weeks.*

  to submit a report: *You need to submit your report to the committee by tomorrow.*

  to submit an argument

  to submit an article (for publication)

submit (v) to let someone or something take control

  voluntarily submit, willingly submit; meekly submit

refuse to submit, be forced to submit, be compelled to submit

submit to authority, submit to force, submit to threats

submittal (n)

submission (n) something that will be considered by others

to require submission, to reject a submission, to accept a submission

[law] to hear a submission, to uphold a submission

a detailed submission, a written submission, an oral submission, a joint submission

submission (n)

to demand submission, to expect submission

to beat into submission, to bomb into submission, to force into submission

to starve into submission

complete submission, total submission

submissible (adj) allowed to be considered

succeed (v) to follow or come after

successor (n) a person who follows another and takes that person's job

to pick a successor, to choose a successor, to appoint a successor, to designate a successor

the chosen successor, logical successor, natural successor, obvious successor

a worthy successor, rightful successor

likely successor, eventual successor, possible successor, potential successor

succession (n)

in logical succession, in quick succession; bewildering succession

rule of succession, line of succession; succession to the throne

succeed (v) to achieve the desired result

thesis (n) [pl: theses] an idea or proposition to be supported or maintained by argument

to write a thesis (about/on), to advance a thesis, to propose a thesis

to challenge a thesis, to refute a thesis

main thesis, major thesis

topic (n) the subject or a talk or of a written text

to choose a topic, to pick a topic, to narrow a topic

to expand on a topic

controversial topic, main topic, sub topic; broad topic, narrow topic

chosen topic, favorite topic, important topic, key topic, principal topic, hot topic

historical topic, philosophical topic, social topic, etc.

a range of topics; related topics

a topic of conversation, a topic of discussion, topic of interest

topical (adj)

transmit (v) to convey or pass on; to send from one place to another

to transmit from ~ to; to transmit by (satellite, radio)

to transmit live: *This program is being transmitted live from New York City.*

to transmit a disease, to transmit malaria: *A certain mosquito transmits malaria.*

sexually transmitted disease, genetically transmitted

actively transmitted, easily transmitted, readily transmitted

automatically transmitted, electronically transmitted

transmission (n) the act of conveying or passing on

direct transmission, one-way transmission

data transmission, voice transmission, fax transmission, cable transmission

radio transmission, television transmission, wireless transmission

live transmission, cultural transmission, simultaneous transmission

transmission (n) the system of gears that transmits power from one mechanism to another

automatic transmission, manual transmission, four-speed transmission, five-speed transmission

transmitter (n)

ultimate (adj) last or final in a series or process; fundamental or basic; most important or greatest

to carry/take something to the ultimate (conclusion): *If we take your argument to its ultimate conclusion, we'd agree that all murderers should be punished by death.*

ultimate achievement, ultimate goal, ultimate conclusion, ultimate sacrifice

ultimately (adv)

ultimate (n) the best, most important or greatest

    the ultimate in: *This car is the ultimate in driving luxury.*

unique (adj) one of a kind; no others are equal to it

    a unique opportunity

    unique in: *Holland is unique in the way it treats drug use.*

    unique in this respect

    unique to: *Kangaroos are unique to Australia.*

    quite unique, totally unique, truly unique

    far from unique, by no means unique: *The ideas in your essay are far from unique. Try to be a little more creative; think outside the box.*

uniquely (adv)

visible (adj) able to be seen

    to remain visible, to become visible, to stay visible

    clearly visible, plainly visible, all too visible

    dimly visible, faintly visible, barely visible

    visible from: *The Great Wall of China is not visible from space as many people think.*

    visible to: *His dissatisfaction was visible to everyone who looked at his face.*

    a highly visible public figure

    visible for miles

    (without) visible traces

    visible to the naked eye: *Mercury is visible to the naked eye just after sunset.*

visibly (adv)

    visibly shaken

visibility (n)

vision (n) ability to see

    excellent vision, perfect vision, 20/20 vision

    normal vision, clear vision ; blurred vision, impaired vision, poor vision

    double vision, tunnel vision

    binocular vision, stereoscopic vision, x-ray vision, night vision, peripheral vision [= side vision]: *After her stroke, Gerry had very limited peripheral vision and had to turn her head to see what was on her right side.*

    field of vision

vision (n) imaginary sight

    to experience a vision, to have a vision, to receive a vision

    to conjure up a vision: *As we prepared for our trip, I conjured up a vision of white sand and warm sunshine.*

    a disturbing vision, a horrible vision

    a spiritual vision, a mystic vision

vision (n) ability to plan for the future

    to develop a vision, to share a vision, to convey a vision, to expand a vision

    a great vision, a broad vision, a comprehensive vision, a global vision, a wide vision

    to outline a vision, to sketch a vision, to promote a vision

    to cloud one's vision [= to make it difficult to plan]: *Elaine was careful not to let Sally's negativity cloud her vision of a better learning environment for the children.*

Synonyms

adapt:	accommodate, arrange, adjust
adult:	grown-up, mature, big
advocate:	recommend, advise, support
aid:	help, assist, serve
channel:	course, bed, waterway
chemical:	substance, element, compound
classic:	model, idea, exemplar
comprehensive:	thorough, complete, extensive
comprise:	contain, include, consist of
confirm:	validate, affirm, verify
contrary:	opposite, conflicting, reverse
convert:	transform, change, remake
couple:	pair, twosome, duo
decade:	ten
definite:	exact, specific, precise
deny:	disallow, negate, forbid
differentiate:	contrast, discriminate, distinguish
dispose:	discard, remove, eliminate
eliminate:	abolish, remove, dispose
empirical:	objective, scientific, verifiable
equip:	furnish, outfit, supply
extract:	pull, remove, derive
file:	catalogue, archive
finite:	limited, constrained
foundation:	base, support, groundwork
globe:	earth, world, sphere
guarantee:	warranty, promise, assurance
hierarchy:	rank, level, status
identical:	same, alike, equal
ideology:	beliefs, principles, thought
infer:	conclude, determine, guess
innovate:	invent, pioneer
insert:	introduce, interject, stick
intervene:	interfere, mediate, intrude
isolate:	separate, seclude, sequester
media:	news, press, publication
mode:	method, way, approach
paradigm:	pattern, model, example
phenomenon:	event, occurrence, happening
priority:	preference, primacy, preeminence
prohibit:	disallow, forbid, ban
release:	liberate, let go, free
reverse:	backward, opposite, inverse
simulate:	imitate, mock, copy
sole:	lone, only, solitary
somewhat:	rather, fairly, pretty
submit:	surrender, resign, yield
succession:	progression, sequence, series
thesis:	premise, proposition, theme
topic:	issue, subject, point
transmit:	send, broadcast, convey
ultimate:	final, last, utmost
unique:	sole, singular, individual
visible:	seen, observable, noticeable

Unit 7

Answers

Definitions

1. convert	16. identical	31. hierarchy	46. chemical
2. equip	17. definite	32. phenomenon	47. reverse
3. infer	18. adult	33. priority	48. comprehensive
4. successor	19. dispose	34. submit	49. confirmed
5. mode	20. isolate	35. comprise	50. guaranteed
6. globe	21. transmit	36. adapt	51. denied
7. contrary	22. paradigm	37. empirical	52. couple
8. solely	23. channel	38. classic	53. foundation
9. somewhat	24. thesis	39. ultimate	54. file
10. releases	25. unique	40. advocate	
11. intervenes	26. visible	41. prohibit	
12. extracts	27. finite	42. innovate	
13. decade	28. simulate	43. aid	
14. ideology	29. insert	44. medium	
15. topic	30. differentiate	45. elimination	

Parts of Speech

1. adaptation / adaptable	12. converted / converts	23. filed / files	34. intervention / intervened
2. adulthood / adult	13. coupled / couple	24. finite / finite	35. isolated / isolation
3. advocates / advocacy	14. decades / decade	25. foundation/ foundations / foundation	36. media / medium
4. aided / aids	15. definite / definitely	26. globe / global	37. modes / mode
5. channeled / channels	16. denied / denial	27. guarantee / guaranteed	38. paradigms / paradigm
6. chemicals / chemical	17. differentiation / differentiate	28. hierarchy / hierarchically	39. phenomenon / phenomena
7. classical / classic	18. disposed / disposable	29. identically / identical	40. prioritize / priorities
8. comprehensively / comprehensives	19. elimination / eliminates	30. ideologies / ideological	41. prohibited / prohibition
9. comprised / comprise	20. empirically / empirical	31. inferable / inferred / inference	42. released / release
10. confirmed/ confirms / confirmation	21. equipped / equips	32. innovation / innovators	43. reverses / reversals
11. contrary / contrary	22. extracted / extract	33. insertion / inserts	44. simulations / simulated

45. sole / solely	49. thesis / thesis	53. unique / uniquely
46. somewhat / somewhat	50. topic / topics	54. visibility / visibly
47. submitted / submission	51. transmitted / transmission	
48. succeed / successor	52. ultimate / ultimately	

Unit 7

Answers

Collocations			
Exercise 1	**Exercise 2**	**Exercise 3**	**Exercise 4**
1. adult Adult adulthood	1. reverse reversal reversible	1. mode mode modes	1. transmit transmitted/ transmissible transmission
2. deny denial denial	2. innovating innovation innovation	2. successor successor succession	2. file file files
3. hierarchy hierarchy hierarchical	3. disposal disposed Disposable	3. topics topic topic	3. advocates advocate advocate
4. differentiate differentiate differential	4. classic classical classics	4. empirical Empirically empirical	4. aid aid aid
5. adapted adaptable adaptation	5. simulation simulate simulates	5. contrary contrary contrary	5. finite finite
6. prohibited prohibition prohibitively	6. elimination eliminate eliminating	6. submit submit submission	6. isolation isolated isolation
7. visible visibly vision	7. guarantee guaranteed guarantee	7. unique unique	7. ultimate ultimate ultimate
8. inferences inference infer	8. confirmed confirm confirmation	8. converted converts convert	8. globe global
9. channel channel channels	9. intervene intervention intervene	9. equipment equipped	9. priority priorities priority
10. chemicals chemical	10. sole solely	10. foundation/~s foundation/~s	10. phenomenon phenomenon

Unit 7

Answers

Synonyms (Crossword)

Across	Down
3. contrary	1. somewhat
6. confirm	2. dispose
10. couple	3. comprise
11. release	4. infer
12. channel	5. aid
14. visible	7. sole
17. adult	8. identical
18. equip	9. paradigm
25. deny	12. comprehensive
26. topic	13. hierarchy
27. eliminate	15. guarantee
28. ultimate	16. globe
30. adapt	19. foundation
	20. prohibit
	21. convert
	22. isolate
	23. unique
	24. definite
	29. mode

Review

1. comprehensive	19. mode	37. prohibit
2. finite	20. hierarchy	38. innovate
3. ultimate	21. channel	39. isolate
4. definite	22. advocate	40. couple
5. somewhat	23. aid	41. comprise
6. identical	24. file	42. adapt
7. classic	25. ideology	43. convert
8. sole	26. paradigm	44. dispose
9. empirical	27. globe	45. infer
10. unique	28. foundation	46. intervene
11. visible	29. phenomenon	47. submit
12. contrary	30. successor	48. reverse
13. adult	31. confirm	49. extract
14. decade	32. deny	50. differentiate
15. guarantee	33. equip	51. eliminate
16. media	34. insert	52. chemicals
17. priority	35. release	53. simulations
18. thesis	36. transmit	54. topics

Unit 8

Word List

n = noun   **v** = verb   **adj** = adjective   **adv** = adverb   **prep** = preposition

abandon (v)
    abandon (n)
    abandonment (n)
accompany (v)
    accompaniment (adj)
accumulate (v)
    accumulation (n)
    accumulative (adj)
ambiguous (adj)
    ambiguously (adv)
    ambiguity (n)
append (v)
    appendage (n)
    appendix (n)
appreciate (v)
    appreciation (n)
    appreciative (adj)
    appreciatively (adv)
arbitrary (adj)
    arbitrarily (adv)
    arbitrate (v)
    arbitration (n)
automate (v)
    automation (n)
bias (n)
    bias (v)
chart (n)
    chart (v)
    chartable (adj)
clarify (v)
    clarification (n)
commodity (n)
complement (n)
    complement (v)
    complementary (adj)
conform (v)
    conformity (n)
    conformance (n)
    conformable (adj)
contemporary (adj)
    contemporary (n)
    contemporaneous (adj)
    contemporaneously (adv)
contradict (v)
    contradiction (n)
    contradictory (adj)
crucial (adj)
    crucially (adv)
currency (n)
denote (v)
    denotation (n)

detect (v)
    detection (n)
    detector (n)
    detectable (adj)
    detective (n)
deviate (v)
    deviation (n)
displace (v)
    displacement (n)
    displaceable (adj)
eventual (adj)
    eventually (adv)
    eventuality (n)
    eventuate (v)
exhibit (v)
    exhibit (n)
    exhibition (n)
exploit (v)
    exploit (n)
    exploitable (adj)
    exploitation (n)
fluctuate (v)
    fluctuation (n)
guideline (n)
highlight (n)
    highlight (v)
implicit (adj)
    implicitly (adv)
    implication (n)
    implicitness (n)
induce (v)
    inducement (n)
inevitable (adj)
    inevitably (adv)
    inevitability (n)
infrastructure (n)
inspect (v)
    inspection (n)
    inspector (n)
intense (adj)
    intensely (adv)
    intensity (n)
    intenseness (n)
    intensify (v)
manipulate (v)
    manipulation (n)
    manipulative (adj)
    manipulator (n)
minimize (v)
    minimization (n)
    minimal (adj)
    minimally (adv)
offset (v)
    offset (n)
    offset (adj)

practitioner (n)
predominant (adj)
    predominantly (adv)
    predominance (n)
prospect (n)
    prospect (v)
    prospects (n. pl.)
radical (adj)
    radical (n)
    radically (adv)
    radicalize (v)
    radicalization (n)
random (adj)
    randomly (adv)
    randomize (v)
    randomization (n)
reinforce (v)
    reinforcement (n)
    reinforcements (n. pl.)
restore (v)
    restoration (n)
    restorable (adj)
revise (v)
    revision (n)
    revisable (adj)
    revisionism (n)
    revisionist (n0
tense (adj)
    tense (n)
    tense (v)
    tenseness (n)
    tension (n)
terminate (v)
    termination (n)
    terminal (adj)
theme (n)
    thematic (adj)
    thematically (adv)
thereby (adv)
uniform (adj)
    uniformly (adv)
    uniform (n)
    uniformity (n)
vehicle (n)
    vehicular (adj)
via (adv)
virtual (adj)
    virtually (adv)
visual (adj)
    visually (adv)
    visual (n)
    visualize (v)
    vision (n)
    visuals (n. pl.)

Unit 8

Definitions Use the definition clues to write the correct words in the blanks.

1.	to give up something completely; to withdraw support *Because we ran out of money, we had to _____ our plans to remodel our house.*	conform clarify induce chart abandon fluctuate
2.	to look like or act in a similar way; to be like all the others *Michele always finds it difficult to _____ to rules.*	
3.	to persuade, influence or stimulate something to happen *We could not _____ Henry to join us for the party.*	
4.	existing at the same time; belonging to the current time *Zoe is a student of _____ music.*	crucial radical arbitrary contemporary predominant minimal
5.	not based on objective principles *The manager's decisions seem _____ to us; they don't make any sense.*	
6.	extreme *Anthony takes the _____ position that all rich people must be taxed heavily.*	
7.	a system of money used in a country *The euro is the _____ used by twelve member nations of the European Union.*	bias currency displacement infrastructure reinforcement inspection
8.	an inclination to favor one side; a prejudicial attitude *The liberal media have a _____ for the president.*	
9.	the physical and organizational structure that allows society to operate *The tsunami destroyed much of the _____ in the area around Fukushima.*	
10.	to strengthen, make more effective, or give additional support *New insights _____ relationships between human social activity and the natural environment as a whole.*	accompany terminate manipulate denote reinforce detect
11.	to represent or to indicate directly *The €, £ and $ _____ various currencies.*	
12.	to go along with; to join as a companion *A colleague will _____ me to the conference.*	
13.	by way of *He drove from Boston to Miami _____ Atlanta.*	arbitrary intensely virtually thereby inevitable via
14.	almost, but not in every way; not exactly *The bus drivers' strike _____ paralyzed the city.*	
15.	by means of that; in that connection *He was late for the interview, _____ losing any chance of getting the job.*	

16. a useful thing that has value and could be bought or sold *Coffee is one of Brazil's most important export _____ .* 17. a statement or policy indicating requirements or recommendations *Be sure to read the author submission _____ before you send in your manuscript.* 18. someone who practices an art, occupation or profession *Medical _____ can advise individuals with a recent history of heart disease on which vitamins to take.*	guidelines practitioners commodities prospects offsets biases
19. to reduce to the smallest amount *We will make every effort to _____ your downtime.* 20. to gather or collect gradually over time *We expect to _____ 20 inches of snow overnight.* 21. to discover or notice the existence of something *The test can _____ the presence of THC in the blood.*	minimize reinforce accumulate visualize detect fluctuate
22. the possibility of success, improvement or recovery *The people will face the _____ of a general election.* 23. a means for moving or transporting people or things *The electric _____ uses a new kind of battery.* 24. an idea or image that is repeated or revisited *The central _____ of the play is morality.*	complement contemporary vehicle prospect termination theme
25. able to be seen *The video gives you a _____ tour of the museum.* 26. alike in most or all ways *Policies on clubs should be _____ from school to school.* 27. a state of emotional or mental strain *During the incredibly _____ moments that followed the shooting, I read a mixture of emotions in his eyes.*	intense visual tense crucial eventual uniform
28. to vary in amount, value or level; to rise and fall *Prices of commodities _____ from day to day.* 29. to control by the hands, especially in a skillful manner *With Photoshop, you can digitally _____ the picture.* 30. to examine something again in order to change or improve it *With the new data, we are able to _____ the economic forecast.*	revise abandon accumulate exploit manipulate fluctuate

31. a graph, table, map or diagram showing data *The organizational _____ is too complex to be useful.* 32. something that provides balance or contrast *A simple green salad makes an excellent _____ to the savory lamb dish.* 33. the most significant, interesting or outstanding feature *The _____ of the Tanzania tour was the visit to Ngorogoro Crater.*	offset complement chart revision highlight deviation
34. to add as a supplement; to affix or attach *We learned how to _____ one text file to another.* 35. to make something clearer or easier to understand *You need to _____ the responsibilities of the researchers in the form of a written contract.* 36. to make the greatest use of something; to take unfair advantage of *These computer viruses _____ some of the weaknesses in the Windows platform.*	induce restore inspect exploit clarify append
37. more frequent; having the greatest importance or power *A paradigm shift occurs when the current _____ paradigm is replaced by a new one.* 38. great or extreme *The campers were not prepared for the _____ desert heat.* 39. without a definite plan, order, pattern or purpose *The fairest thing to do is to choose a name at _____ .*	intense implicit random eventual predominant ambiguous
40. to understand or be aware of the value of something; to be thankful *I really _____ all the help you have given me.* 41. to turn or move away from a planned course or the normal way *They get into trouble when they _____ from the rules.* 42. to examine carefully and critically *First, _____ for any damage to the foundation.*	displace minimize deviate appreciate inspect visualize
43. to return something to the original condition or state *The old farm house was _____ to the way it was in the 1880s.* 44. to counter-balance, counteract or compensate *The expenditures were _____ by an increase in revenue.* 45. to show something publically; to appear *Liz Taylor's diamonds were _____ at the museum.*	exhibited reinforced induced clarified offset restored

Unit 8

46. happening after an unspecified period of time *Her hard work led to her _____ promotion.* 47. unclear; having several possible meanings *The film has an _____ ending in which the fate of the world is left in doubt.* 48. extremely important, essential or vital *There is a _____ difference between a goal and a resolution.*	random eventual predominant contemporary ambiguous crucial
49. to change to way of doing something that requires no manual control *This software _____ the process of backing up files.* 50. to say, write or act in a contrary or opposite way *We are confused because that completely _____ what you told us yesterday.* 51. to bring to an end *The sequence _____ when the value of X becomes zero.*	contradicts abandons automates complements terminates deviates
52. put or taken out of the usual place *More than two thousand workers were _____ when Boeing closed the plant in Kansas.* 53. certain to happen; unable to avoid *Change is _____, so we must prepare ourselves.* 54. implied or meant, but not directly expressed *Such a notion seems _____ in the push for online science lessons today.*	intense radical implicit displaced inevitable exploit

Unit 8

Parts of Speech

Write the parts of speech (noun, verb, adjective or adverb form).
Word Forms: Be careful with nouns and verbs:
      Some *nouns* might need to be plural (~s).
      Some *verbs* might need ~s, ~ed, ~ing.

abandon   1. After the accident, the teenager _____ the car.

                     It was difficult to forgive Mabel for _____ her family.

accompany   2. I played the violin and Madison _____ me on the piano.

                     Madison's _____ was superb.

accumulate   3. We expect an _____ of over a foot of snow tonight.

                     The _____ effects of the marketing campaign were quite noticeable.

ambiguous   4. The _____ worded instructions confused us.

                     The computer cannot tolerate _____ . It cannot think.

append   5. This fish has two leg-like _____ that allow it to crawl on land.

                     It is possible to _____ a date to a filename.

appreciate   6. Lonnie was given a box of chocolates in _____ for the extra help he provided.

                     Emily never felt very _____ for all the support she had given to her family.

arbitrary   7. Sam made a somewhat _____ list of things for us to do over the weekend. There was no logic to it.

                     For their new game, the children invented rules _____ .

automate   8. When the company _____ its production line, some workers will lose their jobs.

                     Office _____ should help to increase efficiency.

bias   9. We stopped reading the newspaper because of its one-sided, _____ reporting.

                     My uncle has a _____ against buying foreign-made goods.

chart   10. After leaving Corsica, the captain _____ a course towards Sicily.

                     The new pie _____ graphically shows how much of the budget goes to the military and how much goes to social security.

clarify   11. Thank you for _____ the ambiguity regarding your marital status.

                     The responsibilities of each participant need to be _____ at the outset.

Unit 8

commodity   12. Open space is a rare _____ in many urban areas.

Coffee and sugar are the country's principal crops and most important export _____ .

complement   13. The usual conference sessions were _____ by optional workshops and discussion sessions.

Qualitative research approaches are considered as _____ to, and not in competition with, quantitative approaches.

conform   14. Their way of living would challenge the dull _____ of everyday life under capitalism.

Ginny's version of last night's shooting _____ with Levi's account, so we are reasonably sure that it is accurate.

contemporary   15. Manchester offers you the opportunity to understand _____ Japan through its language and history.

Strauss and Mahler were _____, and both are considered to have been Romanticists.

contradict   16. Kant resolves this _____ by assuming two points of view or modes of existence.

The reason for these apparently _____ findings is the specific nature of each sport.

crucial   17. It is _____ to understand why a given program works or does not work.

Bernanke is convinced that the success of small businesses is _____ important to the health of the entire economy.

currency   18. Some countries use two different _____ .

You can exchange your foreign _____ at the airport.

denote   19. The expressions '4' and '8/2' have the same _____ but express different senses.

The most important items on the list are _____ with an asterisk (*).

detect   20. Only one test is capable of _____ the virus.

A trace of THC was _____ in the blood sample.

deviate   21. Alan gets upset at any _____ from the normal routine.

His latest film is successful even though it _____ from the formula of the films it is trying to parody.

displace   22. Over 78,000 Kurds were _____ from their homes.

The _____ of an object is defined as the vector distance from some initial point to a final point.

eventual   23. Their _____ downfall was their love of publicity.

They prepared for all _____ before traveling to Peru.

exhibit   24. Rodney is someone who _____ great intelligence.

Details of future _____ are available on line.

exploit   25. Mineral _____ dates back to the times of the Romans.

By _____ a loophole, they saved money on their taxes.

fluctuate   26. Prices _____ markedly from one day to the next.

In this experiment, you must not allow any _____ of the temperature.

guideline   27. Brandy was fired for failure to follow the _____.

None of the _____ helped us make our decision.

highlight   28. The new report _____ the fact that more than half of the inmates have alcohol problems.

A few _____ of the game will be shown later on.

implicit   29. The paper discusses the various _____ of these findings in relation to students' learning.

The lawyer _____ stated her objections.

induce   30. He offered us a cash _____ to get us to vote for him.

What can I give you to _____ you to accept my offer?

inevitable   31. Climate change seems _____, or at least beyond our control.

You must keep trying, despite the _____ that you will make mistakes along the way.

infrastructure 32. The need to rebuild a media _____ from the bottom up is obvious.

Merseyside has a good transport _____ which is being built on to suit the emerging needs of the city center.

inspect   33. It is the responsibility of the buyer to arrange _____ of the goods upon delivery.

The vehicles are visually _____ every three months.

Unit 8

intense   34. The _____ of the light hurt our eyes.

         We were _____ aware that we were being watched.

manipulate   35. Some people are easily _____ by their friends.

         Her political success was achieved via careful _____ of the media.

minimize   36. For some patients, a low-dose aspirin _____ the risk of a heart attack.

         Energy _____, as the name implies, is a procedure that attempts to minimize the potential energy of the system to the lowest possible amount.

offset   37. The company limited the use of its vehicles in order to _____ the increase in fuel costs.

         Our annual tree planting enables us to _____ our carbon emissions, thus making us a carbon-neutral business.

practitioner   38. Ten nurse _____ work in this clinic.

         Video conferencing technology can assist _____ who work in rural areas.

predominant   39. The _____ color in his latest paintings is green.

         The population in the inner city is _____ black and Hispanic.

prospect   40. We are excited by the _____ of training these dentists to provide for local health needs.

         Now that he has graduated, he has more _____ for finding a high-paying job.

radical   41. More than one hundred left-wing _____ descended on the Capital building.

         The new economic policy is a _____ departure from the old policy.

random   42. The victims were not related to each other. The violence seemed totally _____ .

         Be sure to _____ the numbers before you begin testing the hypothesis.

reinforce   43. This understanding has been powerfully _____ by many new insights into relationships between human social activity and the natural environment as a whole.

         Soon, many _____ were sent in to restore order.

restore   44. After the _____ of the monarchy, parliament re-asserted its authority in the Bill of Rights of 1689.

         They _____ the stone wall to its original state.

Unit 8

revise   45. The law is undergoing a _____ to close a rather odd loophole.

The _____ version of the code was approved in July.

tense   46. I was worried and the muscles in my neck were _____.

Everyone in the room _____ when the announcement was made.

terminate   47. All damages should be limited to the immediate _____ of services.

This road _____ at the base of the mountain.

theme   48. A recurring _____ in her work is the romance of the inexplicable.

This paper describes cross-curricular _____ instruction that encourages the exploration of a selected topic.

thereby   49. The villagers repaired the bridge, _____ allowing them access to the neighboring towns.

It's a story about a seagull that steals a video camera, _____ creating a "seagullcam."

uniform   50. All of the cans and jars in the cupboard were _____ arranged in alphabetical order.

Unfortunately, health care laws are not _____ from state to state.

vehicle   51. The popularity of four-wheel drive "sports utility _____" is hurting efforts to cut air pollution on Britain's roads.

There are too many gas-powered _____ on the roads today.

via   52. Nowadays, few people send letters _____ snail mail.

We found out, _____ Twitter, that Charlie was fired from the show.

virtual   53. The students will be expected to undertake learning tasks between classes and to participate in a computer-based _____ learning environment.

Take a _____ tour and find out how you can save energy in your home.

visual   54. The storyline in the movie was boring, but the _____ were stunning.

_____ aids, properly used, are powerful.

Unit 8

Collocations

In each group of sentences, write *one* word from the list which goes with the **highlighted collocations**. Be careful with word forms.

Exercise 1	automate theme abandon restore appreciate commodity
	prospect append currency inevitable fluctuate conform

1. After the President's speech, the stock market _____ **wildly**.

    Good CEOs understand the nature of **seasonal** _____ in the markets.

    Her mood _____ **with** every change to her medication.

2. The police released the children and _____ them **to their fate**.

    The sixteen-year old drove his father's car around town **in wild** _____.

    As the lions approached, we had to **hastily** _____ our camp.

3. Putin's reelection **seems** _____ now.

    We have **to accept the** _____ **of** heavy flooding this year.

    It is becoming increasingly _____ that Dan will not graduate.

4. After the lecture, we **had a deeper** _____ **for** the work of the volunteers in Malawi.

    Recently, home prices have begun to _____ **in value**.

    Julie began **to cultivate an** _____ for 19th century literature.

5. Lisa's _____ **for the future** improved when she married Lionel.

    We are **excited at the** _____ **of** having Yi work for us.

    Waylon **welcomed the** _____ of moving to New York.

6. Alex's degree in art history is not a very **marketable** _____.

    Self-deprecation is **a rare** _____ among politicians these days.

    When the stock market is unstable, it is not wise **to trade in** _____.

7. The police were called in to _____ **order**.

    The law **is aimed at** _____ the state's right to regulate health care.

    Edison's lab is being **carefully** _____ to its original state.

8. Workers in the Middle East get paid **in local** _____.

    If China's _____ **floats**, the balance of trade will shift.

    Before you travel to Canada, check the _____ **exchange rate**.

9. Two **main** _____ **emerge** during the first act of the play.

    Today, we will **explore the** _____ of heroism in Crane's novel.

    Brahms wrote many **variations on a** _____ of Haydn.

10. Many of the steps in the manufacturing **process** are now **fully** _____.

    The lab uses an improved _____ **procedure** for detecting calcium levels.

Unit 8

Collocations

<table>
<tr><td rowspan="2">**Exercise 2**</td><td>accompany</td><td>offset</td><td>arbitrary</td><td>uniform</td><td>conform</td><td>radical</td></tr>
<tr><td>guidelines</td><td>revise</td><td>inspect</td><td>automate</td><td>via</td><td>detect</td></tr>
</table>

1. Our first task is to **draw up new** _____.

    By **following the** _____, you will have more luck in your job hunt.

    The **safety** _____ were not clearly written.

2. You will have one week to _____ **your paper**.

    Estimates for economic growth were _____ **upward**.

    The guidelines will **undergo a complete** _____.

3. I play the piano and my wife _____ me **on the violin**.

    The film benefits from the beautiful **musical** _____.

    Roasted vegetables **make a delicious** _____ to baked fish.

4. Tomorrow, we will **carry out an** _____ of all of the vehicles.

    It looked like paint, but **on closer** _____ it turned out to be ink.

    The fire marshal **conducted a visual** _____ of all the room in the boarding house.

5. Her **decision seemed rather** _____.

    Rather than **make purely** _____ **choices**, you should use a logical system.

    The new rules **seem completely** _____ to us.

6. Students are **required to** _____ **to** the dress code at this institution.

    State laws **must** _____ **with** federal laws.

    If the state laws are not **in** _____ **with** federal laws, the state laws must be altered.

7. Because of their _____ **differences of opinion**, they were unable to come to an agreement.

    The protesters are **becoming increasingly** _____ in their demands.

    The _____ **elements** of the group tried to derail the negotiations.

8. Stir the mixture until it has a _____ **consistency**.

    Pierre wore a **smart military** _____ to the dinner party.

    We want **to ensure broad** _____ in the execution of the orders.

9. Todd _____ **a note of sadness** in Rachael's voice.

    Early _____ of cancer is vital in order to control the disease.

    The apartment must have a working **smoke** _____ installed.

10. Researchers have discovered that two pollutants _____ **each other** in the atmosphere.

    There are several ways you can _____ **your carbon footprint**.

Unit 8

Collocations

<table>
<tr><td>Exercise 3</td><td>accumulate   vehicle   bias   random   contradict   tense
intense   exhibition   highlight   chart   practitioner   virtual</td></tr>
</table>

1. Calcium started to _____ **slowly** in her old bones.

   We were alarmed by the **rapid** _____ of mercury in the organs of people living near the coal plant.

   If fluid is **allowed to** _____ in the lungs, the patient will die.

2. Oddly, the coach has a _____ **in favor of** the shortest players.

   Usually, instructors are not supposed **to show** _____ in their opinions.

   Margie has **a strong personal** _____ for left-wing candidates.

3. The senator's recent stock purchases **came under** _____ **scrutiny**.

   The _____ **of the heat** meant that working outdoors was impossible.

   We were **under** _____ **pressure** to finish before 5:00.

4. Four contestants were **chosen** _____

   The _____ **acts of violence** seemed so senseless to us.

   Ideally, you should **take a** _____ **sample**.

5. He changed his policy concerning welfare **in an apparent** _____ **to** his campaign promise.

   He **completely** _____ what he had said earlier.

   In _____ **to** what you may have heard, I am not going to resign.

6. My daughter is not old enough to **drive a** _____ right now.

   "Paid crowdsourcing" is **a** _____ **for** market **reform**.

   The San Francisco Foundation is a _____ **for change**.

7. If the patient _____ **symptoms** of the flu, contact the doctor immediately.

   You can view her paintings at the _____ **center** downtown.

   The moon rocks will be _____ **to the public** next year.

8. If you **feel** _____ before your speech, do some breathing exercises.

   A light massage can help **to release the** _____ in your face muscles.

   The president tried everything **to ease the** _____ that **was building up** in the Middle East.

9. The _____ **of the evening** was Cynthia's speech.

   The increase in the illness rate **serves to** _____ **the need for** decent hygiene facilities.

   The guide book _____ **the danger of** drinking the water.

10. This **pie** _____ clearly shows the enormity of the nation's debt burden.

   We hope that the new president will _____ **a course** towards greater economic prosperity.

Unit 8

Collocations

Exercise 4	clarify ambiguity crucial induce exploit manipulate
	terminate reinforce deviate visual displace implicit

1. With **clever** _____ , the princess was able to extract a great deal of money from the king.

   We refuse to purchase **genetically** _____ food products.

   The programmer **skillfully** _____ the code to override the controls.

2. Their actions only served to _____ **the stereotype** of the church.

   Social interaction **helps to** _____ **learning**.

   Praise can be a **powerful positive** _____ for people with low self-esteem.

3. Our daughter gave us a **somewhat** _____ answer to our question.

   Before we proceed, we need to **clear up any remaining** _____ .

   To avoid potential _____ , everyone needs to state exactly why he or she wants to be involved in this committee.

4. That's all I have to say for now, but I would **be delighted to** _____ **any points** that are still unclear to you.

   Your resumé looks good, but you need **to provide further** _____ about last year's summer employment.

   Would you please _____ **your position** on women's rights?

5. Before we shoot, we need **to get a** _____ on the enemy's position.

   Because of her _____ **impairment**, she was placed in a special class.

   It is **difficult for me to** _____ peace in the Middle East.

6. The higher salary was **offered as an** _____ to get her to work for us.

   Of course, we can **provide** other _____ to attract the best people to come to work for us.

7. The insurgents' lack of ammunition **proved** _____ to the outcome of the battle.

   Your support is **deemed** _____ to the success of the enterprise.

   There is a _____ **distinction** to be made between intensive and extensive reading.

8. We are considering **early** _____ **of the contract**.

   Erwin received **a notice of** _____ **of employment**.

   The match _____ **in a draw**.

9. So far, the new software has not been **commercially** _____ .

   Newly arrived immigrants are, unfortunately, **vulnerable to** _____ .

   In a game of chess, it is important to know how to _____ **a weakness** in your opponent's game.

10. It's too late to _____ **from the plan**.

    The simplest approach is to calculate the **standard** _____ .

Unit 8

Synonyms Use the synonym clues to solve this crossword puzzle.

Across
1. modern, concurrent, fashionable
7. attend, assist, supplement
8. change, alter, modify
10. outlook, possibility, likelihood
12. money, cash
13. essential, fundamental, extreme
18. add, attach, join
24. map, diagram, outline
25. instruction, procedure, law
27. handle, tamper with, maneuver
29. stray, depart, wander
31. re-establish, revive, renew
32. fortify, strengthen, support
33. check, examine, investigate

Down
2. compensate, counterbalance
3. chance, haphazard, uncontrolled
4. topic, subject, point
5. leave, give up, reject
6. explain, clear up, illuminate
9. persuade, convince, move
11. vital, critical, essential
14. signify, indicate, represent
15. uncertain, unclear, vague
16. end, finish, stop
17. comply, agree, obey
19. find, notice, discover
20. gather, collect, compile
21. prejudice, tendency, inclination
22. extreme, powerful, strong
23. replace, supplant, relocate
26. capitalize, utilize, take advantage of
28. show, display, present
30. rigid, tight, stiff

Unit 8

Review

1. The manufacturing process must be exact if you want to produce a _____ product every time.	uniform
2. The item was picked at _____, just as an example.	random
	appreciative
	ambiguous
3. The first explanation was clear, but the rest of them were somewhat _____.	eventual
	implicit

4. To be fair, we chose a number that was purely _____.	virtual
	radical
5. The idea of socialism was _____ in the speeches of Roosevelt.	arbitrary
	exploitative
6. His needs were _____; all others' needs were subordinate.	implicit
	predominant

7. Martin realized how _____ he had been these past weeks. He really needed to relax.	eventual
	crucial
8. We traveled to Rome _____ London and Paris.	contradictory
	tense
9. It is critical that everyone cooperates when the _____ moment arrives.	via
	appreciative

10. The pain was _____, but he continued to climb to the summit.	thereby
	accumulative
11. They replaced the thin wire with a thicker one, _____ increasing the flow of electricity.	intense
	complementary
12. They patiently awaited the _____ return of Captain John.	ambiguous
	eventual

13. His essay was a _____ copy of one I had seen a few weeks ago.	exploitative
	inevitable
14. We moved a step closer to the _____ conclusion. There could be no other possible way for it to end.	implicit
	intense
15. We need a _____ revolution in our whole outlook.	virtual
	radical

16. Winning the race was the _____ of my career.	vehicle
	uniform
17. He was a medical _____, not a lawyer.	highlight
	practitioner
18. As he offered his hand, she gently stepped from the _____.	theme
	restoration

Unit 8

Review

19. This herbal remedy may be an excellent _____ to the conventional medicine you're already taking. 20. Do not ignore this _____. It tells you exactly what to do in case of an emergency. 21. The collapse of Russia's economic _____ ended the Cold War.	guideline prospect complement inspection fluctuation infrastructure
22. The principle _____ of Thomas's poetry was love. 23. The election system has a built-in _____ towards large political parties. 24. Banks are responsible for foreign _____ transfers.	automation bias conformity currency theme detection
25. They weren't looking forward to the _____ of spending the night out in the cold. 26. True love is supposedly the one _____ that cannot be bought or sold. 27. Kandinsky was not quite as famous as his _____, Picasso.	prospect commodity exhibition contemporary appreciation guideline
28. "Thumbs up" is a hand signal that is used to _____ approval. 29. In this experiment, you need to put water into the container to _____ the air. 30. If you allow snow to _____ on the plants, it will protect them from freezing.	append conform accumulate fluctuate displace denote
31. It's easy to find software that can _____ repetitive tasks. 32. No one was allowed to _____ the conditions in the jail. 33. We hope this year's gains will _____ last year's losses.	revise inspect automate manipulate offset induce
34. They made an effort to end their business relationship, but were legally unable to _____ the contract. 35. They added stone to _____ the wall at its weakest points. 36. Our opponents may _____ our weakness if they discover it.	terminate restore highlight reinforce detect exploit

Unit 8

Review

37. True friends don't _____ their companions when the going gets rough.	demote contradict deviate append terminate abandon
38. You need to _____ a short footnote to your paper.	
39. The new findings seem to _____ earlier claims.	
40. I shall be glad to _____ the evidence to any interested person.	restore abandon manipulate accompany exhibit bias
41. She quickly learned how to _____ her new husband into doing everything that she wanted.	
42. This polishing cream can _____ the brightness to a silver ring.	
43. He used quiet, hypnotic music to _____ me to sleep.	offset clarify induce deviate automate minimize
44. He stayed on the road and did not _____ from the route he had chosen.	
45. The president made use of a press conference to _____ his position on the issue.	
46. She used to like to _____ her parents to concerts in the park.	accompany append clarify tense appreciate detect
47. It's satisfying to know that people _____ what you are doing.	
48. The new procedure can _____ early signs of cancer.	
49. Commodity prices often _____ daily.	abandon fluctuate terminate visualize revise detect
50. The 3-D picture helped me to _____ the relationships between the different parts of the machine.	
51. The new information forced them to _____ their theory radically.	
52. We took a map in order to _____ the chances of getting lost.	exhibit highlight minimize chart contradict conform
53. Having lived overseas for many years, she found it difficult to _____ to the social customs of her native England.	
54. After the ship was blown off course by the violent storm, the captain had to _____ a new course.	

Unit 8

Definitions ₒ Parts of Speech ₒ Collocations

abandon (v) to give something up completely; to withdraw support
to abandon to one's fate: *The soldiers left our village and abandoned us to our fate.*
to hastily abandon, largely abandon, virtually abandon
to voluntarily abandon, to temporarily abandon
to decide to abandon, to be forced to abandon: *When we ran out of money, we were forced to abandon our vacation plans.*
to simply abandon: *During the uprising, all moral principles were simply abandoned.*
to abandon altogether, to abandon completely, to abandon entirely

abandon (n) freedom without restraint
in (with) reckless abandon [= doing something without worrying about the results]: *As soon as the graduation ceremony ended, the students jumped into their cars and drove to the seashore to party with reckless abandon.*
in (with) wild abandon

abandonment (n)

accompany (v) to go along or in company with; join in as a companion
to accompany on: *I played the violin and she accompanied me on the piano.*
to accompany to: *I would like to accompany you to the dance.*

accompaniment (n) to something eaten or drunk with a main meal
a delicious accompaniment, an ideal accompaniment
to make an ideal accompaniment (for): *This wine makes an ideal accompaniment for the baked salmon.*

accompaniment (n) music that is played along with singing or the playing of an instrument
musical accompaniment, instrumental accompaniment, orchestral accompaniment, piano accompaniment, guitar accompaniment

accompaniment (n) an event that happens at the same time as another event
to the accompaniment of: *She entered the hall to the accompaniment of great fanfare.*
with (the) accompaniment of

accompanist (n)

accumulate (v) to gather, collect or pile up, often gradually over time
to accumulate junk: *Over the years, we have accumulated a lot of junk.*
to gradually accumulate, to slowly accumulate, to steadily accumulate: *Over a period of several weeks after her surgery, Lonnie accumulated enough strength to go back to work.*
to begin to accumulate, to be allowed to accumulate: *Under no conditions should dust be allowed to accumulate on the clock's gears.*
to tend to accumulate: *Mercury tends to accumulate in the fish which are higher up on the food chain.*

accumulation (n)
rapid accumulation, steady accumulation, slow accumulation, great accumulation, impressive accumulation, large accumulation
capital accumulation

accumulative (adj)

ambiguous (adj) having several possible meanings or interpretations; doubtful or uncertain
to remain ambiguous, to render something ambiguous [= to make something ambiguous]: *The author's use of strange word combinations rendered most of the passage ambiguous.*
highly ambiguous, rather ambiguous, slightly ambiguous, somewhat ambiguous
deliberately ambiguous, intentionally ambiguous: *Jason was being intentionally ambiguous about where he had been last night.*
an ambiguous statement, an ambiguous answer

ambiguity (n)
to clear up an ambiguity: *I'd like to clear up an ambiguity: I absolutely will not loan you any money.*
to clarify (an/any) ambiguity, to remove an ambiguity
to avoid (all) ambiguity: *To avoid ambiguity, you should give the names of the participants, rather than just refer to them as "he" and "she."*
a possible ambiguity, a potential ambiguity, moral ambiguity, sexual ambiguity
a degree if ambiguity, an element of ambiguity: *There was an element of ambiguity in her statement.*

ambiguity arises, ambiguity occurs

ambiguously (adv)

append (v) to add as a supplement; to affix or attach

append (something) to (something): *At the end of this document, we have appended a list of the people who participated in the survey.*

appendage (n)

appendix (n) a section at the end of a book or document that gives additional information

attached appendix: *See the attached appendix for a complete list of participating pharmacies.*

appendix (n) an organ attached to the intestines

a burst appendix, an inflamed appendix, a ruptured appendix

to remove one's appendix

appreciate (v) to understand or be aware of the value of something; to be grateful or thankful

to appreciate deeply, to appreciate sincerely, to appreciate very much

to fully appreciate, to properly appreciate,

to be generally appreciated, to be widely appreciated

appreciation (n)

a deep appreciation, a fine appreciation, a great appreciation, a real appreciation: *Yesterday's visit to the recording studio gave me a real appreciation for how hard musicians work.*

a lack of appreciation, (as) a token of appreciation [= a small symbol of appreciation]: *Please accept this gift certificate as a token of our appreciation for your fine work.*

a better appreciation, a clear appreciation, a wider appreciation, a keen appreciation

to demonstrate appreciation (for), to show appreciation (for): *We're doing this to show our appreciation for your contribution.*

to cultivate an appreciation of/for: *While I was in Paris, I cultivated an appreciation for Impressionist paintings.*

appreciative (adj)

appreciatively (adv)

appreciate (v) to increase in value

appreciate steeply: *The price of gas has appreciated steeply.*

appreciate in value: *We hope our home will continue to appreciate in value.*

appreciation (n) the amount by which something has increased in value

arbitrary (adj) based on subjective factors or random choice rather than on objective principles

an arbitrary choice, an arbitrary decision: *We feel that the director made an arbitrary decision when she gave a pay raise to the new workers but not to us.*

to seem arbitrary

completely arbitrary, entirely arbitrary, purely arbitrary, quite arbitrary, wholly arbitrary

fairly arbitrary, somewhat arbitrary, to some extent arbitrary: *I think you are being to some extent arbitrary when you exclude the younger workers from the meeting.*

arbitrarily (adv)

arbitrate (v) to act as a judge in settling a dispute

arbitration (n) the act of making a judgment to settle a dispute

automate (v) to change to a way of doing something that requires no manual control

to automate a procedure, to automate a process

to automate fully

Because every step in the process in the manufacture of the plastic furniture was fully automated, many people lost their jobs.

automation (n)

automated teller machine (n) [ATM]

bias (n) an inclination or preference to favor one side, often resulting in prejudicial judgment

to demonstrate, have, display or show bias: *When you say that the cars that are made in your country are better than those made here, you are definitely showing bias.*

to avoid bias, to eliminate bias, to reduce bias, to correct (the) bias, to be free from bias

strong bias, personal bias, obvious bias , marked bias

left-wing bias, right-wing bias, cultural bias, political bias confirmation bias [= the tendency of people to favor information that confirms what they already believe]: *It is difficult for some scientists to conduct fair, objective experiments due to their unconscious confirmation bias.*

racial bias, religious bias, sexual bias

without bias, with bias

a bias against: *Margie seems to have a bias against people who are overweight.*

a bias for, a bias in favor of: *The coach obviously has a bias in favor of the African-American members of the team.*

bias (v) to influence or prejudice someone or something

chart (n) a graph, table, map or diagram showing data

billboard chart, astrological chart, solar chart, flow chart

bar chart, pie chart, line chart

flip chart, wall chart

organizational chart, progress chart, weather chart

aviation chart [= a chart used by aircraft], nautical chart [= a chart used by ships]

navigation chart [= a chart used for finding a route]

chart (v) to make a map, a table, a graph or a plan

to chart a course

chartable (adj)

clarify (v) to make something clearer or easier to understand

to clarify the meaning, to clarify one's position, to clarify a point

to clarify (an/any) ambiguity

to clarify further, to clarify fully

to be delighted to clarify, to be happy to clarify, to be pleased to clarify: *I would be delighted to clarify any points that are still unclear to you.*

clarification (n)

to provide or seek clarification: *Before we decide which engines to purchase, the manufacturer needs to provide clarification about its warranty program.*

additional or further clarification: *Your idea is a little ambiguous. I think it needs additional clarification.*

to require clarification, to provide clarification

commodity (n) a useful thing that has value and could be bought or sold

a marketable commodity: *I think your hand-held video phone can easily become a marketable commodity.*

a basic commodity: *Basic commodities, such as bread and meat, were in short supply.*

primary commodity, cheap commodity

rare commodity, scarce commodity

precious commodity, valuable commodity, expensive commodity

farm commodity, agricultural commodity, industrial commodity

to trade in commodities: *Because the stock market seemed unstable, we decided to stop trading in commodities.*

complement (n) something that provides balance or contrast

a perfect complement (to): *Red wine is a perfect complement to red meat.*

ideal complement, natural complement

complementary (adj) going together to enhance or emphasize the qualities of each other

essentially complementary, mutually complementary: *Diane's wish to live in the city and her husband's desire to have a big garden are not mutually complementary.*

complement (v) to add to something to make it better

Her green and gold necklace complements her dress perfectly.

complement (n) something that completes or perfects

a full complement (of): *There was a full complement of nurses at the meeting.*

conform (v) to look like or act in a similar way; to be like all the others

to be required to conform (to), must conform, should conform

to conform to: *School children often conform with the appearance and behavior of their peers.*

to conform with

conformity (n)
>to achieve conformity, to bring something into conformity with
>complete conformity, outward conformity, strict conformity: *You must operate your business in strict conformity with the law, or the State will shut your business down.*
>in conformity with: *In conformity with the regulations of this institute, you must update your CV annually.*

conformance (n) the act of conforming; conformity
>in conformance with

conformation (n) form, shape, structure or configuration

conformable (adj)

contemporary (adj) existing or relating to the same period of time; modern
>contemporary life, contemporary music, contemporary art, contemporary literature, contemporary history, contemporary culture

contemporary (n) someone or something that exists or existed at the same time
>to be a contemporary of: *Roosevelt was a contemporary of Truman.*

contemporaneous (adj)

contemporaneously (adv)

contradict (v) to express the opposite of or act in the opposite way
>to appear to contradict, to seem to contradict
>to flatly contradict, clearly contradict, completely contradict, directly contradict

contradiction (n) a condition in which two things are in disagreement
>(in an) apparent contradiction: *He changed his policy concerning welfare in an apparent contradiction to his campaign promise.*
>a complete contradiction, a flat contradiction [= a clear and emphatic contradiction], a flagrant contradiction [= a clearly offensive contradition]
>basic contradiction, direct contradiction, outright contradiction, inherent contradiction, glaring contradiction [= highly obvious, very easily seen contradiction]: *There is a glaring contradiction between what she says and how she acts.*
>a contradiction between: *There seems to be a contradiction between what he said he would do and what he has actually done.*
>in contradiction to: *In contradiction to what you may have heard, I am still going to apply to Stanford.*
>a contradiction in terms

contradictory (adj) being a contradiction; disagreeing

crucial (adj) extremely important, essential or vital
>to prove crucial, to become crucial, to remain crucial
>to see as crucial, to consider as crucial, to deem as crucial, to regard as crucial: *We regard everyone's participation as crucial to the success of our work.*
>fairly crucial, hardly crucial, rather crucial, clearly crucial, obviously crucial
>crucial for: *Believing in ourselves is crucial for winning the game.*
>crucial to, to be crucial that: *It is crucial that we believe in ourselves.*
>(to make) a crucial distinction

crucially (adv)

currency (n) a system of money used in a country
>to issue currency, to print currency; to withdraw currency; to devalue currency; to exchange currency
>to be paid in (local) currency: *When I worked in Saudi Arabia, I was paid in the local currency which is the riyal.*
>foreign currency, local currency
>weak currency, strong currency, a major currency
>hard currency [= currency that is not likely to change in value], convertible currency [= currency that is easily changed into gold or another currency]
>currency fluctuates, currency floats, currency rises, currency falls: *Some countries are not interested in allowing their currency to fluctuate in today's market.*
>foreign currency, domestic currency
>currency exchange, currency conversion; currency markets
>currency deal, currency speculation, currency trade

currency (n) widespread acceptance
> to gain currency, to have little currency: *The idea that women should not work outside the home has little currency today.*
> general currency, wide currency, widespread currency: *The belief that inanimate objects have spirits has wide currency among the indigenous people.*

denote (v) to represent or indicate; to be a sign

denotation (n)

detect (v) to discover or notice the existence of something
> to detect an odor; detect smoke
> to detect a note of sadness: *When she spoke to me the day after her party, I detected a note of sadness in her voice.*
> to detect early, to detect late; to detect quickly, to detect easily, to detect readily: *Certain forms of cancer are readily detected during routine blood tests.*
> to be sensitive enough to detect, to be unable to detect, to be designed to detect
> fail to detect, be difficult to detect, be hard to detect, be impossible to detect
> a means of detecting, a method of detecting, a way of detecting

detection (n)
> to avoid detection, to escape detection, to evade detection
> early detection
> detection rate

detector (n)
> a lie detector, a metal detector, a smoke detector

detectable (adj)
> barely detectable, hardly detectable

detective (n) a person who conducts an investigation

deviate (v) to turn or move away from a correct or normal way
> to deviate sharply, to deviate considerably, to deviate significantly, to deviate slightly
> to deviate from: *If we deviate from our plan, we shall surely fail.*
> to deviate from a plan, to deviate from a path, deviate from the script
> to deviate from the mean, to deviate from the norm

deviation (n)
> a standard deviation: *She scored one standard deviation higher than the norm.*

displace (v) to put or take out of the usual place
> to displace as: *He was displaced as chess champion by a new computer program.*

displacement (n)

displaceable (adj)

eventual (adj) happening after an unspecified a period of time
> the eventual outcome: *It grew dark as we patiently awaited the eventual outcome of the battle.*

eventually (adv)
> will eventually happen: *Just wait. Good things will eventually happen.*

eventuality (n) a possible event or outcome
> in the eventuality that: *In the eventuality that I do not survive the operation, please donate my organs to science.*

eventuate (v) to be the final result: *The investigation eventuated in finding the criminal.*

exhibit (v) to show or display publicly
> to exhibit paintings, to exhibit photos
> to exhibit characteristics, to exhibit behavior, to exhibit a tendency, to exhibit symptoms
> to exhibit to the public: *Rocks from the Moon will be exhibited to the public at the Science Museum.*

exhibit (n)
> permanent exhibit, traveling exhibit, temporary exhibit
> on exhibit: *Norm's photos will be on exhibit at the Springfield Museum for two more weeks.*

exhibition (n)
> to have an exhibition, to hold an exhibition, to organize an exhibition, to put on an exhibition, to host an exhibition: *The Smithsonian will host an exhibition of Civil War documents in Washington, D. C.*
> to close an exhibition, to open an exhibition

to be on exhibition: *Her fine paintings are on exhibition at the Guggenheim.*

(the) exhibition features, exhibition includes, exhibition is entitled, exhibition illustrates, exhibition traces: *The current exhibition traces the route that Lewis and Clark took as they explored the Louisiana Purchase.*

an art exhibition, a photo exhibition, a traveling exhibition

a major exhibition, annual exhibition, summer exhibition

international exhibition, local exhibition, private exhibition, public exhibition

permanent exhibition, temporary exhibition, special exhibition

that's just an exhibition: *Don't pay any attention to the way he tosses those heavy rocks into the truck. That's just an exhibition to impress you with his strength.*

an exhibition center, exhibition gallery, exhibition hall, exhibition venue

exploit (v) to make the greatest use of or take unfair advantage of, usually for one's own aims

to deliberately exploit, to sexually exploit, to exploit ruthlessly [to exploit without any feelings for others], to exploit mercilessly [= to exploit without pity]

to exploit a vulnerability, to exploit a weakness

heavily exploit, extensively exploit, fully exploit, exploit to the full

further exploit, widely exploit, profitably exploit, cleverly exploit, skillfully exploit, commercially exploit

exploit (n) [often plural] a heroic or notable deed; extraordinary act, usually dangerous or exciting

a daring exploit, a legendary exploit

a military exploit, a sexual exploit, a sporting exploit

daring exploits, sexual exploits, exciting exploits

legendary exploits [= exploits that people tell stories about for a long time afterwards] : *Mozart's opera,* Don Giovanni, *is about the legendary exploits of a Spanish nobleman.*

exploitable (adj)

exploitation (n)

unfair exploitation, commercial exploitation, capitalist exploitation, industrial exploitation, sexual exploitation

to be open to exploitation, to be vulnerable to exploitation, to be based on exploitation

brutal exploitation, ruthless exploitation: *The shoe manufacturer demonstrated that it was, in fact, not guilty of the ruthless exploitation of the local workforce.*

fluctuate (v) to vary in amount, value, or level; to rise and fall

to fluctuate considerably, to fluctuate sharply, to fluctuate widely, to fluctuate constantly, to fluctuate continually, to fluctuate wildly: *Lately, the stock markets have been fluctuating wildly.*

to fluctuate between: *The temperature in the summer fluctuates between 35 and 40 degrees Celsius.*

to fluctuate with: *The mood of the citizens fluctuates with changes in the economy.*

to fluctuate according to: *The possible length of video recording time for this camera fluctuates according to the temperature.*

to fluctuate around: *The number of frogs in the stream fluctuates around 200 every spring.*

fluctuation (n)

considerable fluctuation, marked fluctuation, sharp fluctuation, wide fluctuation, wild fluctuation

local fluctuation, short term fluctuation, minor fluctuation

cyclical fluctuation, seasonal fluctuation, random fluctuation, climatic fluctuation, temperature fluctuation

currency fluctuation, economic fluctuation, market fluctuation, price fluctuation

fluctuation in: *There is too much fluctuation in the markets these days.*

guideline (n) [often plural] a statement or policy indicating what action is required or recommended

to draw up guidelines (for), to establish guidelines (for), to lay down guidelines, to set out guidelines

to follow guidelines, to adhere to guidelines, to comply with guidelines, to stick to guidelines

to breach guidelines, to ignore guidelines, to violate guidelines

flexible guidelines, rigid guidelines, strict guidelines, tight guidelines

clear guidelines, helpful guidelines, practical guidelines, reliable guidelines,

broad guidelines, general guidelines, simple guidelines

detailed guidelines, explicit guidelines

EU guidelines, government guidelines, planning guidelines, safety guidelines, legal guidelines

Unit 8

within the guidelines, guidelines about, guidelines for, guidelines from

highlight (n) the most significant, interesting or outstanding feature, event, or experience

the highlight of one's life: *My one-month trip to Italy has been the highlight of my life so far.*

the highlight of one's career

the highlight of the day, the highlight of the week, the highlight of the month, the highlight of the year

highlight (v)

serves to highlight: *Unfortunately, the tragic accident serves to highlight how dangerous it is for bicycles and cars to share the narrow road.*

merely highlights, dramatically highlights, graphically highlights, clearly highlights

to highlight the danger, to highlight the need, highlight the lack, highlight the importance

implicit (adj) implied or meant, even though not directly expressed

implicit in: *I knew from the tone of her voice that there was a threat implicit in what she said.*

implicit that: *It was implicit that he wanted us to stay and comfort him.*

implicitly (adv)

implication (n)

by implication

implicitness (n)

induce (v) to persuade, influence or stimulate someone to do something

to induce someone to do something: *Nothing could induce me to move from my quiet country home to New York City.*

to induce labor [= to force the birth of a baby]: *If the baby doesn't come soon, we will have to induce labor.*

to induce flowering: *Altering the amount of daylight that the plants receive will help to induce early flowering.*

inducement (n)

to offer an inducement, to provide an inducement, to receive an inducement

a massive inducement, a powerful inducement, a strong inducement, sufficient inducement, extra inducement, further inducement, positive inducement

cash inducement, financial inducement

inevitable (adj) certain to happen; unable to avoid

to appear inevitable, to look inevitable, to seem inevitable, to become inevitable

to make something inevitable, to regard something as inevitable

absolutely inevitable, increasingly inevitable, almost inevitable, virtually inevitable

(It is) inevitable that: *It is inevitable that glory will come once again to our country.*

inevitable demise: *The generals were anxiously awaiting the inevitable demise of the dictator.*

inevitably (adv)

inevitability (n)

terrible inevitability, tragic inevitability, a certain inevitability: *There was a certain inevitability about Mitch being nominated for the post.*

to accept the inevitability

a feeling of inevitability, a sense of inevitability

infrastructure (n) the physical and organizational structure that allows society to operate

to set up the infrastructure

the market infrastructure, the economic infrastructure

inspect (v) to examine carefully and critically, often to find faults or mistakes

to inspect closely, to inspect thoroughly, to inspect carefully, to inspect regularly

to allow something to be inspected, to entitle to inspect

to inspect for: *All of the jets will be inspected for cracks in the wings.*

inspection (n)

to carry out an inspection, to conduct an inspection, to make an inspection

an on-site inspection, a visual inspection, a safety inspection

on closer inspection: *It looked like a piece of glass. On closer inspection, it turned out to be a diamond.*

to be ready for inspection: *The soldiers were ordered to be ready for inspection by noon.*

inspector (n)

Unit 8

inspector general (n) an investigative officer within a government organization who reports on the operation of that organization

intense (adj) great or extreme

to become intense, to remain intense

to come under intense scrutiny [= to be examined intensely]

extremely intense, incredibly intense, fairly intense, pretty intense: *Because the fire was pretty intense, the entire trailer burned down in less than a quarter of an hour.*

under intense pressure: *We were under intense pressure to recommend him for a promotion.*

intense emotion, intense hatred, intense feelings

intense light, intense heat

labor intensive [= requiring much work]: *Gardening is often labor intensive. Little of it can be done by machine.*

intensely (adv)

intensity (n)

to grow in intensity, to decrease in intensity

fierce intensity, great intensity; high intensity, low intensity

emotional intensity, passionate intensity

intensify (v)

to appear to intensify, to seem to intensify, to tend to intensify, to serve to intensify

greatly intensify, sharply intensify; further intensify: *The Prime Minister's words will only serve to further intensify the already serious situation.*

intenseness (n)

manipulate (v) to control or influence someone or something cleverly and unscrupulously, especially to one's own advantage

to manipulate someone: *They tried to manipulate us by promising us powerful positions in their new government.*

to manipulate a situation, to manipulate the data, to manipulate variables

easily manipulate, successfully manipulate, deftly manipulate, delicately manipulate, skillfully manipulate, artificially manipulate

deliberately manipulate, systematically manipulate, genetically manipulate

manipulation (n)

careful manipulation, clever manipulation, skillful manipulation, conscious manipulation, cynical manipulation, deliberate manipulation, systematic manipulation

political manipulation; genetic manipulation

manipulate (v) to operate or control by the hands, especially in a skillful manner

to manipulate a machine, to manipulate a tool

manipulation (n) the operation or control of a tool or machine

manipulative (adj) characterized by control of a situation or person in a dishonest or unfair way

Kim was immature, selfish and very manipulative, always getting other people to do things for her.

manipulator (n)

minimize (v) to reduce to the smallest amount

to minimize the danger, to minimize the risk, to minimize the damage: *The politician tried to minimize the damage caused by his careless remarks.*

minimization (n)

minimal (adj)

minimally (adv)

offset (v) to counter-balance, counteract or compensate for something

(two things) offset each other

to offset carbon emissions

largely offset, substantially offset, completely offset, more than offset: *The loss of value of my home is more than offset by the recent rise in the stock market.*

offset (n)

offset (adj)

offset printing (n) a printing process in which the inked impression is made on a rubber roller or blanket, from which it is then transferred to paper

practitioner (n) someone who practices an art, occupation, technique or profession medical practitioner, family practitioner, general practitioner, health practitioner

predominant (adj) more frequent; having the greatest importance or power

predominant paradigm

predominance (n)

take predominance over: *The needs of the common man should take predominance over the wants of the wealthy.*

predominantly (adv)

prospect (n) possibility of success, improvement, recovery; something expected

to have (no) prospect for; to face the prospect, to offer the prospect

to be excited at the prospect, to relish the prospect, to welcome the prospect

an attractive prospect, a reasonable prospect, immediate prospect

bleak prospect, daunting prospects: *Right now, we are facing the daunting prospect of having to find office space for all of the new employees.*

prospect (v) to search for minerals in the earth

to prospect for gold, to prospect for silver, to prospect for uranium

prospects (n. pl.) chances of being successful

prospects for the future: *Sally's prospects for the future are looking pretty good right now.*

bright prospects, exciting prospects; limited prospects, poor prospects; future prospects

economic prospects, development prospects, growth prospects

career prospects, employment prospects, job prospects, promotion prospects, election prospects

prospects for the future: *The economy isn't very good right now, the prospects for the future are great.*

long-term prospects, short-term prospects

prospects will improve: *Right now things are looking bad, but we hope that prospects will improve.*

radical (adj) extreme

radical treatment, radical group, radical change, radical procedure, radical nature, radical views, radical innovation

radical elements: *The government tried to get rid of the radical elements that opposed its policies.*

increasingly radical, fairly radical, genuinely radical, truly radical

radical (adj) basic, fundamental

radical differences: *There are radical differences between your political views and mine.*

radical reform, radical change, radical transformation

radical (n)

political radical, conservative radical, left-wing radical, religious radical, Islamic radical

radically (adv)

radicalize (v)

radicalization (n)

radical (n) [Mathematics] the root of a quantity

radical (n) [Chemistry] a group of two or more atoms, arranged in a specific way, that acts as a single atom in chemical reactions

free radicals: *As plants evolved, they developed antioxidants to fight free radicals.*

random (adj) without a definite plan, order, pattern or purpose

to choose at random; to select at random

at random: *He placed stones at random all around the garden.*

to take a random sample; random access; random acts of violence

random number generator

completely random, entirely random, purely random, totally random

fairly random, apparently random, seemingly random

randomly (adv)

randomize (v)

randomization (n)

random access (adj) [computer] relating to computer memory, allowing the retrieval of data directly

random access memory (RAM)

reinforce (v) to strengthen, make more effective or give additional support

to reinforce an opinion, to reinforce learning, to reinforce a stereotype

to serve to reinforce, to help to reinforce, to tend to reinforce enormously reinforce, greatly reinforce, massively reinforce, powerfully reinforce, strongly reinforce

further reinforce, merely reinforce, simply reinforce

constantly reinforce, continually reinforce, repeatedly reinforce, implicitly reinforce

unwittingly reinforce, positively reinforce, negatively reinforce

heavily reinforce (with): *The huge wooden doors were heavily reinforced with iron.*

reinforced concrete

reinforcement (n)

to provide reinforcement, to receive reinforcement

positive reinforcement, negative reinforcement

powerful reinforcement

reinforcements (n. pl) extra soldiers, police, etc.

to bring in reinforcements: *If he were to win the battle, he knew he had to bring in reinforcements.*

to call for reinforcements, to send for reinforcements

reinforceable (adj)

restore (v) to return to a previous condition or state

to restore confidence in, restore faith in: *Her kindness has restored my faith in humanity.*

to restore to: *The police were able to restore the stolen car to its rightful owner.*

to restore to original state/condition: *Young Marvin took pride in his ability to restore old cars to their original condition.*

to restore order: *During the protest, the soldiers arrived and quickly restored order.*

quickly restore, soon restore

formally restore

to attempt to restore, to help to restore, to be designed to restore, to be intended to restore, to take measures to restore

aimed at restoring: *The new laws are aimed at restoring workers' rights.*

tastefully restored, carefully restored, handsomely restored, lovingly restored, painstakingly restored

restoration (n)

restorable (adj)

revise (v) to examine something again in order to change or improve

to revise an answer; to revise a paper; to revise a position

to revise downward, to revise upwards: *The estimates for the Gross National Product were revised upward after the latest economic figures.*

extensively revise, drastically revise, heavily revise, radically revise, substantially revise

completely revise, fully revise, thoroughly revise, slightly revise, constantly revise

revision (n)

to undergo (a) revision, to agree to revision, to announce a revision, to approve a revision

to bring about a revision, to lead to revision, to result in revision

to carry out revision, to complete a revision, to conduct a revision, to undertake a revision

a proposed revision, minor revision, major revision, radical revision

the process of revision

exam revision

complete revision, considerable revision, drastic revision, fundamental revision, major revision, radical revision, substantial revision, thorough revision

slight revision, minor revision

revisable (adj)

revisionism (n) any doctrine or view of history that departs from a longstanding or widely accepted doctrine or view, esp. from orthodox Marxism, or that advocates practices that depart from it.

revisionist (n)

tense (adj) a state of emotional, nervous or mental strain; tightly stretched

to feel tense, to look tense, to seem tense, to sound tense

to become tense, to get tense, to grow tense

a little tense, a bit tense, rather tense

extremely tense, incredibly tense

tensely (adv)

tenseness (n)

Unit 8

tension (n) physical or emotional strain
> to suffer from tension, to feel tension, to sense tension
> to cause tension, to create tension, to relieve tension, to release tension
> a release of tension, a sign of tension
> inner tension, emotional tension, muscle/muscular tension, nervous tension
> sexual tension

tension (n) bad feeling between people
> to ease tension, to reduce tension, to defuse tension [= to reduce tension]: *Bart tried to defuse the tension between his brother and sister by inviting them both to dinner.*
> tension builds up, tension grows, tension mounts
> palpable tension [= tension that can be felt], mounting tension [increasing tension]
> unresolved tension [= tension that has not been reduced]: *For several days, there was mounting, palpable tension in Maidan Square.*
> ethnic tension, political tension, racial tension, religious tension, social tension
> communal tension, family tension, internal tension, international tension

tense (v)
> to tense up under pressure

tense (n) [grammar] a category of verb inflection that indicates time
> past tense, present tense, etc.

terminate (v) to bring to an end
> to terminate in: *The match terminated in a draw.*
> abruptly terminate, prematurely terminate, swiftly terminate, automatically terminate
> the right to terminate someone

termination (n)
> voluntary termination, early termination, premature termination, sudden termination
> termination date, termination of employment, termination of a contract, notice of termination

terminal (adj) the end of something; leading to death
> terminal velocity [= the highest speed reached by a falling object, when the forces of gravity and air resistance are in equilibrium]: *Will a dropped feather and a dropped brick reach terminal velocity at the same time?*

theme (n) an idea or image that is repeated or revisited
> to develop a theme, to discuss a theme, to examine a theme, to explore a theme
> a theme emerges, a theme runs through something
> a basic theme, central theme, dominant theme, main theme, underlying theme, key theme
> broad theme, general theme; a common theme, popular theme, universal theme
> contemporary theme; a recurrent theme
> campaign theme, conference theme, research theme
> a theme for (a discussion)
> variations on a theme; theme song, theme music
> on the theme of

thematic (adj)
thematically (adv)
> to be related thematically

theme park (n) an amusement park designed around a common theme

theme song (n) a specific song associated with a play, movie or television program

thereby (adv) by means of that; in that connection
> *He was late for the interview, thereby losing any chance of getting the job.*

uniform (adj) alike in most or all ways
> a uniform code
> uniform consistency

uniformly (adv)
uniformity (n)
> to achieve uniformity, to ensure uniformity, to impose uniformity
> broad uniformity, great uniformity
> bland uniformity, dull uniformity, drab uniformity [= uniformity resulting in a lack of brightness]: *We were shocked by the drab uniformity of the housing in the village near the coal mine.*

uniform (n) a specific set of clothes that members of a group must wear

to be in uniform, to be out of uniform

to put on a uniform, to wear a uniform; to take off a uniform

a dress uniform, a regulation uniform; school uniform

a smart uniform, a traditional uniform, a dress uniform

army uniform, navy uniform, marine uniform, air force uniform

prison uniform

out of uniform: *The sergeant punished the soldier for being out of uniform.*

vehicle (n) a means for moving or transporting people or things

to drive a vehicle, to operate a vehicle, to own a vehicle, to hire a vehicle

to park a vehicle, to impound a vehicle, to tow away a vehicle

to abandon a vehicle [= to leave a vehicle and not care for it any more]: *The snow was coming down so intensely that we had to abandon our vehicle and try to walk the rest of the way home.*

vehicles collide, a vehicle crashes (into)

an all-purpose vehicle; an armored vehicle

a motor vehicle, a passenger vehicle

a vehicle for ~ing: *That small-town newspaper is just a vehicle for spreading rumors.*

a vehicle for/of reform, a vehicle for change

vehicular (adj)

vehicular homicide

via (adv) by way of; by means of

to travel via: *We hope to travel to Rome from Paris via Genoa.*

via an alternative route: *The dog sled had to return to camp via an alternative route.*

virtual (adj) almost but not in every way; not exactly

virtual reality, virtual tour

virtually (adv)

virtually unharmed, virtually unscathed: *They came away from the explosion virtually unscathed. They had only minor cuts and scratches.*

visual (adj) pertaining to sight

visual impairment

visual arts

visually (adv)

visually impaired

visual (n)

to get a visual, to have a visual (on): *Now that the fog has lifted, we have a visual on the plane.*

visualize (v)

try to visualize, to be easy to visualize, to be difficult to visualize, to be hard to visualize

to visualize as: *Gerald visualized himself as a much greater intellect than he actually was.*

vision (n)

visuals (n. pl.) the pictorial characteristics of film or television: *The story was not especially interesting, but the visuals were spectacular.*

Synonyms

abandon:	leave, give up, reject
accompany:	attend, assist, supplement
accumulate:	collect, gather, compile
ambiguous:	uncertain, unclear, vague
append:	add, attach, join
appreciate:	value, admire, acknowledge
arbitrary:	random, fanciful, haphazard
automated:	mechanical
bias:	inclination, prejudice, tendency
chart:	map, diagram, outline
clarify:	explain, clear up, illuminate
commodities:	goods, things, products, wares
complement:	supplement, accompaniment, addition
conform:	comply, agree, obey
contemporary:	concurrent, modern, fashionable
contradict:	oppose, refute, disagree
crucial:	vital, critical, essential
currency:	cash, money
denote:	signify, represent, stand for
detect:	find, perceive, discover
deviate:	stray, depart, wander
displace:	replace, supplant, relocate
eventual:	coming, future, upcoming
exhibit:	show, present, display
exploit:	capitalize, take advantage of, utilize
fluctuate:	waver, vary, change
guideline:	instruction, procedure, law
highlight:	emphasize, underscore, stress
implicit:	apparent, tacit, implied
induce:	persuade, convince, move
inevitable:	unavoidable, certain, sure
infrastructure:	facilities
inspect:	check, examine, investigate
intense:	extreme, powerful, strong
manipulate:	handle, maneuver, tamper with
minimize:	lessen, reduce, belittle
offset:	compensate, counterbalance, correct
practitioner:	doctor, nurse
predominant:	chief, foremost, prevailing
prospect:	outlook, possibility, likelihood
radical:	essential, fundamental, extreme
random:	chance, haphazard, uncontrolled
reinforce:	fortify, strengthen, support
restore:	re-establish, revive, renew
revise:	change, alter, modify
tense:	tight, rigid, stiff
terminate:	end, stop, finish
theme:	topic, subject, point
thereby:	resulting in
uniform:	constant, invariable, regular
vehicle:	car, conveyance, transportation
via:	through, by way of
virtually:	practically, essentially
visual:	visible

Unit 8

Answers

Definitions

1. abandon	16. commodities	31. chart	46. eventual
2. conform	17. guidelines	32. complement	47. ambiguous
3. induce	18. practitioners	33. highlight	48. crucial
4. contemporary	19. minimize	34. append	49. automates
5. arbitrary	20. accumulate	35. clarify	50. contradicts
6. radical	21. detect	36. exploit	51. terminates
7. currency	22. prospect	37. predominant	52. displaced
8. bias	23. vehicle	38. intense	53. inevitable
9. infrastructure	24. theme	39. random	54. implicit
10. reinforce	25. visual	40. appreciate	
11. denote	26. uniform	41. deviate	
12. accompany	27. tense	42. inspect	
13. via	28. fluctuate	43. restored	
14. virtually	29. manipulate	44. offset	
15. thereby	30. revise	45. exhibited	

Parts of Speech

1. abandoned / abandoning	12. commodity / commodities	23. eventual / eventualities	34. intensity / intensely
2. accompanied / accompaniment	13. complemented / complementary	24. exhibits / exhibitions	35. manipulated / manipulation
3. accumulation / accumulative / accumulated	14. conformity / conformed / conforms	25. exploitation / exploiting	36. minimizes / minimization
4. ambiguously / ambiguity	15. contemporary / contemporaries	26. fluctuate/~d / fluctuation	37. offset / offset
5. appendages / append	16. contradiction / contradictory	27. guideline/~s / guidelines	38. practitioners / practitioners
6. appreciation / appreciated	17. crucial / crucially	28. highlights / highlights	39. predominant / predominantly
7. arbitrary / arbitrarily	18. currencies / currency	29. implications / implicitly	40. prospect / prospects
8. automates / automation	19. denotation / denoted	30. inducement / induce	41. radicals / radical
9. biased / bias	20. detecting / detected	31. inevitable / inevitability	42. random / randomize
10. charted / chart	21. deviation / deviates	32. infrastructure / infrastructure	43. reinforce / reinforcements
11. clarifying / clarified	22. displaced / displacement	33. inspection / inspected	44. restoration / restored

45. revision / revised	49. thereby / thereby	53. virtual / virtual
46. tense / tensed	50. uniformly / uniform	54. visuals / Visual
47. termination / terminates	51. vehicles / vehicles	
48. theme / thematic	52. via / via	

Unit 8

Answers

Collocations

Exercise 1	Exercise 2	Exercise 3	Exercise 4
1. fluctuated fluctuations fluctuates / fluctuated	1. guidelines guidelines guidelines	1. accumulate accumulation accumulate	1. manipulation manipulated manipulated
2. abandoned abandon abandon	2. revise revised revision	2. bias bias/biases bias	2. reinforce reinforce reinforcement
3. inevitable inevitability inevitable	3. accompanies accompaniment accompaniment	3. intense intensity intense	3. ambiguous ambiguity ambiguity
4. appreciation appreciate appreciation	4. inspection inspection inspection	4. randomly random random	4. clarify clarification clarify
5. prospects prospect prospect	5. arbitrary arbitrary arbitrary	5. contradiction contradicted contradiction	5. visual visual visualize
6. commodity commodity commodities	6. conform conform conformance	6. vehicle vehicle vehicle	6. inducement inducements
7. restore restoring restored	7. radical radical radical	7. exhibits exhibition exhibited	7. crucial crucial crucial
8. currency currency currency	8. uniform uniform uniformity	8. tense tension tension	8. termination termination terminated
9. themes theme theme	9. detected detection detector	9. highlight highlight highlights	9. exploited exploitation exploit
10. automated automatic/ automated	10. offset offset	10. chart chart	10. deviate deviation

Unit 8

Answers

<table>
<tr><td colspan="2">Synonyms (Crossword)</td></tr>
<tr><td>Across</td><td>Down</td></tr>
<tr><td>

1. contemporary
7. accompany
8. revise
10. prospect
12. currency
13. radical
18. append
24. chart
25. guideline
27. manipulate
29. deviate
31. restore
32. reinforce
33. inspect

</td><td>

2. offset
3. random
4. theme
5. abandon
6. clarify
9. induce
11. crucial
14. denote
15. ambiguous
16. terminate
17. conform
19. detect
20. accumulate
21. bias
22. intense
23. displace
26. exploit
28. exhibit
30. tense

</td></tr>
</table>

<table>
<tr><td colspan="3">Review</td></tr>
<tr><td>

1. uniform
2. random
3. ambiguous
4. arbitrary
5. implicit
6. predominant
7. tense
8. via
9. crucial
10. intense
11. thereby
12. eventual
13. virtual
14. inevitable
15. radical
16. highlight
17. practitioner
18. vehicle

</td><td>

19. complement
20. guideline
21. infrastructure
22. theme
23. bias
24. currency
25. prospect
26. commodity
27. contemporary
28. denote
29. displace
30. accumulate
31. automate
32. inspect
33. offset
34. terminate
35. reinforce
36. exploit

</td><td>

37. abandon
38. append
39. contradict
40. exhibit
41. manipulate
42. restore
43. induce
44. deviate
45. clarify
46. accompany
47. appreciate
48. detect
49. fluctuate
50. visualize
51. revise
52. minimize
53. conform
54. chart

</td></tr>
</table>

Unit 9

Word List

n = noun   **v** = verb   **adj** = adjective   **adv** = adverb   **prep** = preposition

accommodate (v)
   accommodation (n)
   accommodations (n. pl.)
analogy (n)
   analogous (adj)
   analogously (adj)
anticipation (n)
   anticipate (v)
   anticipatory (adj)
assure (v)
   assurance (n)
attain (v)
   attainment (n)
   attainable (adj)
behalf (n)
bulk (n)
   bulk up (v)
cease (v)
   cessation (n)
coherent (adj)
   coherently (adv)
   coherence (n)
   cohere (v)
coincide (v)
   coincidence (n)
   coincidental (adj)
   coincidentally (adv)
commence (v)
   commencement (n)
compatible (adj)
   compatibly (adv)
   compatibility (n)
concurrent (adj)
   concurrently (adv)
   concurrence (n)
   concur (v)
confine (v)
   confinement (n)
   confines (n. pl.)
converse (n)
   converse (v)
   converse (adj)
   conversely (adv)
device (n)
devote (v)
   devotion (n)
   devotions (n. pl.)

diminish (v)
   diminution (n)
distort (v)
   distortion (n)
duration (n)
   durable (adj)
erode (v)
   erosion (n)
ethic (n)
   ethical (adj)
   ethically (adv)
   ethics (n. pl.)
format (n)
   format (v)
found (v)
   foundation (n)
   founder (n)
inherent (adj)
   inherently (adv)
insight (n)
   insightful (adj)
   insightfully (adv)
integral (adj)
   integrally (adv)
   integrate (v)
   integration (n)
intermediate (adj)
   intermediary (n)
manual (n)
   manual (adj)
   manually (adv)
mature (adj)
   maturely (adv)
   mature (v)
mediate (v)
   mediation (n)
medium (n)
   medium (adj)
military (n)
   military (adj)
mutual (adj)
   mutually (adv)
norm (n)
overlap (n)
   overlap (v)
passive (adj)
   passively (adv)

portion (n)
   portion (v)
preliminary (adj)
   preliminarily (adv)
   preliminaries (n. pl.)
protocol (n)
qualitative (adj)
   qualitatively (adv)
refine (v)
   refinement (n)
   refinery (n)
relax (v)
   relaxation (n)
restrain (v)
   restraint (n)
revolution (n)
   revolve (v)
   revolutionary (adj)
   revolutionarily (adv)
   revolutionary (n)
rigid (adj)
   rigidly (adv)
   rigidity (n)
   rigidness (n)
   rigidify (v)
   rigidification (n)
route (n)
   route (v)
sphere (n)
   spherical (adj)
   spherically (adv)
subordinate (n)
   subordinate (v)
   subordinate (adj)
   subordinately (adv)
supplement (n)
   supplement (v)
   supplemental (adj)
   supplementary (adj)
suspend (v)
   suspension (n)
team (n)
   team up (v)
temporary (adj)
   temporarily (adv)
   temporary (n)
trigger (n)
   trigger (v)

Unit 9

Definitions Use the definition clues to write the correct words in the blanks.

1.	the expectation of something; feeling or realizing beforehand *Our _____ of winning grew stronger as the game reached its final minutes.*	behalf duration format portion sphere anticipation
2.	the length of time that something lasts; continuation in time *After her injury, Pat sat on the bench for the _____ of the game.*	
3.	part of a whole *The largest _____ of the treasure went to the captain.*	
4.	to make looser; to reduce the intensity or stress *After you finish working, you can watch TV and _____.*	suspend assure cease diminish confine relax
5.	to inform positively and confidently; to guarantee *I can _____ you that I will do everything I can to help you.*	
6.	to restrict or limit; to shut in; to imprison *Please _____ your remarks to the topic which is currently under discussion.*	
7.	marked by a consistent, logical relationship between parts *We changed our minds after we heard Kathy's _____ argument.*	coherent intermediate integral mutual temporary rigid
8.	in the middle; between the beginning and the end *Yumi is at the _____ level in her English studies.*	
9.	not flexible *We can't work with you if you continue to be so _____.*	
10.	a likeness or similarity in some respects *If you argue by _____, your opponent will point out the ways in which the two situations are not entirely the same.*	trigger supplement protocol route device analogy
11.	something that is used for a special purpose, such as a tool *Your passenger seat can be used as a flotation _____.*	
12.	correct formal or diplomatic etiquette, ceremony or procedure *According to established _____, you cannot talk to the dean directly. You need to go to the associate dean first.*	
13.	to remove unsuitable elements; to make more elegant or cultured *If you _____ your manners, you will be invited to more dinner parties.*	devote refine coincide distort attain cease
14.	to gain, achieve or reach an objective or goal *Sean worked hard to _____ the position he is now in.*	
15.	to concentrate on a particular purpose; to love or be loyal to *She's the kind of person who will _____ herself to whatever she is working on.*	

Unit 9

16. by hand *It is sometimes relaxing to do _____ work after a long day at the office.* 17. in a lower rank; of a lower level of importance *A lieutenant is _____ to a captain.* 18. associating, performing or agreeing harmoniously *Old versions of the Word document are still _____ with new versions.*	qualitative subordinate preliminary passive compatible manual
19. a set of principles or rules of moral or correct behavior *We hired Nancy because she has a strong work _____.* 20. a group that works or plays together *No one on the volleyball _____ had ever been to the championships.* 21. the ability to have a clear and deep understanding of the true nature of a situation *Her latest book contains meaningful _____ into human nature.*	insight military ethic portion device team
22. to provide for; to hold comfortably without crowding; to adapt *The small sports car can only _____ two people.* 23. to act to get two sides to agree or come together *Diplomats find it difficult to _____ between the quarreling states.* 24. to prevent someone or something from doing something *We did everything to _____ from hurting Vera's feelings.*	accommodate coincide mediate restrain distort erode
25. occurring simultaneously or side by side *We were shocked by the earthquake and the _____ tsunami.* 26. existing as a natural, essential or permanent quality or characteristic *There is _____ danger in hiking across glaciers.* 27. grown up; adult *Kyan is not _____ enough to start kindergarten.*	coherent intermediate concurrent inherent mature passive
28. as a representative of someone or something else *On _____ of the entire team, I accept this trophy.* 29. the design, plan or shape of something *The _____ of this magazine article makes it easy to read.* 30. a field of activity; a circle of influence or knowledge *I feel very uncomfortable outside my social _____.*	analogy converse format sphere behalf medium

Unit 9

31. to temporarily or permanently stop or prevent *When the heavy snow begins, we will _____ classes until the crews have time to clear the roads.* 32. to bring or come to an end; to discontinue *The friendship that can _____ was never true friendship in the first place.* 33. to lessen or reduce; to cause to be smaller or less important *The fact that you did not get the promotion does not _____ my opinion of you.*	assure cease suspend format diminish commence
34. essential for the complete thing *The marketing campaign is an _____ component of our business plan.* 35. having the same relationship with respect to each other *Cultural fears can be removed when there is _____ respect on both sides.* 36. limited to a short period of time; not permanent *This will be your _____ office until we can find a permanent one for you.*	integral mutual temporary intermediate compatible ethical
37. fundamental, far-reaching change in ideas, ways of doing things, etc. *Trotsky's leadership during the Russian civil war probably saved the Bolshevik _____ of November 1917.* 38. very large size, mass or volume; the major portion of something *Many athletes who want to remain legal and yet gain muscle _____ and energy use creatine instead of steroids.* 39. something by which something else is produced or carried *Tom expertly expresses himself though the _____ of photography.*	analogy device medium revolution bulk overlap
40. to happen at the same time; to be the same; to agree in some way *This year, Hal's birthday and his graduation _____ with the full moon.* 41. to twist out of the usual shape; to change the meaning of something *We are very upset at the way they _____ everything we say.* 42. The model or standard that is generally accepted or followed *Wearing a mustache is not the _____ in America.*	coincide refine trigger converse distort norm
43. relating to the quality or standard of something *Problems of economic policy also involve political and ethical criteria that are essentially _____ in nature.* 44. prior to or preparing for what comes next *We intend to start as soon as possible, and some very _____ work has already begun in London.* 45. accepting without rejecting; not participating actively *Ken was so _____ that he did everything his wife told him without question or complaint.*	coherent passive concurrent preliminary integral qualitative

46. a device or event that causes something to begin *Cigarette smoke is the second most common* _____ *of asthma in the workplace.* 47. something added to something else to make it complete *Many people take a fish oil* _____ *to get more omega-3 in their diet.* 48. a road, course or way for traveling; a means for reading a destination *We took the longer* _____ *because it was more scenic.*	supplement revolution format trigger route bulk
49. to start or begin *We will* _____ *operations on May 3.* 50. to eat away or wear away *The citizens fear that the new laws will* _____ *many of their civil liberties.* 51. to start or establish, especially by providing for future existence *The princess decided to* _____ *a school for underprivileged children in Malawi.*	assure devote mediate erode found commence
52. something which is opposite or contrary in direction, action or sequence *It didn't seem logical to be going downhill to get a better view. It seemed we should be doing the* _____. 53. the armed forces *We are partners in the war against terrorism and we continue to build a strong* _____ *and security partnership.* 54. something that partially covers another thing, or occupies the same time or space *It is normal for there to be a small amount of* _____ *between the two types of assessment.*	converse sphere protocol military manual overlap

Parts of Speech

Write the parts of speech (noun, verb, adjective or adverb form).
Word Forms: Be careful with nouns and verbs:
Some *nouns* might need to be plural (~s).
Some *verbs* might need ~s, ~ed, ~ing.

accommodate 1. When you visit campus, you can find _____ nearby.

The executive suite _____ four adults.

analogy 2. Brad uses many sports _____ when he teaches.

Junk email is closely _____ to junk snail mail.

anticipate 3. We're looking forward with _____ to your next book.

It is _____ that the new version will be released soon.

assure 4. The witness was _____ that her identity would be safe.

Can you give me your _____ that you will try harder?

attain 5. Their newest album has not _____ the popularity of their first album.

We think that _____ of the goals can be done quickly.

behalf 6. I come to you on _____ of all the shareholders.

In _____ of the board, I want to thank all of you for coming here today.

bulk 7. The net effect would be a reduction in choice for the customer for narrowband services, which constitute the _____ of the market.

The _____ of the population live beyond their means.

cease 8. This regulation _____ to apply once the new regulation is in place.

After Charles' latest story, Tina _____ to believe anything he said.

coherent 9. The ideas in this essay seem to lack _____.

We cannot begin the campaign without a _____ plan.

coincide 10. Several theories can explain this remarkable _____.

Yesterday's BlackBerry outage _____ with a reduced number of traffic accidents.

commence 11. During the week _____ on May 3, you may begin to pick up your class schedules.

Prior to the _____ of a bankruptcy, a bankruptcy estate is created.

Unit 9

compatible 12. It is difficult to find ink cartridges that are _____ with my old printer.

The following tables summarize the _____ of our products with different versions of Joomla! and PHP.

concurrent 13. Because the accounting year was not _____ with the tax year, additional audit visit was necessary.

The judge ordered her to two twelve-year sentences to be served _____.

confine 14. He had been brought up in strict _____ in his father's castle.

British troops are largely _____ to their bases for fear of much higher casualties.

converse 15. Troy worked on the conclusion of the essay before working on the introduction. The _____ would have been easier.

Poor people sometimes dream about becoming rich. _____, rich people rarely dream about becoming poor.

device 16. Wi fi reception is poor when other wireless _____ are used in the vicinity.

To see how the page would look on a mobile _____, click the preview button.

devote 17. Despite Wentworth's single-minded _____ to the king's interest, Charles had never entirely trusted him.

The two sisters were entirely _____ to serving their elder brother.

diminish 18. Within weeks, the horrible nightmares had _____.

For many people, due to the changing nature of work, the concept of a job career for life is rapidly _____.

distort 19. Photoshop elements also allows consumers to easily correct camera lens _____.

It seems they have _____ their records for propaganda purposes.

duration 20. Season tickets of varying _____ are available at all of our city center car parks.

Agency contracts may have an indefinite _____.

erode 21. _____ of civil liberties is threatened by the measures contained in the prevention of terrorism bill.

Your right to privacy has been severely _____.

ethic 22. The _____ of individualism leads to social disintegration.

Web bloggers may be producing "news" articles without any journalistic _____.

Unit 9

format 23. These books are in .pdf _____, for which you need an Acrobat reader.

The magazine articles are specially _____ for hand-held devices.

found 24. The museum was originally _____ as a monastery.

The Muslim Brotherhood was _____ in 1928 in Egypt.

inherent 25. There are too many _____ weaknesses in the design.

The two points of view are _____ contradictory.

insight 26. Thank you for your _____ comments.

The new book gives _____ into how the Beatles lived.

integral 27. In the past, kitchens were not _____ parts of the home.

This DVD player is an _____ component of the entertainment system.

intermediate 28. The express train does not stop at _____ stations.

A commission is money paid to an independent _____ or an agent for selling policies.

manual 29. All the on-line _____ are no longer on the web site.

The fruit must be picked _____, not by machine.

mature 30. Whiskey worth millions of pounds lies _____ in barrels on the estate.

The footballer says he has _____ since his mistakes in last season's games.

mediate 31. These issues raise more general questions about the future of scientific discourse in an electronically _____ world.

When _____ a conflict, you should begin by defining winning and losing.

medium 32. Twitter has played an important role as the _____ of revolution in several countries.

Simply put, the interstellar _____ is the material which fills the space between the stars.

military 33. In her new book, she shatters myths about history, especially _____ history.

Any _____ action will have to be approved by the United Nations under international law.

Unit 9

mutual   34. We talked until we reached a _____ understanding.

Tsar Nicholas and Emperor Napoleon seemed to regard each other with _____ respect.

norm   35. In the post-cold war world, effective _____ against proliferation are inseparable from standards against nuclear weapons.

Dr. Malachi proposes the concept of mutual value-creation as a behavioral _____ for the new era.

overlap   36. This plugin detects if one or more elements are _____.

The scheduled time for both meetings _____, so I had to leave the first meeting early.

passive   37. Levi sat _____ watching the trucks go by.

People don't realize how dangerous _____ smoking is.

portion   38. You may not reproduce any _____ of this book without prior written permission.

You need to eat five _____ of fruits and vegetables every day.

preliminary   39. The _____ results showed no signs of disease.

The transit workers have _____ approved the right for their leadership to call a strike

protocol   40. We have many _____ with the police to help us handle domestic violence cases effectively.

The center follows a strict _____ in the development of the guideline.

qualitative   41. Andrew's main job is to conduct _____ interviews on the behalf of various manufacturers.

Problems of economic policy also involve political and ethical criteria that are essentially _____ in nature.

refine   42. Crude oil is _____ to produce useable gasoline and other products.

"Cupellation" is the most ancient way of _____ silver.

relax   43. Atheists are questioning the _____ of tax laws for the benefit of religious organizations.

Annie looks forward to _____ with her friends after work.

restrain   44. Iris had to be _____ by the nurses on staff.

If you are the victim of abuse, you can get a _____ order from the court.

Unit 9

revolution   45. The new phones may update some small features, but they are hardly _____.

Much of Asia's transformation is being driven by the twin _____ of domestic consumption and outsourcing.

rigid   46. His eyes moved, but his body remained _____.

It was difficult to resolve the conflict because of the _____ of Edward's position on the matter.

route   47. We can save money by _____ the delivery trucks around the more congested highways.

We had a choice of several _____ for getting back to the hotel.

sphere   48. Von Guericke had prepared a large hollow _____ from which he had removed the air using a vacuum pump of his invention.

Wi fi solutions are entering the private _____.

subordinate   49. The Republicans generally favor the _____ of the public interest to the needs of private profit.

Careful use of _____ clauses can help you to focus on the more important ideas.

supplement   50. Recipients of Medicare often purchase _____ health care insurance.

Fortunately, Karen had _____ her income by working part-time at a local nursery.

suspend   51. The former Southampton defender will be back following his one-match _____ last week.

General Motors is _____ production of the Volt until further safety tests are carried out.

team   52. A _____ of experts will join our staff.

His mother and his lawyer _____ up to prove his innocence.

temporary   53. Facebook users suddenly found that their accounts had been _____ suspended.

The city wants to provide _____ shelters for the homeless this winter.

trigger   54. The aggregation of platelets _____ the cascade of reactions that lead to blood clot formation.

The intense rains are sure to _____ mudslides.

Unit 9

Collocations

In each group of sentences, write *one* word from the list which goes with the **highlighted collocations**. Be careful with word forms.

Exercise 1	distort route diminish concur accommodate medium
	portion integrate sphere assure cease behalf team

1. Her sense of humor **never** _____ **to amaze** me.

    If sea levels rise, some island nations will _____ **to exist**.

    After ten hours of fighting, we decide **to call a** _____ **fire**.

2. We hope to quickly **reach an** _____ **with** North Korea on the matter of border security.

    We can wait until we arrive in the city **to look for** _____.

    Each limousine can **comfortably** _____ eight people.

3. The committee **unanimously** _____ on the budget bill.

    In _____ **with** the new law, airlines now post all ticket costs.

4. I don't know anyone who _____ **the truth** the way Sheila does.

    That's a **deliberate** _____ **of** what I said yesterday.

    The government-controlled media try to _____ **the reality** of what really happened.

5. Little children who have emotional problems can express themselves **through the** _____ **of** puppets.

    Moist sand is a good **storage** _____ for potatoes.

    I know we disagree, but I think we can **find a happy** _____.

6. The mayor **played an** _____ **part** in building consensus on the matter.

    I like the way the poetry **is seamlessly** _____ **into** the opera's libretto.

    The nations of Europe discussed the question of **monetary** _____.

7. Kurds **make up a** _____ of the population of northern Iraq.

    Each **individual** _____ of food was rather small.

    Groceries **take up a sizeable** _____ of our weekly budget.

8. Kissinger's _____ **of influence** was considerable.

    Laurent's lack of interest was not very important **in the wider** _____ of things.

9. The **shortest** _____ to the summit is also the steepest.

    They were late because they took the **scenic** _____.

    They were last seen **en** _____ to Kandahar.

10. Ken and Amy make an excellent **husband and wife** _____.

    We like Harriet because she is a _____ **player**.

Unit 9

Collocations

Exercise 2	preliminary coherent military duration subordinate team
	confine analogy restrain intermediate trigger devote

1. The speaker **drew a useful** _____ that made the complex ideas much more clear to the audience.

    It is not always a good idea **to reason by** _____

    A camera lens **is roughly** _____ to the eye.

2. **According to** _____ **findings**, the new drug may not be as safe as the pharmaceutical company claims.

    After **the usual** _____, the two leaders began serious discussions.

    The Palestinians demanded the release of the prisoners **as a** _____ **to** further talks.

3. The queen **is largely** _____ **to** ceremonial roles in the government.

    The artist's actions were not **within the** _____ **of** socially-accepted behavior.

    The demonstrators were **held in** _____ for twenty-four hours.

4. We had to remain in our seats **for the** _____ **of** the flight.

    Fortunately, the solar flares were **of short** _____.

5. The ideas in this essay seem **to lack** _____.

    Alison succeeded because she had a _____ **approach** to running the program.

    Logical _____ is important in a well-written essay.

6. **At the** _____ **level**, language students start to greatly expand their vocabulary.

    The US negotiates with Iran **though an** _____.

    Justin agreed **to act as an** _____ between Phil and Charlene.

7. **Compulsory** _____ **service** is required of all young Korean men.

    During the riots, the governor **called in the** _____.

    The United Nations **condemned the use** _____ **power** in Sudan.

8. I know you are excited, but **try to** _____ **yourself**.

    The police **exercised voluntary** _____ during the riots.

    Due to **budgetary** _____, we cannot afford to remodel the schools.

9. Check all around you before you **pull the** _____.

    Be care what you say. She has **a hair** _____ temper.

    Lack of fresh water has _____ **a fight** between the clans.

10. Meg could not be **completely** _____ **to** her husband.

    The use of _____ **clauses** will make your paragraph more interesting.

Unit 9

Collocations

Exercise 3	bulk ethic mutual protocol device refine supplement
	manual passive anticipate format mature coincide

1. Our visit **is timed to** _____ with the full moon rising.

   Steve ran into Molly **by pure** _____.

   A series of _____ eventually led to the discovery of the ancient Indian burial grounds.

2. **It is widely** _____ **that** Karin will marry Andrew.

   The children **look forward** to Christmas **with keen** _____.

   Everyone could feel **the thrill of** _____ before the big boxing match.

3. Modern American kitchens are full of **labor-saving** _____.

   Left to her own _____, Maria created extraordinary artwork.

   In the event of an emergency landing over water, your seat cushion can be used as a **flotation** _____.

4. For years, American educators have been touting the rise of the "knowledge economy" and shifting focus away from _____ **labor**.

   Everything you need to know is in the **instruction** _____

   According to the _____, e-FAXes should print automatically.

5. Perry was given a promotion because of his excellent **work** _____.

   The Penn State scandal was really **a matter of** _____.

   The concept of **professional** _____ is partly comprised of what a professional should or should not do in the work place.

6. Using Photoshop, Kevin created **a slightly** _____ version of his sunset photo.

   Beatrice is a woman **of great** _____.

   There are many **oil** _____ near New Orleans.

7. To have peace, we must **have** _____ **trust for** each other.

   Where residents **hold** the neighborhood **in high** _____ **regard**, there is a noticeable reduction in the crime rate.

   We have a _____ **agreed upon** plan for improving the neighborhood.

8. If you don't get enough iron in your diet, you need **to take a** _____.

   The New York Times Magazine is a Sunday **magazine** _____ included with the Sunday edition of The New York Times.

   I had to pay extra for a **single** _____ when I booked my tour.

9. **The vast** _____ **of** the manufacturing is now done by robots.

   It is much cheaper **to buy** supplies **in** _____.

10. _____ **demands that** everyone in the room stands at attention when the queen enters.

    During the experiments, you must prepare the starch samples **according to established** _____.

Unit 9

Collocations

Exercise 4	insight erode mediate devote norm relax diminish
	revolution compatible suspend relax assure qualitative

1. Village officials **hasten to** _____ us that the water is safe to drink.

   The new regulations **provide reasonable** _____ to part-time teachers that they will still have jobs if enrollment drops.

   Despite _____ **to the contrary**, Russia continues to fear that US missiles will be aimed at Moscow.

2. I agree that free will and determinism can be **perfectly** _____.

   Sexual _____ is important because failure in intimacy can spell trouble in many other areas in the marriage.

   The problems of _____ **between** the 32-bit and 64-bit versions of Office have been solved.

3. I can do a good job of _____ **between** the two **parties** if they don't have a basic level of trust to begin with.

   When _____ **efforts failed**, rioting began.

   The process of _____ should be flexible for everyone concerned.

4. We encourage students **to think outside the** _____.

   "Nixon in China" is an opera whose **departure from the** _____ will startle and amaze most audiences.

   If no one every dared defy **the accepted** _____ **of society**, women would not be playing sports in college.

5. _____ **techniques** can help you get a good night's sleep.

   The **gradual** _____ of the muscles reduces the heart beat.

   Come in, **sit back**, _____ **and enjoy yourself**.

6. Copley is an artist who is **entirely** _____ **to** his art.

   Ron Paul had a unique way of **inspiring** _____ among his followers.

   The danger of **blind** _____ is that it prevents you from understanding other people's points of view.

7. What he **lacks in** _____, he makes up for in hard work.

   She made some **remarkably** _____ comments on the manuscript.

8. The regime **put down a violent** _____ in the countryside.

   Before 1789, universal education was a _____ **idea** in France.

   In February of 1914, the first _____ **broke out** in Russia.

9. As you listen, try to _____ **judgment**.

   After a brief _____ , the meeting resumed.

10. Homes tend to appreciate rather than _____ **in value** over time.

    The **point of** _____ **returns** depends upon the effect the variable has on production.

Unit 9

Synonyms Use the synonym clues to solve this crossword puzzle.

Across
2. similarity, comparison
7. concur, synchronize, match
8. set off, actuate, initiate
10. inspiration, perception, realization
11. agreeable, harmonious, fitting
12. stop, conclude, finish
16. length, period, span, time
17. cultivate, purify, process
18. limit, restrain, restrict
19. domain, realm, circle
20. reach, achieve, accomplish
21. common, joint, shared
24. hang, postpone, delay
27. opposite, reverse, contrary
29. preparatory, introductory
30. deform, misshape, contort
31. inborn, natural, built-in

Down
1. etiquette, formality
3. lap, converge, cover
4. grown up, adult, ripe
5. lap, converge, cover
6. tool, gadget, instrument
9. set up, establish, support
12. begin, start, initiate
13. look for, expect, foresee
14. consistent, cohesive, orderly
15. referee, moderate, intercede
17. stiff, unbending, inflexible
22. guarantee, ensure, promise
23. size, mass, volume
25. part, piece, fraction
26. dedicate, commit, pledge
28. wear away, corrode, scour

Unit 9

Review

1. We were too tired and upset to carry on a _____ conversation.	coherent compatible intermediate converse concurrent military
2. On the contrary, our analysis shows that the _____ is true.	
3. We carried out tests on short-range, _____ and long-range missiles.	
4. We were able to resolve our differences because of our _____ trust.	rigid distorted qualitative supplemental mutual subordinate
5. The numbers reflect _____, not quantitative, characteristics in the data.	
6. She was at first assigned to a _____ position, but she soon rose in the ranks of her department.	
7. We were pleased that _____ results confirmed our suspicions.	integral preliminary mutual passive united mature
8. When these trees are _____, they will stand about 60 feet tall.	
9. We thought the reference to the jewelry was insignificant, but it soon became one of the _____ parts of the story.	
10. The office issued us a _____ license and said we could get a permanent license after six months.	analogous preliminary compatible temporary inherent diminished
11. State laws must be _____ with federal laws.	
12. There are some _____ difficulties in her proposal.	
13. He was sentenced to six hours of _____ labor a day.	intermediate mature rigid manual spherical passive
14. Assertive people don't suddenly become _____, unless something is wrong.	
15. The rules are too _____. They need to be more flexible.	
16. By _____, we could say that the brain is similar to a computer.	device analogy concurrence assurance behalf format
17. This new _____ is so sensitive that you can detect objects buried three meters underground.	
18. The new TV program followed the usual _____ for prime-time situational comedies.	

Unit 9

Review

19. The decision to go to war must be made by the legislature, not by the _____.	behalf format revolution sphere military bulk
20. The next _____ in computer technology will probably be social.	
21. Pakistan was not willing to come under America's _____ of influence.	
22. Her vocabulary range is well within the _____ for children of her age.	norm team route converse revolution protocol
23. Because of the incredible _____ effort, we were able to exceed our goal.	
24. He did not know that _____ required him to give advance notice before arriving.	
25. She expressed her feelings through the _____ of painting.	unity bulk medium ethic device confines
26. Because of his strong work _____, he often wore himself out.	
27. The _____ of the estate was owned by the daughter; the son owned only a very small share.	
28. On _____ of the citizens of Arles, I would like to thank you.	scenario mediation duration behalf insight revolution
29. I kept my seat belt fastened for the _____ of the flight.	
30. We asked them if they could offer any _____ into this matter.	
31. The smallest _____ of the inheritance went to Henry.	route medium cessation device portion supplement
32. The quickest _____ to safety is along the river bed.	
33. He added an iron _____ to his diet.	
34. This room can easily _____ the 80 people who want to attend your meeting.	accommodate commence devote attain coincide distort
35. It took him five years to _____ his ultimate goal.	
36. The ceremony will _____ at exactly 7:00.	

Unit 9

Review

#	Sentence	Words
37.	If you _____ more time to exercising, you will be healthier.	devote
38.	As his confidence began to _____, his willingness to fight diminished.	commence erode converse
39.	Because the aims of the two businesses _____ so much, we are thinking of merging them.	found overlap

#	Sentence	Words
40.	I will _____ my final decision until you give me more information.	restrain violate
41.	The Prime Minister could not _____ with the suggestions that members of his own party put forth.	coincide suspend concur
42.	No one had the power to _____ them from entering the building.	attain

#	Sentence	Words
43.	They sent someone to _____ with the two warring factions.	devote relax
44.	It seemed he wanted to _____ the facts to make himself appear to be innocent.	mediate distort unify
45.	Let's sit down and _____ before we head home.	subordinate

#	Sentence	Words
46.	The slightest movement will _____ an interesting reaction.	trigger assure
47.	Major religious holidays _____ with the early part of winter.	cease devote coincide
48.	I can _____ you that you will always have my support.	confine

#	Sentence	Words
49.	We don't _____ any problems with the new computer system.	attain cease
50.	Without the sun's warmth, most life on earth would _____ to exist.	accommodate anticipate confine
51.	We were asked to _____ our comments to the topic under discussion.	refine

#	Sentence	Words
52.	They tried to _____ their opponents' political power and make their own positions stronger.	diminish unify
53.	The billionaire decided to _____ a new university.	refine supplement
54.	During the next two years, he began to _____ his writing style.	concur found

Unit 9

Definitions ° Parts of Speech ° Collocations

accommodate (v) to provide for; to supply with; to hold comfortably without crowding; to adapt
    comfortably accommodate, easily accommodate: *The dance hall can easily accommodate 100 people.*
    to accommodate to [= adapt to]: *The tropical fish accommodated themselves to the environment of the new aquarium.*

accommodation (n) a place to live or stay
    to look for accommodation, to seek accommodation, to secure accommodation, to provide accommodation
    comfortable accommodation, decent accommodation, suitable accommodation
    inadequate accommodation, substandard accommodation; luxurious accommodation
    overnight accommodation, temporary accommodation, residential accommodation

accommodations (n. pl.) places to stay, such as hotel rooms or apartments

accommodation (n) satisfactory arrangement or agreement
    to reach an accommodation, to work out an accommodation, to seek an accommodation
    an accommodation between, an accommodation with

analogy (n) a likeness or a similarity in some respects
    to make an analogy, to draw an analogy: *It's not hard to draw an analogy between their methods of reporting the news and the methods used by their counterparts in the Soviet Union.*
    to reason by analogy; an appropriate analogy, an apt analogy, a useful analogy
    a close analogy, a superficial analogy
    an analogy between: *There is an analogy between growing a garden and raising children.*
    an analogy with: *Past events form analogies with our present fears.*
    by analogy: *Ships at sea take refuge in clam harbors during storms. By analogy, young adults sometimes return to the home of their parents when life takes a bad turn.*
    argument by analogy, argument from analogy

analogous (adj)
    closely analogous, directly analogous, roughly analogous to, analogous with

analogously (adv)

anticipation (n) the expectation of something; feeling or realizing beforehand
    to be full of anticipation; to look forward with anticipation
    in anticipation of: *In anticipation of the upcoming holiday, we are decorating our house.*
    in/with anticipation, in/with eager anticipation, in/with keen anticipation, in/with happy anticipation, in/with pleasurable anticipation: *We look forward to your visit with eager anticipation.*
    a sense of anticipation, a feeling of anticipation, a shiver of anticipation, a thrill of anticipation

anticipate (v)
    to keenly anticipate, to eagerly anticipate: *At Christmas, children eagerly anticipate a visit from Santa Clause.*
    to be widely anticipated: *It is widely anticipated that sanctions will be imposed on Iran.*

anticipatory (adj)

assure (v) to inform positively and confidently; to guarantee
    to assure (someone) of (something): *The assassins were assured of a place in paradise.*
    to assure that: *We were assured that we would get our money back.*
    to hasten to assure; let me assure you

assurance (n)
    to provide assurance, to offer assurance, to gain assurance, to obtain assurance, to receive assurance
    to ask for assurance, to seek assurance; to accept assurance, to be satisfied with assurance
    to go back on assurances, to renege on assurances; despite assurances, in spite of assurances
    reasonable assurance, absolute assurance, categorical assurance, further assurance
    formal assurance, official assurance, personal assurance, verbal assurance, written assurance
    assurances to the contrary: *Despite assurances to the contrary, our neighbors eventually built a fence between our properties.*

attain (v) to gain, achieve, or reach an objective
    to attain success

to attain nirvana [= to reach a state of perfect peace and happiness]: *The young seeker followed the teachings of Buddha in hopes of attaining nirvana.*

attainment (n)

attainable (adj)

to become attainable, to seem attainable; readily attainable, easily attainable; attainable by

behalf (n) as a representative of someone else; for the benefit of someone else

in behalf of: *In behalf of all of us who work here, I would like to present you with this gold watch.*

on behalf of: *The chief decided, on behalf of the village, to kill all the stray dogs.*

bulk (n) very large (sometimes awkward) size, mass or volume

to ease one's bulk, to heave one's bulk, to shift one's bulk

considerable bulk, formidable bulk, huge bulk, massive bulk, sheer bulk, solid bulk

looming bulk [= a dangerous, shadowy large object or person]: *Traders were setting up their tables under the looming bulk of St. Martin's Church.*

bulk (n) the major portion of something

the vast bulk of: *The vast bulk of America's trade is with China.*

in bulk: *These apples are less expensive in bulk.*

to buy in bulk: *We get our goods cheaply because we buy them in bulk.*

bulk up (v) to increase in size or amount

The weight-lifters eat lots of food in order to bulk up before the big contest.

cease (v) to bring or come to an end; to discontinue

to cease to exist: *If more nations obtain nuclear weapons, life as we know it may cease to exist.*

to cease fire [= to stop shooting]: *The artillerymen were ordered to cease fire.*

to cease ~ing: *We ceased trading with them when we learned that they used slave labor.*

never cease to amaze: *It never ceases to amaze me that you can get so much done in a day.*

cease altogether, cease completely, cease entirely

all but cease, almost cease, virtually cease; largely cease, effectively cease

cease forthwith, cease immediately; cease abruptly, cease suddenly

rapidly cease, gradually cease, eventually cease; long (since) cease: *Jed's problems had long since ceased to interest me.*

without ceasing

cessation (n)

coherent (adj) marked by a consistent, logical relationship between the parts; sticking together

to become coherent, to seem coherent

a coherent approach to: *The introduction will help students develop a coherent approach to the subject.*

remarkably coherent, perfectly coherent, reasonably coherent; a coherent argument

coherent argument, coherent ideas, coherent remarks

coherently (adv)

coherence (n)

to lack coherence: *Your topic is interesting, but the essay lacks coherence.*

to achieve coherence, to create coherence, to give something coherence, to maintain coherence

internal coherence, ideological coherence, intellectual coherence, logical coherence, theoretical coherence; a degree of coherence, a sense of coherence

coherence between: *There seems to be no coherence between the ideas in the second and third paragraphs.*

cohere (v)

coincide (v) to happen at the same time; to be the same; agree in some way

to be planned to coincide, to be timed to coincide

to coincide with: *His football success coincided with an increase in his attention to his workout routine.*

to coincide in: *The dimensions of the three rooms coincide in length but not in width.*

closely coincide, exactly coincide, roughly coincide

coincidence (n)

mere, pure, or sheer coincidence: *It was a pure coincidence that I happened to be in New York when the Twin Towers were struck.*

an amazing coincidence, a happy coincidence, a remarkable coincidence, a wonderful coincidence
an odd coincidence, a strange coincidence, a weird coincidence, a curious coincidence, a funny
coincidence; a complete coincidence, pure coincidence, sheer coincidence
a string of coincidences, a set of coincidences, a series of coincidences
by coincidence: *She and I both ended up in Venice at the same time by sheer coincidence.*

coincidental (adj)

purely coincidental, entirely coincidental, merely coincidental, largely coincidental

coincident (adj)

Japan's index of coincident economic indicators rose a preliminary 2.5 points in January from the previous month.

coincidentally (adv)

commence (v) to start or begin

to commence by ~ing; to commence with: *The film commences with a scene from the past.*
commence firing! [= start shooting]
Let the ~ commence: *Everyone in the stadium stood up when the host of the Olympic Games shouted "Let the Games commence."*

commencement (n) the act of beginning

commencement (n) graduation day

Two hundred and ten students received their degrees on commencement day this year.

compatible (adj) able to associate, perform or coexist agreeably and harmoniously

to seem compatible
perfectly compatible, entirely compatible, fully compatible, quite compatible, totally compatible, wholly compatible
directly compatible, hardly compatible, sexually compatible, technologically compatible
compatible with: *I don't know why you two don't get married. I think you are perfectly compatible with each other.*

compatibility (n)

compatibility between or with: *The two brothers don't behave alike and really don't like the same things. There doesn't seem to be much compatibility between them.*

compatibly (adv)

concurrent (adj) occurring or existing simultaneously or side by side; being harmonious or in agreement

concurrent with: *The policeman's testimony was concurrent with that of the chief witness.*

concurrently (adv)

concurrently with: *In the final term of your master's program, you must do student teaching concurrently with writing your dissertation.*

concurrence (n) agreement

in complete, full or unanimous concurrence: *The workers were in unanimous concurrence with management's decision to cut back on overtime pay.*
in concurrence with: *In concurrence with the laws of the land, you must pay your taxes just like everyone else when they are due.*
with the concurrence of: *We can only build a new fence on our property line with the concurrence of our neighbors.*

concur (v)

to strongly concur, to fully concur, to completely concur: *He said we should invest in bonds rather than stocks right now, and we completely concur.*
to concur in, to concur with
to concur that: *The judge concurred that the lawyer's comments should be stricken from the records.*

confine (v) to restrict or limit; to shut in; to imprison

entirely confine, exclusively confine, solely confine, strictly confine, totally confine
increasingly confine, largely confine, mainly confine, principally confine
generally confine, normally confine
effectively confine, not necessarily confine, by no means confine: *Ignorance of the agreement was by no means confined to the media; many senators were also unaware of it.*

to confine to; to be confined to quarters [= to keep soldiers in their barracks/rooms]: *The soldiers were confined to quarters after they disobeyed the captain's orders.*

confinement (n)

to be held in confinement, to be kept in confinement, to be placed in confinement

solitary confinement: *The prisoner was released from solitary confinement after one month.*

close confinement; in confinement: *You'll have to stay in confinement until your fever subsides.*

confines (n)

to leave the confines

close confines, cramped confines, limited confines, narrow confines, strict confines

immediate confines, comfortable confines, comfy confines, safe confines

within the confines of: *We had to get the job done within the confines of our budget.*

outside the confines, beyond the confines

converse (n) something which is opposite or contrary in direction, action, sequence, etc.; turned around

the converse is true: *Most people think that Hans the horse was very clever. However, the converse was true; he was just stupidly reacting to signals from his trainer.*

in converse: *In converse with you, I feel we can solve the problem diplomatically.*

converse (adj)

conversely (adv) *Cusco is situated in a high, dry Andean mountain valley. Conversely, Machu Picchu is located on a lower peak just above the warm, moist Amazon jungles.*

converse (v) to speak; to engage in oral communication

to converse fluently: *My sister can converse fluently in Chinese.*

to converse about: *We were just conversing about the fact that the stock market looks like a bad investment these days.*

to converse with

conversation (n)

device (n) something used for a special purpose, such as a tool or instrument

a laborsaving device, a timesaving device

an explosive device, an incendiary device (= a device that will cause a fire)

a clever device, an ingenious device, a labor-saving device, useful device

a simple device, complex device, complicated device, sophisticated device

an automatic device, a mechanical device, an electronic device

a contraceptive device, a measuring device, a safety device, a timing device, a warning device

a mnemonic device [= a technique to aid memory]: *You can use mnemonic devices to acquire vocabulary words quickly and efficiently.*

a literary device: *The use of symbolism is a literary device used by many skillful writers.*

a flotation device: *Planes are equipped with flotation devices in case they go down over water.*

a listening device: *In the 1950s, the Soviets planted listening devices in the offices of American diplomats.*

left to one's own devices [= allowed to do as you please]: *He's so lazy that, if he were left to his own devices, he would soon stop working.*

devote (v) to concentrate on a particular purpose; to love or be loyal to

to devote oneself to; to devote one's attention to

to devote a song/poem to

blindly devoted to, completely devoted to, deeply devoted to, utterly devoted to, absolutely devoted to

entirely devoted to: *She was entirely devoted to her children.*

devotion (n)

to demonstrate devotion, to show devotion, to inspire devotion

absolute devotion, great devotion, unflagging devotion, selfless devotion

deep devotion, enormous devotion, fanatical devotion, intense devotion, single-minded devotion

religious devotion; blind devotion

with devotion: *We worked with great devotion to rebuild our community after the tornado.*

devotion to family, devotion to duty, devotion to a/the cause

an object of devotion

devotions (n. pl.) prayers, worship or religious services

morning devotions, evening devotions

diminish (v) to lessen or reduce; to cause to be or seem smaller, less important, etc.
>   to diminish in: *Your failure to win the election does not diminish you in our eyes.*
>   to diminish the problem: *The fact that you needed the money doesn't diminish the problem. You should not have taken the money.*
>   to diminish in value: *Homes tend to appreciate rather than diminish in value over time.*
>   diminishing returns: *The law of diminishing returns states that if one input in the production of a commodity is increased while all other inputs are held fixed, a point will eventually be reached at which additions of the input yield progressively smaller, or diminishing, increases in output.*

diminution (n)

distort (v) to twist out of the usual shape; to give false meaning to
>   to distort the truth, to distort reality
>   grossly distort, seriously distort, severely distort
>   completely distort, slightly distort, deliberately distort

distortion (n)
>   a deliberate distortion, a crude distortion, a willful distortion
>   a malicious distortion: *Her version of the story is a malicious distortion of the truth.*

duration (n) the length of time that something lasts; continuation in time
>   for the duration: *It looks as though the storm is going to last for a very long time, so we had better plan to just stay here at the hotel for the duration.*
>   for the duration of: *After she fell ill, she stayed inside the cabin for the duration of the visit.*
>   a long duration, a moderate duration, a short duration, a brief duration; of a certain duration
>   of short duration: *The flowers on this tree are of short duration. They last only two or three days.*

durable (adj) able to last for a long time

erode (v) to eat or wear away
>   badly erode, deeply erode, seriously erode, severely erode
>   further erode, gradually erode, slowly erode, completely erode
>   to threaten to erode, to tend to erode; to erode someone's trust

erosion (n)
>   to contribute to erosion, to lead to erosion, to result in erosion, to suffer from erosion
>   the rate of erosion, to slow the rate of erosion
>   seriously erosion, severe erosion, rapid erosion, gradual erosion, steady erosion
>   coastal erosion, soil erosion, water erosion, wind erosion, glacial erosion, acid erosion

ethic (n) a set of principles or rules of moral or correct behavior
>   the work ethic: *Americans are sometimes frustrated when their version of the work ethic is not followed in other countries.*

ethical (adj)

ethically (adv)

ethics (n. pl.)
>   a code of ethics, personal ethics
>   a matter of ethics, a question of ethics: *The editors decided not to publish the photo of the victim, saying it was a question of ethics, not journalism.*
>   business ethics, medical ethics, professional ethics

format (n) the design, plan, shape or organization of something
>   a suitable format: *The content of your essay is quite interesting. Now you need to put it into a suitable format so that it will be easier to read.*

format (v)

found (v) to start or establish, especially by providing for future existence
>   to be founded on: *The country was founded on certain moral principles.*

founder (n)

foundation (n) [see Unit 7]

inherent (adj) existing as a natural, essential or permanent quality or characteristic
>   inherent in, inherent to

inherently (adv)
>   inherently true, inherently false

insight (n) the ability to have a clear and deep understanding of the true and usually complex nature of a situation

to gain insight, to have (an) insight

to give insight, to offer insight, to provide insight

to be lacking in insight; a lack of insight

a deep insight, a profound insight, considerable insight, significant insight, deep insight, remarkable insight

a new insight, fresh insight, original insight, startling insight

penetrating insight, revealing insight, illuminating insight, crucial insight, invaluable insight

to have the insight to do something: *Benjamin Franklin had the insight to realize that lightening was somehow related to the electricity he had observed in his laboratory.*

a person of great insight

insightful (adj)

insightfully (adv)

integral (adj) essential for the complete thing

an integral part of: *Sessions in the computer lab are an integral part of the course.*

an integral whole; an integral unit

integrally (adv)

integral (n) a mathematical object that can be interpreted as an area or a generalization of area

integral calculus; definite integral, indefinite integral

integrate (v)

closely integrate, tightly integrate, completely integrate, fully integrate: *Only one in five businesses has fully integrated sustainability into their business practices.*

seamlessly integrate, successfully integrate

highly integrated, well integrated

integration (n)

true integration, complete integration, full integration, close integration, seamless integration, rapid integration

economic integration, monetary integration, political integration, racial integration, social integration

a move toward integration, a need for integration

intermediate (adj) in the middle; between the beginning and the end

intermediate level

intermediate range missiles

intermediary (n)

to act as an intermediary: *The President decided to send the Secretary of State to the Middle East to act as an intermediary between the Israelis and the Palestinians.*

through an intermediary, via an intermediary

manual (adj) by hand

manual labor: *Farmers in the United States depend to a great extent on manual labor.*

manually (adv)

manual (n) a booklet that provides instructions on how to do something

to check the manual, to consult the manual, to look at the manual

instruction manual, training manual, owner's manual, user manual

car manual, computer manual, sewing manual, software manual

maintenance manual, operating manual, operational manual, reference manual, technical manual

according to the manual

mature (adj) grown up; adult

to allow something to mature, to leave something to mature: *After you make the cheese, leave it to mature for at least two weeks.*

emotionally mature, mentally mature, physically mature, fully mature

to be mature for: *Margaret is only twelve, but she's quite mature for her age.*

maturely (adv)

mature (v)

to mature early, to mature quickly, to mature on time, to mature slowly

to mature into: *William matured into a handsome young man.*

mediate (v) to act to get two sides to agree or come together
> to mediate between parties: *The Secretary of State found it difficult to mediate between the warring parties.*

mediation (n)
> to offer mediation, to accept mediation
> mediation efforts fail, mediation process fails
> through someone's mediation, under someone's mediation
> mediation between, mediation by

medium (n) something by or through which something else is produced or carried on
> through a (the) medium of: *She eloquently expresses herself through the medium of poetry.*
> a medium for: *copper wire is the most common medium for conducting electricity.*

medium (n) an instrument, means or agency
> *In some island countries, sea shells were used as a medium of exchange.*
> a storage medium
> a medium of instruction: *In many African countries, French is the medium of instruction.*

medium (n) a middle way, thing or condition
> happy medium: *I wanted to keep the house at 68° but my husband wanted to keep it at 74°, so we chose the happy medium of 71°.*

medium (n) [media = n.pl] [see Unit 7] a means of mass communication, such as TV, Internet, newspapers, magazines, etc.
> mass media, mixed media, multi-media

medium (n) a person who is believed to be in contact with spirits
> *Karen went to a medium to try to get a message from her dead father.*

medium (adj) in the middle; a middle amount
> of medium height, of medium build

military (n) the armed forces
> to serve in the military
> to call in the military: *When the enemy started to cross our border, the President called in the military.*
> the military seizes power, the military takes power
> a member of the military

military (adj)
> compulsory military service, universal military service, voluntary military service

militarily (adv)

mutual (adj) having the same relationship with respect to each other; reciprocal
> to hold in mutual regard
> mutual admiration, mutual understanding, mutual respect
> mutual fund
> mutual regard: *Even though we disagree on many things, we still hold each other in high mutual regard.*

mutually (adv)
> mutually agreeable, mutually agreed upon

norm (n) the model or standard that is generally accepted or followed
> to think outside the norm, to act outside the norm, to deviate from the norm [= to behave in a way that is not generally accepted]: *Some people deviate from the norm simply because they are not satisfied with their lives or because they just want to be different.*
> the accepted norm, the established norm, ethical norm, moral norm, cultural norm, social norm
> community norm, family norm, group norm
> outside the norm, above the norm, below the norm, over the norm
> the norm for: *One snowstorm for the year is the norm for this part of the country.*
> a departure from the norm, a deviation from the norm
> an exception to the norm; the norm rather than the exception

norm (n) an average
> *A reading rate of 125 words per minute is the norm for children at that age.*
> statistical norm

overlap (v) to lie over and partially cover; to occupy some of the same space or time
    overlap with: *My German class overlaps with my lunch time so I tend to get very hungry.*
    almost overlap, partially overlap, partly overlap, slightly overlap
    overlap to some extent; overlap with
overlap (n) something that partially covers or partially occupies the same space or time
passive (adj) accepting without rejecting; not participating readily or actively; inactive
    to seem passive, to remain passive
    extremely passive, essentially passive
    passive aggression: *When she stops responding to your questions, you should suspect her of passive aggression.*
passively (adv)
portion (n) a part of a whole
    to make up a portion of: *Bonds make up a small portion of my total investments.*
    to take up a portion of: *Finding substitute teachers takes up a considerable portion of the director's time.*
    an individual portion, a considerable portion, a large portion, a significant portion, a sizeable portion, a substantial portion
    (in) equal portions
portion (v) to divide into parts and distribute
    portion out: *When the fishing boats returned, the fish were portioned out to everyone in the village.*
preliminary (adj) prior to or preparing for what comes next
    preliminary results, preliminary findings, preliminary investigation, preliminary assessment
    preliminary hearing, preliminary ruling
    an essential preliminary, a necessary preliminary, a useful preliminary
    the usual preliminaries: *After the usual preliminaries, Carla launched into her speech.*
    preliminary to: *Preliminary to tomorrow's meeting, you should all read the article I gave you.*
    as a preliminary to: *The two ministers met privately as a preliminary to making the announcement.*
preliminarily (adv)
preliminaries (n. pl.) the first round of elections
protocol (n) correct formal or diplomatic etiquette, ceremony or procedure
    established protocol
    to observe protocol
    protocol demands that, protocol requires that
    according to protocol
qualitative (adj) relating to the quality or standard of something
    qualitative analysis
qualitatively (adv)
refine (v) to remove course or unsuitable elements; to make more elegant, cultured or pure
    to attempt to refine, to try to refine, to help to refine
    to refine on; to refine on a method
    to refine into: *Corn can be refined into ethanol.*
    slightly refine, further refine, increasingly refine, constantly refine, continuously refine
    refined version
refinement (n)
    considerable refinement, great refinement, extra refinement, further refinement
    continuous refinement, endless refinement
    of great refinement: *Though she was born to a poor family, Emily educated herself and became a woman of great refinement.*
refinery (n) an industrial plant where natural resources are purified into usable products.
    oil refinery, sugar refinery
relax (v) to make looser or less tight; to reduce the intensity or stress
    to learn to relax, to begin to relax, to try to relax
    to relax one's hold
    deeply relax, completely relax, totally relax; relax a little, relax slightly
    to relax against, to relax into

come in and relax, sit back and relax, relax and enjoy yourself

relaxation (n)

to promote relaxation, to aid relaxation

deep relaxation, great relaxation, complete relaxation, total relaxation

muscle relaxation; relaxation exercises, relaxation techniques; relaxation therapy, relaxation class

an aid to relaxation; rest and relaxation; a state of relaxation

relaxation (n) making rules less strict

further relaxation, gradual relaxation

to call for relaxation, to seek relaxation: *The president is seeking a gradual relaxation of the regulations governing oil drilling in the Gulf.*

restrain (v) to prevent from doing something

to restrain someone/something from: *The only thing we ask is that you restrain your dog from getting into our garden.*

to manage to restrain, to try to restrain: *Don't eat so much. Try to restrain yourself.*

an effort to restrain, an attempt to restrain

effectively restrain, forcibly restrain, physically restrain

remarkably restrained, unusually restrained

restraint (n)

to show some restraint, to exercise restraint

effective restraint, voluntary restraint, conventional restraint

budgetary restraint, economic restraint, financial restraint, fiscal restraint, monetary restraint, spending restraint, wage relaxation, pay restraint

a call for restraint, an appeal for restraint

revolution (n) fundamental and usually far-reaching change in ideas, social habits, ways of doing things, etc.

to stir up a revolution, to organize a revolution, to foment revolution

to carry out a revolution, to conduct a revolution

to fight a revolution, crush a revolution, put down a revolution, defeat a revolution, quash a revolution [= to stop a revolution]: *The dictator acted quickly to quash a revolution that would have threatened his power.*

a revolution breaks out, spreads, overthrows, topples

cultural revolution, industrial revolution, sexual revolution

a bloody revolution, a violent revolution; bloodless revolution, peaceful revolution

popular revolution, anti-communist revolution, anti- democratic revolution, proletarian revolution

world revolution, socialist revolution

quiet revolution, virtual revolution, agrarian revolution, political revolution, scientific revolution

the threat of revolution ,the outbreak of revolution

a revolution in: *When computers became cheap and powerful, there was a revolution in how our classes were taught.*

revolutionary (n) a person who works for radical political change

revolutionary (adj)

revolutionary war, revolutionary idea

revolutionarily (adv)

revolution (n) the act of moving around a center point; rotation

complete revolution: *The earth makes one complete revolution around the sun every 365 days.*

revolutions per minute

revolve (v) to go around a center point; to rotate

The moon revolves around the earth.

rigid (adj) not flexible

to grow rigid, to lie rigid, to go rigid

rigid about: *She was very rigid about starting the meeting on time.*

rigid with: *At the sound of something pounding in the attic, we went rigid with fear.*

rigidly (adv)

rigidity (n)

rigidness (n)

rigidify (v)

rigidification (n)

route (n) road, course or way for traveling; a means for reaching a destination

to map out a route: *I think we can get to the ski slopes quickly if we just map out a route through these mountains.*

to follow a route, to take a route, to choose a route, to map out a route, to run a route

the route crosses, flows, goes, passes through, climbs, turns, leads, lies

an alternate route, a circuitous route, a direct route, an indirect route; an escape route

a scenic route, a beautiful route, an attractive route

main route, trunk route, air route, overland route, shipping route, tourist route

a quick route, short route, convenient route, easy route; the shortest route

along the route, on the route, the route between, the route through

en route [= on the way]: *The packages are en route to you right now. They should be there tomorrow.*

route (v) to send along a certain way

The email messages from Dakar was routed through London, Dallas, Mountain View and Chicago before arriving in New York.

sphere (n) a field of activity

wider sphere: *Speranski's ideas started to influence a wider sphere than the emperor's immediate circle.*

academic sphere, cultural sphere, domestic sphere, social sphere

economic sphere, military sphere, political sphere

(under) a sphere of influence: *Several of the South American nations resisted coming under America's sphere of influence.*

within the sphere, outside the sphere

sphere (n) a round ball-like object

sphere (n) a planet or the world

spherical (adj)

spherical object

spherically (adv)

subordinate (adj) in a lower rank; of a lower level of importance

completely subordinate, totally subordinate, wholly subordinate, largely subordinate

subordinate to: *A wife's needs should never be subordinate to her husband's needs.*

subordinate clause

subordinately (adv)

subordinate (n) a person or thing that is of a lower level or rank

subordinate (v)

to completely subordinate, to totally subordinate, to wholly subordinate, to largely subordinate

supplement (n) something added to something else to make it complete

to take a supplement: *I don't get enough iron in my diet, so I take a supplement.*

a dietary supplement, an iron supplement, mineral supplement, vitamin supplement

a valuable supplement, a magazine supplement

supplement (n) extra amount of money

to charge a supplement, to add a supplement; a supplement is payable

$/€/£ supplement: *Extra legroom on the flight is available for a $60 supplement.*

flight supplement, single room supplement

earnings-related supplement, means-tested supplement

supplement (v)

to supplement with: *You should supplement your diet with more fresh fruit.*

to supplement by: *He supplements his income by selling vacuum cleaners.*

supplementary (adj)

supplemental (adj)

suspend (v) to temporarily or permanently stop or prevent

to suspend judgment, to suspend belief

to agree to suspend, to decide to suspend, to vote to suspend

to threaten to suspend, to be forced to suspend

to have the power to suspend

suspend (v) to hang

to suspend from: *Decorations for the birthday party were suspended from the ceiling.*

suspension (n)

a brief suspension, total suspension, temporary suspension, sudden suspension, immediate suspension

to give someone a suspension, to impose a suspension, to order a suspension

to be under suspension: *Work on the bridge is under temporary suspension until more funding is found.*

suspension (n) part of a vehicle that holds the body up

front suspension, rear suspension, independent suspension; suspension system

suspended animation (n) a state in which life functions are temporarily stopped

Future space travelers will be in suspended animation during their long space flights.

team (n) a group that works or plays together

to field a team, to choose a team, to get a team together; to coach a team, to play for a team, to manage a team

to make the team [= to be chosen for the team]: *Shelly is working hard to make the baseball team.*

to be dropped from the team, to get kicked off the team; to sign for a team

a team player, team member; a team of oxen, a team of horses

a baseball team, a football team, a basketball team, etc.

the home team, the away team, the opposing team, the rival team, the visiting team

dream team, winning team, strong team; junior team, senior team, local team, national team

team effort, team performance, team talk

husband and wife team, joint team

editorial team, management team, marketing team, production team

team building, team development

team up (v) to join together with

teamwork (n)

effective teamwork, to emphasize teamwork, to encourage teamwork

through teamwork

temporary (adj) limited to a short period of time; not permanent

temporary arrangements, temporary quarters, temporary accommodations

temporarily (adv)

temporary (n) a person who works for a short period of time

trigger (n) a device or event that causes something to begin; a small lever on a gun that fires the bullet

to have your finger on the trigger

to press a trigger, to pull a trigger, to release a trigger, to squeeze a trigger

quick on the trigger; a hair trigger [= to be very quick to act]: *Don't get him angry. He has a hair trigger temper and will start fighting before you know what's happening.*

to trigger a mechanism

trigger finger; an itchy trigger finger [= always ready for a fight]: *Sam was always getting into trouble with the police. He had an itchy trigger finder and was fond of getting very drunk.*

trigger (v) to set off; to initiate; to cause to explode

to trigger a war, to trigger a fight, to trigger a conflict

to trigger a response: *We were hoping that the offer of food and medicine would trigger a more positive response from them.*

Synonyms

accommodate:	contain, hold, house
analogy:	similarity, comparison, resemblance
anticipate:	look for, expect, foresee
assure:	guarantee, ensure, promise
attain:	reach, achieve, accomplish
behalf:	representation, proxy, support
bulk:	size, mass, volume
cease:	stop, conclude, finish
coherent:	consistent, cohesive, orderly
coincide:	concur, synchronize, match
commence:	begin, start, initiate
compatible:	agreeable, harmonious, fitting
concurrent:	simultaneous, harmonious
confine:	limit, restrain, restrict
converse:	opposite, reverse, contrary
device:	tool, gadget, instrument
devote:	dedicate, commit, pledge
diminish:	decrease, lessen, weaken
distort:	deform, misshape, contort
duration:	length, period, span, time
erode:	wear away, corrode, scour
ethic:	code, moral
format:	layout, form, pattern
found:	set up, establish, initiate
inherent:	inborn, natural, built-in
insight:	inspiration, perception, realization
integral:	intrinsic, essential, indispensable
intermediate:	medium, middle, central
manual:	by hand
mature:	grown up, adult, ripe
mediate:	referee, moderate, intercede
medium:	vehicle, means, instrument
military:	martial, warlike, army
mutual:	common, joint, shared
norm:	average, standard, usual
overlap:	lap, converge, cover
passive:	receptive, inactive, accepting
portion:	part, piece, fraction
preliminary:	preparatory, introductory, advance
protocol:	etiquette, convention, formality
qualitative:	attributive, native
refine:	cultivate, purify, process
relax:	let go, loosen, tone down
restrain:	hold back, confine, control
revolution:	revolt, upheaval, uprising
rigid:	stiff, unbending, inflexible
route:	path, way, road
sphere:	domain, realm, circle
subordinate:	inferior, lesser, lower
supplement:	augment, add, extend
suspend:	hang, postpone, delay
team:	squad, gang, crew
temporary:	short-term, momentary, brief
trigger:	set off, actuate, initiate

Unit 9

Answers

Definitions

1. anticipation	16. manual	31. suspend	46. trigger
2. duration	17. subordinate	32. cease	47. supplement
3. portion	18. compatible	33. diminish	48. route
4. relax	19. ethic	34. integral	49. commence
5. assure	20. team	35. mutual	50. erode
6. confine	21. insight	36. temporary	51. found
7. coherent	22. accommodate	37. revolution	52. converse
8. intermediate	23. mediate	38. bulk	53. military
9. rigid	24. restrain	39. medium	54. overlap
10. analogy	25. concurrent	40. coincide	
11. device	26. inherent	41. distort	
12. protocol	27. mature	42. norm	
13. refine	28. behalf	43. qualitative	
14. attain	29. format	44. preliminary	
15. devote	30. sphere	45. passive	

Parts of Speech

1. accommodations accommodates	12. compatible compatibility	23. format formatted	34. mutual mutual
2. analogies analogous	13. concurrent concurrently	24. founded founded	35. norms norm
3. anticipation anticipated	14. confinement confined	25. inherent inherently	36. overlapping overlapped
4. assured assurance	15. converse Conversely	26. insightful insights	37. passively passive
5. attained attainment	16. devices device	27. integral integral	38. portion portions
6. behalf behalf	17. devotion devoted	28. intermediate intermediary	39. preliminary preliminarily
7. bulk bulk	18. diminished diminishing	29. manuals manually	40. protocols protocol
8. ceases ceased	19. distortion distorted	30. maturing matured	41. qualitative qualitative
9. coherence coherent	20. duration duration	31. mediated mediating	42. refined refining
10. coincidence coincided	21. Erosion eroded	32. medium medium	43. relaxation relaxing
11. commencing commencement	22. ethic/ethics ethics	33. military military	44. restrained restraining

45. revolutionary revolutions	49. subordination subordinate	53. temporarily temporary
46. rigid rigidity	50. supplemental supplemented	54. triggered trigger
47. routing routes	51. suspension suspending	
48. sphere sphere	52. team teamed	

Unit 9

Answers

Collocations

Exercise 1	Exercise 2	Exercise 3	Exercise 4
1. ceases cease cease	1. analogy analogy analogous	1. coincide coincidence coincidences	1. assure assurance assurances
2. accommodation accommodations accommodate	2. preliminary preliminaries preliminary	2. anticipated anticipation anticipation	2. compatible compatibility compatibility
3. concurred / concurs concurrence	3. confined confines confinement	3. devices devices device	3. mediating mediation mediation
4. distorts distortion distort	4. duration duration	4. manual manual manual	4. norm norm norm
5. medium medium medium	5. cohesion coherent cohesion	5. ethic ethics ethics	5. Relaxation relaxation relax
6. integral integrated integration	6. intermediate intermediary intermediary	6. refined refinement refineries	6. devoted devotion devotion
7. portion portion portion	7. military military military	7. mutual mutual mutually	7. insight insightful
8. sphere sphere	8. restrain restraint restraints	8. supplement supplement supplement	8. revolution revolutionary revolution
9. route route route	9. trigger trigger triggered	9. bulk bulk	9. suspend suspension
10. team team	10. subordinate subordinate	10. Protocol protocol	10. diminish diminishing

Unit 9

Answers

Synonyms (Crossword)

Across
2. analogy
7. coincide
8. trigger
10. insight
11. compatible
12. cease
16. duration
17. refine
18. confine
19. sphere
20. attain
21. mutual
24. suspend
27. converse
29. preliminary
30. distort
31. inherent

Down
1. protocol
3. overlap
4. mature
5. diminish
6. device
9. found
12. commence
13. anticipate
14. coherent
15. mediate
17. rigid
22. assure
23. bulk
25. portion
26. devote
28. erode

Review

1. coherent
2. converse
3. intermediate
4. mutual
5. qualitative
6. subordinate
7. preliminary
8. mature
9. integral
10. temporary
11. compatible
12. inherent
13. manual
14. passive
15. rigid
16. analogy
17. device
18. format
19. military
20. revolution
21. sphere
22. norm
23. team
24. protocol
25. medium
26. ethic
27. bulk
28. behalf
29. duration
30. insight
31. portion
32. route
33. supplement
34. accommodate
35. attain
36. commence
37. devote
38. erode
39. overlap
40. suspend
41. concur
42. restrain
43. mediate
44. distort
45. relax
46. trigger
47. coincide
48. assure
49. anticipate
50. cease
51. confine
52. diminish
53. found
54. refine

Unit 10

Word List

n = noun   **v** = verb   **adj** = adjective   **adv** = adverb
prep = preposition   **conj** = conjunction

adjacent (adj)
albeit (conj)
assemble (v)
    assembly (n)
    assemblage (n)
collapse (v)
    collapse (v)
colleague (n)
compile (v)
    compilation (n)
    compiler (n)
conceive (v)
    conception (n)
    conceivable (adj)
    conceivably (adv)
controversy (n)
    controversial (adj)
    controversially (adv)
convince (v)
    convinced (adj)
    convincing (adj)
    convincingly (adv)
depression (n)
    depress (v)
    depressed (adj)
    depressing (adj)
drama (n)
    dramatics (n. pl.)
    dramatic (adj)
    dramatically (adv)
    dramatize (v)
dynamic (adj)
    dynamically (adv)
    dynamics (n. pl.)
    dynamism (n)
encounter (n)
    encounter (v)
enormous (adj)
    enormously (adv)
    enormity (n)
estate (n)
ethnic (adj)
    ethnicity (n)
expand (v)
    expansion (n)
    expandable (adj)
external (adj)
    externalize (v)
    externalization (n)
    externally (adv)

forthcoming (adj)
gender (n)
incentive (n)
    incentivize (v)
incidence (n)
incline (v)
    incline (n)
    inclined (adj)
integrity (n)
intrinsic (adj)
    intrinsically (adv)
invoke (v)
    invocation (n)
    invocable (adj)
involve (v)
    involved (adj)
    involvement (n)
levy (v)
    levy (n)
medical (adj)
    medically (adv)
    medical (n)
modify (v)
    modification (n)
    modified (adj)
    modifier (n)
nonetheless (adv)
notwithstanding (prep)
    notwithstanding (conj)
nuclear (adj)
    nucleus (n)
odd (adj)
    oddly (adv)
    odds (n. pl)
    oddity (n)
overall (adj)
    overall (n)
overseas (adj)
    overseas (adv)
panel (n)
    panel (v)
persist (v)
    persistence (n)
    persistent (adj)
    persistently (adv)

pose (n)
    pose (v)
professional (adj)
    professionally (adv)
    professional (n)
    professionalize (v)
    professionalism (n)
publication (n)
    publish (v)
quote (v)
    quote (n)
    quotation (n)
reluctance (n)
    reluctant (adj)
    reluctantly (adv)
scenario (n)
secure (adj)
    securely (adv)
    security (n)
    secure (v)
straightforward (adj)
    straightforward (adv)
    straightforwardly (adv)
    straightforwardness (n)
survive (v)
    survival (n)
    survival (adj)
    surviving (adj)
    survivor (n)
    survivable (adj)
tradition (n)
    traditional (adj)
    traditionally (adv)
undergo (v)
unify (v)
    unification (n)
    unified (adj)
    unifying (adj)
violate (v)
    violation (n)
voluntary (adj)
    voluntarily (adv)
    volunteer (n)
    volunteer (v)
whereby (conj)
widespread (adj)

Unit 10

Definitions Use the definition clues to write the correct words in the blanks.

1. relating to medicine *Laura has to go in for a minor _____ procedure.* 2. essential and inherent to the nature of something *The notion of abstract time has become _____ to most people's lives.* 3. next to, near *We heard a loud noise in the _____ room.*	medical overall intrinsic external adjacent dynamic
4. to put or come together into a group *In the US, all citizens have the right to _____ in groups for any lawful purposes.* 5. to imagine, think or envision *Let's go to a baseball game. I can't _____ of a better way to spend my day off.* 6. to increase, make larger, spread or develop *As the snow melted, the pool of water in my driveway began to _____.*	expand collapse assemble convince conceive survive
7. a serious theatrical work; a play *We stayed up late last night watching a _____ about the life of an autistic boy.* 8. sex; male or female *There are noticeable _____ differences among boys and girls of kindergarten age.* 9. strong honesty and morality *You can't help but to admire Will's honesty and _____.*	gender drama integrity colleague incentive incline
10. relating to a profession or career *It is sometimes difficult to separate one's _____ life from one's private life.* 11. deliberate; by free choice *Karen engages in many _____ activities, such as helping disadvantaged children learn to read.* 12. constantly active, changing, moving forward in a positive manner *A _____ weather front is moving across the Midwest.*	dynamic voluntary professional nuclear ethnic odd
13. to fall down; to stop functioning *It looks like the old barn is ready to _____.* 14. to make someone accept or believe *There is no way you can _____ me to jump into the icy water.* 15. to call out for support, protection or inspiration *In ancient times, certain names were used to _____ protection by supernatural forces.*	collapse modify depress undergo convince invoke

Unit 10

16. a person who works in the same profession *Tonight there is a retirement party for a _____ who has worked here for 27 years.* 17. a motivation or ambition *Terry has a strong _____ to do well in college this year. He wants to land a good job at Microsoft.* 18. a group of people who investigate or examine something *No one on the _____ believed that the climate scientists were telling the complete truth.*	incentive drama quote levy panel colleague
19. open, honest unambiguous *I was surprised at how _____ Ruth was as she told me what I needed to know about teaching at the university.* 20. huge, immense *There was an _____ shining object hovering above us. It filled the sky.* 21. of a distinctive culture, race or national heritage *Despite their different _____ origins, the neighbors got along with each other quite well.*	straightforward widespread enormous external secure ethnic
22. to gather pieces together *It will take weeks to _____ all the data that we have collected.* 23. to push down *The decline in the housing market will continue to _____ the entire economy for a few more years.* 24. to contain or include *Digging a new drainage ditch will _____ bringing in some heavy machinery.*	compile involve assemble unify persist depress
25. a huge area of land including a large home and other buildings *Count Rostov had to sell his huge _____ in order to pay all of his creditors.* 26. frequency of occurrence *After the video cameras were installed, the _____ of cheating during exams diminished.* 27. a book, magazine, journal or other work *"Discovery" is a _____ about science news written for non-scientists.*	publication tradition incidence scenario estate pose
28. even though *She sings with enthusiasm, _____ poorly.* 29. despite what has gone before *The weather worsened; the ships sailed on _____.* 30. in spite of *I succeeded in winning _____ a great effort by the opposition to stop me.*	whereby nonetheless forthcoming notwithstanding widespread albeit

31. on the outside *The _____ surface of the pipe is rough, while the internal surface is smooth.* 32. relating to the core of an atom *Scientists detected a _____ explosion somewhere in the western part of the country.* 33. strange, unusual or unexpected *It is not at all _____ to find life forms several miles below the surface of the earth.*	adjacent intrinsic dynamic external odd nuclear
34. to make changes *This design is just a sketch. We can _____ it to suit your needs.* 35. to stay in existence *Pierre wondered if he could _____ much longer in the terrible heat without fresh water to drink.* 36. to experience, sustain or be subjected to *All new recruits will have to _____ a complete physical examination.*	violate involve survive depress undergo modify
37. the exact words taken from a publication, speech or other source *"If a million people say a foolish thing, it is still a foolish thing" is a famous _____ by Anatole France.* 38. a custom that is habitually followed from one generation to the next *My family has a _____ of eating turkey at Christmas.* 39. a predicted sequence of events *Witnesses described the _____ as one of utter devastation.*	quote tradition scenario encounter controversy publication
40. generally, on the whole *The _____ opinion was that Travis should remain in the army for two more years.* 41. abroad, beyond the sea *Gerry had never traveled _____ before her trip to South Africa.* 42. safe from danger, fear, attack or worry *Mandy said she would not feel _____ until all the doors and windows were locked.*	nuclear overall enormous overseas medical secure
43. to unite or form a single unit *When East Germany and West Germany were ready to _____, many people became nervous.* 44. to continue stubbornly or insistently *If the sunny skies _____ this week, we can start planting the garden.* 45. to break a law, regulation or contract *You should consult with your lawyer. It seems you are about to _____ the terms of your contract.*	assemble violate persist convince undergo unify

46. unwillingness *Because of Ted's _____ to cooperate with us, we decided to do without his financial support.* 47. a tax or charge *Mr. Osborne also announced Tuesday that he would impose a _____ on banks to raise £2 billion per year.* 48. a position; a way of positioning oneself in front of a camera *Al made himself comfortable on the sofa, then adopted a _____ that made the cameraman laugh.*	reluctance publication integrity panel levy pose
49. about to appear or happen *In preparation for the _____ senior prom, the students worked late into the night to decorate the gym.* 50. covering a large area *There is a _____ belief among some conservatives that President Obama is not a US citizen.* 51. by which, through which *The police were amazed at the method _____ the prisoner had managed to escape.*	albeit whereby nonetheless widespread forthcoming notwithstanding
52. a dispute, argument or debate *In Myanmar, _____ over a massive dam on the Irrawaddy River caused a public outcry.* 53. a slope; something that slants *We stayed on our horses and rode them down the gentle _____ to the shore of the mountain lake.* 54. a meeting which is brief or unexpected *While I was snorkeling around the reef, I had a sudden _____ with a small shark.*	controversy encounter incline quote scenario incentive

Unit 10

Parts of Speech

Write the parts of speech (noun, verb, adjective or adverb form).
Word Forms: Be careful with nouns and verbs:
  Some *nouns* might need to be plural (~s).
  Some *verbs* might need ~s, ~ed, ~ing.

adjacent   1. The fire quickly spread to the _____ buildings.

             At the first table, pick up your registration forms. On the _____ table, pick up the conference program.

albeit   2. Sally is a shy, _____ very intelligent, girl.

             Bernard plays basketball with enthusiasm, _____ without much skill.

assemble   3. The lawn mower comes in a box. It requires a bit of _____ before you can use it.

             Within an hour, Kevin had _____ a crew.

collapse   4. The peace talks had already _____ by the time the Secretary arrived.

             To prevent the roof from _____, we need to strengthen the beams.

colleague   5. Most of my _____ are fun to work with.

             None of Hal's former _____ is still in touch with him.

compile   6. It took a long time, but we finally _____ the statistics.

             The _____ of the bibliography took a long time.

conceive   7. It doesn't seem _____ that Sebastian is ready for college.

             Whoever _____ of assemble-it-yourself furniture was a genius.

controversy 8. The announcement to build a nuclear power plant near the city stirred up a bitter _____.

             Gun control laws are generally _____ across the US.

convince   9. Everything that the mayor said about the downtown redevelopment plan sounded _____ to us.

             Rita was not at all _____ that her daughter would pay back the loan.

depress   10. After just two weeks away from home, Wilson missed his family and felt mildly _____.

             Upon losing her job, Nora fell into a black _____.

drama   11. The _____ events in Egypt fascinated TV viewers all over the world.

             Prospects for Glenda's recovery after the car accident have _____ improved.

dynamic 12. The presence of the reporters changed the _____ of the entire meeting.

Lamar turned out to be a _____ force in leading the discussions.

encounter 13. When they entered the coffee shop, they _____ several strange people.

Upon _____ the wolf cubs, the hunters wondered where the mother was.

enormous 14. During the early 20th Century, Europe and America experienced _____ social upheaval.

The first responders were aghast at the _____ of the damage caused by the floods.

estate 15. Tyshawn inherited an _____ valued at over seven million dollars.

Aunt Britney lives alone on a sizeable _____ in Connecticut.

ethnic 16. The _____ minorities in some countries are starting to fight for their rights.

It is illegal in the US to discriminate against people due to their _____ background.

expand 17. The solar energy plant is due for _____ later this year.

Last month, the city _____ the industrial zone.

external 18. I paid for one-day delivery, but it was delayed due to "_____ factors."

The university has just published a guide to _____ funded research programs.

forthcoming 19. The senator was urged to be more _____ about her involvement in insider trading.

This page contains a list of our _____ articles.

gender 20. Some parents in India, because of their preference to have male children, are very interested in _____ prediction.

The undergraduate program includes biology of human reproduction and the psychology of _____ identity.

incentive 21. Yvonne no longer has an _____ to work harder.

The car dealership offers cash _____ for new buyers.

incidence 22. There is a greater _____ of flu among the elderly this year.

The _____ of polio has sharply declined.

Unit 10

incline   23. Boris is _____ to take long naps after dinner.

Now that Natalie is single again, she seems to be rather romantically _____ .

integrity   24. A single soldier's misbehavior can seriously impair the _____ of military operations.

Xavier was shocked at the way everyone started to attack his personal _____ .

intrinsic   25. There is _____ value in reading good literature.

They believe that biodiversity is _____ valuable.

invoke   26. The governor was praised for _____ the ideals of the Rev. Dr. Martin Luther King Jr.

German President Joachim Gauck _____ Mahatma Gandhi in his first public speech.

involve   27. In 1970, Safdie established a Jerusalem branch office, commencing an intense _____ with the rebuilding of Jerusalem.

It is this level of personal _____ that makes each project a true collaboration.

levy   28. The shippers were angry with the port authority for _____ a surcharge on their operations.

Most people do not realize that taxes are _____ for their benefit.

medical   29. The knee replacement was a _____ necessary procedure.

Some _____ procedures are performed by robots.

modify   30. They returned to us with a slightly _____ version of the original document.

There is a huge controversy over genetic _____ of food.

nonetheless   31. Mary Hardison was 101 years old. _____, she wanted to try paragliding.

Facebook promised better privacy. _____, many users remained skeptical.

notwithstanding   32. Some Hizbullah members might be willing to chat with a foreigner whom they trust, _____ the "veil of secrecy."

A narrow, long streak of light showed that, _____ the late hour, the outer door was ajar.

nuclear   33. Here and there piles of drift-wood were to be found forming the _____ of some future island.

_____ power produces around 11% of the world's energy needs

Unit 10

odd
34. What were the _____ that the Giants would defeat the Patriots yet again?

NASA's Hubble Space Telescope zoomed in on a space _____, one of the strangest space objects ever seen.

overall
35. The business schools are listed by _____ ranking.

Rumi Punku is a wonderful hotel _____.

overseas
36. I would be interested in finding an _____ assignment.

Florence does not like to travel _____.

panel
37. The _____ discussion lasted over an hour.

Paul agreed to serve on the advisory _____.

persist
38. The blood stains _____ despite every effort to remove them.

Because of her dogged _____, Janice was able to get an interview with Clooney.

pose
39. At yesterday's shooting, little Kyle _____ for the camera with unusual charm.

Ignore her. She's just _____.

professional
40. Christine and her husband are real estate _____ who really care about their clients.

Some people believe that college athletes should be paid a salary, just like _____ athletes.

publication
41. There are several professional _____ that you can subscribe to when you begin your career as a teacher.

When you select articles for your research paper, be sure to look at the date of _____.

quote
42. Randy _____ us a price of $200 to fix our broken sink.

By _____ well-known authorities, you can strengthen the arguments in your paper.

reluctance
43. We can understand your _____ to giving up one of your days off to come and help us at the fundraiser.

Rob tried to persuade his wife to overcome her _____ to try out the new Chinese restaurant.

scenario
44. A clear, unequivocal victory in Afghanistan is an unlikely _____.

In the worst-case _____, we would have to lay off about a dozen employees.

Unit 10

secure
45. In the expanding jobs market of the 1960s, many American women _____ a measure of economic independence.

Some software packages provide more Internet _____ than others.

straightforward
46. Tammy usually takes a _____ approach to problem solving.

The process is fairly _____.

survive
47. Polar bears are barely _____ in some regions.

Santorum's political _____ depended on support from social conservatives.

tradition
48. In this valley lies the _____ burial grounds of the Hopi Indians.

_____, in Mexico the transition from childhood to womanhood is marked with the celebration of the *Quinceañera*.

undergo
49. Right now, we are _____ an audit.

Last year, the Dell Corporation _____ a major reorganization.

unify
50. In 1810, King Kamehameha achieved the _____ of the Hawaiian Islands.

Author Brian Greene explains why string theory might hold the key to _____ the four forces of nature.

violate
51. The U.S. may have _____ domestic and international law in capturing and holding a Somali for months at sea.

Drugs were found in the car after the driver was stopped for a minor traffic _____.

voluntary
52. He had _____ put himself in a position to be insulted.

As we came out upon the floor of the church again, another priest _____ to show us the treasures of the church.

whereby
53. Learning a language is a process _____ new vocabulary and grammar are acquired.

The U.S. had a law enforcement system _____ companies that committed crimes were prosecuted criminally.

widespread
54. There is a _____ rumor that Apple will pay dividends to stockholders.

The increased demand for electricity caused _____ blackouts all along the east coast.

- 314 -

Unit 10

Collocations

In each group of sentences, write *one* word from the list which goes with the **highlighted collocations**. Be careful with word forms.

Exercise 1	tradition conceivable adjacent publication incline external
	medical panel encounter intrinsic dynamic expand

1. Protesters tried **to halt the** _____ **of** the subdivision.

   The **period of colonial** _____ lasted until the middle of the 20th century.

   The Bretton Woods conference facilitated **global** _____ of multinational corporations.

2. The Trans-Pacific Partnership is **easy to** _____ , but difficult to deliver.

   This collection of **brilliantly** _____ recipes has quickly become one of my favorites.

3. Our experts will help you **prepare your manuscript for** _____ .

   In the citations, be sure to indicate the _____ **date**.

   Four Courts Press has announced several **forthcoming** _____ including *Benedict XVI and Beauty in Sacred Art and Architecture.*

4. This week, Earth and Mars are having a **close** _____ .

   Rebecca **briefly** _____ a mountain lion while jogging yesterday.

   I would love to have a **face-to-face** _____ with a gorilla.

5. I **feel somewhat** _____ to tell you what I think of this whole idea.

   Tom bought a guitar, even though he was not at all **musically** _____ .

   Gas prices are **on the** _____ due to tensions in the Middle East.

6. Your insurance will not pay for an unnecessary _____ **procedure**.

   Margaret was thinking of going into the _____ **profession**.

   When you enter the service, you have **to undergo a** _____ **exam**.

7. Atomic reactors **immediately** _____ **to** Prairie Island Indian Community are leaking toxins and radioactivity yet again.

   The neighborhoods **directly** _____ **to** the campus are pretty well established, white, and affluent.

8. The tea is **a time-honored** _____ that dates back to 1947.

   The rosary is one of the most **cherished** _____ of the Catholic faith.

   These revolutionary paintings were **a departure from** _____ .

9. Dr. Bradford was elected **to serve on a** _____ .

   Mrs. Henley is **a distinguished** _____ **member**.

   A _____ **of experts** will examine the report in depth.

10. You should know the _____ **value** of a company before you buy stocks in it.

    An external incentive, such as a reward, decreases a person's _____ **motivation** to perform a particular task.

Unit 10

Collocations

Exercise 2	undergo quote gender convince integrity modify
	persist controversy compile assemble unify forthcoming

1. Not all behavior differences in boys and girls can be explained by
    _____ **differences**. Some are caused by socialization differences.

    Women's and _____ **studies programs** have grown over the years.

    Lack of access to health care and to education, _____ **inequality** and
    limited access to credit pose challenges for women.

2. The scooter **comes fully** _____, so you can start riding it right away.

    A new **peaceful** _____ law in Malaysia was harshly criticized.

    Karzai plans **to hold an** _____ of elders to decide the peace strategy.

3. The voter ID law is sure **to stir up a** _____.

    Gadhafi's 42-year reign was **marked by** _____.

    Brizard tried to defend the _____ **decision** to close schools.

4. Arguments of convenience **lack** _____ and can backfire on you.

    The UN envoy encouraged Iraqi leaders **to safeguard the** _____ of
    democracy in that country.

    Our company offers **structural** _____ services for offshore
    installations with the aim of extending service life of floating installations.

5. The debate over **genetic** _____ **of food** will go on for a long time.

    We purchased a **slightly** _____ **version** of the software.

    Aviation experts say the helicopter may have been **heavily** _____ to
    avoid detection by the enemy.

6. Ryan was **not at all** _____ to become a vegan.

    Scientific jargon often **sounds** _____ to lay people.

    Bernadette was **only half** _____ by her own arguments.

7. Slower internet service in Alaska **is likely to** _____ for some time.

    _____ **paid off** for Dr. Shechtman who was recently awarded the
    Nobel Prize in Chemistry for his observations of quasicrystals.

    She suffered during her captivity, but **doggedly** _____ in trying to
    escape.

8. Martin is able to _____ **verbatim** lines from his favorite movies.

    Ben's **widely** _____ "facts" turned out to be somewhat inaccurate.

    We were _____ **a price** of $2,500 to install a new air conditioner.

9. Global warming skeptics try to _____ **their opposition** to my theory.

    The newly _____ **nation** faced political crisis when an estimated
    800000 Yemeni nationals and overseas workers were sent home by Saudi Arabia

    In 1450, **political** _____ began in Iberia.

10. The DOD does not _____ **statistics** on civilian casualties.

    _____ **a database** is a fundamental part of the research process.

Unit 10

Collocations

<table>
<tr><td>Exercise 3</td><td>scenario   depression   incentive   nuclear   involve   overseas
violate   estate   straightforward   collapse   widespread   pose</td></tr>
</table>

1. Even young children can **suffer from** _____.

   Mara experienced **a bout of** _____ after the birth of her child.

   We **find it** _____ that so many animals are used for testing cosmetics.

2. The trade talks _____ **in the face of** pressure from the CEO.

   The **sudden** _____ of the overpass was caused by a small earthquake.

   The old table _____ **from the weight** of the books.

3. Jean **lacks** _____ to go to college now that he has inherited the estate.

   Perhaps a pay raise will **act as an** _____ for you to stay with the company.

   The **tax** _____ were just what we needed to expand our business.

4. Dr. Thompson **left an** _____ worth millions to his son Jean.

   Jean doesn't have the skill **to manage an** _____ of that size.

   The _____ **is valued at** over $5,000,000.

5. The inspectors found nothing wrong with the _____ **reactor**.

   Physicists studied the _____ **explosion** at Los Alamos.

   France depends on _____ **power** for much of its electricity.

6. Francine's **day-to-day** _____ in the discussions led to success.

   Andrew is **romantically** _____ with a beautiful German woman.

   You need to stay **actively** _____ in your children's lives.

7. **In the unlikely** _____ that I do not return by evening, you should go ahead and start dinner without me.

   In a worst-case _____, the city would have to lay off ten policemen.

   The Prime Minister **painted a rosy** _____ despite mounting protests.

8. We have to hospitalize Irene because she _____ **a danger** to everyone around her.

   We would like you to _____ **for a picture** with us.

   Cameramen like Cindy because she knows how **to strike a** _____.

9. If you _____ **the law**, you go to jail.

   Beth has several unpaid **traffic** _____.

   Forcing the ten-year old boys to join the armed forces constitutes a _____ **of their human rights**.

10. The chairwoman impresses everyone with her _____ **manner** and no-nonsense approach to problem solving.

    Don't try to evade the question. Just give us a _____ **answer**.

    There is no reason not to believe Justin. He is being **perfectly** _____.

Unit 10

Collocations

Exercise 4	drama	colleague	professional	incidence	ethnic	levy
	odd	survive	secure	panel	voluntary	enormous

1. According to the Koran, a Muslim country cannot _____ **war on** another Muslim country.

    The federal government has the power to _____ **taxes** to "pay the debts and provide for the common defense . . . of the United States."

    Ireland's government will **impose a** _____ on domestic private pension savings, raising as much as 1.9 billion euros ($2.7 billion).

2. A large multi-national state, China is composed of 56 _____ **groups**.

    The study highlights the fact that a person's _____ **background** can give an idea about his or her fat and muscle mass.

    The Sri Lankan government has been accused of launching a campaign of _____ **cleansing** following its victory over the Tamil Tigers.

3. One of my **business** _____ is getting married next month.

    Marissa is **a trusted** _____ and friend. I wish her the best.

    In the case of a conflict of interest, you are obligated to refer the matter to a **professional** _____ .

4. Bill works at the library **on a** _____ **basis**.

    We are **calling for** _____ to help out at the upcoming conference.

    Grandmother is **a part-time** _____ at the local food bank.

5. After the accident at Chernobyl, there was **increased** _____ **of** cancer in the region.

    The report indicates **a lower** _____ of cancer **in** vegetarians.

6. The women's team **beat the** _____ and made it to the regional finals.

    I **find it somewhat** _____ that anyone would like that horrible movie.

    Jim Yong Kim **seemed an** _____ **choice** for World Bank President.

7. Jeanne is an art teacher who **turned** _____ several years ago.

    The **health-care** _____ on our staff are always ready to serve you.

8. The soldiers put up a barbed-wire fence to _____ **the perimeter**.

    Optimism should not comfort us or **lull us into a false sense of** _____ .

    To improve your **chances at** _____ a high valuation on your property, clean it up and make it as presentable as possible.

9. In "The Story of an Hour," Chopin employs specific structural and stylistic techniques **to heighten the** _____ of the hour.

    There is a way to use shutter speed **for** _____ **effects** in your photos.

    We worried about Cathy's health, but **things have improved** _____ since we last saw her.

10. A *Hunger Games* _____ **-of-the-fittest** mentality seemed to prevail.

    After the civil war, people still **struggle to** _____ in Mogadishu.

    Remarkably, an iPad fell 1300 feet from a plane and _____ **unscathed**.

Unit 10

Synonyms Use the synonym clues to solve this crossword puzzle.

Across
1. outline, plot, story line, sketch
5. unite, join, merge, group
8. by which, through which
12. expert, accomplished, master
13. strange, unusual, unexpected
16. fall down, break down, crash
17. outlive, persist, outlast, overcome
19. next to, near, close
23. continue, persevere, remain
25. atomic, central
29. even though, notwithstanding
31. include, call for, engage
32. general, far-flung, popular
33. abroad, foreign

Down
2. imagine, think, envision
3. total, entire, complete
4. endure, stand, suffer, sustain
6. impending, prospective
7. custom, practice, habit, ritual
9. immense, huge, massive
10. persuade, induce, win over
11. assemble, gather, collect
12. committee, commission, jury
14. performance, play, show
15. repeat, recite, retell, cite
18. weigh down, dishearten, deject
20. join, collect, gather, group
21. energetic, lively, active
22. motivation, enticement, ambition
24. include, call for, engage
26. clannish, social, cultural
27. safe, unafraid, protected
28. disobey, disrespect, assault
30. put forth, present, propose

Unit 10

Review

Write the correct word in each sentence.

1. The firemen prevented the fire from spreading to the _____ buildings. 2. The judge told the lawyer to stop circling around the issue and give a more _____ response to her question. 3. Everyone at the charity fund-raiser was there on a _____ basis.	voluntary straightforward adjacent professional external overall
4. After we _____ all of the key players, we can start to discuss our strategy. 5. It would be difficult to _____ of a greater joy than to have the whole family together during Ramadan. 6. Mark worked hard to _____ his sphere of influence.	conceive assemble collapse expand invoke compile
7. Susan is a trusted _____ who works tirelessly. 8. Young people who struggle with _____ identity can get help from the school counselor. 9. Rothko considered the critic's remark as an attack on his artistic _____ .	gender colleague integrity estate gender incentive
10. The music coming from the chapel was hauntingly beautiful, _____ dark and moody. 11. Albert's wishes _____, we will prepare to leave as soon as possible. 12. When the king announced that the hated tax would be done away with, there was _____ joy in the kingdom.	albeit notwithstanding widespread forthcoming nonetheless whereby
13. Coaches know that _____ motivation is more powerful than threats of punishment. 14. The _____ dog that greeted us at the gate frightened us at first, be we soon saw that it was a friendly giant. 15. Alice always conducts herself in a highly _____ manner.	professional enormous intrinsic ethnic nuclear medical
16. Too tired to stay on his feet, Brendan _____ against the wall. 17. We were _____ that Kory was innocent, but we had no way to prove it. 18. The defiant young woman had not _____ her right to be represented by a lawyer.	convinced collapsed invoked modified underwent persisted

Unit 10

Review

19. Everyone stopped and watched in amazement as the _____ unfolded. 20. Now, the CEO has a strong _____ to make sure that the corporation makes a better profit this year. 21. I won't be able to serve on the advisory _____ .	integrity publication quote panel drama incentive
22. The actor forgot his lines; _____ , he managed to fool the audience by coming up with new lines. 23. Tad was able to create a program _____ users' files would be automatically saved to the cloud. 24. Rick was confident about the _____ elections which he hoped to win by a landslide.	whereby albeit forthcoming nonetheless widespread notwithstanding
25. Some of the most expensive _____ treatments work no better than some of the least expensive ones. 26. We need a more _____ approach to creating a better curriculum for the Intensive English Program. 27. Frank's _____ background included Italian, Hopi Indian and Irish.	dynamic overseas medical intrinsic ethnic overall
28. It will only take a few minutes to _____ the statistics that you asked for. 29. High interest rates are likely to _____ consumer demand for automobiles. 30. We didn't want to _____ you in the controversy.	violate survive involve persist compile depress
31. The old baron rarely visited his country _____ after his wife passed away. 32. The _____ of burglary has decreased in the past several years. 33. After the _____ of his new book, he decided he need a long vacation.	reluctance estate levy pose incidence publication
34. Luckily, I saved all of my work to the _____ hard drive before my computer crashed. 35. Few people believe that a _____ war is likely nowadays. 36. The _____ consensus is that we should spend more on academics and less on sports.	overall adjacent voluntary secure nuclear external

Unit 10

Review

37. Gus _____ his car's engine to make it more gas efficient.	compiled
	conceived
38. Few fruit trees _____ the bitterly cold winter.	survived
	modified
39. The coalition forces were _____ under the command of the British general.	unified
	depressed
40. That particular _____ is often attributed to Mark Twain, but in fact, he never uttered or wrote those words.	colleague
	quote
41. Because of Shirley's _____ to serve as chairperson, we had to find someone else.	drama
	reluctance
42. The _____ over the health-care bill caused a split among party members.	estate
	controversy
43. A very _____ animal, the platypus is a native of Australia.	adjacent
	overseas
	odd
44. Foreign language students have the option of studying for one year _____.	secure
	medical
45. We cannot open the secret documents until we are in a more _____ environment.	enormous
46. The Jewish _____ traces its roots to Abraham, who is known as Ibrahim among Muslims.	controversy
	encounter
47. We created a future _____ in which we examined how each decision point would play out.	scenario
	tradition
48. Because the _____ was so steep, we struggled to get to the top.	incline
	panel
49. It is understandable that you are afraid to _____ the surgery.	collapse
	invoke
50. If you _____ in begging me for more time, you will do nothing more than make me angry.	undergo
	violate
51. Student athletes who _____ school regulations will not be allowed to compete.	persist
	unify
52. Most business people think the _____ imposed on them is too severe.	integrity
	encounter
53. The painter did not like the model's _____, so he asked her to turn slightly toward the window.	incidence
	pose
54. After the unexpected _____ with his former wife, Glen became rather nostalgic.	tradition
	levy

Unit 10

Definitions ∘ Parts of Speech ∘ Collocations

adjacent (adj) next to, near
> to be situated adjacent (to), to lie adjacent (to), to stand adjacent (to)
> directly adjacent, immediately adjacent: *Springfield lies immediately adjacent to Eugene.*
> the adjacent room, the adjacent building: *My office is on the third floor, and my library is located in the adjacent room.*
> adjacent to

albeit (conj) even though, notwithstanding
> *Eileen works hard, albeit slowly.*
> *The hotel in Lyon is in the same style as the one in Paris, albeit slightly smaller.*

assemble (v) to put or come together into a group; to join parts together
> to be easy to assemble, difficult to assemble, manage to assemble, to assemble at home, to assemble yourself
> fully assembled: *You can purchase the furniture fully assembled or assemble it yourself.*

assembly (n) an elected group
> to elect an assembly
> to form an assembly, to set up an assembly; elected assembly, representative assembly, general assembly
> legislative assembly, regional assembly, provincial assembly, state assembly, national assembly
> assemblyman, assemblywoman

assembly (n) a gathering of people in general
> to hold an assembly
> a peaceful assembly, a public assembly, a lawful assembly, an unlawful assembly
> freedom of assembly, the right of assembly

assembly (n) putting parts together to create a whole
> easy assembly, home assembly: *The inexpensive bookshelves featured easy home assembly.*
> assembly line, assembly plant, assembly work

assembly (n) a gathering of students at a school
> to hold an assembly, to have an assembly
> assembly hall

assemblage (n)

collapse (v) to fall down; to stop functioning
> to suddenly collapse, to virtually collapse, to collapse from/under the weight of
> completely collapsed: *The roof completely collapsed under the weight of the snow.*
> to collapse against: *After the marathon race, the runners collapsed against the parked vans.*
> to collapse from: *The soldiers eventually collapsed from cold and hunger.*
> to collapse in the face of [= to fail because of something]: *Efforts to revive the talks collapsed in the face of threats from the hostile crowds.*

collapse (n) a breakdown or fall
> to result in a collapse, to contribute to a/the collapse of, to lead to a/the collapse of
> to be in danger of collapse
> sudden collapse: *After the earthquake, the bridges were in danger of sudden collapse.*

collapse (n) a very bad medical condition
> to have a collapse, to be in a state of collapse, to be on the verge of collapse
> a sudden collapse, a nervous collapse, a mental collapse, a physical collapse: *Dora worked twenty hours a day until she was ready to have a mental and physical collapse.*

colleague (n) a person who works in the same profession
> professional colleague, business colleague
> a close colleague, a trusted colleague, a junior colleague, a senior colleague

compile (v) to gather pieces together
> to compile a list, to compile statistics, to compile a bibliography, to compile a dossier, to compile a database

compilation (n) a collection
> *The new album is a compilation mostly of earlier songs plus a few new ones.*

compiler (n) a computer program that translates programming language into machine language

conceive (v) to imagine, think or envision in one's mind

 cannot conceive, difficult to conceive, easy to conceive, possible to conceive

 originally conceived, carefully conceived, brilliantly conceived

 poorly conceived: *The scheme to raise money failed because it was so poorly conceived.*

conceive (v) to become pregnant

 to be able to conceive, to be unable to conceive

 to naturally conceive

conception (n) formation of an idea; plan

conception (n) beginning of pregnancy

conceivable (adj)

 to seem conceivable, to become conceivable

 perfectly conceivable, entirely conceivable

 every conceivable ~ : *We used every conceivable argument to try to persuade George to quit his job.*

conceivably (adv)

controversy (n) a dispute, argument or debate

 to stir up a controversy, to give rise to a controversy, to cause a controversy, to provoke a controversy

 to spark a controversy: *The scientific finding sparked a controversy among conservatives.*

 to be surrounded by controversy, to be marked by controversy, to be involved in controversy

 to be dogged by controversy [= to be constantly bothered by controversy]: *The CEO's endorsement of the new marketing scheme has been dogged by controversy since day one.*

 considerable controversy, bitter controversy, fierce controversy, violent controversy, lively controversy

 fresh controversy, renewed controversy, long-standing controversy

 academic controversy, scholarly controversy, political controversy, religious controversy

 no stranger to controversy [= seems to always be involved in controversy]: *We were not surprised that Jeremiah jumped into the debate. He is no stranger to controversy.*

 controversy rages, controversy centers on, controversy surrounds

 amid controversy, controversy surrounding

 a storm of controversy, a source of controversy

controversial (adj)

 a controversial decision, a controversial ruling

controversially (adv)

convince (v) to make someone accept or believe

convinced (adj)

 to become convinced, to sound convinced: *You don't sound very convinced by these arguments.*

 deeply convinced, firmly convinced, absolutely convinced, completely convinced, fully convinced

 utterly convinced, increasingly convinced: *I'm becoming increasingly convinced that moving to Canada was the right thing to do.*

 by no means convinced, not at all convinced, not entirely convinced, not easily convinced

 only half convinced: *Tom was only half convinced to sell the house and move into a bigger place.*

 convinced of

convincing (adj)

 sounds convincing: *The financial advisor said we would be better off getting out of the stock market right now because of what is going on in Europe at this time. That sounds convincing to me.*

 totally convincing, utterly convincing; hardly convincing, not altogether convincing, far from convincing

convincingly (adv)

depression (n) a mental state in which a person feels extremely sad and sometimes suicidal

 to fall into depression, to suffer from depression, to be treated for depression, to come out of depression

 deep depression, black depression, clinical depression

 acute depression [= a short but intense period of depression]

 chronic depression [= depression of long duration]

manic depression [= alternating between extremes of high-energy excitement and low energy depression]

post-natal depression [= extreme sadness just after giving birth]

a bout of depression, a fit of depression, a period of depression

a cause for depression, the depths of depression, symptoms of depression, a state of depression

the onset of depression [= the beginning of depression]

depression (n) a dip in the surface of something

to leave a depression

shallow depression, slight depression, deep depression: *His thumb left a shallow depression on my forearm.*

depressed (adj) being in a state of depression

to feel depressed, to seem depressed, to sound depressed, to become depressed

to get depressed: *I get depressed just thinking about Susan losing her job.*

acutely depressed, mildly depressed, chronically depressed, clinically depressed [= very seriously depressed]: *Because Sarah was clinically depressed, she needed to take strong anti-depression medications as well as go to therapy sessions every week.*

depressed about, depressed by

depressing (adj) causing the feeling of depression

to find something depressing: *Mother finds all this talk about war to be rather depressing.*

deeply depressing, profoundly depressing, infinitely depressing

depress (v) to cause to be extremely unhappy

depress (v) to push down: *To open the lid, you have to depress the button.*

depress (v) to weaken in force or value: *The news in the housing sector will surely depress the economy.*

drama (n) a serious theatrical work; a play

to put on a drama, to act in a drama, to write a drama, to produce a drama

a powerful drama, a musical drama, a radio drama, a TV drama, an historical drama, a police drama

drama production, drama series, drama festival, drama critic

a drama about

drama (n) a strong emotional event

(to add) a touch of drama, to heighten the drama, a moment of drama

a drama unfolds [= a drama evolves]: *We watched in horror as the drama unfolded before our eyes.*

a real-life drama, human drama

dramatics (n. pl.) acting, directing and stagecraft

Gene developed a love of dramatics when he was in college.

dramatics (n. pl.) exaggerated behavior

I've had enough of your dramatics. Stop arguing and get to work.

dramatic (adj)

a dramatic entrance, for dramatic effect: *As she spoke, Susan raised her eyebrow for dramatic effect.*

dramatically (adv)

dramatically improved, dramatically altered, dramatically changed

dramatize (v) to make a book or event into a play, TV show or movie

to dramatize the situation [= to exaggerate, overdo or overstate a situation]: *The YouTube videos had the effect of dramatizing the events that took place in Maidan Square.*

dynamic (adj) constantly active, changing, moving forward in a positive manner

dynamic personality: *Rachael has one of those dynamic personalities that attracts everyone who meets her.*

dynamically (adv)

dynamic (n) basic energy force

dynamics (n) in physics, the study of motion and force

fluid dynamics, hydrodynamics, thermodynamics

dynamics (n. pl.) interacting forces; driving forces: *You can understand students' behavior better if you study some of the dynamics of certain classroom situations.*

dynamics (n. pl.) in music, the variation in the intensity of sound

dynamism (n) in philosophy, the theory that natural events are based in force or energy

dynamism (n) being vigorous and energetic

Unit 10

encounter (n) a meeting which is brief or unexpected

    a brief encounter, a casual encounter, a chance encounter, an unexpected encounter

    a close encounter, a face-to-face encounter

    an unpleasant encounter: *Wendy had an unpleasant encounter with a skunk this morning.*

    social encounter, sexual encounter

    an encounter between, an encounter with

encounter (v) [often used in the passive voice] to meet

    to encounter difficulties, to encounter a problem commonly encountered, frequently encountered, often encountered, regularly encountered: *Joggers are regularly encountered on this stretch of the road.*

    rarely encounter: *You will rarely encounter any difficulties with these patients.*

    inevitably encounter [= very certainly encounter]: *In Cairo, we inevitably encountered beggars in almost every street.*

encounter (n) a conflict or battle

    military encounter

encounter (v) to confront

enormous (adj) huge, immense

enormously (adv)

enormity (n) hugely immoral, offensive or disgraceful character or quality

enormity (n) the great or extreme scale, seriousness, or extent of something which seems bad or immoral

    to appreciate the enormity, to grasp the enormity, to realize the enormity

    the full enormity, the sheer enormity: *The general public had difficulty grasping the sheer enormity of the looming financial meltdown.*

    the enormity of the situation: *After he was elected, George Bush said that he could not believe the enormity of the situation.*

estate (n) a huge area of land including a large home and other buildings

    a massive estate, a private estate

estate (n) all the property owned by a person or a family; property left to heirs after someone's death

    to manage an estate, to own an estate, to inherit an estate

    to leave an estate, bequeath an estate [=to leave in a will upon one's death]

    a sizeable estate, an heir to an estate; a country estate

    an estate valued at, an estate worth: *Elizabeth inherited a sizeable estate worth five million dollars.*

estate (n) one's social rank

estate (n) [British] housing development

estate agent (n) [British] [= real estate agent (American)] a person who helps clients buy and sell property

ethnic (adj) of a distinctive culture, race or national heritage

    ethnic cleansing [= removing people who are not of the same ethnic group]: *Ratko Mladic was accused of ordering ethnic cleansing in Bosnia to remove non-Serbs from the territory.*

    ethnic minority, ethnic background, ethnic group

ethnicity (n)

expand (v) to increase, make larger, spread or develop in greater detail

expansion (n)

    to be ripe for expansion, to provide for expansion, to call for expansion, to encourage expansion

    to be set for expansion, to facilitate expansion, to promote expansion

    to stop expansion, to prevent expansion, to halt expansion: *Neighbors tried to halt the expansion of the industrial zone near their homes.*

    major expansion, significant expansion, vast expansion [= expansion covering a huge area]: *Los Angeles underwent a vast expansion from a city of 102,000 people in 1900 to a city of over 3.5 million people one hundred years later.*

    rapid expansion, unchecked expansion, steady expansion, sustained expansion

    uncontrolled expansion, unprecedented expansion, aggressive expansion

    global expansion, world-wide expansion, colonial expansion, imperial expansion

    a period of expansion, rate of expansion, room for expansion, space for expansion

expandable (adj)

external (adj) on the outside

external links, external control, external auditor [= a financial expert who examines the accounts of an enterprise of which he or she is not an employee]

external hard drive

due to external factors: *There was a delay in delivery due to external factors.*

externally (adv)

externally funded, externally funded research, externally funded scholarships

externalize (v)

externalization (n)

forthcoming (adj) honest, helpful, informative or frank

not very forthcoming, unusually forthcoming

forthcoming about: *He was unusually forthcoming about his college exploits.*

forthcoming (adj) about to appear or happen

forthcoming events

duly forthcoming: *Aid to the victims of the floods was duly forthcoming, so people stopped worrying.*

gender (n) sex; male or female

gender identity, gender role, gender relations, gender studies program

gender stereotype, gender differences, gender bias, gender imbalance, gender inequality

gender issues, gender politics

gender (n) grammatical group membership; masculine, feminine or neuter

incentive (n) a motivation or ambition

to have an incentive, to offer an incentive, to act as an incentive, to have little incentive, to have no incentive

a tax incentive, price incentive, cash incentive, economic incentive, financial incentive

a powerful incentive, a massive incentive, an added incentive: *The new tax rates should act as an added incentive for companies to hire new workers.*

a lack of incentive

incentivize (v) to motivate

to incentivize employees

incidence (n) frequency of occurrence

to increase the incidence of/for, to decrease the incidence of/for

to measure the incidence, to compare the incidence

greater incidence, increased incidence, rising incidence, lower incidence

incidence in: *There is now a lower incidence of tooth decay in communities that fluoridate the water supply.*

incidence (n) the arrival of a light ray or projectile at a surface

incline (v) to move up and away; to slant

to incline slightly, to incline gently, to incline steeply

to incline towards

inclined (adj) wanting or tending to do or have something

to feel inclined, to seem inclined, to grow inclined

a bit inclined, half inclined, rather inclined, slightly inclined: *After the long walk, I was half inclined to fall asleep on the sofa, but I decided to watch TV instead.*

naturally inclined, liberally inclined, romantically inclined

to incline towards: *When it comes to sports, Ned inclines more towards basketball than baseball.*

inclined (adj) a natural tendency

artistically inclined, musically inclined, academically inclined

incline (n) a slope; something that slants

a gentle slope, a slight slope, a steep slope

an incline bench [= a sloped bench used in weight training]: *Jordan is able to bench press over 200 pounds on the incline bench.*

incline (n) an increase

on the incline: *Gasoline prices have been on the incline lately.*

integrity (n) strong honesty and morality; firm ethical character

to compromise one's integrity, to lack integrity, to lose integrity, to restore integrity personal integrity, artistic integrity, moral integrity, professional integrity

an attack on one's integrity, a challenge to one's integrity, a threat to one's integrity

integrity (n) condition of being whole and unbroken

to maintain the integrity, to preserve the integrity: *US forces tried their best to maintain the territorial integrity of Iraq.*

to safeguard the integrity: *The provider should deliver reliable and secure connectivity to safeguard the integrity and confidentiality of corporate data.*

to compromise the integrity, to impair the integrity, to undermine the integrity, to destroy the integrity

physical integrity, structural integrity, territorial integrity

intrinsic (adj) essential and inherent to the nature of something

intrinsic value, intrinsic motivation, intrinsic brightness

intrinsic to: *The Greek army's practice of self-sacrifice of a few for the benefit of the many was almost intrinsic to their success on the battlefield.*

intrinsically (adv)

invoke (v) to call out for support, protection or inspiration

invoke the wrath of God/Allah [= call upon God's anger]: *The duke invoked the wrath of God upon his enemies, but to no avail.*

invoke (v) to appeal or refer to an authority

invoke Constitutional rights

invoke the Fifth Amendment [= In the US during a trial, to ask for the right to remain silent as guaranteed by the Fifth Amendment to the Constitution of the United States]: *When a suspect invokes his or her Fifth Amendment right to remain silent, this is referred to in the vernacular as "pleading the Fifth." It should not by any means be taken as a sign of guilt, but it is generally portrayed as such in courtroom television dramas.*

invocation (n)

invocable (adj)

involve (v) to contain as a part; to include

to actively involve, to directly involve

involve (v) to make something necessary

inevitably involve, necessarily involve

ordinarily involve, usually involve, typically involve: *Kim's duties as marketing manager typically involve an extensive amount of travel.*

involved (adj) to take part in something

to become involved, to get involved: *When she retired, she became heavily involved in community service.*

actively involved, deeply involved, heavily involved, directly involved

personally involved: *The bill passed in the Senate because the President was personally involved in making sure that it would succeed.*

involved in, involved with

involved (adj) to be emotionally connected

to become involved, to get involved: *I know that you and Jim are not speaking to each other, but I really don't want to get involved.*

personally involved, emotionally involved, romantically involved, sexually involved

involved (adj) complicated

terribly involved: *I tried to understand the plot of Tolstoy's novel, but it was terribly involved.*

involvement (n)

to accuse someone of involvement (in), to suspect someone of involvement (in)

to deny involvement (in), to admit involvement (in)

day-to-day involvement: *Eventually, Arthur grew tired of the day-to-day involvement with his colleagues.*

active involvement, intense involvement

personal involvement, emotional involvement, romantic involvement, sexual involvement

political involvement, military involvement: *The flag-lowering ceremony brings to an end just over a dozen years of Canada's military involvement in the war-wasted nation.*

involvement by, involvement from, involvement with, involvement in

Unit 10

levy (v) to impose or collect money
>to levy a tax, to levy a surcharge, to levy a toll [= to collect money for using a highway]: *In order to pay for the new highway, the state decided to levy a toll on all traffic.*
>to levy a penalty: *Because the contractor did not finish the work by the specified time, she was levied a penalty of $400.*

levy (v) to declare and wage war
>to levy war (on/against)

levy (n) a tax or charge
>to impose a levy, a mandatory levy; a tax levy

[levee (n) = a raised wall of earth or other material used to contain flood waters along a river]

medical (adj) relating to medicine
>a medical procedure, a medical exam, medical treatment, medical help, medical care
>medical advice, medical insurance; medical profession, medical practitioner, medical institution

medically (adv)

medical (n) a physical examination by a doctor
>to have a medical, to undergo a medical
>to pass a medical: *Sheila was very overweight, so she was unable to pass her medical.*

modify (v) to make changes
>heavily modify, drastically modify, substantially modify, radically modify
>slightly modify, gradually modify
>modify genetically: *Much of the corn that we consume has been genetically modified.*
>modify accordingly: *The heavy rain washed out the road to Big Sur, so we had to modify our travel plans accordingly.*

modify (v) in grammar, to describe or qualify something

modification (n)

modifier (n) in grammar, a word or phrase that describes or qualifies something

modified (adj)
>slightly modified, somewhat modified
>heavily modified, drastically modified, substantially modified, radically modified
>in (a) modified form: *The basic curriculum is still being used, albeit in a somewhat modified form.*
>a modified version

nonetheless (adv) despite what has gone before: *It was raining heavily. Nonetheless, Betty went for her usual evening run.*

notwithstanding (prep) in spite of; despite [often used after its object]: *Tickets to the opera were extremely expensive, but we decided to get them, the expense notwithstanding.*

notwithstanding (conj) in spite of the fact that; although: *The young terrorist was not well-known to his neighbors, notwithstanding he had lived among them for many years.*

notwithstanding (adv) all the same; nevertheless; even so: *Janine was not qualified to teach the children, but she was hired notwithstanding.*

nuclear (adj) in physics, relating to the core of an atom
>nuclear reactor, nuclear reaction, nuclear energy, nuclear power
>nuclear explosion, nuclear weapons, nuclear deterrence, nuclear disarmament [= removing nuclear weapons]
>nuclear war, nuclear winter, nuclear holocaust [= nuclear war killing millions of people]
>nuclear medicine

nuclear (adj) in biology, relating to the core of a cell

nucleus (n) [nuclei = n. pl.] the central part of something; the kernel
>galactic nucleus [= the center of a galaxy]

nucleus (n) [nuclei = n. pl] in biology, the central part of a cell

nucleus (n) [nuclei = n. pl] in physics, the positively charged central region of an atom
>atomic nucleus

odd (adj) strange, unusual, unexpected
>to find something odd, to consider something odd [=to think that something is odd]: *Australians consider it odd that Americans eat pie with a fork rather than with a spoon.*
>odd behavior, odd choice

decidedly odd, rather odd, a bit odd, somewhat odd

odd (adj) left over, remaining
We didn't know what to do with the odd pieces of fabric.

odd (adj) in math, not able to be divided by two
odd-numbered

oddly (adv)

odds (n. pl.)
to offer odds, to quote odds; to reduce the odds, to shorten the odds
to beat the odds, to defy the odds, to overcome the odds
considerable odds, impossible odds, overwhelming odds, terrible odds, all odds
against the/all odds: *Luke was young and inexperienced, but he won the race against all odds.*
odds against: *The odds against peace in the Middle East have never been so high.*
What are the odds? [= Who would have guessed.] *I hadn't seen Charlie in over ten years when I saw him last week, then again yesterday. What are the odds?*

odd (n) a thing that is strange: *Marvin is attracted to the odd and the exotic.*

oddity (n) *The quality of Yuki's written English is quite good, and the occasional oddity is quite charming.*

overall (adv) generally, on the whole: *Nina plays well with other children and is well-liked overall.*
to rank ~ overall, to place ~ overall, to come in ~ overall [= to rank overall]: *The Jets played well and came in third overall this season.*

overall (adj) entire; from one end to the other

overall (n) [often plural] loose-fitting clothing: *Pat put on her overalls and went out to work in the garden.*

overseas (adv) abroad, beyond the sea
to travel overseas, to live overseas, to study overseas

overseas (adj)
an overseas assignment

panel (n) a group of people who investigate or evaluate something
to select a panel, to serve on a panel, to participate on a panel
to chair a panel [= to serve as the chairperson of a panel]: *Senator Feinstein will chair a panel responsible for coming up with new guidelines.*
distinguished panel, advisory panel, review panel
panel member, panel discussion, panel interview
a panel of experts, a panel of judges

panel (n) a flat section of a structure
door panel, wall panel, ceiling panel, floor panel; a sliding panel

panel (n) a part of a machine containing dials and controls
instrument panel, control panel, display panel

panel (v) to decorate with panels: *Instead of painting the walls, we decided to panel them with real wood.*

persist (v) to continue stubbornly or insistently
to be likely to persist: *Rain is likely to persist through the weekend.*
to tend to persist, to be allowed to persist: *If such rude behavior is allowed to persist in these meetings, I will have to stop attending.*
persist to this day: *John died on a beach in Hawaii at age 42, and rumors persist to this day that it wasn't necessarily a heart attack.*
doggedly persist [= stubbornly persist]: *They want answers and they will doggedly persist until they get them.*
persist in: *No one agreed with him, but he persisted in telling everyone what he thought.*

persistence (n)
persistence pays off [= persistence succeeds]: *Jan's persistence paid off. She was elected to the board.*
dogged persistence, sheer persistence
by persistence, through persistence

persistent (adj)

persistently (adv)
The new federal law requires states to provide supplemental funding to "persistently dangerous" schools.

pose (v) to put forth or present
>to pose a danger, to pose a threat, to pose a challenge, to pose a risk
>to pose a suggestion

pose (v) to arrange, take or hold a position
>Hold that pose! [= stay in that position; don't move]: *You look great. Now, hold that pose!*
>to pose for a picture/photo, to pose for a portrait
>to pose naked, to pose nude, to pose topless

pose (v) to pretend: *The boss posed as a worker so that she could get in with the staff to see how they were doing.*

pose (n) a position; a way of positioning oneself in front of a camera or a painter
>to strike a pose, to adopt a pose

pose (n) a false identity or mannerism

professional (adj) relating to an occupation or a career
>highly professional, truly professional
>a professional manner, a professional way: *We were impressed by the highly professional manner in which the director handled the dispute.*

professionally (adv)
>to carry oneself professionally, to behave professionally

professional (n) a person who is an expert at something
>to look professional, to turn professional: *Sam is an excellent amateur athlete, but now he wants to turn professional.*
>a committed professional, a true professional, a committed professional, a dedicated professional
>health care professional, medical professional

professionalize (v)

professionalism (n)
>to commend someone for his or her professionalism

publication (n) putting out a book or other text
>to begin publication: *Random House will begin publication of my new book later this year.*
>to prepare something for publication, to be due for publication, to be scheduled for publication , to be accepted for publication; to stop publication
>publication date; the date and time of publication

publication (n) a book, magazine, journal or other work
>a major publication, a best-selling publication, a leading publication
>a recent publication, a forthcoming publication
>a government publication, an official publication, a scientific publication, an academic publication
>a business publication, a trade publication
>a sister publication: *An investigative reporter for* Creative Loafing*'s sister publication, the* Scene, *was arrested along with 25 Occupy Nashville demonstrators and hauled off to jail.*

publication (n) making some information public

publish (v) to put out a book or other text
>*The second edition of this book was first published in 2014.*

quote (v) to repeat the exact words from a publication, speech or other source; to cite as proof
>to quote verbatim [= to quote exactly], to quote at length
>to quote chapter and verse [slang: to cite a passage from a relevant source, originally the Bible]
>to quote out of context
>widely quoted, frequently quoted

quote (n) the exact words taken from a publication, speech or other source
>a famous quote/quotation, a memorable quote/quotation
>a quotable quote, a verbatim quote, a quote taken out of context, a quote taken from

quotation (n) the exact words taken from a publication, speech or other source
>quotation marks, quotation rules, quotation examples

quote (v) to offer a price, usually for work to be performed

quote (n) price
>to get a quote/quotation, to accept a quote/quotation
>a written quote, a free quote

Unit 10

reluctance (n) unwillingness
> to express reluctance, to indicate reluctance, to show reluctance
> to pretend reluctance, to overcome reluctance, to sense reluctance; to explain the reluctance
> to understand one's reluctance: *I can understand your reluctance about going to the conference.*

reluctance (n) in physics, a measure of the opposition to magnetic flux

reluctant (adj)
> to seem reluctant

reluctantly (adv)
> *Andy reluctantly agreed to play tennis with his little sister.*

scenario (n) a predicted sequence of events
> to imagine a scenario (in which): *First, I would like you to imagine a scenario in which you find yourself alone on a deserted island.*
> to describe a scenario, to paint a scenario [= to describe a scenario]
> an unlikely scenario, a future scenario, a likely/more likely scenario, a possible scenario
> a rosy scenario [= a somewhat optimistically predicted event]
> a doomsday scenario [= a prediction that the world will end]
> worst-case scenario [= the worst possible event that could happen]: *In a worst-case scenario, The terrorist will overthrow the dictator, then tear the country apart in a civil war.*

scenario (n) an outline of a play; summary of a plot
> a scenario unfolds, a scenario plays out

secure (adj) safe from danger, attack, fear or worry
> to feel secure, to make something secure, to keep secure
> to make sure against: *The city built a high wall to make itself secure against the invaders.*
> perfectly secure, reasonably secure, relatively secure, sufficiently secure
> safe and secure: *You can keep your valuable papers safe and secure in a fire-proof box.*
> secure enough: *The baby ducks felt secure enough to venture out on the water on their own.*
> financially secure, economically secure

securely (adv)

secure (v) to protect from danger
> to secure the perimeter, to secure the borders, to secure the area

security (n) protection from danger or worry
> to provide security, to give security, to ensure security, to strengthen security
> to compromise security, to undermine security [= to weaken security]
> to perform a security check, to make security arrangements
> to be lulled into a false sense of security [= to be quietly, almost without noticing made to feel secure]
> emotional security, financial security, economic security
> heightened security, tight security, lax security [= weak security]: *Because of lax security, Hamad was able to get a bomb aboard the plane.*
> a feeling of security, a sense of security
> (for) maximum security, national security, personal security, home security, Internet security
> security apparatus, security forces, security services; security guard, security personnel, security staff
> security matters, security measures, security policy
> security system [= an electronic system installed in buildings to protect them from thieves or terrorists]

secure (v) to obtain or achieve something:
> to manage to secure: *They managed to secure a promise from the Prime Minister.*
> to make an attempt at securing, to be aimed at securing, to make an effort at securing
> to have a chance at securing, to have some hope of securing
> to secure a promise, to secure a victory, to secure passage [= to achieve the passage of a piece of legislation]: *In 1963, Kennedy secured passage of the Equal Pay Act.*

secure (adj) held tightly; not loose
> firmly secure, properly secure, tightly secure: *Make sure that all the boxes are tightly secured in the back of the truck before you drive away.*

secure (v) to obtain or guarantee a loan or payment
> to secure a loan, to secure a payment

security (n) [usually plural] stocks and bonds
> to issue securities, to buy securities, to sell securities, to trade securities
> listed securities, unlisted securities; government securities, foreign securities, overseas securities

straightforward (adj) honest, open, unambiguous
> to seem straightforward enough: *Your suggestion seems straightforward enough to us, so we will agree to it.*
> fairly straightforward, perfectly straightforward, remarkably straightforward
> far from straightforward/by no means straightforward [= not at all straightforward]: *The task of creating an up-to-date database is far from straightforward.*
> deceptively straightforward: *Richman's deceptively straightforward songs embody timeless qualities of humanity, optimism, emotional insight and a boundless sense of humor.*
> a straightforward response, straightforward answer: *Don't try to evade the issue. Just give me a straightforward answer.*

straightforward (adv) *In this game, you close your eyes and walk straightforward toward the blackboard.*

straightforwardly (adv)

straightforwardness (n)
> *Many of the students appreciated the straightforwardness with which their instructor told them that they were not working hard enough to pass the course.*

survive (v) to stay in existence
> to struggle to survive, to manage to survive, to be lucky to survive: *We were lucky to survive the tornado.*
> to survive remarkably well, to survive fairly well
> to survive intact [= to survive unchanged], to survive unscathed [= to survive unharmed]
> to barely survive, to narrowly survive, to just survive
> to be likely to survive, to be unlikely to survive
> to survive as: *After the trials, Mindy will be lucky to survive as the champion.*
> to survive from, to survive through
> to survive on: *When the lost hikers ran out of food, they survived on wild berries.*

surviving (adj)
> the sole surviving: *The sole surviving son or daughter may request a discharge from the armed services.*

survival (adj)
> survival instinct [= a natural way of knowing how to survive]: *The young wolves had a strong survival instinct and were able to avoid danger while their mother was away.*

survival (n) continuing to live or exist, usually in spite of an accident or difficult events
> to fight for survival, to ensure survival, to threaten survival: *The destruction of the old-growth forest threatens the survival of the owls.*
> to be essential, necessary, vital, crucial for/to the survival of: *Loose, well-drained soil is vital for the survival of these rare plants.*
> long-term survival, chances of survival, day-to-day survival
> human survival, economic survival, political survival
> survival depends on
> chances of survival, instinct for survival, a threat to the survival
> survival of the fittest [=the continued existence of organisms that are best adapted to their environment while other organisms die out]: *In most cases, "survival of the fittest" has been replaced by the idea of "reproduction of the fittest."*

survivor (n)

survivable (adj)

tradition (n) a custom that is habitually followed from one generation to the next
> to follow a tradition, to cherish a tradition, to honor a tradition, to observe a tradition
> a time-honored tradition, ancient tradition, old tradition, age-old tradition, centuries-old tradition, deep-rooted tradition, long-established tradition, enduring tradition
> local tradition, oral tradition, folk tradition, family tradition
> cherished tradition, time-honored tradition, hallowed tradition
> religious tradition, philosophical tradition, pagan tradition

sporting tradition, theatrical tradition, musical tradition
democratic tradition, liberal tradition, radical tradition
according to the tradition, a departure from tradition, in the best tradition; respect for tradition

traditional (adj)

traditionally (adv)

undergo (v) [past = underwent] to experience, sustain or be subjected to
to undergo a change, to undergo a transformation, to undergo a revision, to undergo an audit

unify (v) to unite or form a single unit
to unify a nation, to unify a country, to unify the opposition, to unify the army, to unify forces
to unify opposing/conflicting theories

unification (n)
political unification, German unification, European unification; unification process

unified (adj)
unified theory [=in particle physics, an attempt to describe all fundamental forces and the relationships between elementary particles in terms of a single theoretical framework]: *For nearly 30 years Einstein had pursued a goal: the creation of a unified field theory to describe all the forces of nature and to demystify the quantum world.*

unifying (adj)
a unifying principle

violate (v) to break a law, regulation or contract
to shamelessly violate, to flagrantly violate [= to violate in a clearly noticeable way]
to violate the law, to violate the terms of a contract
systematically violate, brutally violate

violate (v) to disturb or interrupt

violate (v) to disrespect or desecrate

violate (v) to rape or sexually assault

violation (n)
to constitute a violation
human rights violation: *The* Human Rights *Record of the US in 2007 lists a multitude of cases to show its human rights violation.*
blatant violation, clear violation, flagrant violation
clear violation, wholesale violation [= a great amount of violation]
continued violation, repeated violation; traffic violation
in violation of; a violation against

voluntary (adj) deliberate, by free choice
largely voluntary, purely voluntary, entirely voluntary, completely voluntary
(on a) voluntary basis

voluntarily (adv)

volunteer (n)
to ask for a volunteer, to work as a volunteer; to recruit volunteers, to call for volunteers
an army volunteer, a Red Cross volunteer, a Red Crescent volunteer
a part-time volunteer, a full-time volunteer: *Amy works two hours a week as a part-time volunteer at the Community Center.*
a team of volunteers, a network of volunteers, a band of volunteers, an army of volunteers

volunteer (v)
kindly volunteer
to volunteer for, to volunteer as

whereby (conj) by which, through which: *Researchers are studying the mechanism whereby black cohosh inhibits the growth of cancer cells.*

widespread (adj) covering a large area
widespread blackout [= loss of electric power over a large region]
widespread destruction: *The world was shocked by the widespread destruction caused by the earthquake and tsunami in Japan.*

widespread (adj) believed by or happening to many people
widespread panic, widespread fear, widespread rumor, widespread outrage, widespread concern

Synonyms

adjacent:	next to, near, close
albeit:	even though, notwithstanding
assemble:	join, collect, gather, group
collapse:	fall down, break down, crash
colleague:	associate, coworker, partner
compile:	assemble, gather, collect
conceive:	imagine, think, envision
controversy:	dispute, debate, argument
convince:	persuade, induce, win over
depress:	weigh down, dishearten, deject
drama:	performance, play, show
dynamic:	energetic, lively, active
encounter:	meeting, conflict, battle
enormous:	immense, huge, massive
estate:	property
ethnic:	clannish, social, cultural
expand:	increase, enlarge, spread
external:	outside, outward, visible
forthcoming:	impending, prospective
gender:	sex
incentive:	motivation, enticement, ambition
incidence:	occurrence, episode, case
incline:	slope, lean, tend, tilt
integrity:	honor, morality, virtue
intrinsic:	essential, fundamental, inherent
invoke:	call, pray, appeal, beseech
involve:	include, call for, engage
levy:	impose, collect, tax, charge
medical:	medicinal
modify:	alter, change, qualify
nonetheless:	despite, however, nevertheless
notwithstanding:	in spite of, nevertheless, after all
nuclear:	atomic, central
odd:	strange, unusual, unexpected
overall:	total, entire, complete
overseas:	abroad, foreign
panel:	committee, commission, jury
persist:	continue, persevere, remain
pose:	put forth, present, propose
professional:	expert, accomplished, master
publication:	issue, book, magazine, journal
quote:	repeat, recite, retell, cite
reluctance:	unwillingness, disinclination, hesitancy
scenario:	outline, plot, story line, sketch
secure:	safe, unafraid, protected
straightforward:	honest, open, unambiguous
survive:	outlive, persist, outlast, overcome
tradition:	custom, practice, habit, ritual
undergo:	endure, stand, suffer, sustain
unify:	unite, join, merge, group
violate:	disobey, disrespect, assault
voluntary:	freewill, deliberate, purposeful
whereby:	by which, through which
widespread:	general, far-flung, popular

Unit 10

Answers

<table>
<tr><th colspan="4">Definitions</th></tr>
<tr><td>

1. medical
2. intrinsic
3. adjacent
4. assemble
5. conceive
6. expand
7. drama
8. gender
9. integrity
10. professional
11. voluntary
12. dynamic
13. collapse
14. convince
15. invoke

</td><td>

16. colleague
17. incentive
18. panel
19. straightforward
20. enormous
21. ethnic
22. compile
23. depress
24. involve
25. estate
26. incidence
27. publication
28. albeit
29. nonetheless
30. notwithstanding

</td><td>

31. external
32. nuclear
33. odd
34. modify
35. survive
36. undergo
37. quote
38. tradition
39. scenario
40. overall
41. overseas
42. secure
43. unify
44. persist
45. violate

</td><td>

46. reluctance
47. levy
48. pose
49. forthcoming
50. widespread
51. whereby
52. controversy
53. incline
54. encounter

</td></tr>
</table>

<table>
<tr><th colspan="4">Parts of Speech</th></tr>
<tr><td>

1. adjacent
adjacent
2. albeit
albeit
3. assembling
assembled
4. collapsed
collapsing
5. colleagues
colleagues
6. compiled
compilation
7. conceivable
conceived
8. controversy
controversial
9. convincing
convinced
10. depressed
depression
11. dramatic
dramatically

</td><td>

12. dynamics
dynamic
13. encountered
encountering
14. enormous
enormity
15. estate
estate
16. ethnic
ethnic
17. expansion
expanded
18. external
externally
19. forthcoming
forthcoming
20. gender
gender
21. incentive
incentives
22. incidence
incidence

</td><td>

23. inclined
inclined
24. integrity
integrity
25. intrinsic
intrinsically
26. invoking
invoked
27. involvement
involvement
28. levying
levied
29. medically
medical
30. modified
modification
31. Nonetheless
Nonetheless
32. notwithstanding
notwithstanding
33. nucleus
Nuclear

</td><td>

34. odds
oddity
35. overall
overall
36. overseas
overseas
37. panel
panel
38. persist/persisted
persistence
39. posed
posing
40. professionals
professional
41. publications
publication
42. quoted
quoting
43. reluctance
reluctance
44. scenario
scenario

</td></tr>
<tr><td>

45. secured
security
46. straightforward
straightforward
47. surviving
survival
48. traditional
Traditionally

</td><td>

49. undergoing
underwent
50. unification
unifying
51. violated
violation
52. voluntarily
volunteered

</td><td colspan="2">

53. whereby
whereby
54. widespread
widespread

</td></tr>
</table>

Answers

Collocations			
Exercise 1	**Exercise 2**	**Exercise 3**	**Exercise 4**

1. expansion
  expansion
  expansion
	1. genetic
	  gender
	  gender
		1. depression
		  depression
		  depressing
			1. levy
			  levy
			  levy

2. conceive
  conceived
	2. assembled
	  assembly
	  assembly
		2. collapsed
		  collapse
		  collapsed
			2. ethnic
			  ethnic
			  ethnic

3. publication
  publication
  publications
	3. controversy
	  controversy
	  controversial
		3. incentive
		  incentive
		  incentives
			3. colleagues
			  colleague
			  colleague

4. encounter
  encountered
  encounter
	4. integrity
	  integrity
	  integrity
		4. estate
		  estate
		  estate
			4. voluntary
			  volunteers
			  volunteer

5. inclined
  inclined
  incline
	5. modification
	  modified
	  modified
		5. nuclear
		  nuclear
		  nuclear
			5. incidence
			  incidence

6. medical
  medical
  medical
	6. convinced
	  convincing
	  convinced
		6. involvement
		  involved
		  involved
			6. odds
			  odd
			  odd

7. adjacent
  adjacent
	7. persist
	  Persistence
	  persisted
		7. scenario
		  scenario
		  scenario
			7. professional
			  professionals

8. tradition
  traditions
  tradition
	8. quote
	  quoted
	  quoted
		8. poses
		  pose
		  pose
			8. secure
			  security
			  securing

9. panel
  panel
  panel
	9. unify
	  unified
	  unification
		9. violate
		  violations
		  violation
			9. drama
			  dramatic
			  dramatically

10. intrinsic
  intrinsic
	10. compile
	  Compiling
		10. straightforward
		  straightforward
			10. survival
			  survive
			  survived

Unit 10

Answers

Synonyms (Crossword)

Across
1. scenario
5. unify
8. whereby
12. professional
13. odd
16. collapse
17. survive
19. adjacent
23. persist
25. nuclear
29. albeit
31. invoke
32. widespread
33. overseas

Down
2. conceive
3. overall
4. undergo
6. forthcoming
7. tradition
9. enormous
10. convince
11. compile
12. panel
14. drama
15. quote
18. depress
20. assemble
21. dynamic
22. incentive
24. involve
26. ethnic
27. secure
28. violate
30. pose

Review

1. adjacent
2. straightforward
3. voluntary
4. assemble
5. conceive
6. expand
7. colleague
8. gender
9. integrity
10. albeit
11. notwithstanding
12. widespread
13. intrinsic
14. enormous
15. professional
16. collapsed
17. convinced
18. invoked
19. drama
20. incentive
21. panel
22. nonetheless
23. whereby
24. forthcoming
25. medical
26. dynamic
27. ethnic
28. compile
29. depress
30. involve
31. estate
32. incidence
33. publication
34. external
35. nuclear
36. overall
37. modified
38. survived
39. unified
40. quote
41. reluctance
42. controversy
43. odd
44. overseas
45. secure
46. tradition
47. scenario
48. incline
49. undergo
50. persist
51. violate
52. levy
53. pose
54. encounter

Word + Unit

abandon 8	attain 9	comprise 7	crucial 8
abstract 6	attitude 4	compute 2	culture 2
academy 5	attribute 4	conceive 10	currency 8
access 4	authority 1	concentrate 4	cycle 4
accommodate 9	automate 8	concept 1	data 1
accompany 8	available 1	conclude 2	debate 4
accumulate 8	aware 5	concurrent 9	decade 7
accurate 6	behalf 9	conduct 2	decline 5
achieve 2	benefit 1	conference 4	deduce 3
acknowledge 6	bias 8	confine 9	definite 7
acquire 2	bond 6	confirm 7	demonstrate 3
adapt 7	brief 6	conflict 5	denote 8
adequate 4	bulk 9	conform 8	deny 7
adjacent 10	capable 6	consent 3	depression 10
adjust 5	capacity 5	consequence 2	derive 1
administer 2	category 2	considerable 3	design 2
adult 7	cease 9	consist of 1	despite 4
advocate 7	challenge 5	constant 3	detect 8
affect 2	channel 7	constitute 1	deviate 8
aggregate 6	chapter 2	constrain 3	device 9
aid 7	chart 8	construct 2	devote 9
albeit 10	chemical 7	consult 5	differentiate 7
allocate 6	circumstance 3	consume 2	dimension 4
alter 5	cite 6	contact 5	diminish 9
alternative 3	civil 4	contemporary 8	discrete 5
ambiguous 8	clarify 8	context 1	discriminate 6
amend 5	classic 7	contract 1	displace 8
analogy 9	code 4	contradict 8	display 6
analysis 1	coherent 9	contrary 7	dispose 7
annual 4	coincide 9	contrast 4	distinct 2
anticipate 9	collapse 10	contribute 3	distort 9
apparent 4	colleague 10	controversy 10	distribute 1
append 8	commence 9	convene 3	diverse 6
appreciate 8	comment 3	converse 9	document 3
approach 1	commission 2	convert 7	domain 6
appropriate 2	commit 4	convince 10	domestic 4
arbitrary 8	commodity 8	cooperate 6	dominate 3
area 1	community 2	coordinate 3	draft 5
aspect 2	compatible 9	core 3	drama 10
assemble 10	compensate 3	corporate 3	duration 9
assessment 1	compile 10	correspond 3	dynamic 10
assign 6	complement 8	couple 7	edit 6
assumption 1	component 3	creation 1	element 2
assure 9	compound 5	credit 2	eliminate 7
attach 6	comprehensive 7	criteria 3	emerge 4

emphasis 3
empirical 7
enable 5
encounter 10
energy 5
enforce 5
enhance 6
enormous 10
ensure 3
entity 5
environment 1
equate 2
equip 7
equivalent 5
erode 9
error 4
establish 1
estate 10
ethic 9
ethnic 10
evaluate 2
eventual 8
evident 1
evolve 5
exceed 6
exclude 3
exhibit 8
expand 10
expert 6
explicit 6
exploit 8
export 1
expose 5
external 10
extract 7
facilitate 5
factor 1
feature 2
federal 6
fee 6
file 7
finance 1
finite 7
flexible 6
fluctuate 8

focus 2
format 9
formula 1
forthcoming 10
found 9
foundation 7
framework 3
function 1
fund 3
fundamental 5
furthermore 6
gender 10
generate 5
generation 5
globe 7
goal 4
grant 4
guarantee 7
guideline 8
hence 4
hierarchy 7
highlight 8
hypothesis 4
identical 7
identify 1
ideology 7
ignorant 6
illustrate 3
image 5
immigrate 3
impact 2
implement 4
implicate 4
implicit 8
imply 3
impose 4
incentive 10
incidence 10
incline 10
income 1
incorporate 6
index 6
indicate 1
individual 1
induce 8

inevitable 8
infer 7
infrastructure 8
inherent 9
inhibit 6
initial 3
initiate 6
injure 2
innovate 7
input 6
insert 7
insight 9
inspect 8
instance 3
institute 2
instruct 6
integral 9
integrate 4
integrity 10
intelligent 6
intense 8
interact 3
intermediate 9
internal 4
interpret 1
interval 6
intervene 7
intrinsic 10
invest 2
investigate 4
invoke 10
involve 10
isolate 7
issue 1
item 2
journal 2
justify 3
label 4
labor 1
layer 3
lecture 6
legal 1
legislate 1
levy 10
liberal 5

license 5
link 3
locate 3
logic 5
maintain 2
major 1
manipulate 8
manual 9
margin 5
mature 9
maximize 3
mechanism 4
media 7
mediate 9
medical 10
medium 9
mental 5
method 1
migrate 6
military 9
minimize 8
minimum 6
ministry 6
minor 3
mode 7
modify 10
monitor 5
motive 6
mutual 9
negate 3
network 5
neutral 6
nevertheless 6
nonetheless 10
norm 9
normal 2
notion 5
notwithstanding 10
nuclear 10
objective 5
obtain 2
obvious 4
occupy 4
occur 1
odd 10

offset 8
optional 4
orient 5
outcome 3
output 4
overall 10
overlap 9
overseas 10
panel 10
paradigm 7
parallel 4
parameter 4
participate 2
passive 9
perceive 2
percent 1
period 1
persist 10
perspective 5
phase 4
phenomenon 7
philosophy 3
physical 3
policy 1
portion 9
pose 10
positive 2
potential 2
practitioner 8
precede 6
precise 5
predict 4
predominant 8
preliminary 9
presume 6
primary 2
prime 5
principal 4
prior 4
priority 7
proceed 1
process 1
professional 10
prohibit 7
project 4

promote 4
proportion 3
prospect 8
protocol 9
psychology 5
publication 10
purchase 2
pursue 5
qualitative 9
quote 10
radical 8
random 8
range 2
ratio 5
rational 6
react 3
recover 6
refine 9
regime 4
region 2
regulate 2
reinforce 8
reject 5
relax 9
release 7
relevant 2
reluctance 10
rely 3
require 1
research 1
reside 2
resolve 4
resource 2
restore 8
restrain 9
restrict 2
retain 4
reveal 6
revenue 5
reverse 7
revise 8
revolution 9
rigid 9
role 1
route 9

scenario 10
scheme 3
scope 6
section 1
sector 1
secure 10
seek 2
select 2
sequence 3
series 4
shift 3
significant 1
similar 1
simulate 7
site 2
sole 7
somewhat 7
source 1
specific 1
specify 3
sphere 9
stable 5
statistic 4
status 4
straightforward 10
strategy 2
stress 4
structure 1
style 5
submit 7
subordinate 9
subsequent 4
subsidy 6
substitute 5
successor 7
sufficient 3
sum 4
summary 4
supplement 9
survey 2
survive 10
suspend 9
sustain 5
symbol 5
tape 6

target 5
task 3
team 9
technical 3
technique 3
temporary 9
tense 8
terminate 8
text 2
theme 8
theory 1
thereby 8
thesis 7
topic 7
trace 6
tradition 10
transfer 2
transform 6
transit 5
transmit 7
transport 6
trend 5
trigger 9
ultimate 7
undergo 10
underlie 6
undertake 4
uniform 8
unify 10
unique 7
utilize 6
valid 3
vary 1
vehicle 8
version 5
via 8
violate 10
virtual 8
visible 7
visual 8
volume 3
voluntary 10
welfare 5
whereby 10
widespread 10